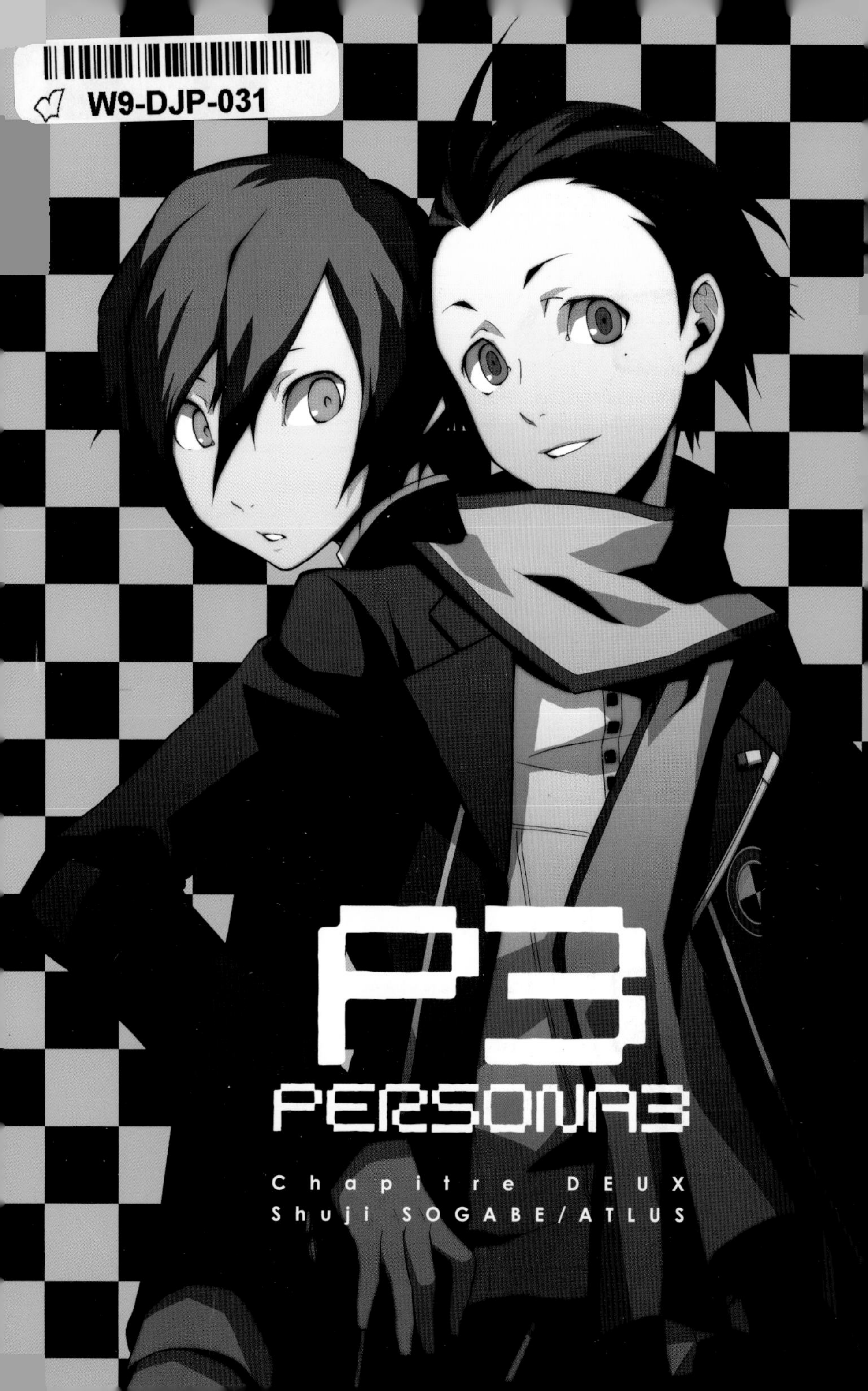
P3
PERSONA3
Chapitre DEUX
Shuji SOGABE/ATLUS

story

In April of 2009, Minato Arisato discovered a formidable power within himself. This discovery landed him in the hospital for a whole week, where he awoke to a most unsettling truth. Following his recovery, Minato would come to be familiar with the way his school transformed into a frightening tower every night at midnight, during the mysterious hour between one day and the next.

This tower was known as Tartarus, and served as the nesting ground for the creatures called Shadows. Minato, Yukari, and Junpei ventured into this tower together, but Yukari and Junpei's lack of combat experience resulted in Minato being seriously injured. Driven to action by Minato's self-sacrifice, Yukari finally pulled the trigger.

In May of 2009, Mitsuru detected the presence of an unusually large Shadow. The trio once again set out together, making their way to the monorail where the Shadow was detected. But a minor altercation leads to Junpei acting on his own.

Shaken by Mitsuru's warning that they only had three minutes before the train car they were on would crash into the train car ahead of them, the three friends manage to overcome their differences in order to work together once again. After fighting their way through their enemies, Minato, Yukari, and Junpei were met by the large Shadow Mitsuru had originally detected: the Arcana Priestess.

In November of 2009, the members of S.E.E.S. were enjoying a relatively normal day. But the knowledge that everything merely existed between the past and the future was ever present. Any given day when the past could be resurrected would in turn be recalled with nostalgia in the future. That is the essence of memory.

2007 08~12

COMIC
149/162p
91.9%

monochrome
B6

#05 特別課外活動部 Piece04 P3 PERSONA3

P3 PERSONA3 #06 piece:05 squared3

P3 PERSONA3 #07 Tight high tide

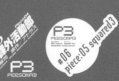

Subtitle logo
#08 #07.5 none

Chapitre DEUX

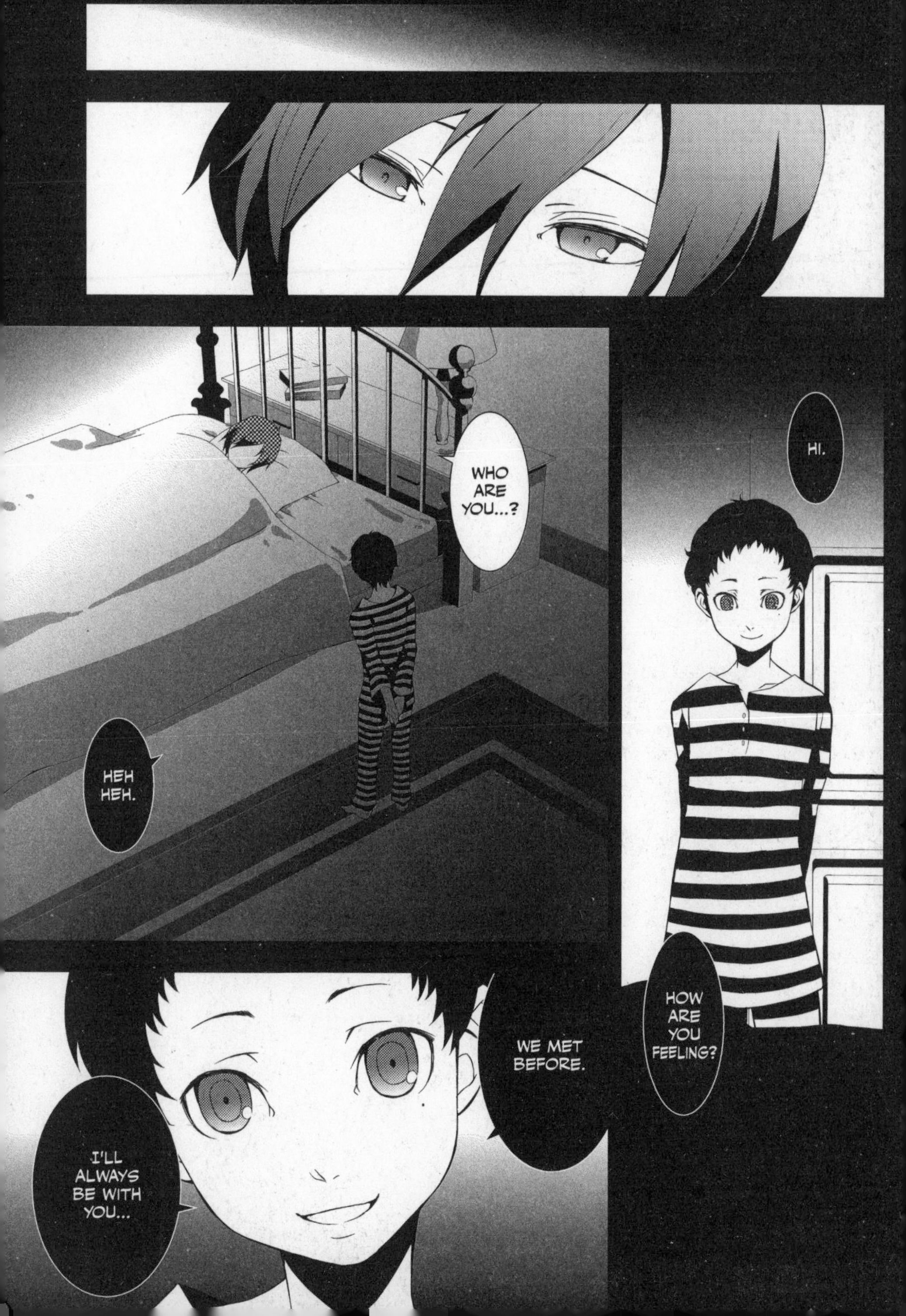
HI.
HOW ARE YOU FEELING?
WHO ARE YOU...?
HEH HEH.
WE MET BEFORE.
I'LL ALWAYS BE WITH YOU...

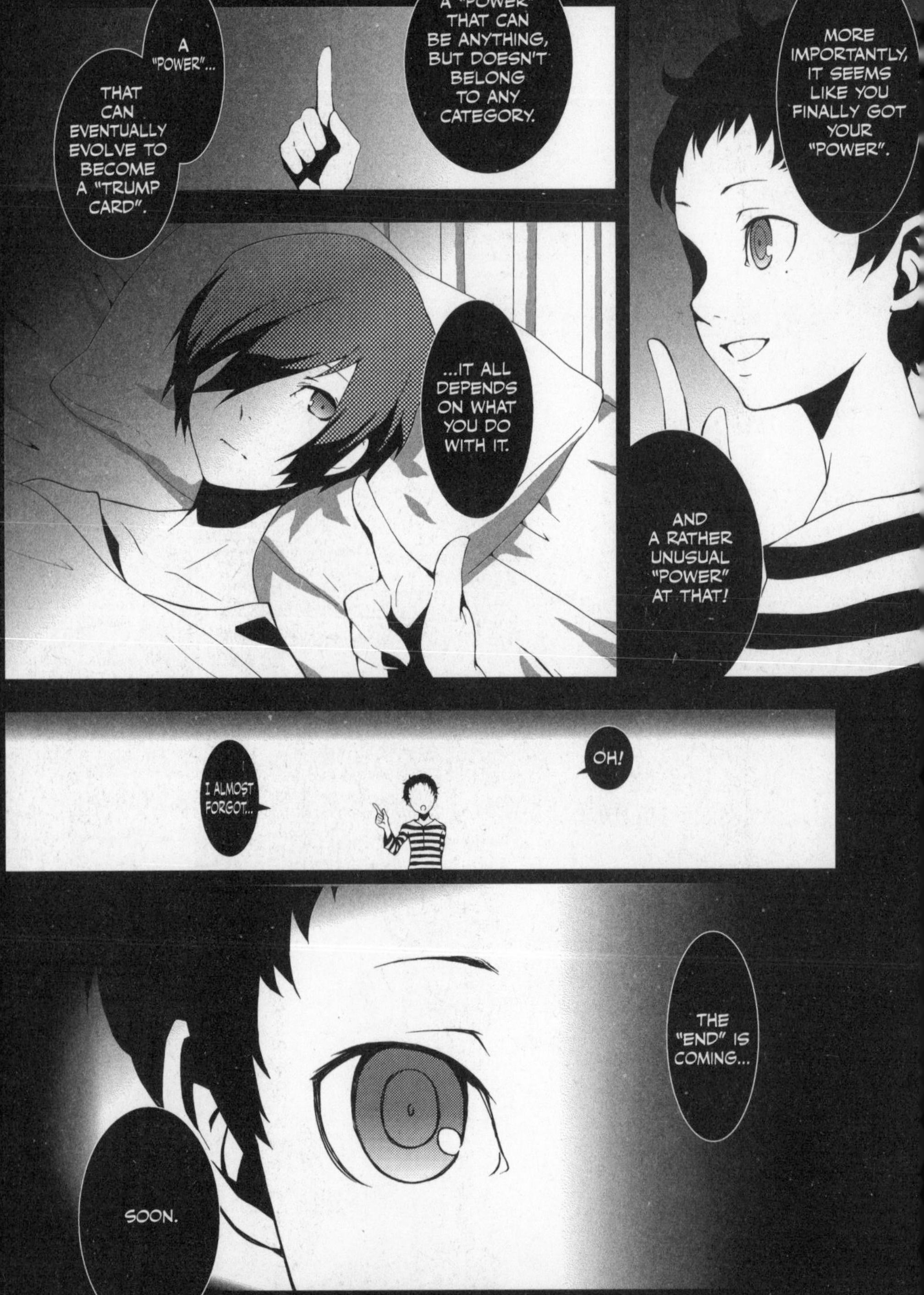
MORE IMPORTANTLY, IT SEEMS LIKE YOU FINALLY GOT YOUR "POWER".
AND A RATHER UNUSUAL "POWER" AT THAT!
A "POWER" THAT CAN BE ANYTHING, BUT DOESN'T BELONG TO ANY CATEGORY.
A "POWER"...
THAT CAN EVENTUALLY EVOLVE TO BECOME A "TRUMP CARD".
...IT ALL DEPENDS ON WHAT YOU DO WITH IT.
OH!
I ALMOST FORGOT...
THE "END" IS COMING...
SOON.

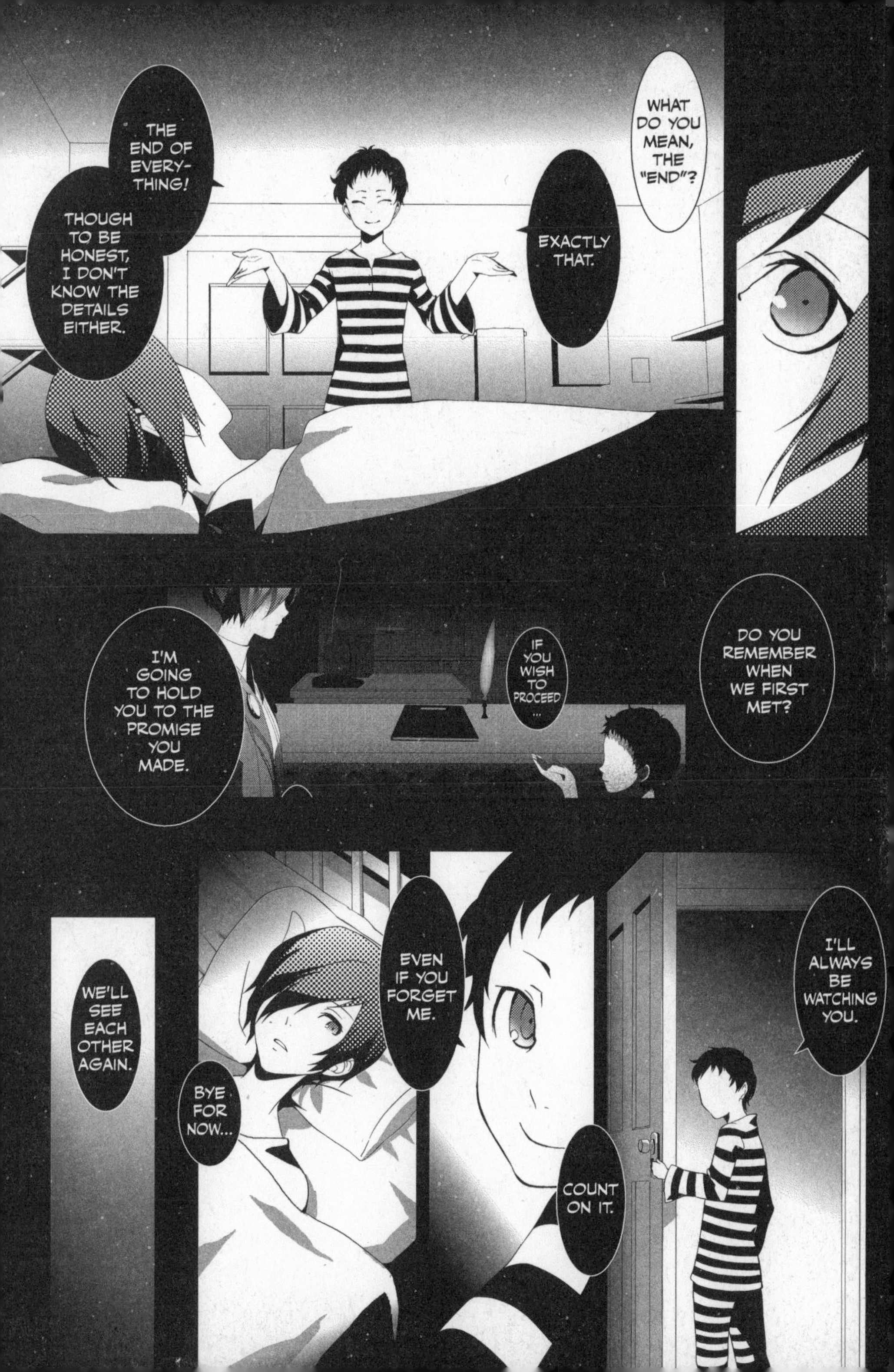
WHAT DO YOU MEAN, THE "END"?
EXACTLY THAT.
THE END OF EVERY-THING!
THOUGH TO BE HONEST, I DON'T KNOW THE DETAILS EITHER.
DO YOU REMEMBER WHEN WE FIRST MET?
IF YOU WISH TO PROCEED ...
I'M GOING TO HOLD YOU TO THE PROMISE YOU MADE.
I'LL ALWAYS BE WATCHING YOU.
COUNT ON IT.
EVEN IF YOU FORGET ME.
BYE FOR NOW...
WE'LL SEE EACH OTHER AGAIN.

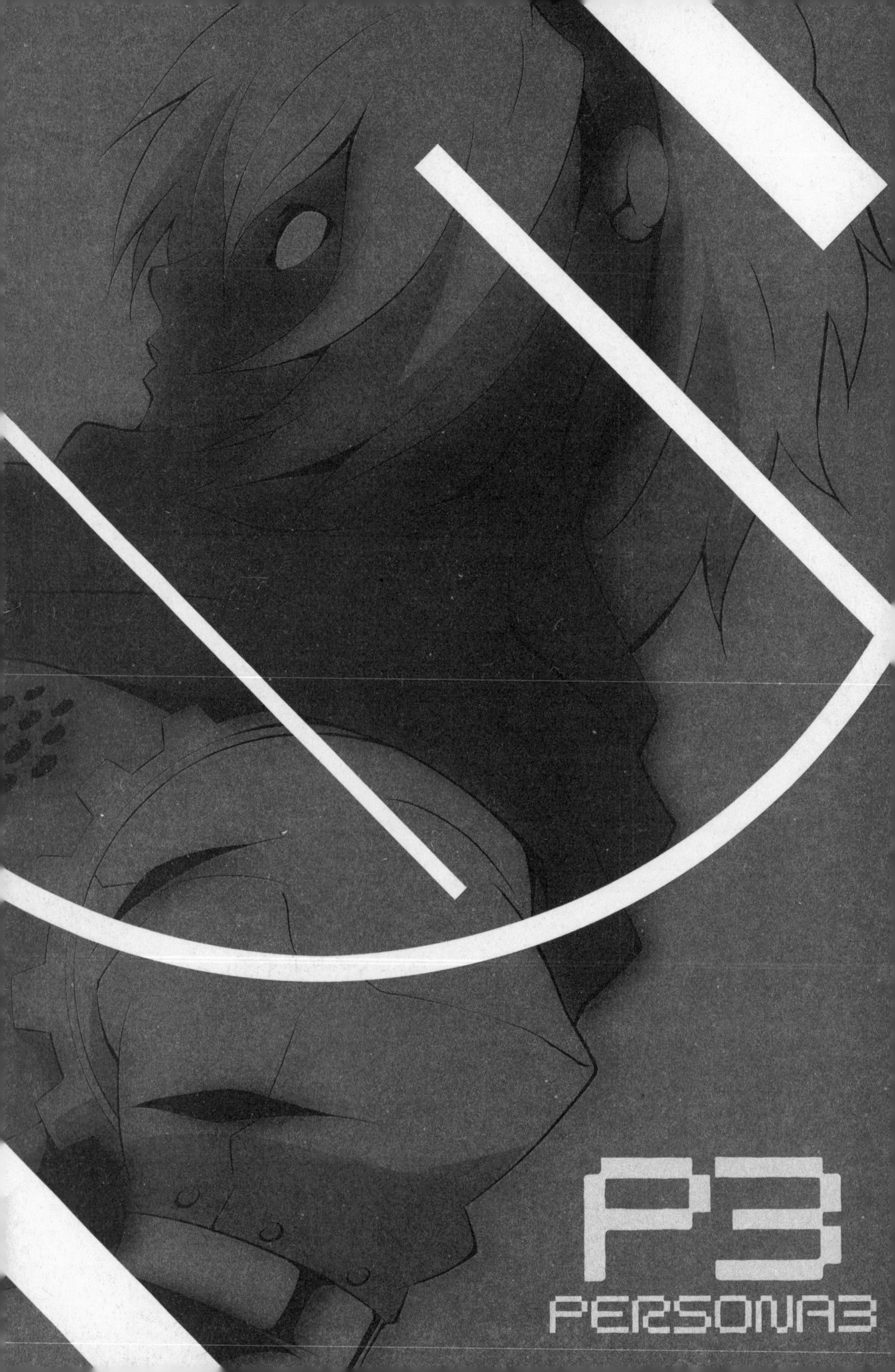
P3
PERSONA3

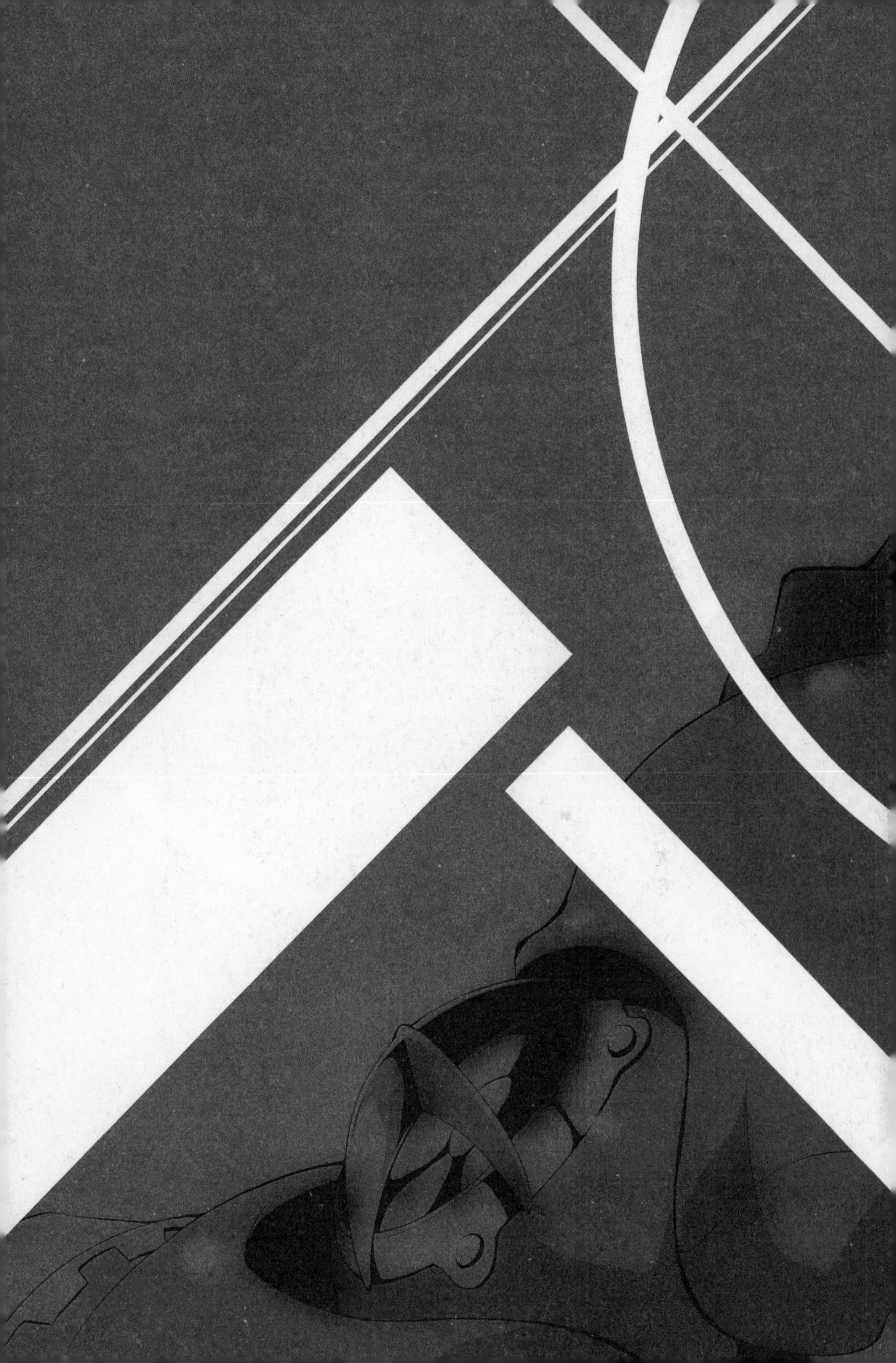

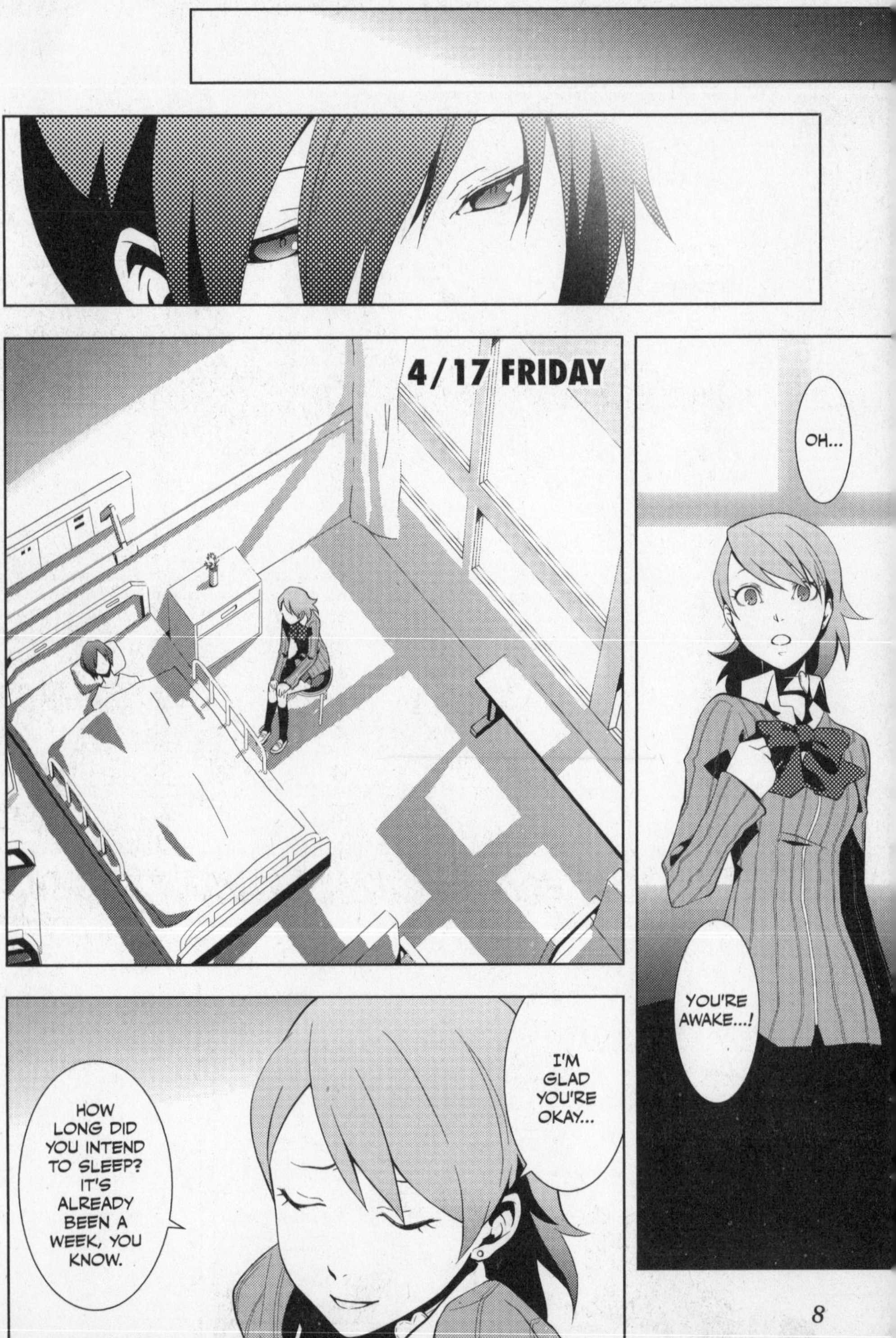
OH...
YOU'RE AWAKE...!
4/17 FRIDAY
I'M GLAD YOU'RE OKAY...
HOW LONG DID YOU INTEND TO SLEEP? IT'S ALREADY BEEN A WEEK, YOU KNOW.

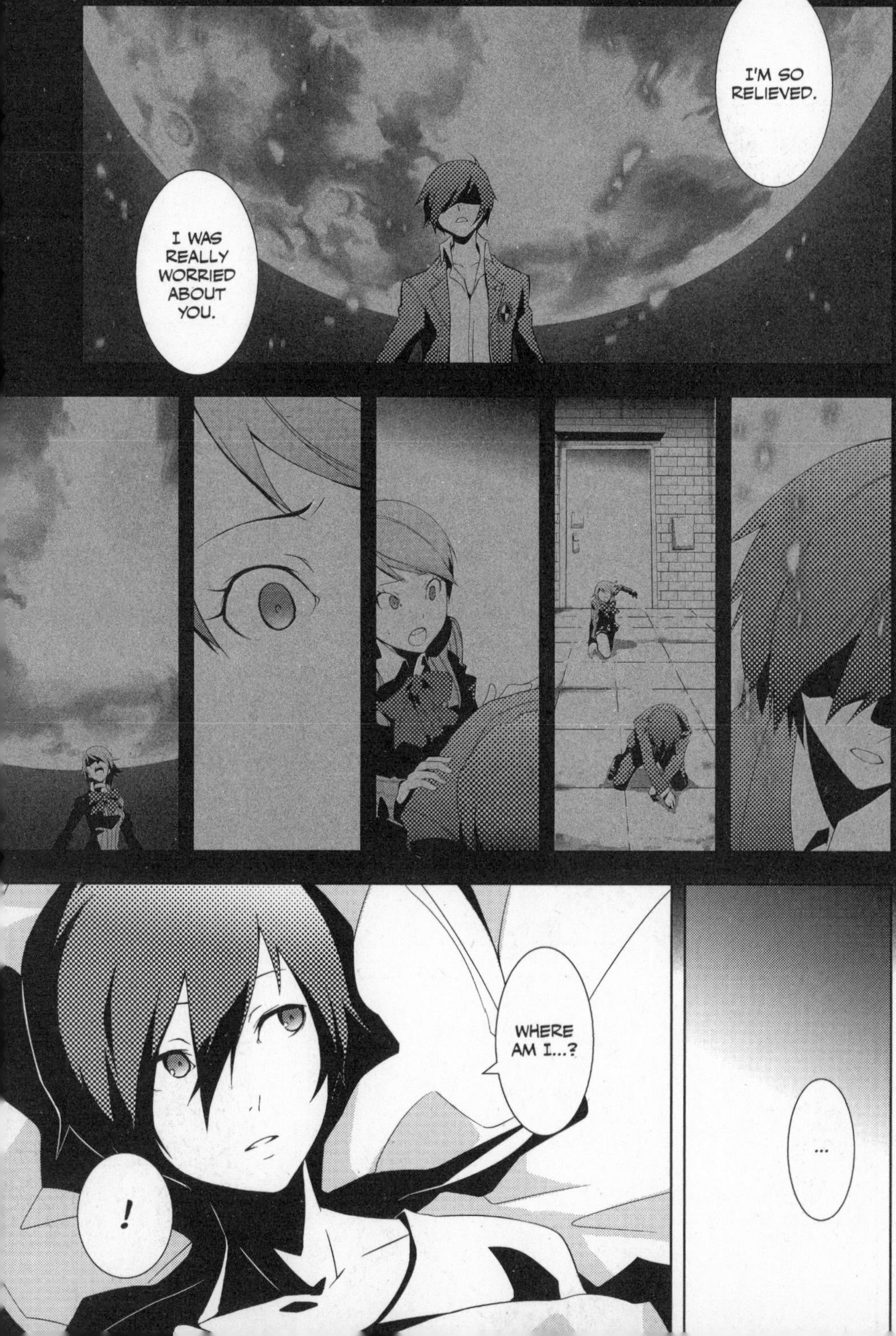
I'M SO RELIEVED.
I WAS REALLY WORRIED ABOUT YOU.
...
WHERE AM I...?
!

WHY ARE YOU HERE?

OH, THIS IS THE TATSUMI MEMORIAL HOSPITAL. IT'S NOT TOO FAR FROM THE STATION.

...

I'M SORRY I COULDN'T DO ANYTHING TO HELP AT THE TIME...

MITSURU AND THE OTHERS TOLD ME IT WAS MY JOB TO PROTECT YOU, BUT I OBVIOUSLY FAILED AT THAT.

I COULDN'T LEAVE YOU ALONE... I MEAN...

YOU DID SAVE ME, AFTER ALL.

... POWER.

YOUR, UH...

IT WAS SO AMAZING, BY THE WAY!

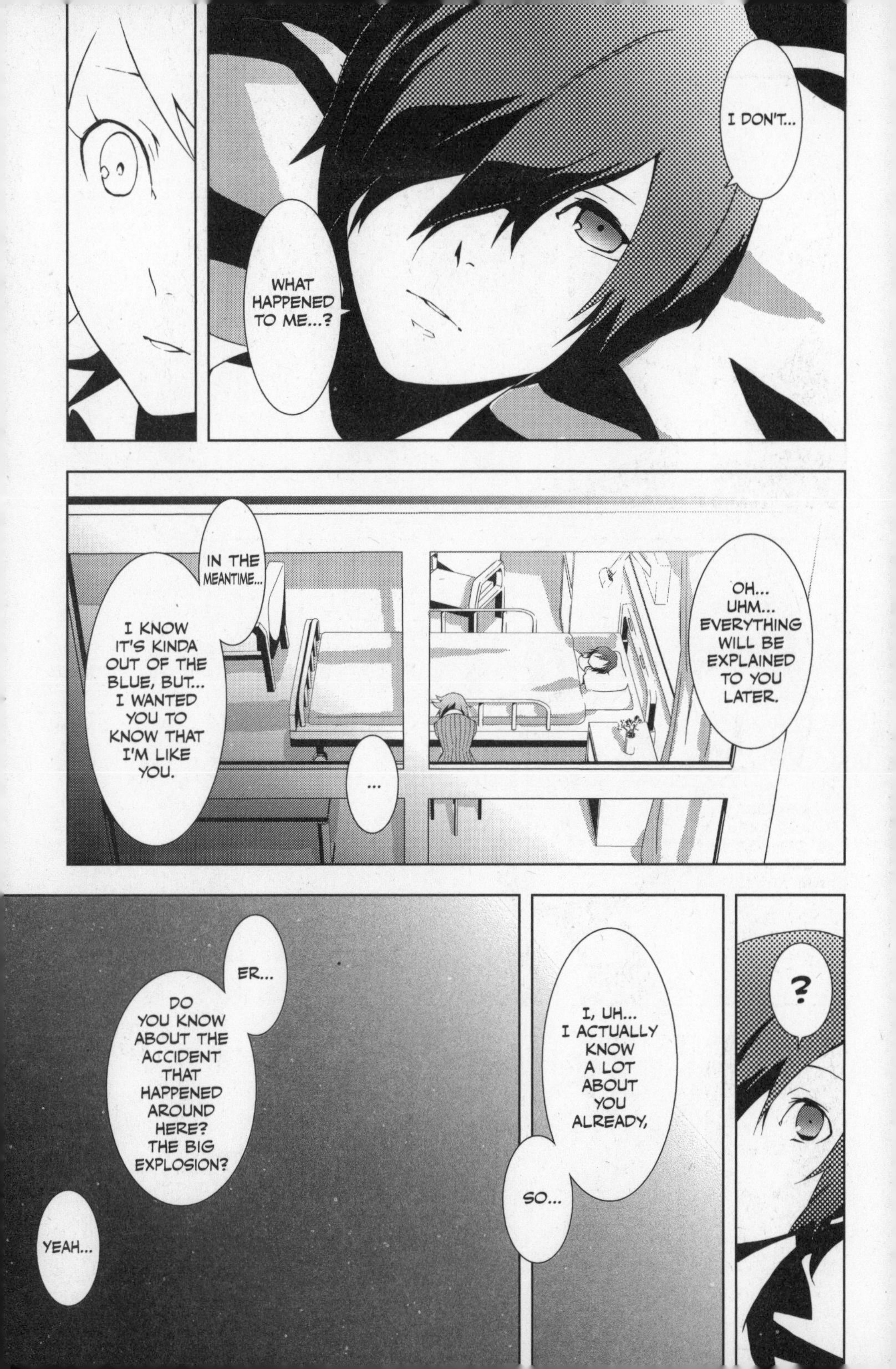
I DON'T...
WHAT HAPPENED TO ME...?
OH... UHM... EVERYTHING WILL BE EXPLAINED TO YOU LATER.
...
IN THE MEANTIME...
I KNOW IT'S KINDA OUT OF THE BLUE, BUT... I WANTED YOU TO KNOW THAT I'M LIKE YOU.
?
I, UH... I ACTUALLY KNOW A LOT ABOUT YOU ALREADY,
SO...
ER...
DO YOU KNOW ABOUT THE ACCIDENT THAT HAPPENED AROUND HERE? THE BIG EXPLOSION?
YEAH...

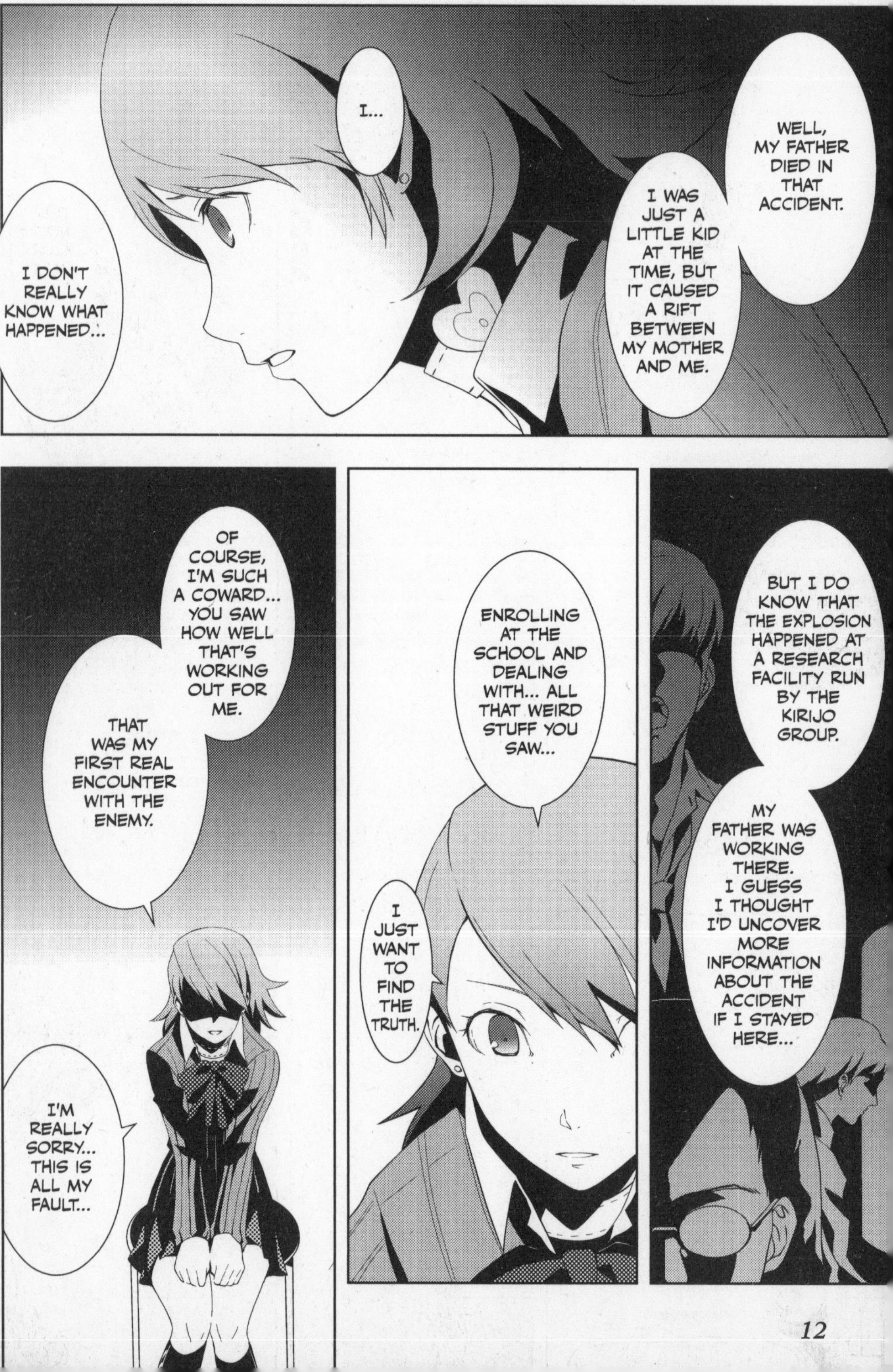
WELL, MY FATHER DIED IN THAT ACCIDENT.
I WAS JUST A LITTLE KID AT THE TIME, BUT IT CAUSED A RIFT BETWEEN MY MOTHER AND ME.
I...
I DON'T REALLY KNOW WHAT HAPPENED...
BUT I DO KNOW THAT THE EXPLOSION HAPPENED AT A RESEARCH FACILITY RUN BY THE KIRIJO GROUP.
MY FATHER WAS WORKING THERE. I GUESS I THOUGHT I'D UNCOVER MORE INFORMATION ABOUT THE ACCIDENT IF I STAYED HERE...
ENROLLING AT THE SCHOOL AND DEALING WITH... ALL THAT WEIRD STUFF YOU SAW...
I JUST WANT TO FIND THE TRUTH.
OF COURSE, I'M SUCH A COWARD... YOU SAW HOW WELL THAT'S WORKING OUT FOR ME.
THAT WAS MY FIRST REAL ENCOUNTER WITH THE ENEMY.
I'M REALLY SORRY... THIS IS ALL MY FAULT...

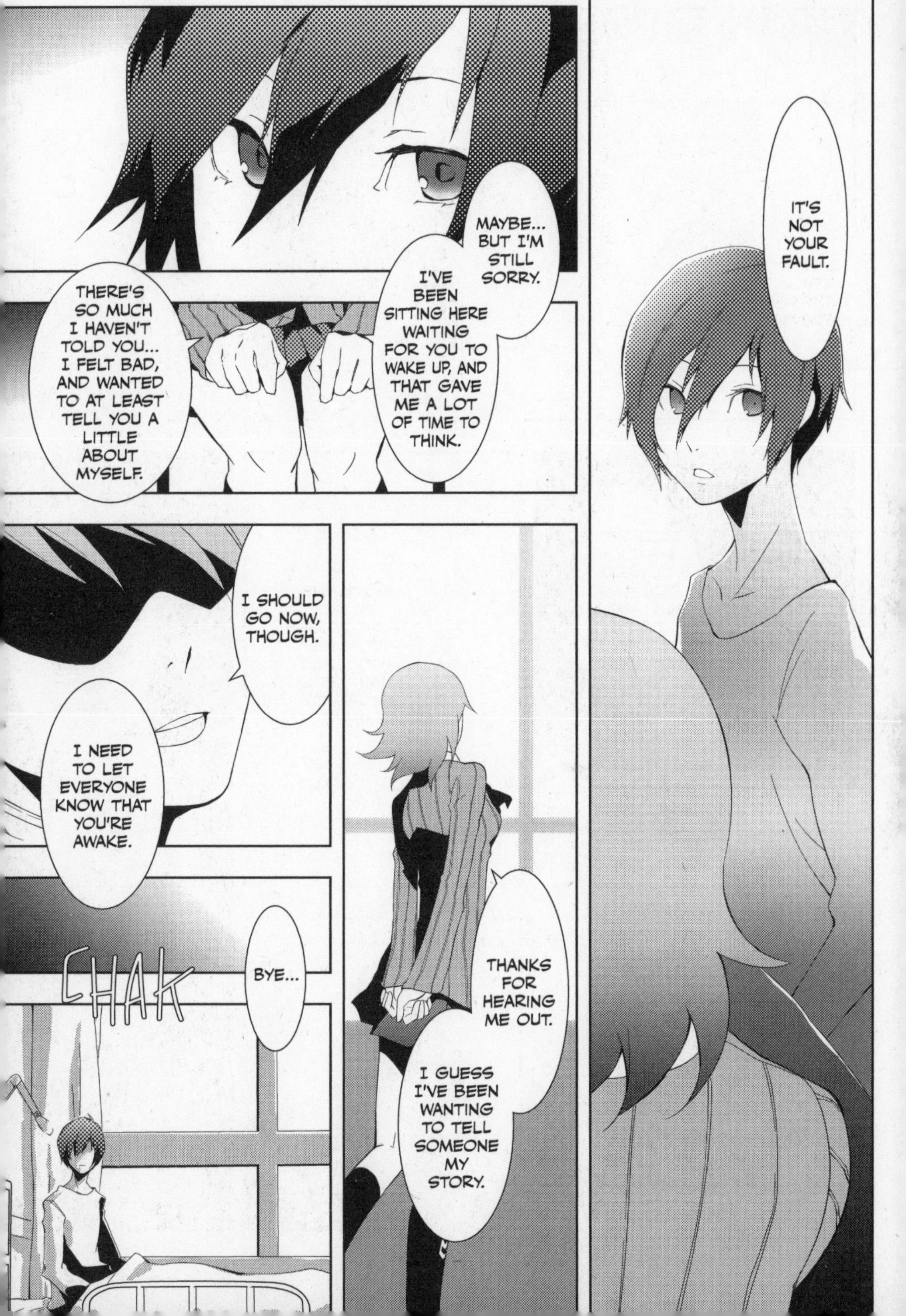
IT'S NOT YOUR FAULT.
MAYBE... BUT I'M STILL SORRY.
I'VE BEEN SITTING HERE WAITING FOR YOU TO WAKE UP, AND THAT GAVE ME A LOT OF TIME TO THINK.
THERE'S SO MUCH I HAVEN'T TOLD YOU... I FELT BAD, AND WANTED TO AT LEAST TELL YOU A LITTLE ABOUT MYSELF.
THANKS FOR HEARING ME OUT.
I GUESS I'VE BEEN WANTING TO TELL SOMEONE MY STORY.
I SHOULD GO NOW, THOUGH.
I NEED TO LET EVERYONE KNOW THAT YOU'RE AWAKE.
CHAK
BYE...

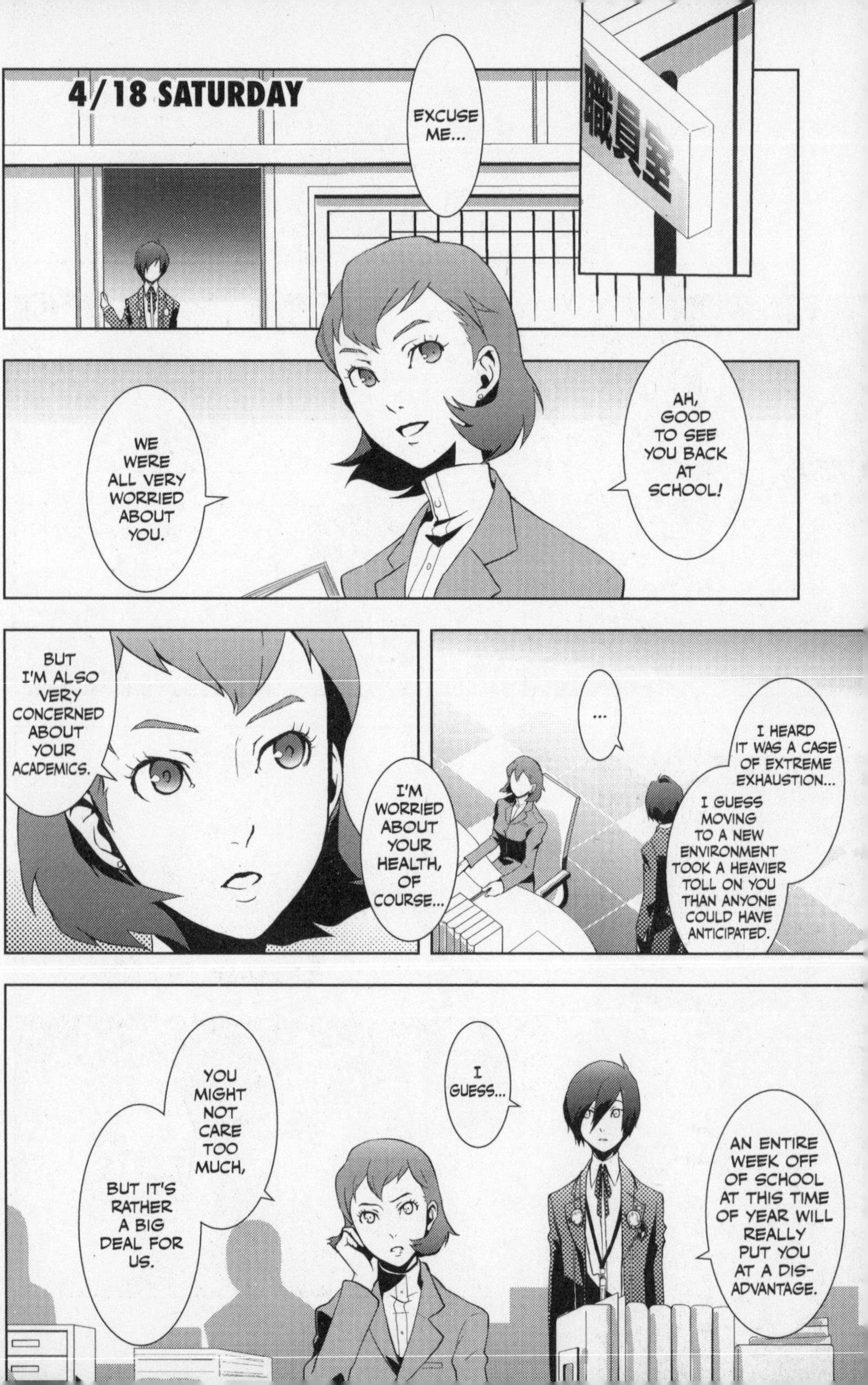
職員室
EXCUSE ME...
4/18 SATURDAY
AH, GOOD TO SEE YOU BACK AT SCHOOL!
WE WERE ALL VERY WORRIED ABOUT YOU.
I HEARD IT WAS A CASE OF EXTREME EXHAUSTION...
I GUESS MOVING TO A NEW ENVIRONMENT TOOK A HEAVIER TOLL ON YOU THAN ANYONE COULD HAVE ANTICIPATED.
...
I'M WORRIED ABOUT YOUR HEALTH, OF COURSE...
BUT I'M ALSO VERY CONCERNED ABOUT YOUR ACADEMICS.
AN ENTIRE WEEK OFF OF SCHOOL AT THIS TIME OF YEAR WILL REALLY PUT YOU AT A DIS-ADVANTAGE.
I GUESS...
YOU MIGHT NOT CARE TOO MUCH,
BUT IT'S RATHER A BIG DEAL FOR US.

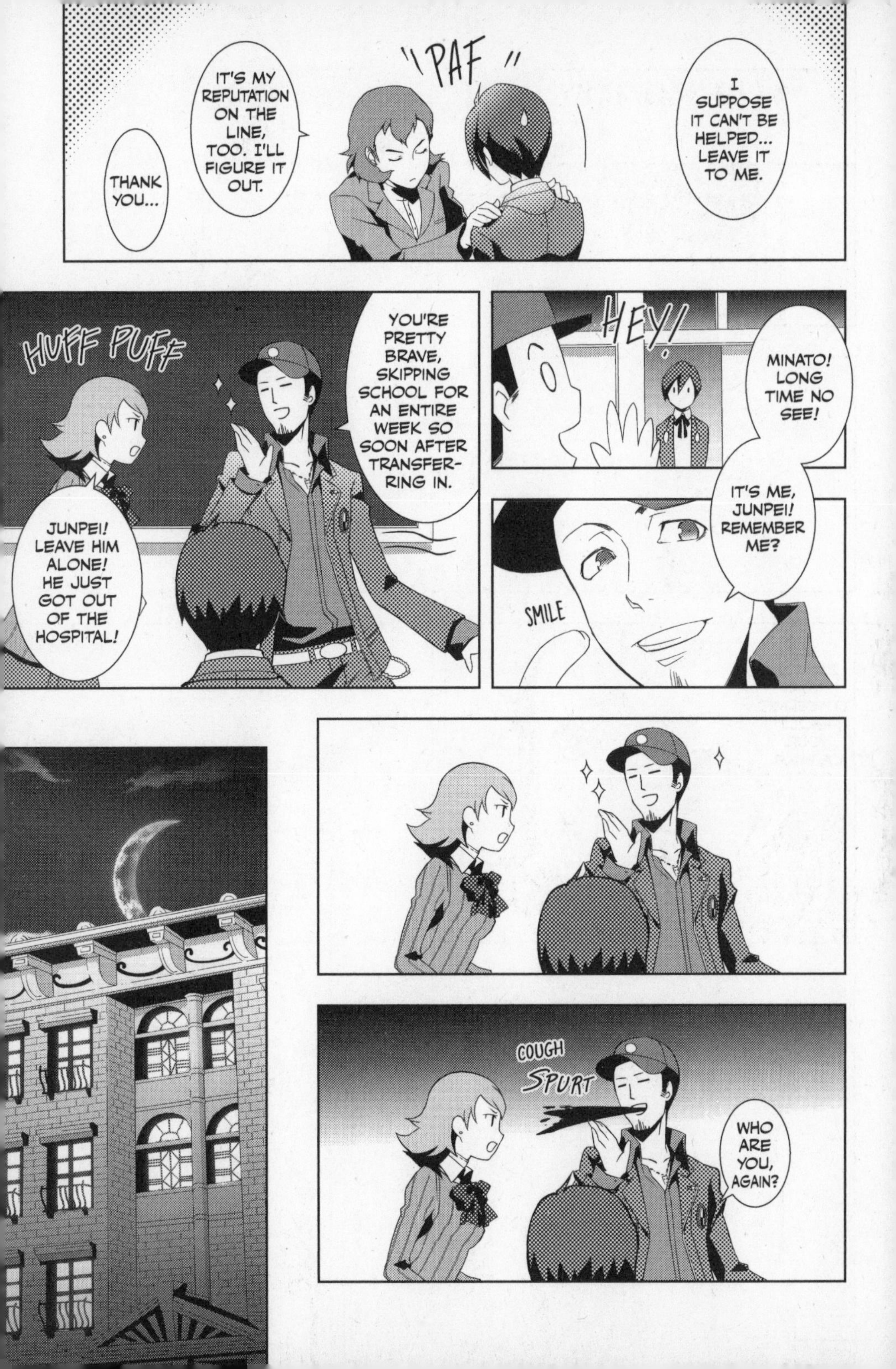
I SUPPOSE IT CAN'T BE HELPED... LEAVE IT TO ME.
PAF
IT'S MY REPUTATION ON THE LINE, TOO. I'LL FIGURE IT OUT.
THANK YOU...
HEY!
MINATO! LONG TIME NO SEE!
IT'S ME, JUNPEI! REMEMBER ME?
SMILE
HUFF PUFF
YOU'RE PRETTY BRAVE, SKIPPING SCHOOL FOR AN ENTIRE WEEK SO SOON AFTER TRANSFERRING IN.
JUNPEI! LEAVE HIM ALONE! HE JUST GOT OUT OF THE HOSPITAL!
COUGH
SPURT
WHO ARE YOU, AGAIN?

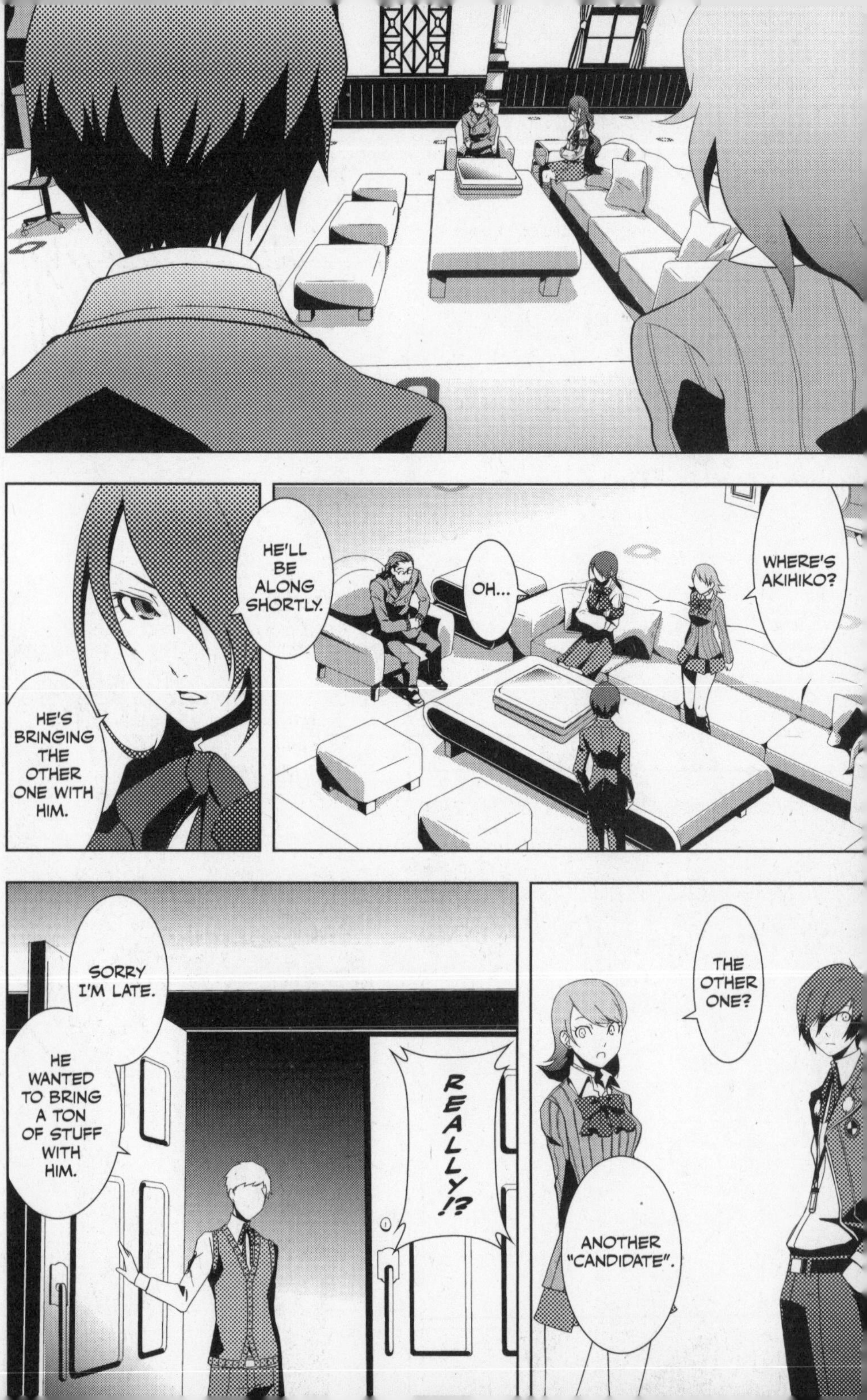
WHERE'S AKIHIKO?
OH...
HE'LL BE ALONG SHORTLY.
HE'S BRINGING THE OTHER ONE WITH HIM.
THE OTHER ONE?
ANOTHER "CANDIDATE".
REALLY!?
SORRY I'M LATE.
HE WANTED TO BRING A TON OF STUFF WITH HIM.

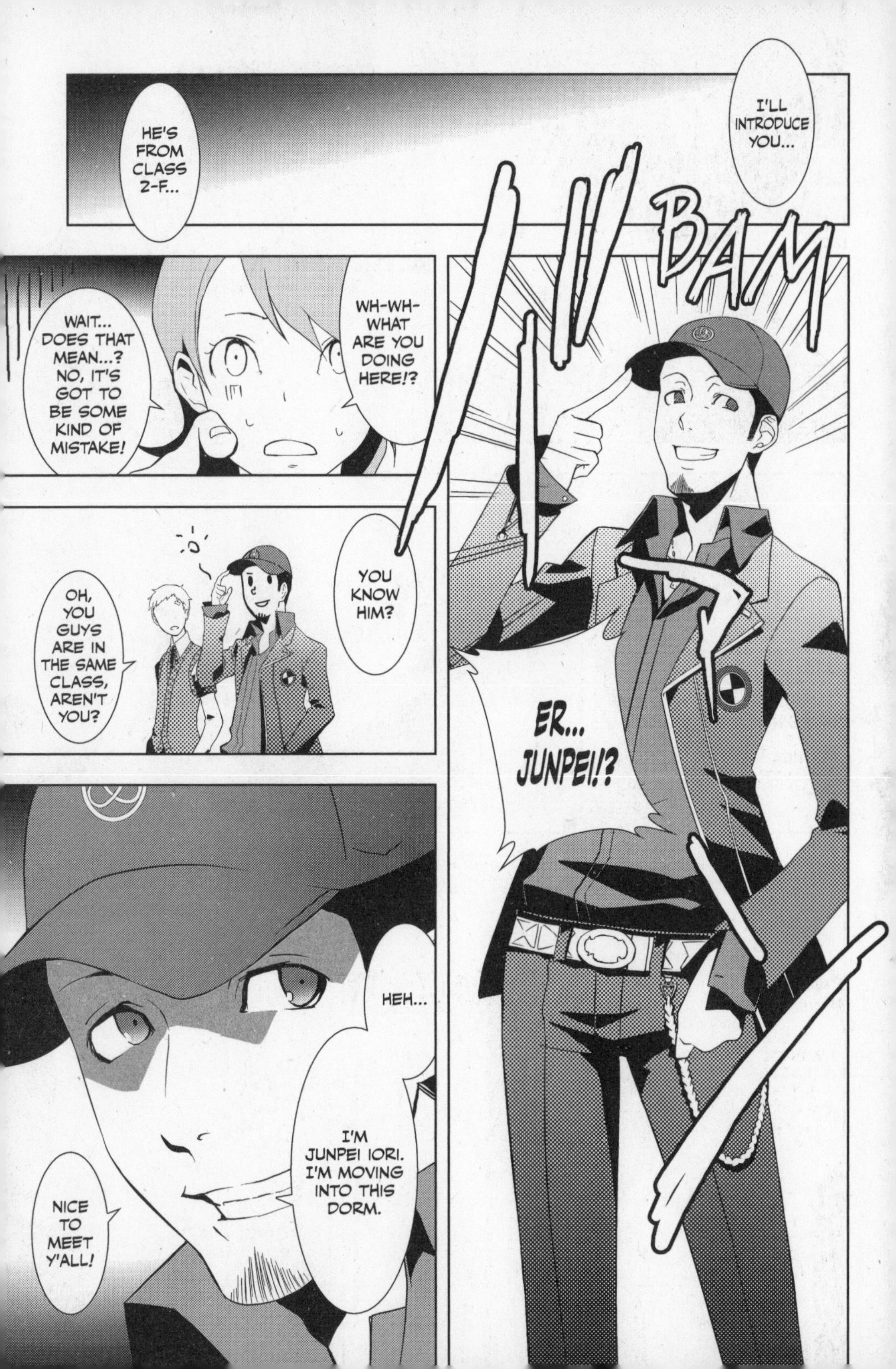
I'LL INTRODUCE YOU...
HE'S FROM CLASS 2-F...
BAM
ER... JUNPEI!?
WH-WH-WHAT ARE YOU DOING HERE!?
WAIT... DOES THAT MEAN...? NO, IT'S GOT TO BE SOME KIND OF MISTAKE!
YOU KNOW HIM?
OH, YOU GUYS ARE IN THE SAME CLASS, AREN'T YOU?
HEH...
I'M JUNPEI IORI. I'M MOVING INTO THIS DORM.
NICE TO MEET Y'ALL!

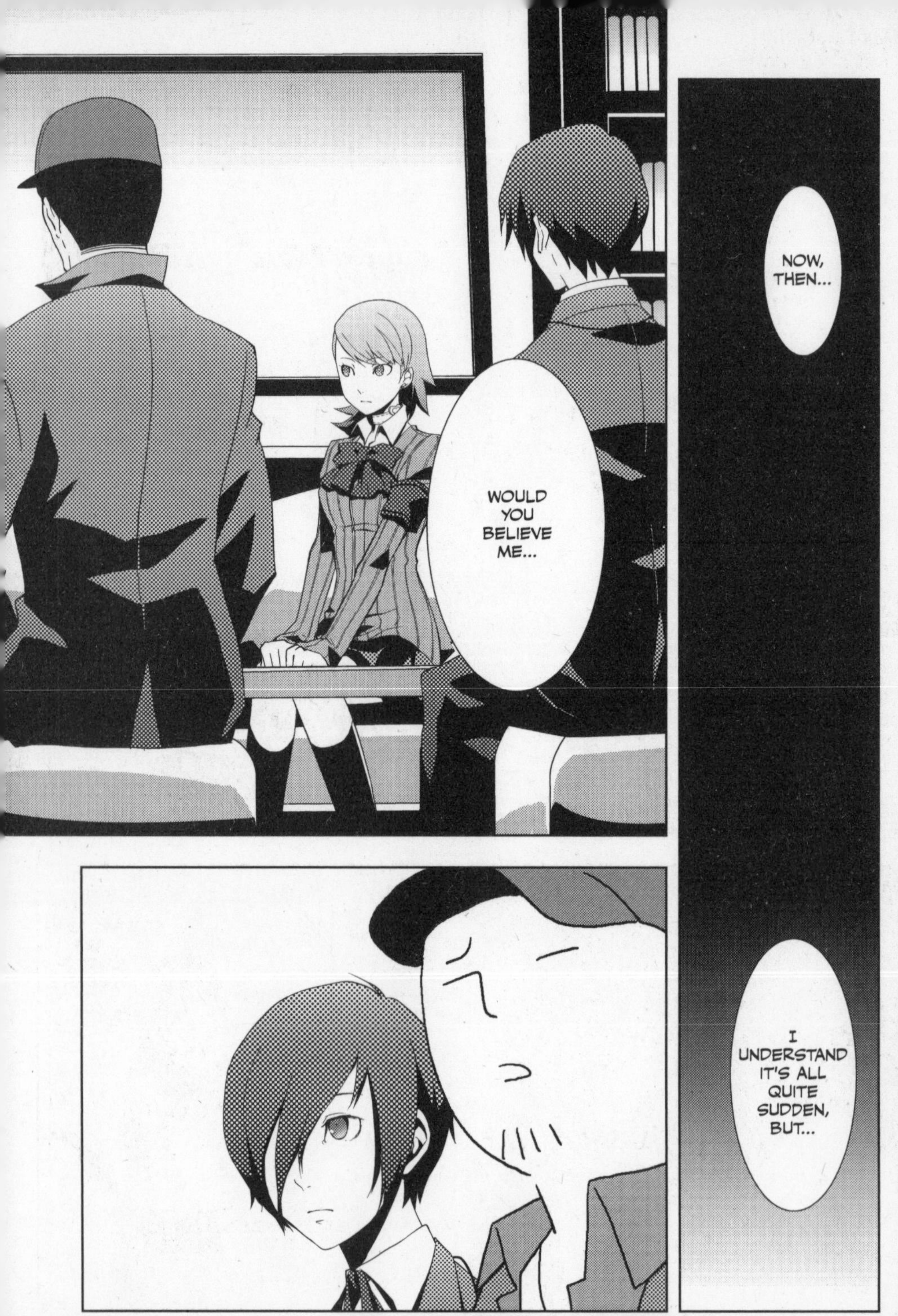
NOW, THEN...
I UNDERSTAND IT'S ALL QUITE SUDDEN, BUT...
WOULD YOU BELIEVE ME...

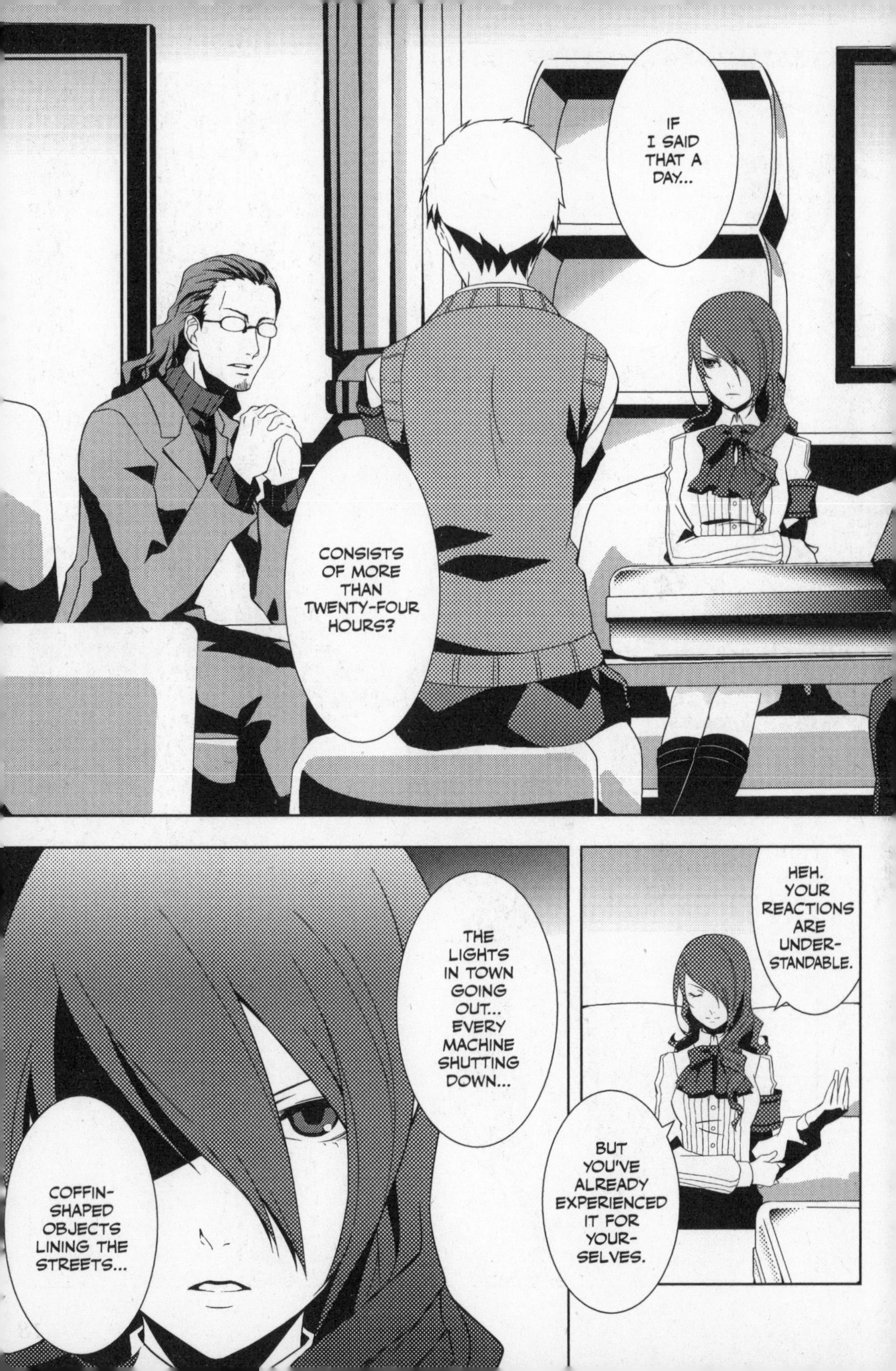
IF I SAID THAT A DAY...
CONSISTS OF MORE THAN TWENTY-FOUR HOURS?
HEH. YOUR REACTIONS ARE UNDER-STANDABLE.
BUT YOU'VE ALREADY EXPERIENCED IT FOR YOUR-SELVES.
THE LIGHTS IN TOWN GOING OUT... EVERY MACHINE SHUTTING DOWN...
COFFIN-SHAPED OBJECTS LINING THE STREETS...

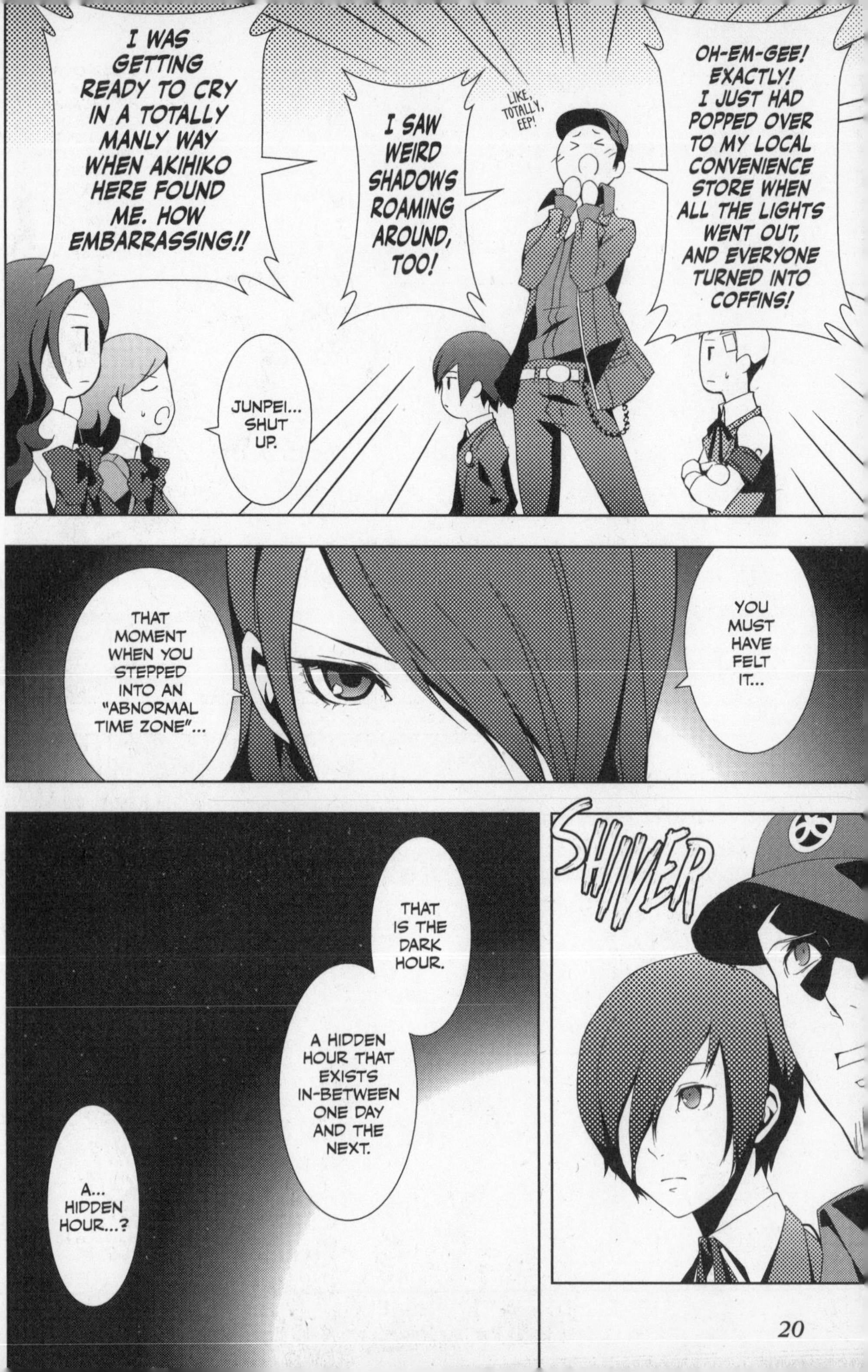
OH-EM-GEE! EXACTLY! I JUST HAD POPPED OVER TO MY LOCAL CONVENIENCE STORE WHEN ALL THE LIGHTS WENT OUT, AND EVERYONE TURNED INTO COFFINS!
LIKE, TOTALLY, EEP!
I SAW WEIRD SHADOWS ROAMING AROUND, TOO!
I WAS GETTING READY TO CRY IN A TOTALLY MANLY WAY WHEN AKIHIKO HERE FOUND ME. HOW EMBARRASSING!!
JUNPEI... SHUT UP.
YOU MUST HAVE FELT IT...
THAT MOMENT WHEN YOU STEPPED INTO AN "ABNORMAL TIME ZONE"...
SHIVER
THAT IS THE DARK HOUR.
A HIDDEN HOUR THAT EXISTS IN-BETWEEN ONE DAY AND THE NEXT.
A... HIDDEN HOUR...?

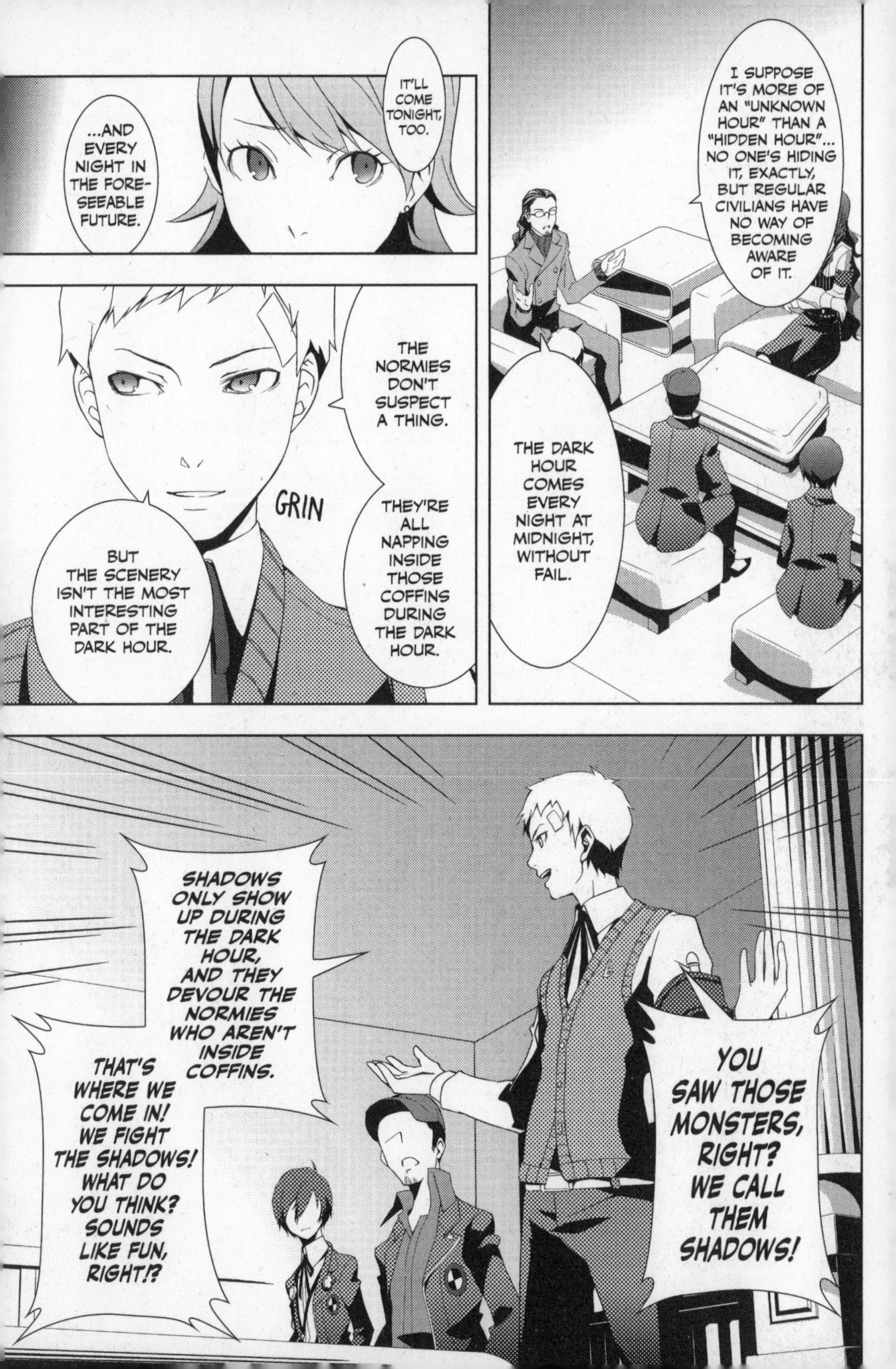
I SUPPOSE IT'S MORE OF AN "UNKNOWN HOUR" THAN A "HIDDEN HOUR"... NO ONE'S HIDING IT, EXACTLY, BUT REGULAR CIVILIANS HAVE NO WAY OF BECOMING AWARE OF IT.
THE DARK HOUR COMES EVERY NIGHT AT MIDNIGHT, WITHOUT FAIL.
IT'LL COME TONIGHT, TOO.
...AND EVERY NIGHT IN THE FORE-SEEABLE FUTURE.
THE NORMIES DON'T SUSPECT A THING.
THEY'RE ALL NAPPING INSIDE THOSE COFFINS DURING THE DARK HOUR.
GRIN
BUT THE SCENERY ISN'T THE MOST INTERESTING PART OF THE DARK HOUR.
YOU SAW THOSE MONSTERS, RIGHT? WE CALL THEM SHADOWS!
SHADOWS ONLY SHOW UP DURING THE DARK HOUR, AND THEY DEVOUR THE NORMIES WHO AREN'T INSIDE COFFINS.
THAT'S WHERE WE COME IN! WE FIGHT THE SHADOWS! WHAT DO YOU THINK? SOUNDS LIKE FUN, RIGHT!?

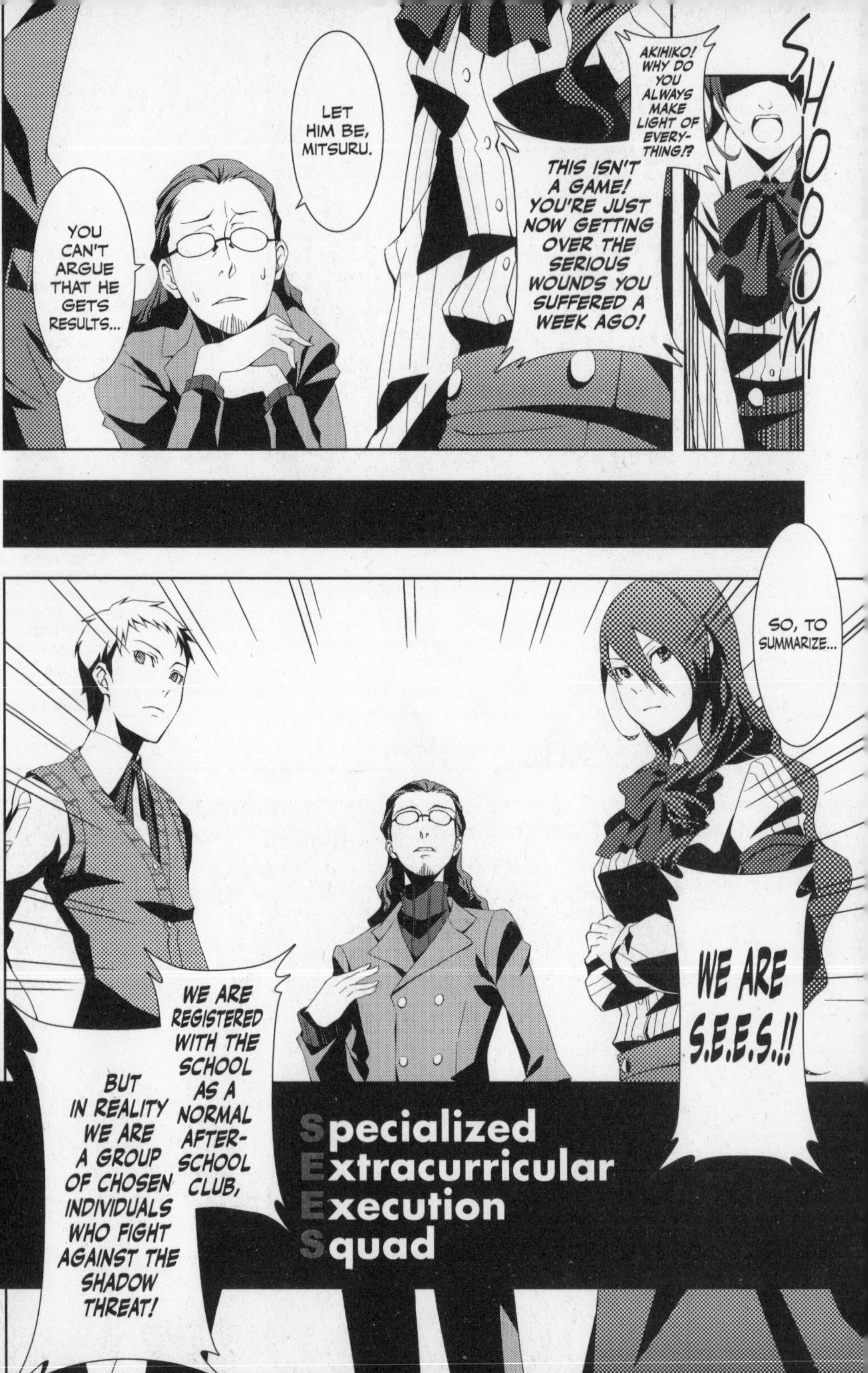
SHOOOOM!
AKIHIKO! WHY DO YOU ALWAYS MAKE LIGHT OF EVERY-THING!?
THIS ISN'T A GAME! YOU'RE JUST NOW GETTING OVER THE SERIOUS WOUNDS YOU SUFFERED A WEEK AGO!
LET HIM BE, MITSURU.
YOU CAN'T ARGUE THAT HE GETS RESULTS...
SO, TO SUMMARIZE...
WE ARE S.E.E.S.!!
WE ARE REGISTERED WITH THE SCHOOL AS A NORMAL AFTER-SCHOOL CLUB,
BUT IN REALITY WE ARE A GROUP OF CHOSEN INDIVIDUALS WHO FIGHT AGAINST THE SHADOW THREAT!
Specialized
Extracurricular
Execution
Squad

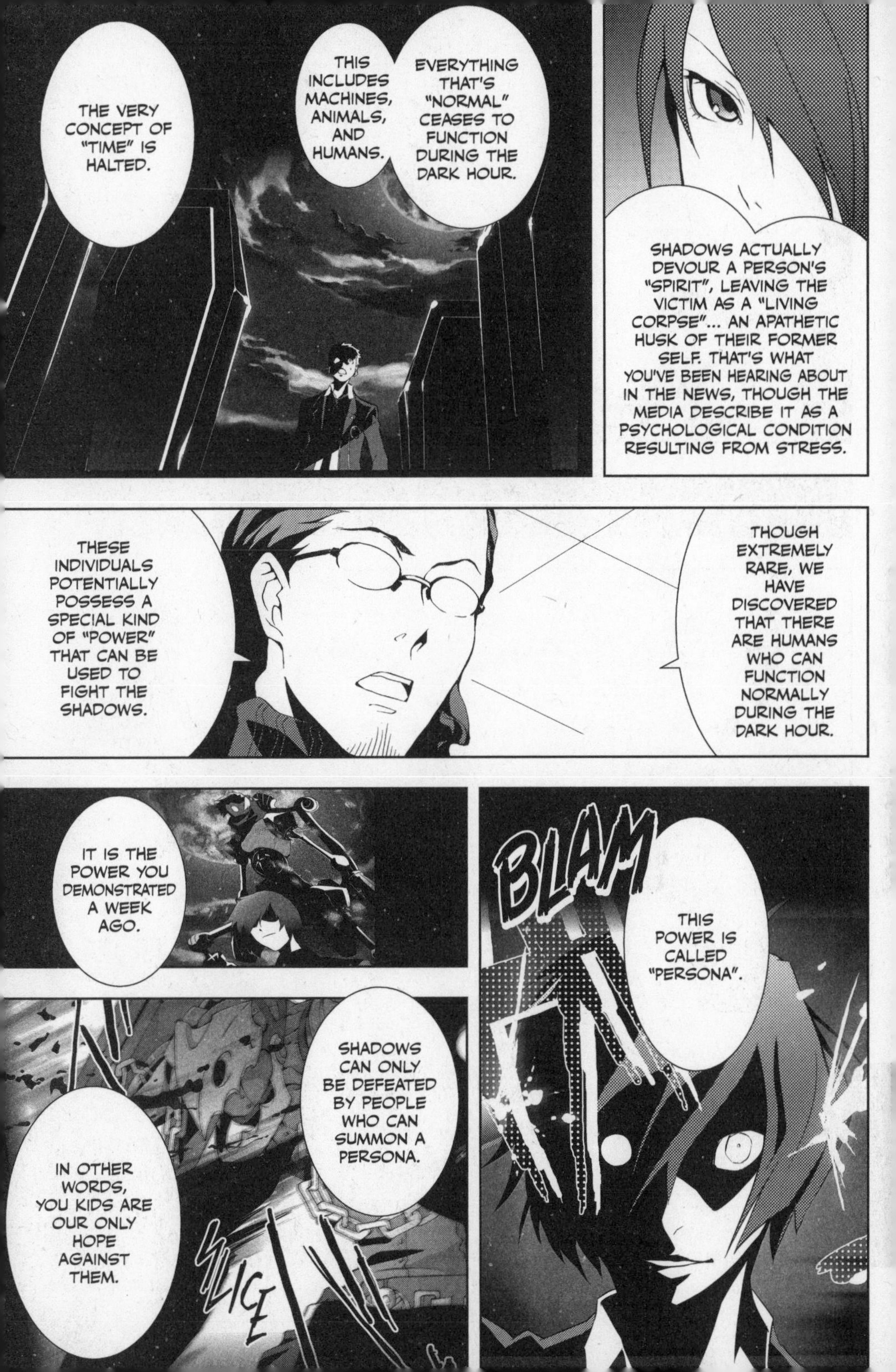
SHADOWS ACTUALLY DEVOUR A PERSON'S "SPIRIT", LEAVING THE VICTIM AS A "LIVING CORPSE"... AN APATHETIC HUSK OF THEIR FORMER SELF. THAT'S WHAT YOU'VE BEEN HEARING ABOUT IN THE NEWS, THOUGH THE MEDIA DESCRIBE IT AS A PSYCHOLOGICAL CONDITION RESULTING FROM STRESS.
EVERYTHING THAT'S "NORMAL" CEASES TO FUNCTION DURING THE DARK HOUR.
THIS INCLUDES MACHINES, ANIMALS, AND HUMANS.
THE VERY CONCEPT OF "TIME" IS HALTED.
THOUGH EXTREMELY RARE, WE HAVE DISCOVERED THAT THERE ARE HUMANS WHO CAN FUNCTION NORMALLY DURING THE DARK HOUR.
THESE INDIVIDUALS POTENTIALLY POSSESS A SPECIAL KIND OF "POWER" THAT CAN BE USED TO FIGHT THE SHADOWS.
BLAM
THIS POWER IS CALLED "PERSONA".
IT IS THE POWER YOU DEMONSTRATED A WEEK AGO.
SHADOWS CAN ONLY BE DEFEATED BY PEOPLE WHO CAN SUMMON A PERSONA.
IN OTHER WORDS, YOU KIDS ARE OUR ONLY HOPE AGAINST THEM.
SLICE

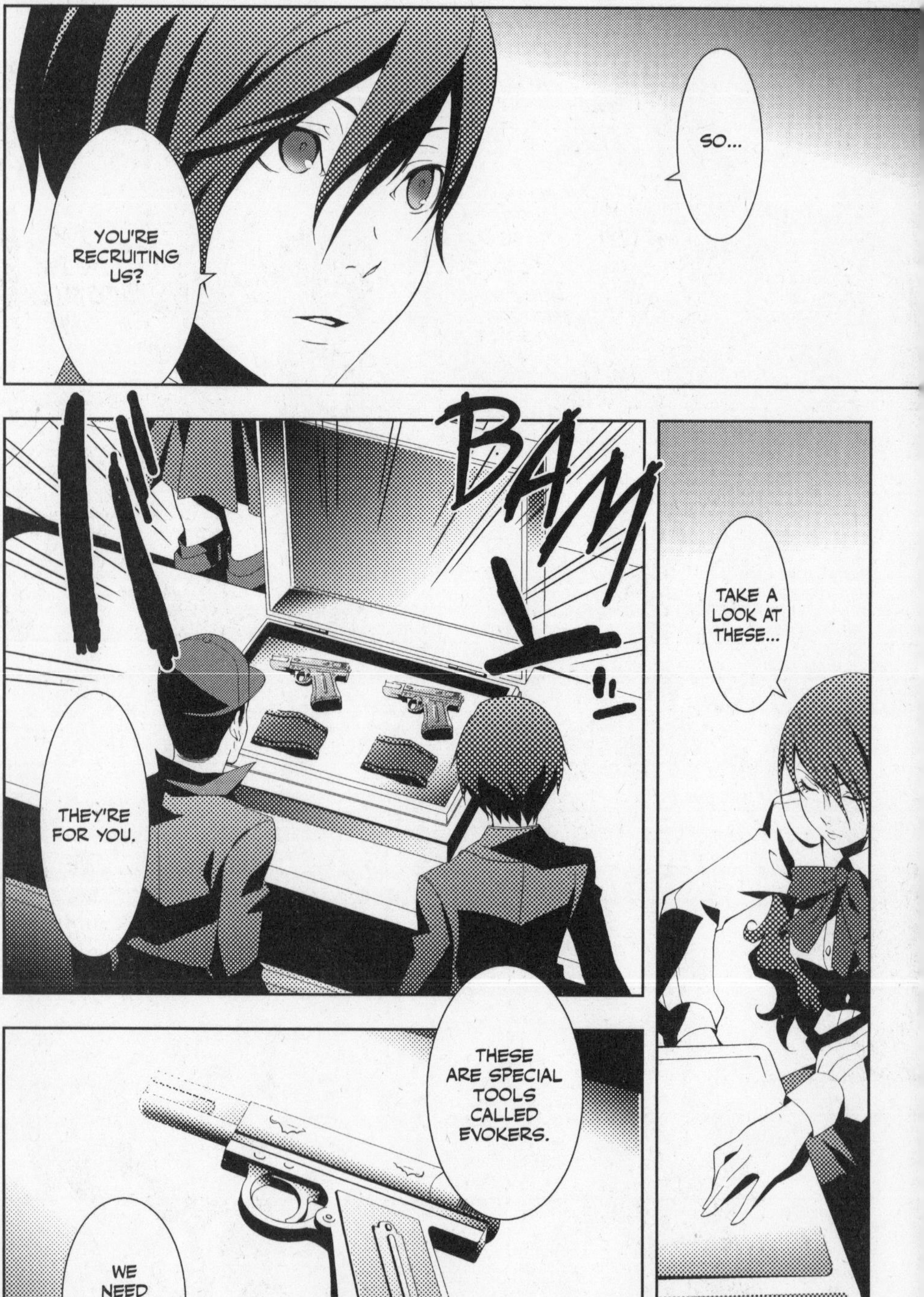
SO...
YOU'RE RECRUITING US?
TAKE A LOOK AT THESE...
BAM
THEY'RE FOR YOU.
THESE ARE SPECIAL TOOLS CALLED EVOKERS.
WE NEED YOUR HELP.

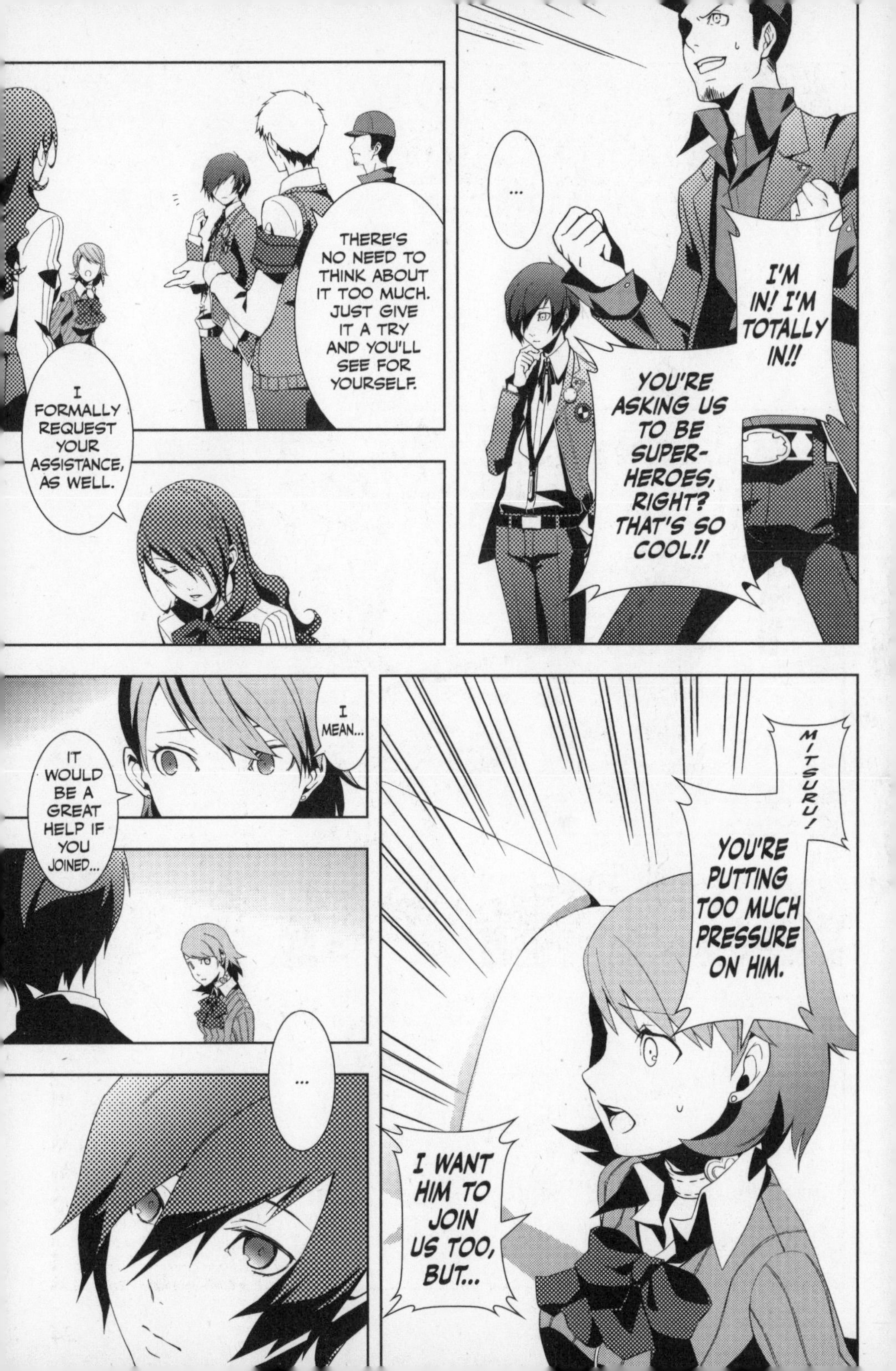
I'M IN! I'M TOTALLY IN!!
YOU'RE ASKING US TO BE SUPER-HEROES, RIGHT? THAT'S SO COOL!!
...
THERE'S NO NEED TO THINK ABOUT IT TOO MUCH. JUST GIVE IT A TRY AND YOU'LL SEE FOR YOURSELF.
I FORMALLY REQUEST YOUR ASSISTANCE, AS WELL.
MITSURU!
YOU'RE PUTTING TOO MUCH PRESSURE ON HIM.
I WANT HIM TO JOIN US TOO, BUT...
I MEAN...
IT WOULD BE A GREAT HELP IF YOU JOINED...
...

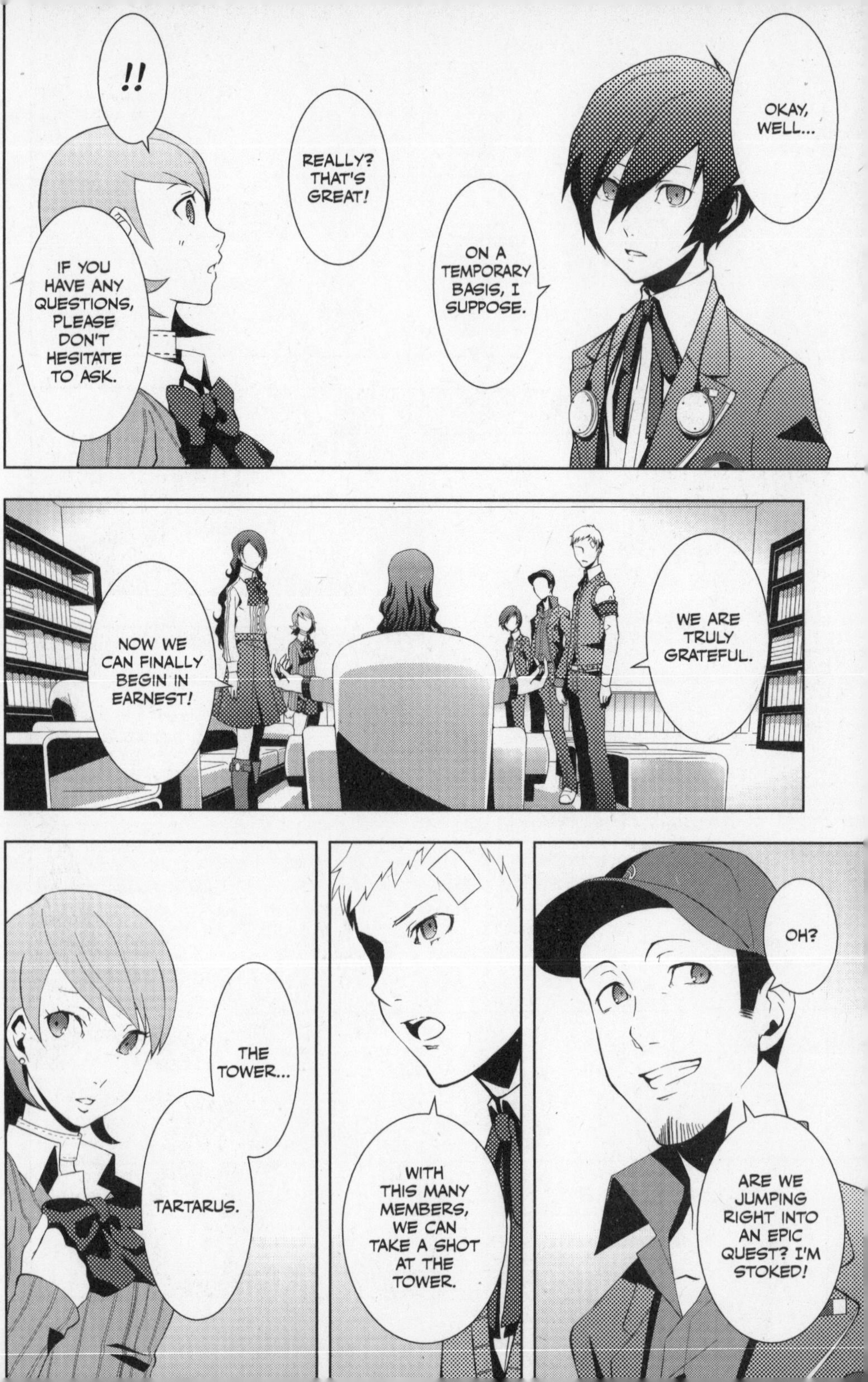
OKAY, WELL...
ON A TEMPORARY BASIS, I SUPPOSE.
REALLY? THAT'S GREAT!
!!
IF YOU HAVE ANY QUESTIONS, PLEASE DON'T HESITATE TO ASK.
WE ARE TRULY GRATEFUL.
NOW WE CAN FINALLY BEGIN IN EARNEST!
OH?
ARE WE JUMPING RIGHT INTO AN EPIC QUEST? I'M STOKED!
WITH THIS MANY MEMBERS, WE CAN TAKE A SHOT AT THE TOWER.
THE TOWER...
TARTARUS.

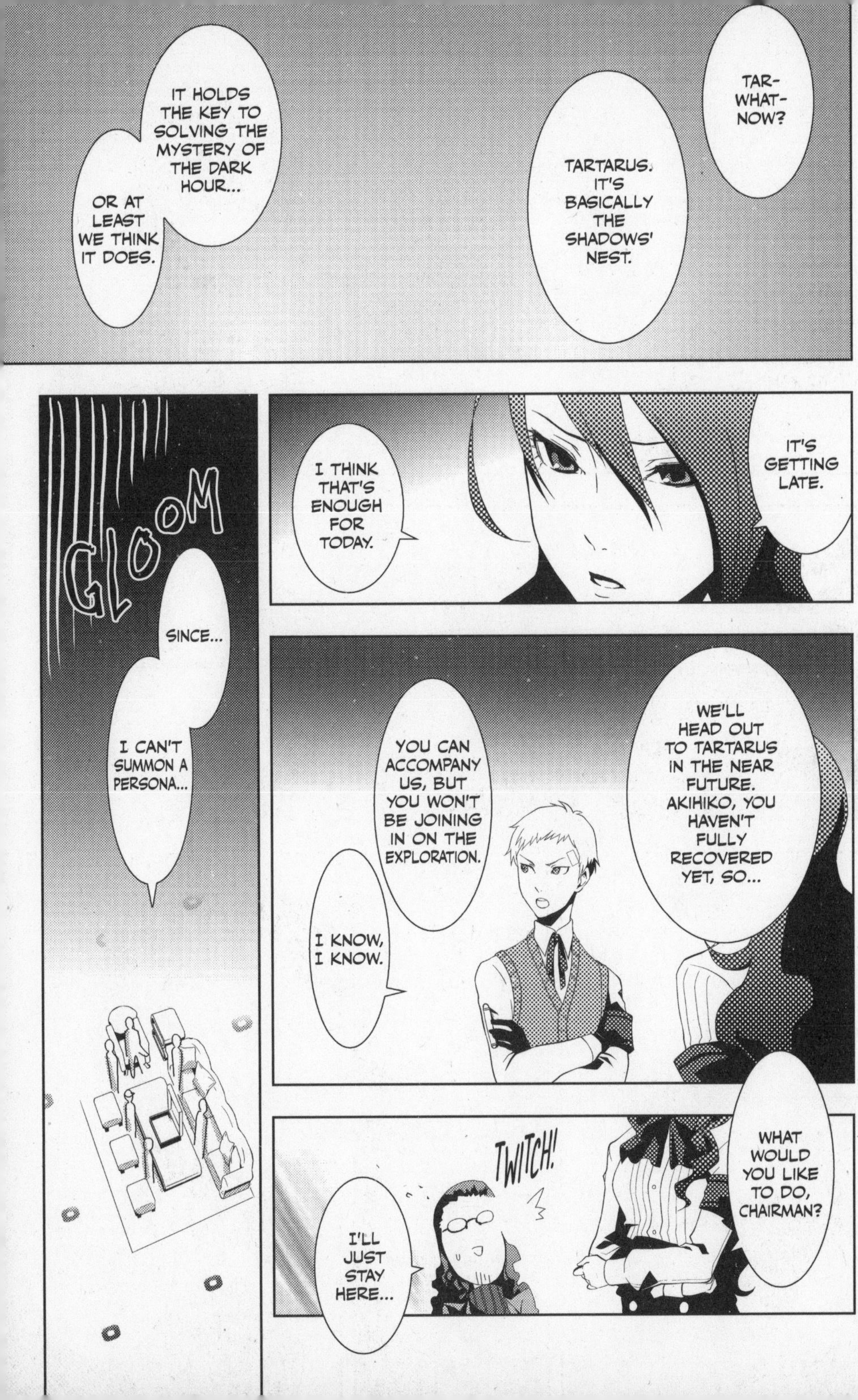
TAR-WHAT-NOW?
TARTARUS. IT'S BASICALLY THE SHADOWS' NEST.
IT HOLDS THE KEY TO SOLVING THE MYSTERY OF THE DARK HOUR...
OR AT LEAST WE THINK IT DOES.
IT'S GETTING LATE.
I THINK THAT'S ENOUGH FOR TODAY.
WE'LL HEAD OUT TO TARTARUS IN THE NEAR FUTURE. AKIHIKO, YOU HAVEN'T FULLY RECOVERED YET, SO...
YOU CAN ACCOMPANY US, BUT YOU WON'T BE JOINING IN ON THE EXPLORATION.
I KNOW, I KNOW.
WHAT WOULD YOU LIKE TO DO, CHAIRMAN?
TWITCH!
I'LL JUST STAY HERE...
GLOOM
SINCE...
I CAN'T SUMMON A PERSONA...

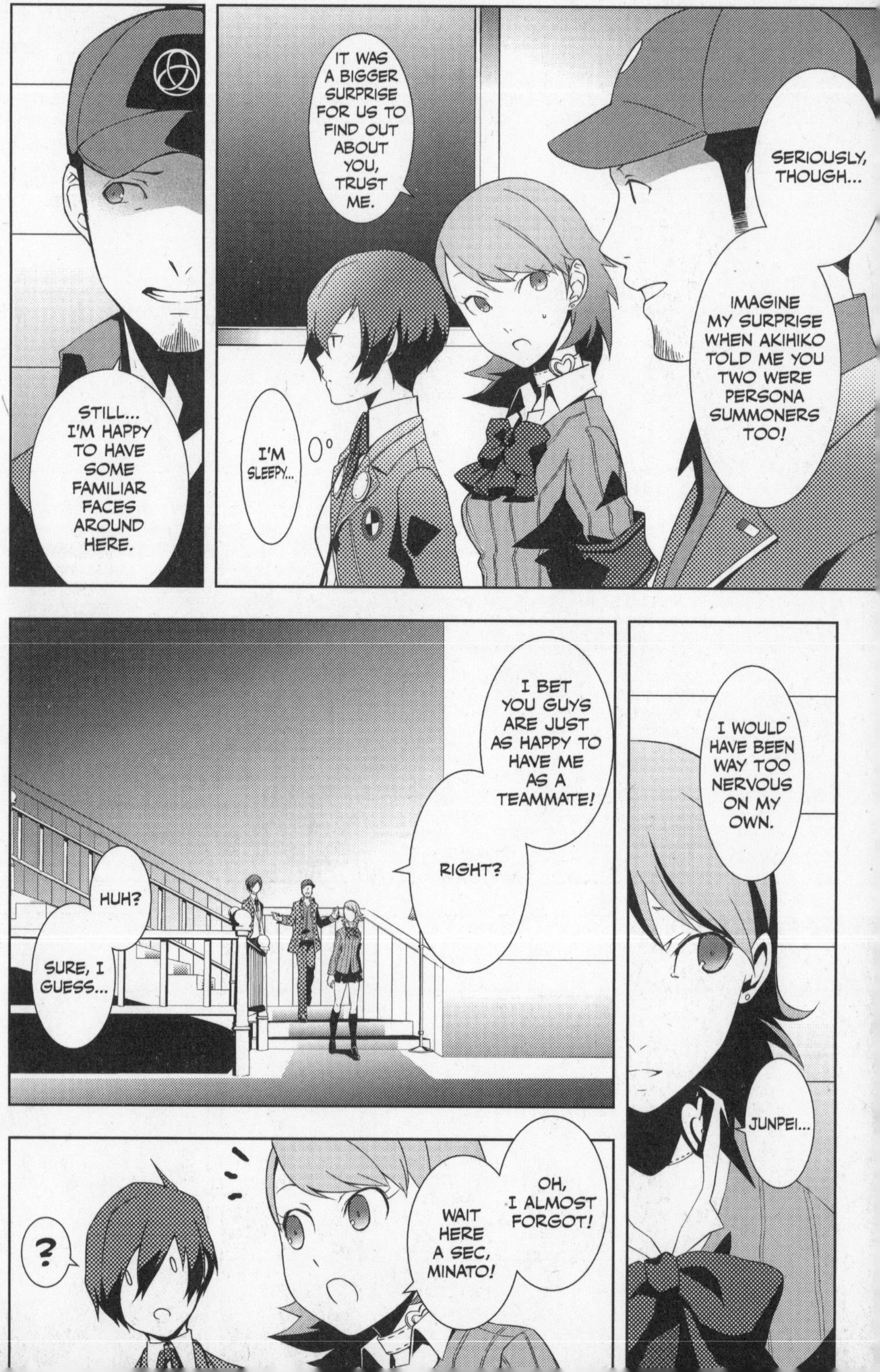
SERIOUSLY, THOUGH...
IMAGINE MY SURPRISE WHEN AKIHIKO TOLD ME YOU TWO WERE PERSONA SUMMONERS TOO!
IT WAS A BIGGER SURPRISE FOR US TO FIND OUT ABOUT YOU, TRUST ME.
I'M SLEEPY...
STILL... I'M HAPPY TO HAVE SOME FAMILIAR FACES AROUND HERE.
I WOULD HAVE BEEN WAY TOO NERVOUS ON MY OWN.
JUNPEI...
I BET YOU GUYS ARE JUST AS HAPPY TO HAVE ME AS A TEAMMATE!
RIGHT?
HUH?
SURE, I GUESS...
OH, I ALMOST FORGOT!
WAIT HERE A SEC, MINATO!
?

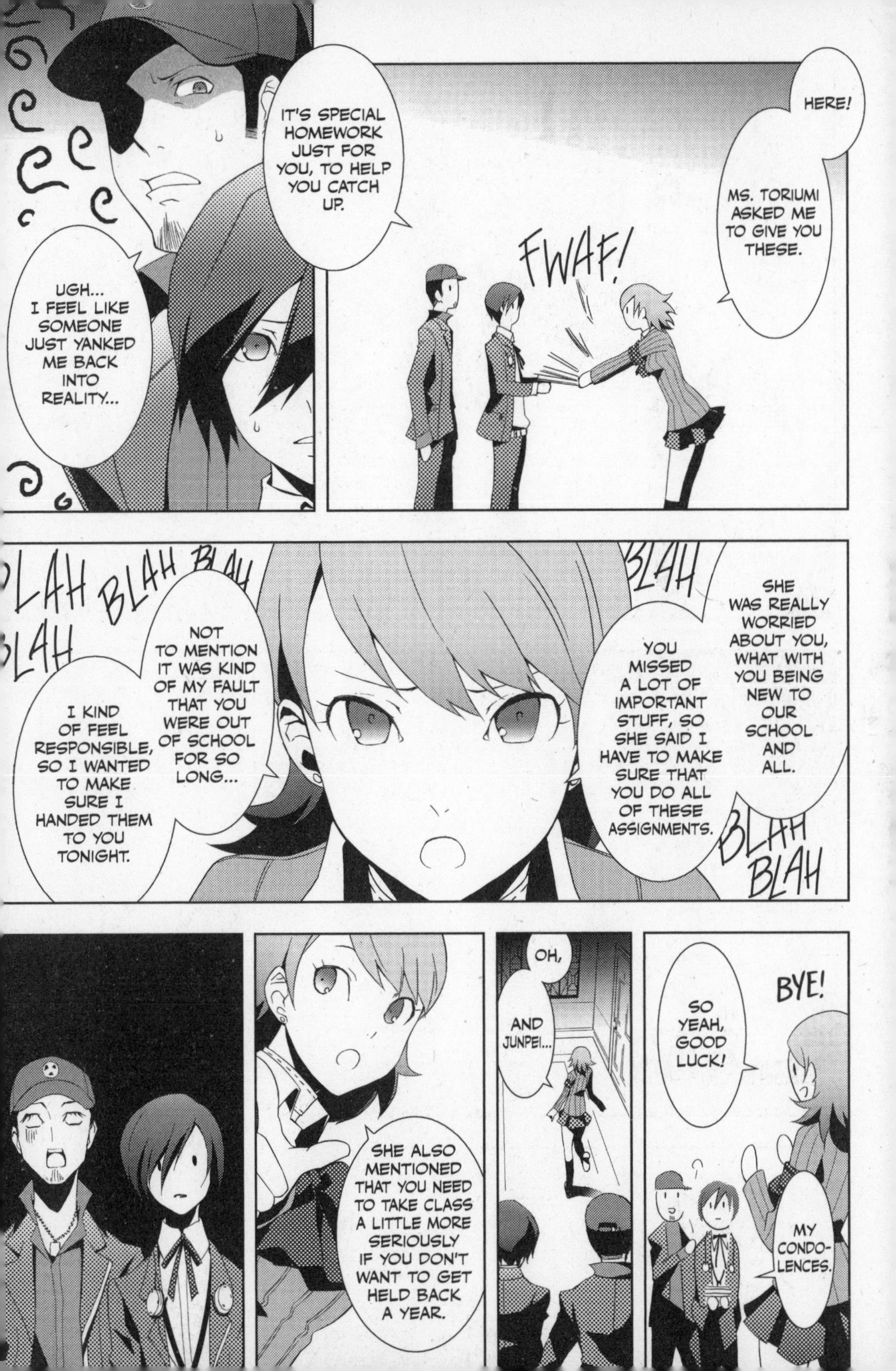
HERE!
MS. TORIUMI ASKED ME TO GIVE YOU THESE.
FWAF!
IT'S SPECIAL HOMEWORK JUST FOR YOU, TO HELP YOU CATCH UP.
UGH... I FEEL LIKE SOMEONE JUST YANKED ME BACK INTO REALITY...
BLAH
SHE WAS REALLY WORRIED ABOUT YOU, WHAT WITH YOU BEING NEW TO OUR SCHOOL AND ALL.
YOU MISSED A LOT OF IMPORTANT STUFF, SO SHE SAID I HAVE TO MAKE SURE THAT YOU DO ALL OF THESE ASSIGNMENTS.
BLAH BLAH
NOT TO MENTION IT WAS KIND OF MY FAULT THAT YOU WERE OUT OF SCHOOL FOR SO LONG...
I KIND OF FEEL RESPONSIBLE, SO I WANTED TO MAKE SURE I HANDED THEM TO YOU TONIGHT.
BLAH BLAH BLAH
BLAH BLAH
BYE!
SO YEAH, GOOD LUCK!
MY CONDO-LENCES.
OH,
AND JUNPEI...
SHE ALSO MENTIONED THAT YOU NEED TO TAKE CLASS A LITTLE MORE SERIOUSLY IF YOU DON'T WANT TO GET HELD BACK A YEAR.

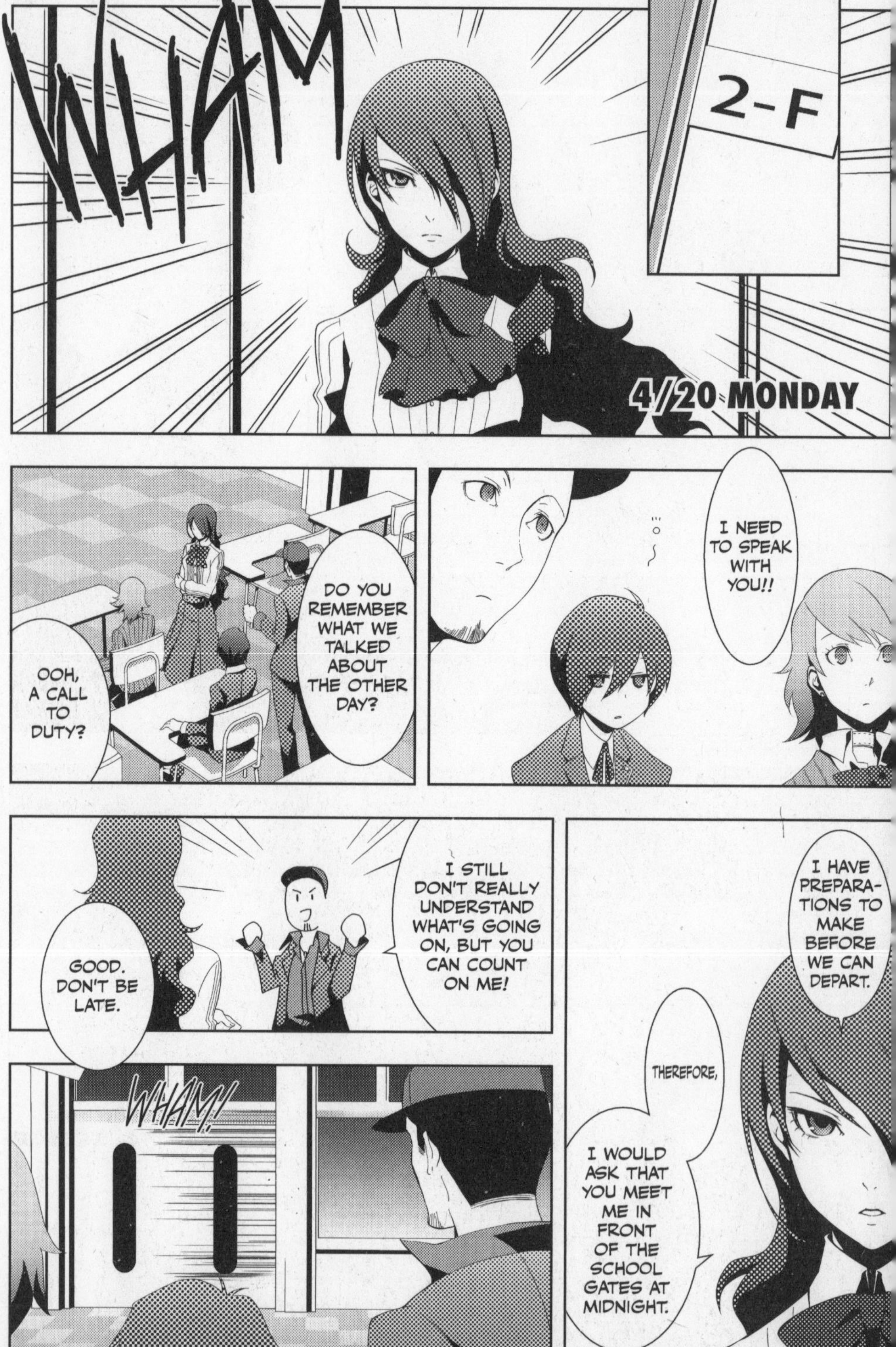
2-F
WHAM
4/20 MONDAY
I NEED TO SPEAK WITH YOU!!
...
DO YOU REMEMBER WHAT WE TALKED ABOUT THE OTHER DAY?
OOH, A CALL TO DUTY?
I HAVE PREPARATIONS TO MAKE BEFORE WE CAN DEPART.
THEREFORE,
I WOULD ASK THAT YOU MEET ME IN FRONT OF THE SCHOOL GATES AT MIDNIGHT.
I STILL DON'T REALLY UNDERSTAND WHAT'S GOING ON, BUT YOU CAN COUNT ON ME!
GOOD. DON'T BE LATE.
WHAM!

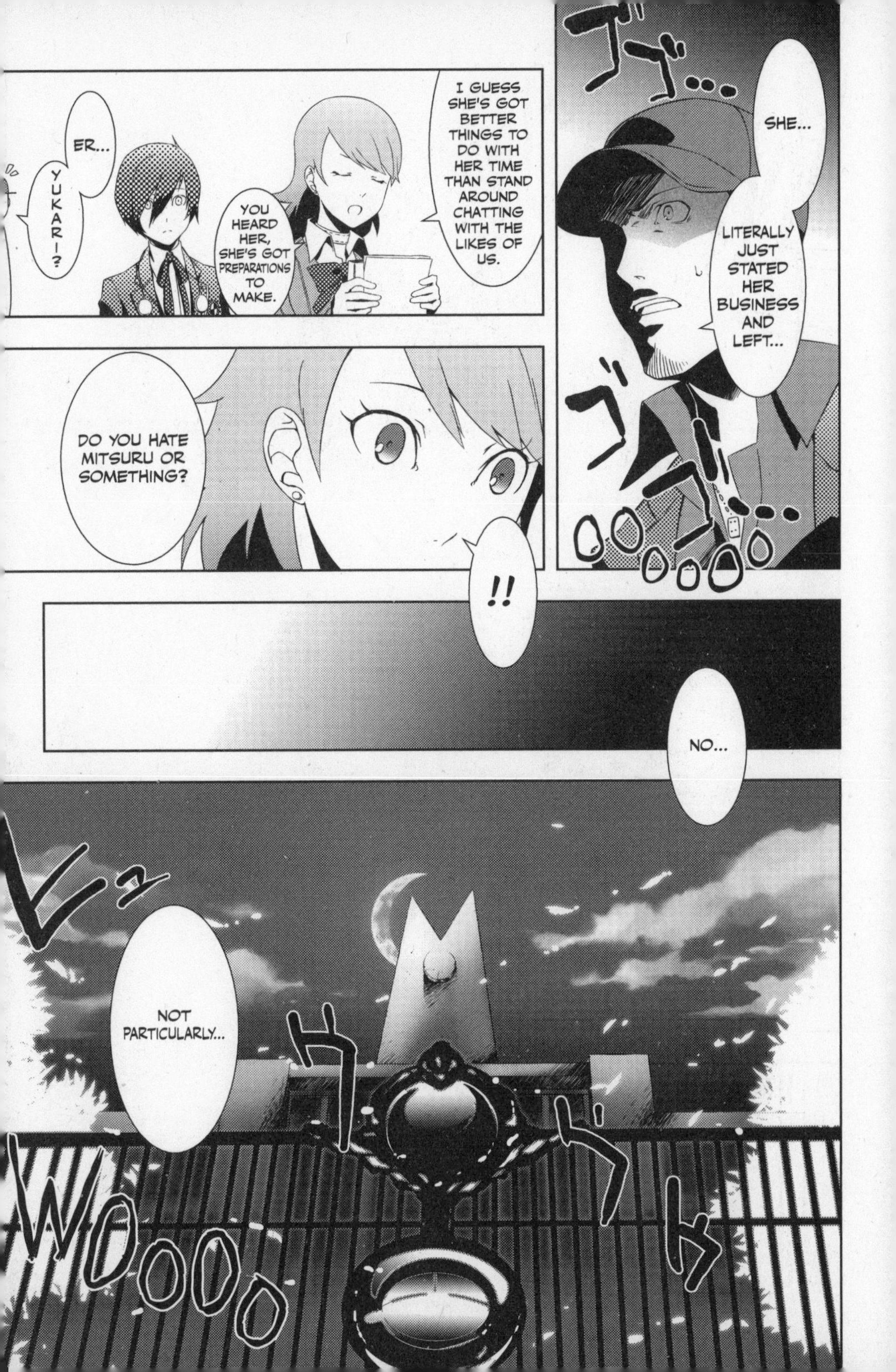
ゴゴ...
SHE...
LITERALLY JUST STATED HER BUSINESS AND LEFT...
I GUESS SHE'S GOT BETTER THINGS TO DO WITH HER TIME THAN STAND AROUND CHATTING WITH THE LIKES OF US.
YOU HEARD HER, SHE'S GOT PREPARATIONS TO MAKE.
ER...
YUKARI?
DO YOU HATE MITSURU OR SOMETHING?
!!
NO...
NOT PARTICULARLY...
WOOOOO

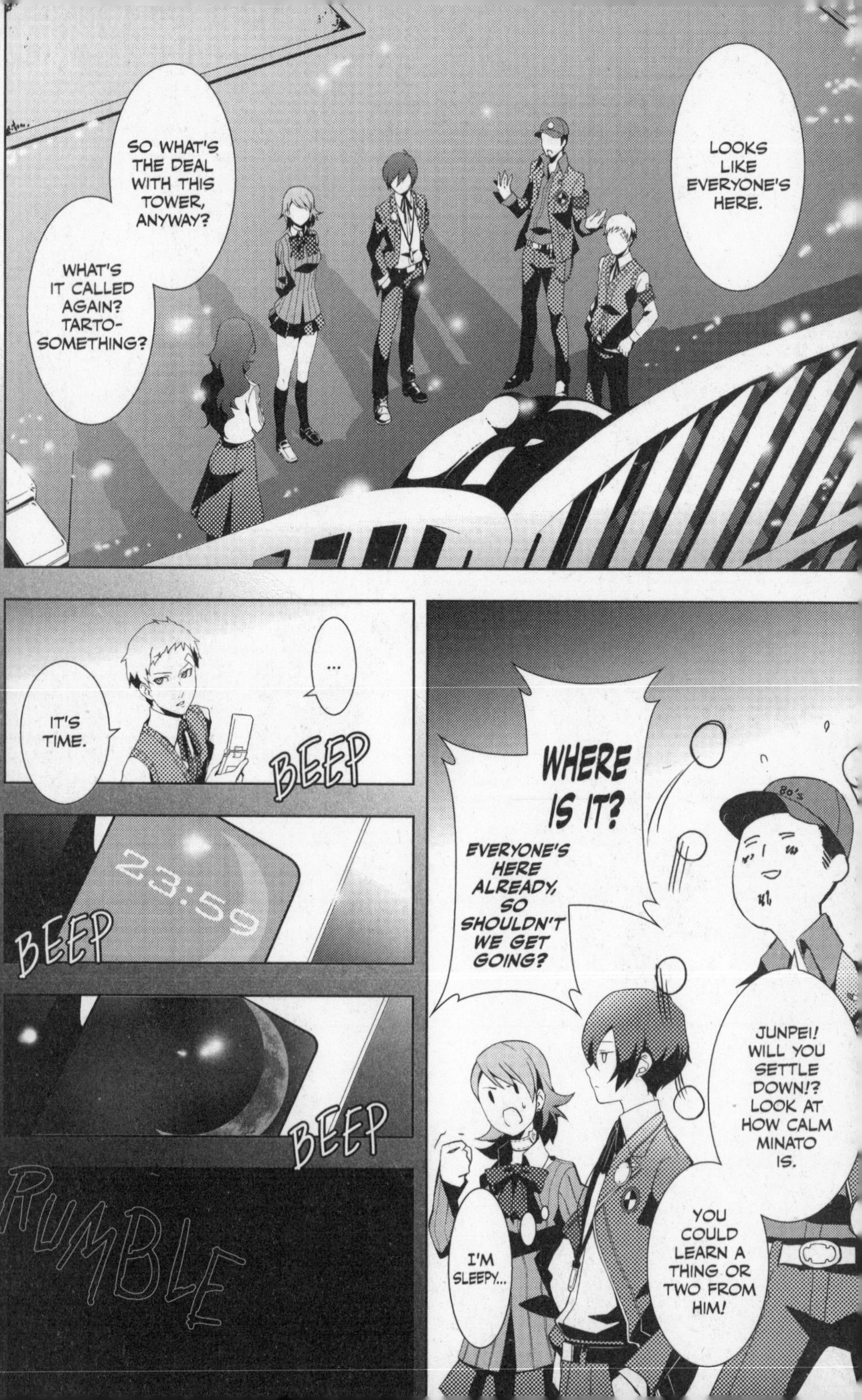
LOOKS LIKE EVERYONE'S HERE.
SO WHAT'S THE DEAL WITH THIS TOWER, ANYWAY?
WHAT'S IT CALLED AGAIN? TARTO-SOMETHING?
WHERE IS IT?
EVERYONE'S HERE ALREADY, SO SHOULDN'T WE GET GOING?
JUNPEI! WILL YOU SETTLE DOWN!? LOOK AT HOW CALM MINATO IS.
YOU COULD LEARN A THING OR TWO FROM HIM!
I'M SLEEPY...
...
IT'S TIME.
BEEP
23:59
BEEP
BEEP
RUMBLE

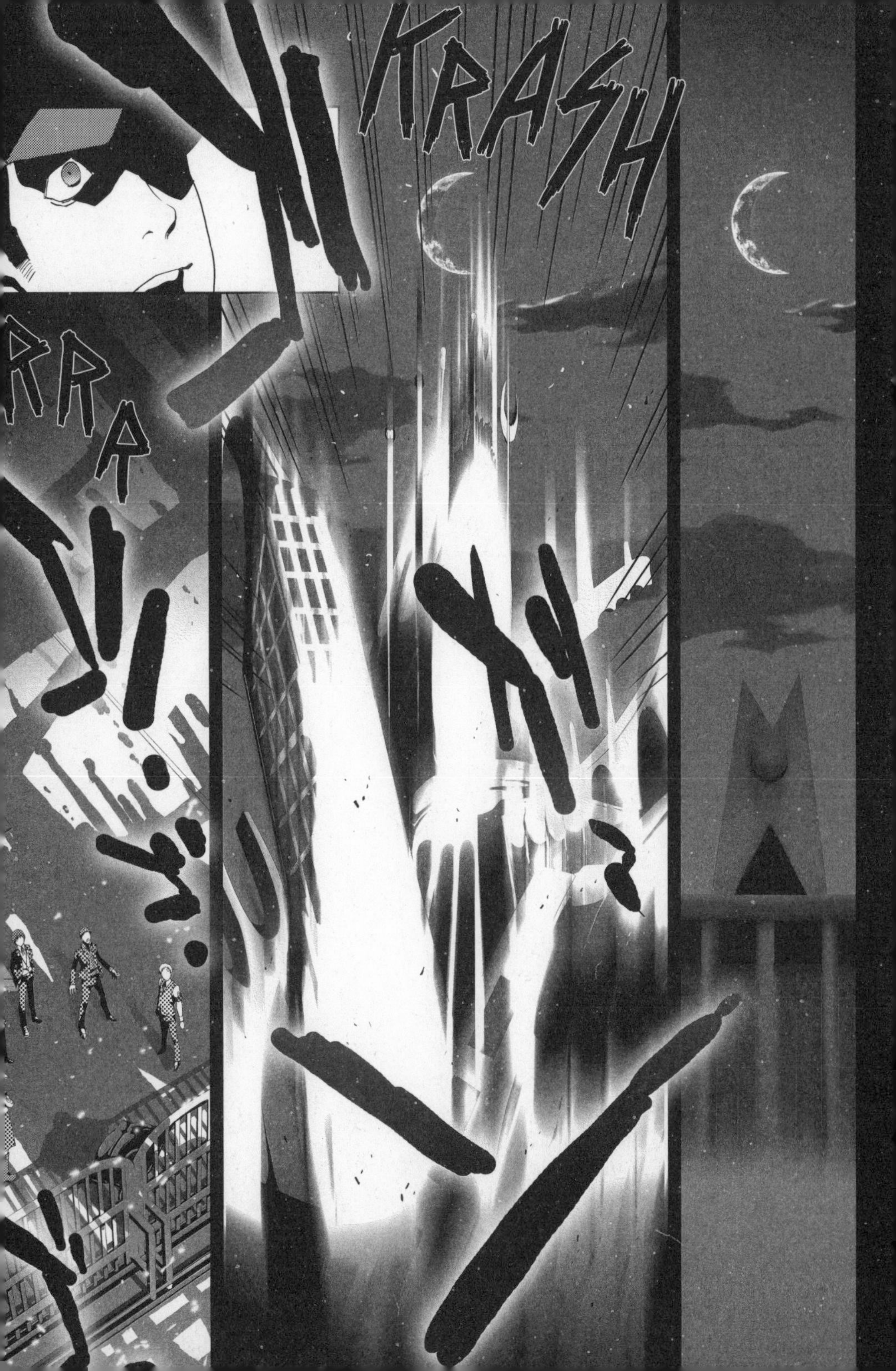
KRASH

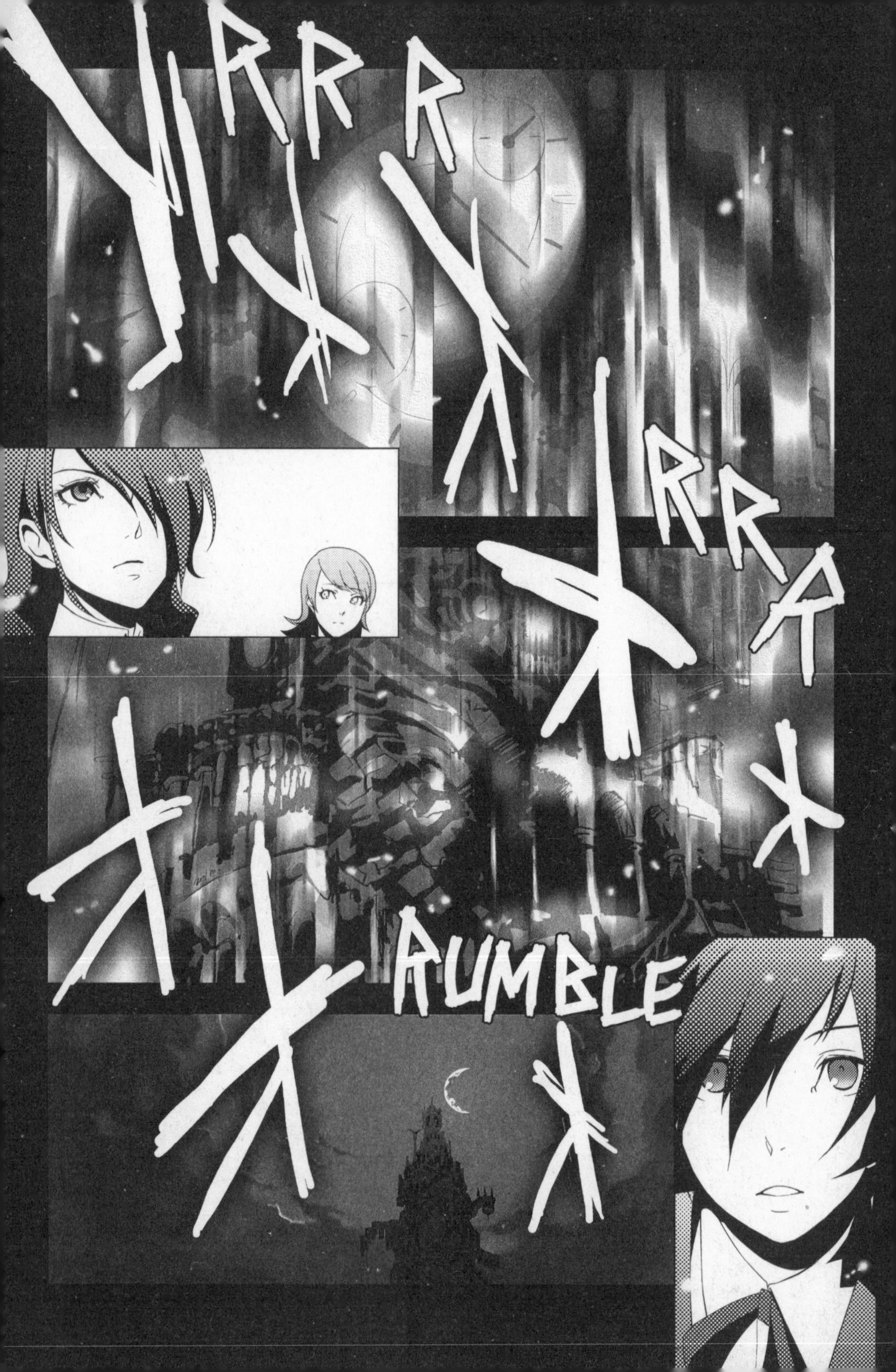
RUMBLE

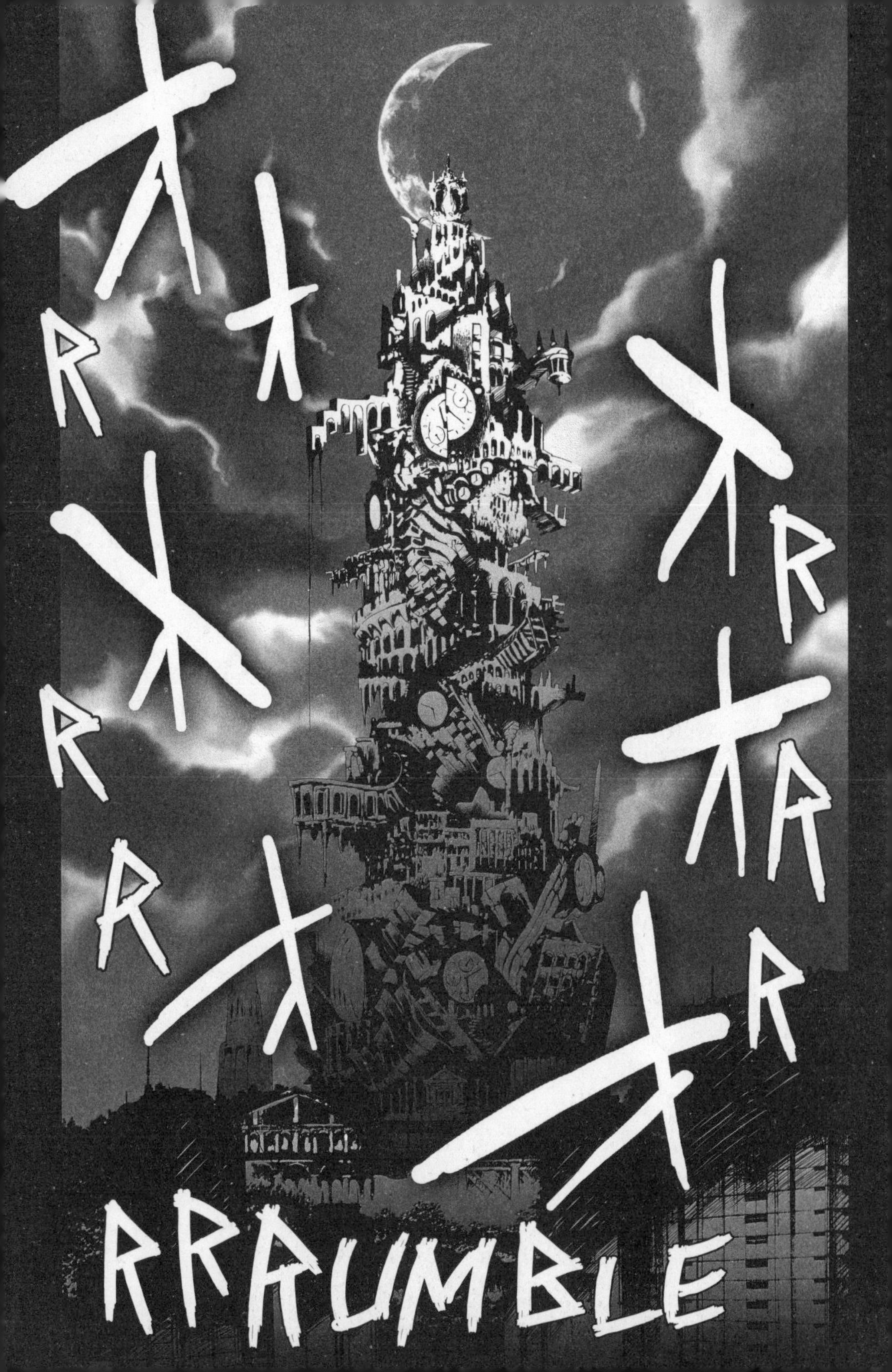
RRRUMBLE

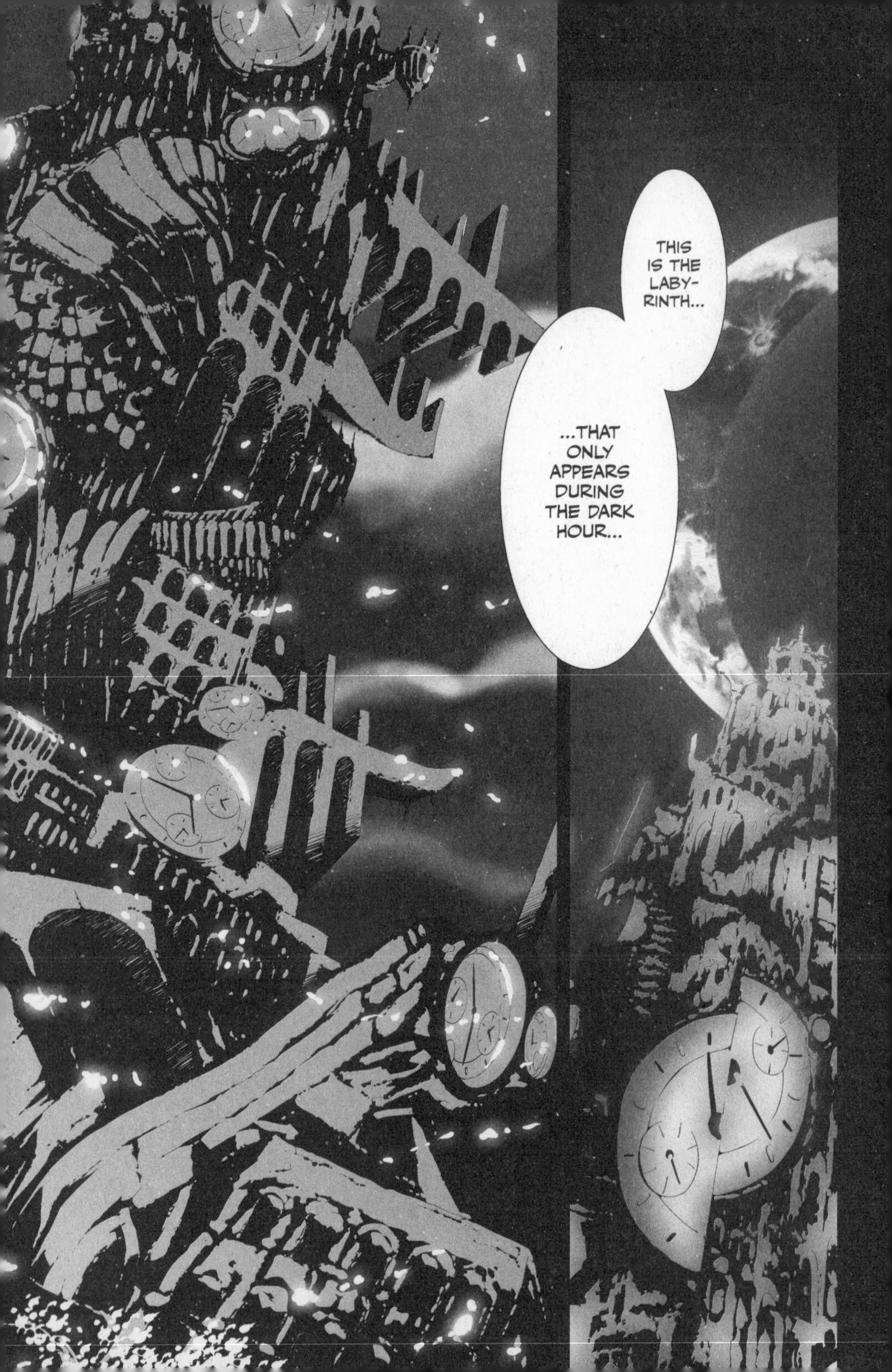
THIS IS THE LABY-RINTH...
...THAT ONLY APPEARS DURING THE DARK HOUR...

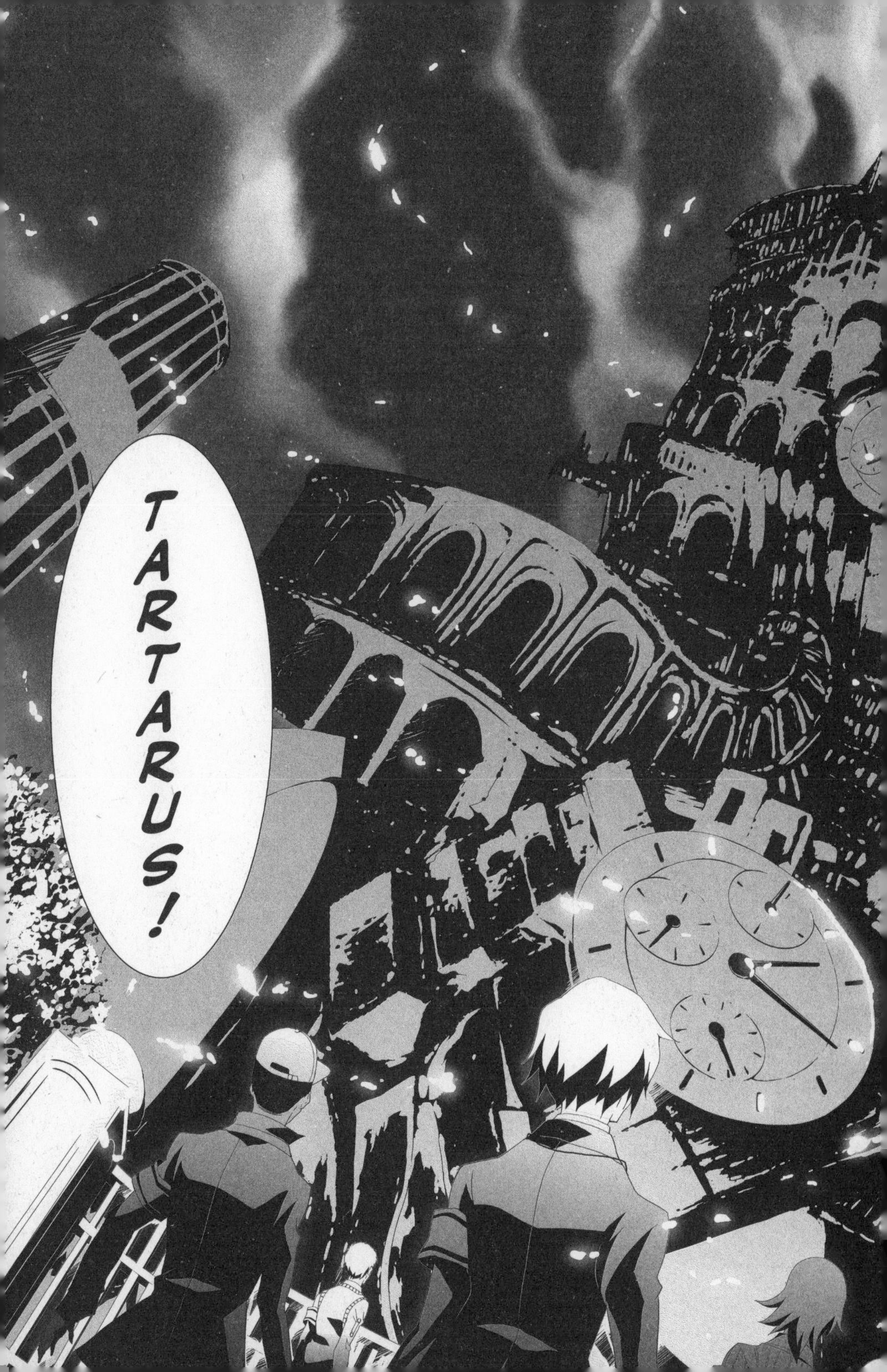
TARTARUS!

そしてラストに[redacted]として出て来る[redacted]なんですが、
[redacted]では割とそこまでの出番、絡みが少なかったので
この漫画ではその辺、とくに主人公達との[redacted]的なものを重点的に話の軸とし

特に紙面に表記はしないですが、大まかにこのような順序で進めていきます。

1	・主人公紹介編	・[redacted]救出編		基本的な世界観
2	・[redacted]編	・[redacted]、[redacted]編		[redacted]の事件を
3	・[redacted]編	・[redacted]、[redacted]編		[redacted]、[redacted]、[redacted]
4	・[redacted]編			上の二つとほぼ
5	・[redacted]編	・[redacted]編	・[redacted]編	最終局面。[redacted]

話数表記について

#02　Piece:01 転校生

#は雑誌の掲載順。
Piece:01はカテゴリとそのナンバリングです。

Piece　キャラクタ　ト
Perspective　話の流れ
[redacted]　ス

P3だけに3　ば#0　はologueとか
時間軸が　してはなるべく明快にすべきと
このようにタ　[redacted]算段で
[redacted]

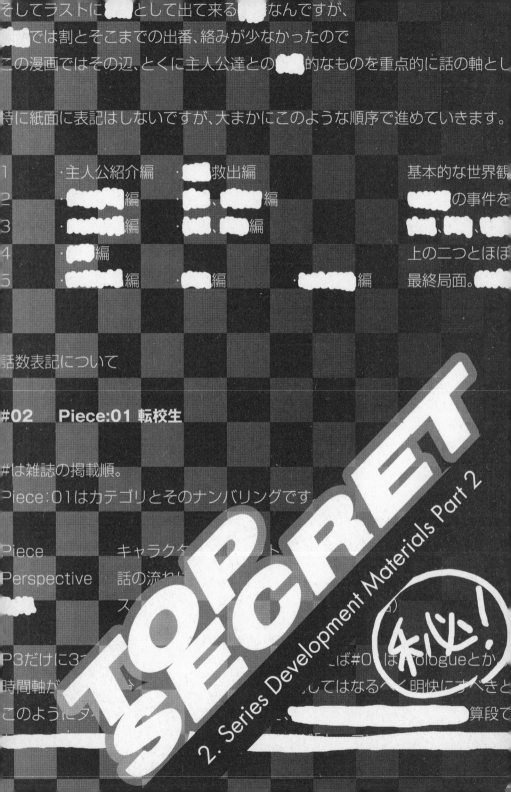

TOP SECRET

2. Series Development Materials Part 2

秘!

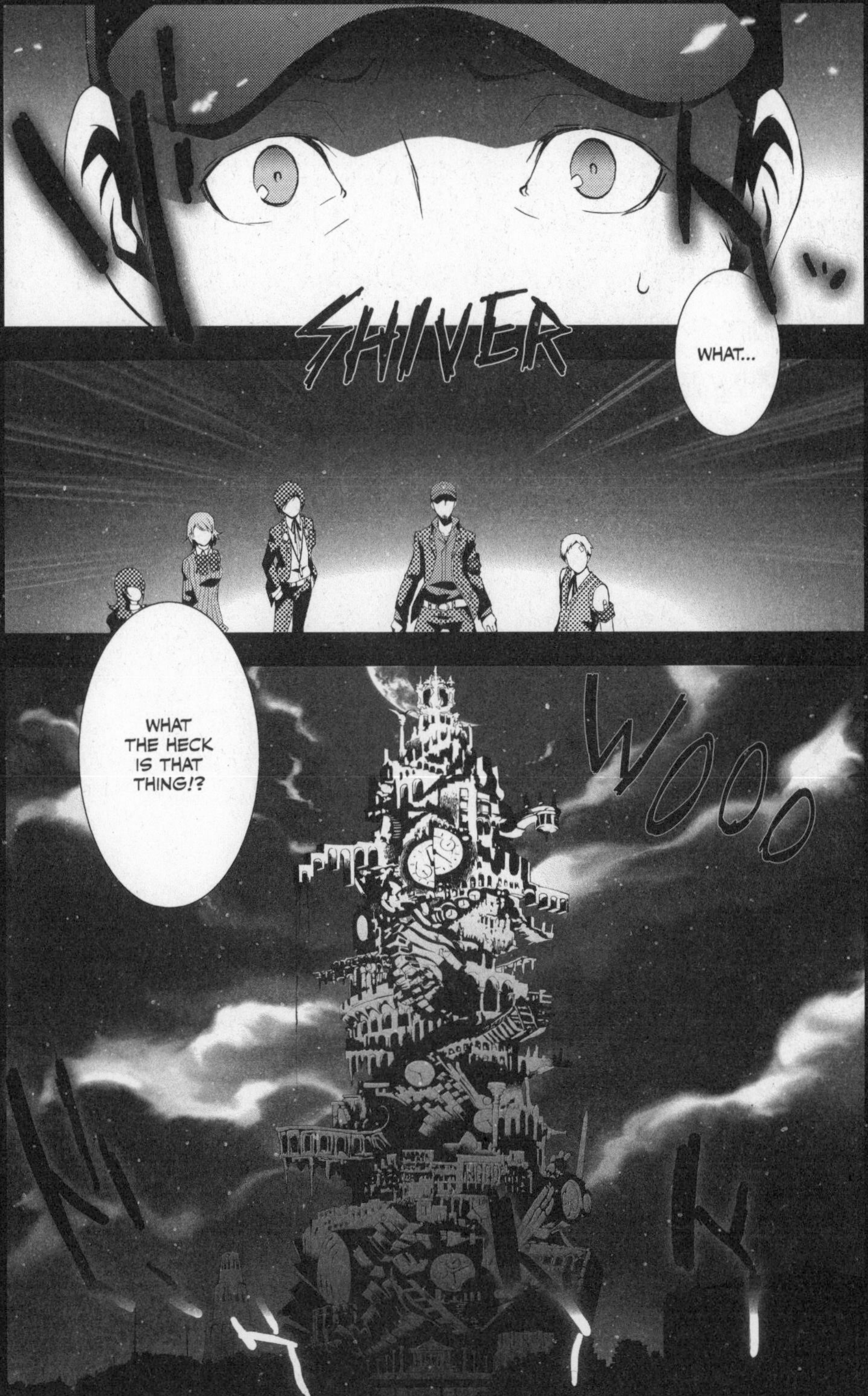
SHIVER
WHAT...
WHAT THE HECK IS THAT THING!?
WOOO

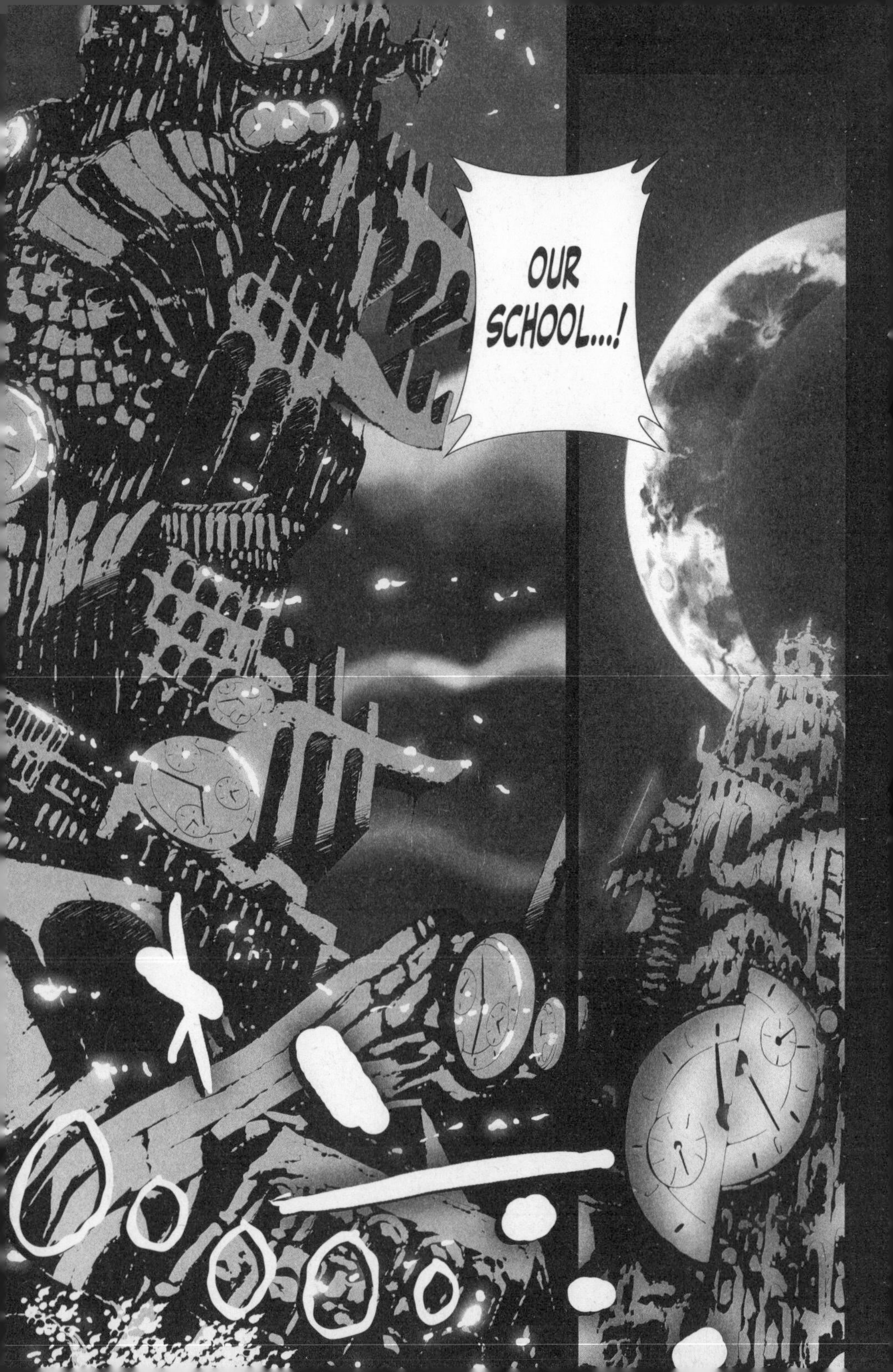
OUR SCHOOL...!

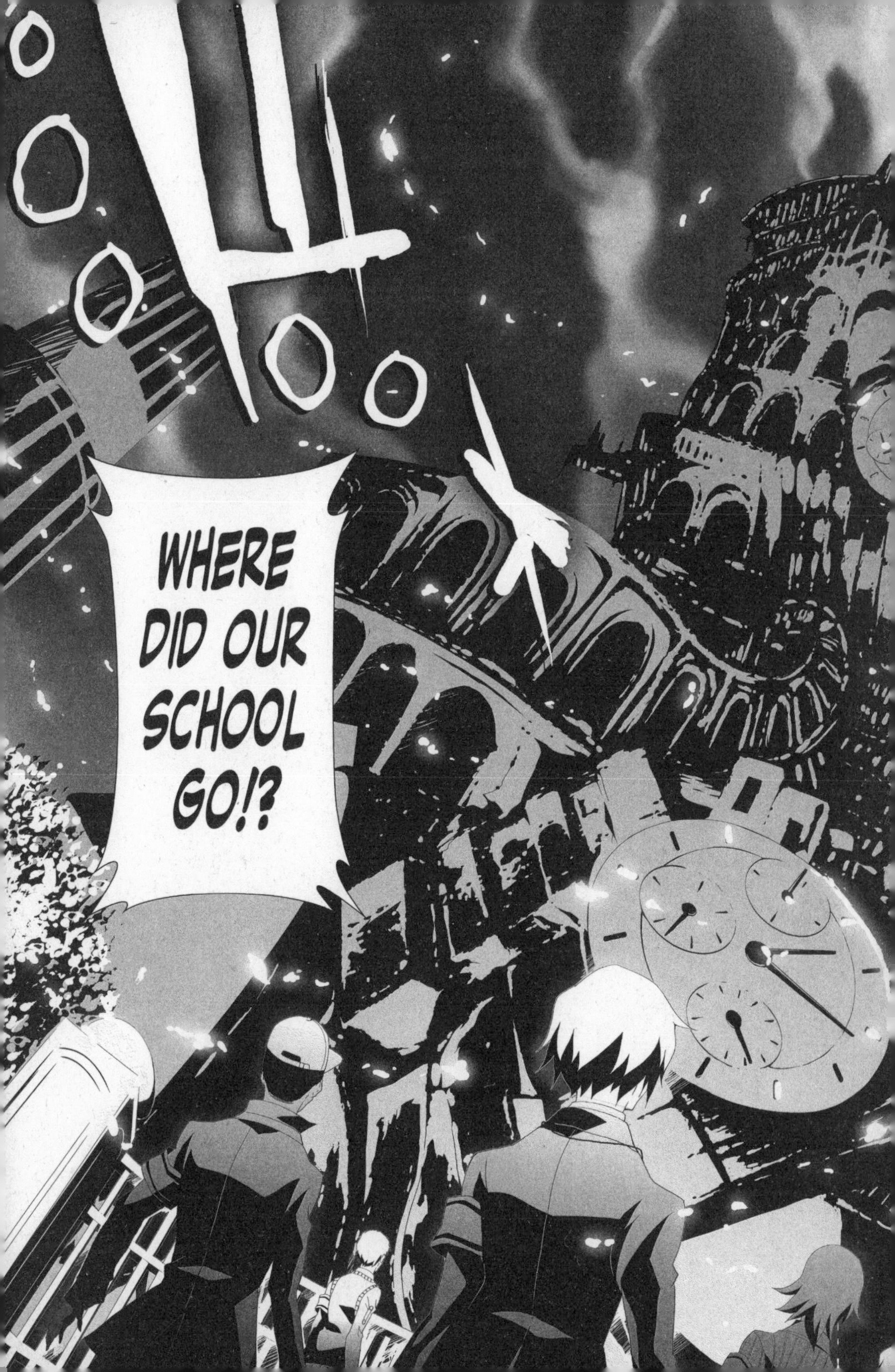
WHERE DID OUR SCHOOL GO!?

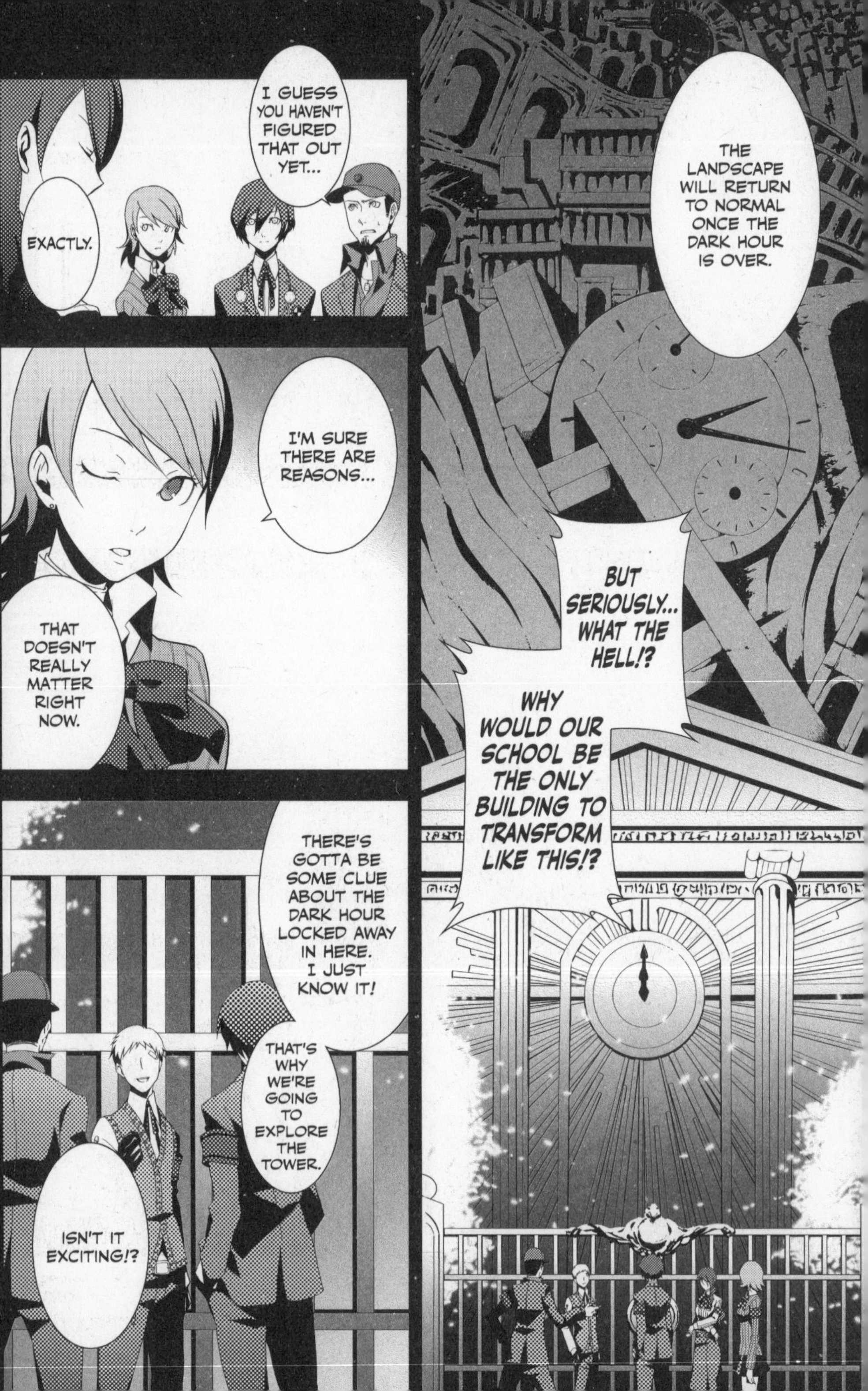
THE LANDSCAPE WILL RETURN TO NORMAL ONCE THE DARK HOUR IS OVER.
BUT SERIOUSLY... WHAT THE HELL!?
WHY WOULD OUR SCHOOL BE THE ONLY BUILDING TO TRANSFORM LIKE THIS!?
I GUESS YOU HAVEN'T FIGURED THAT OUT YET...
EXACTLY.
I'M SURE THERE ARE REASONS...
THAT DOESN'T REALLY MATTER RIGHT NOW.
THERE'S GOTTA BE SOME CLUE ABOUT THE DARK HOUR LOCKED AWAY IN HERE. I JUST KNOW IT!
THAT'S WHY WE'RE GOING TO EXPLORE THE TOWER.
ISN'T IT EXCITING!?

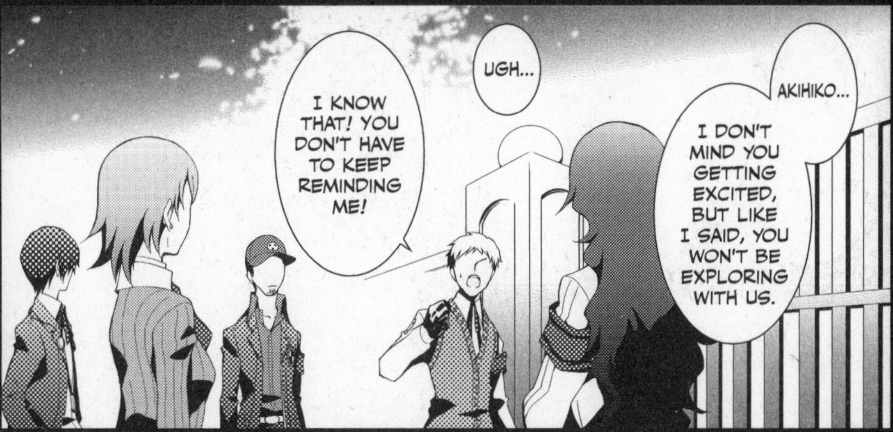
AKIHIKO...
I DON'T MIND YOU GETTING EXCITED, BUT LIKE I SAID, YOU WON'T BE EXPLORING WITH US.
UGH...
I KNOW THAT! YOU DON'T HAVE TO KEEP REMINDING ME!

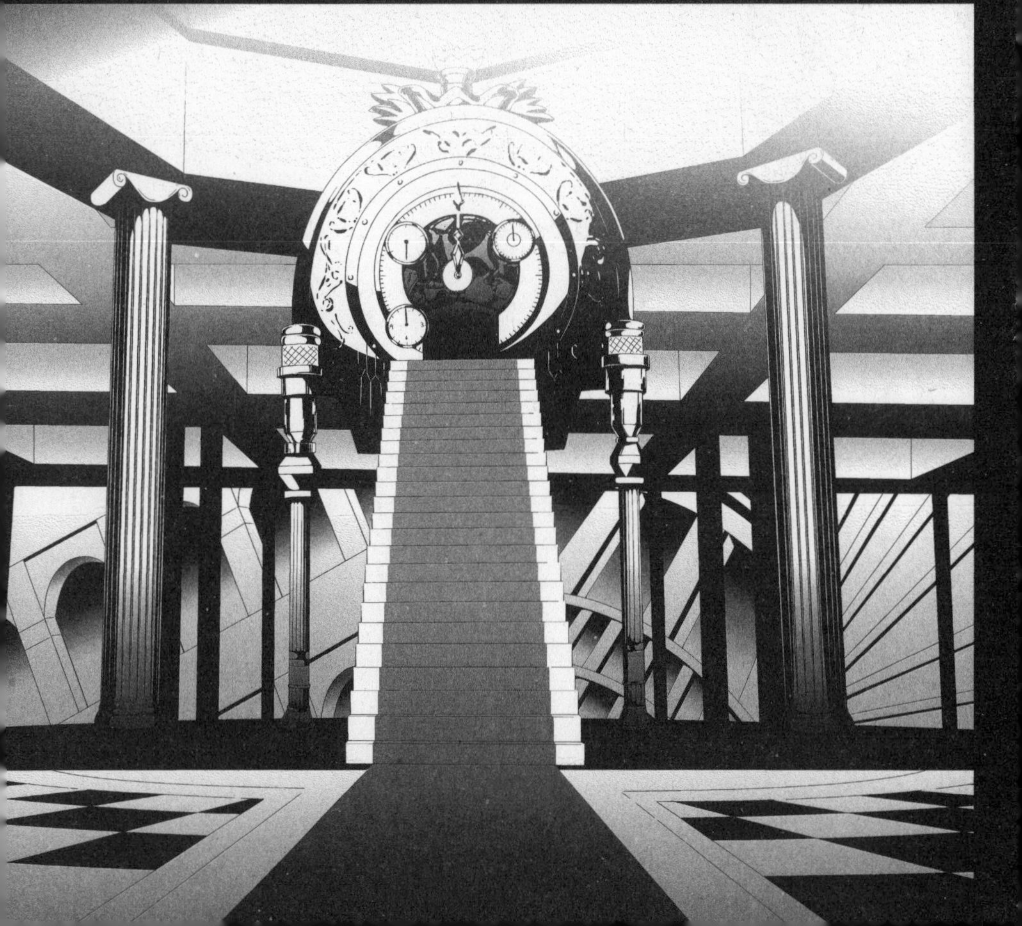

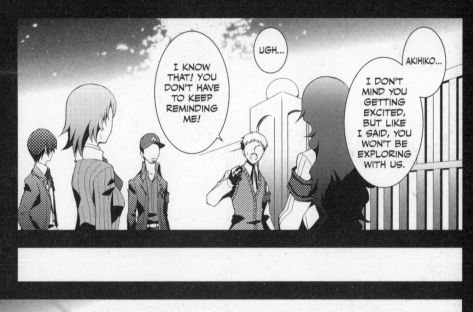

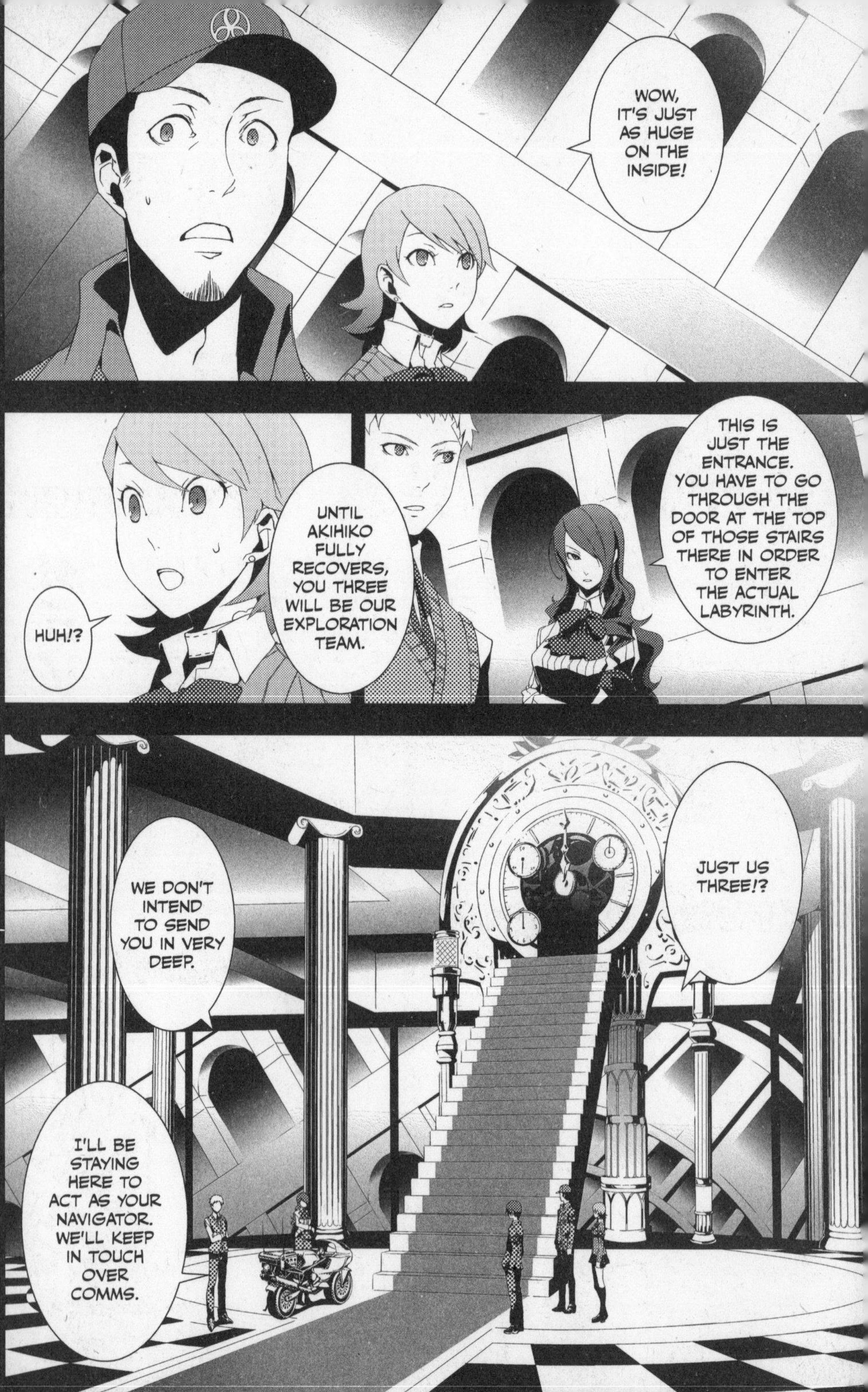
WOW, IT'S JUST AS HUGE ON THE INSIDE!
THIS IS JUST THE ENTRANCE. YOU HAVE TO GO THROUGH THE DOOR AT THE TOP OF THOSE STAIRS THERE IN ORDER TO ENTER THE ACTUAL LABYRINTH.
UNTIL AKIHIKO FULLY RECOVERS, YOU THREE WILL BE OUR EXPLORATION TEAM.
HUH!?
JUST US THREE!?
WE DON'T INTEND TO SEND YOU IN VERY DEEP.
I'LL BE STAYING HERE TO ACT AS YOUR NAVIGATOR. WE'LL KEEP IN TOUCH OVER COMMS.

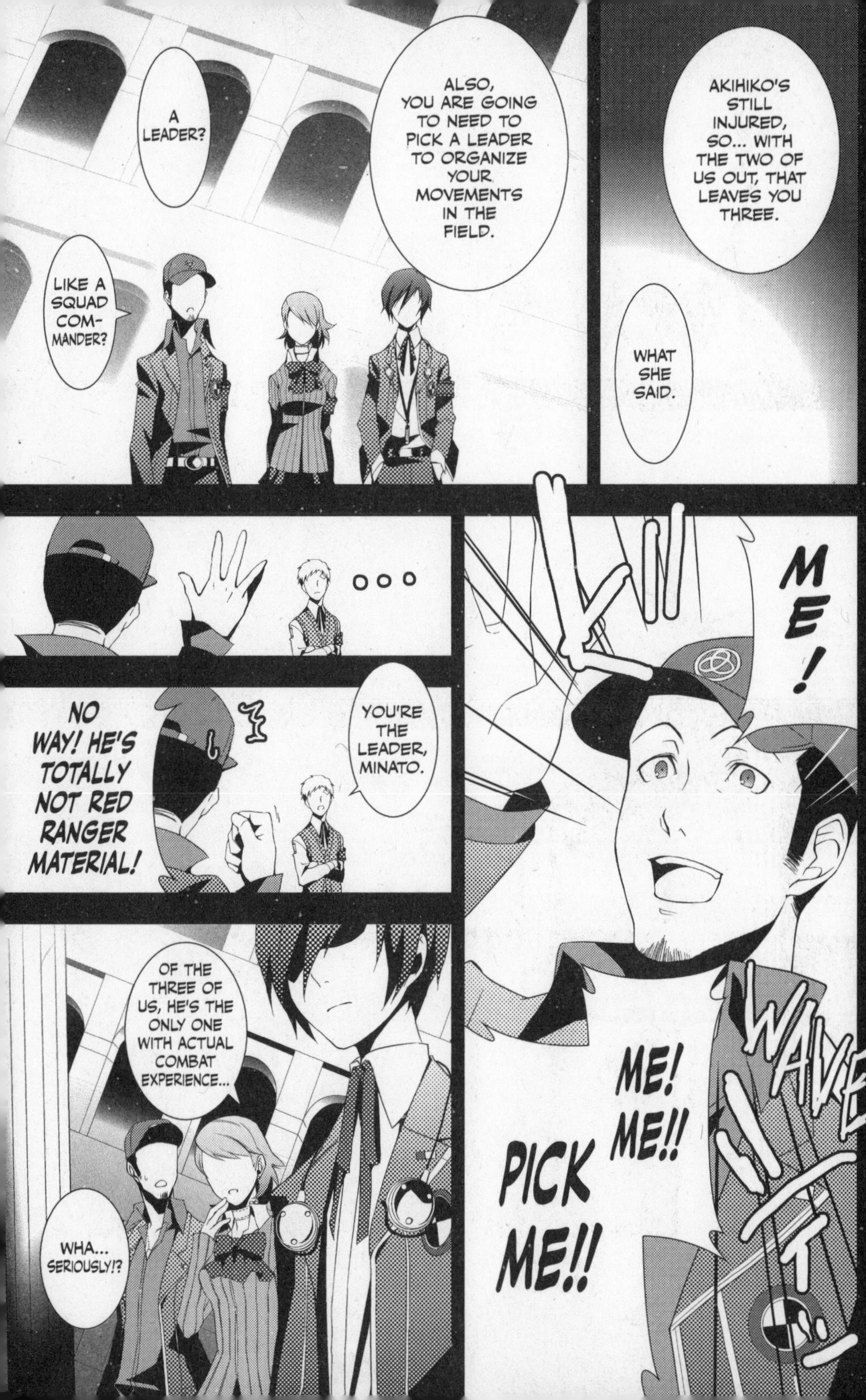
AKIHIKO'S STILL INJURED, SO... WITH THE TWO OF US OUT, THAT LEAVES YOU THREE.
WHAT SHE SAID.
ALSO, YOU ARE GOING TO NEED TO PICK A LEADER TO ORGANIZE YOUR MOVEMENTS IN THE FIELD.
A LEADER?
LIKE A SQUAD COM-MANDER?
ME!
WAVE
ME! ME!!
PICK ME!!
...
YOU'RE THE LEADER, MINATO.
NO WAY! HE'S TOTALLY NOT RED RANGER MATERIAL!
OF THE THREE OF US, HE'S THE ONLY ONE WITH ACTUAL COMBAT EXPERIENCE...
WHA... SERIOUSLY!?

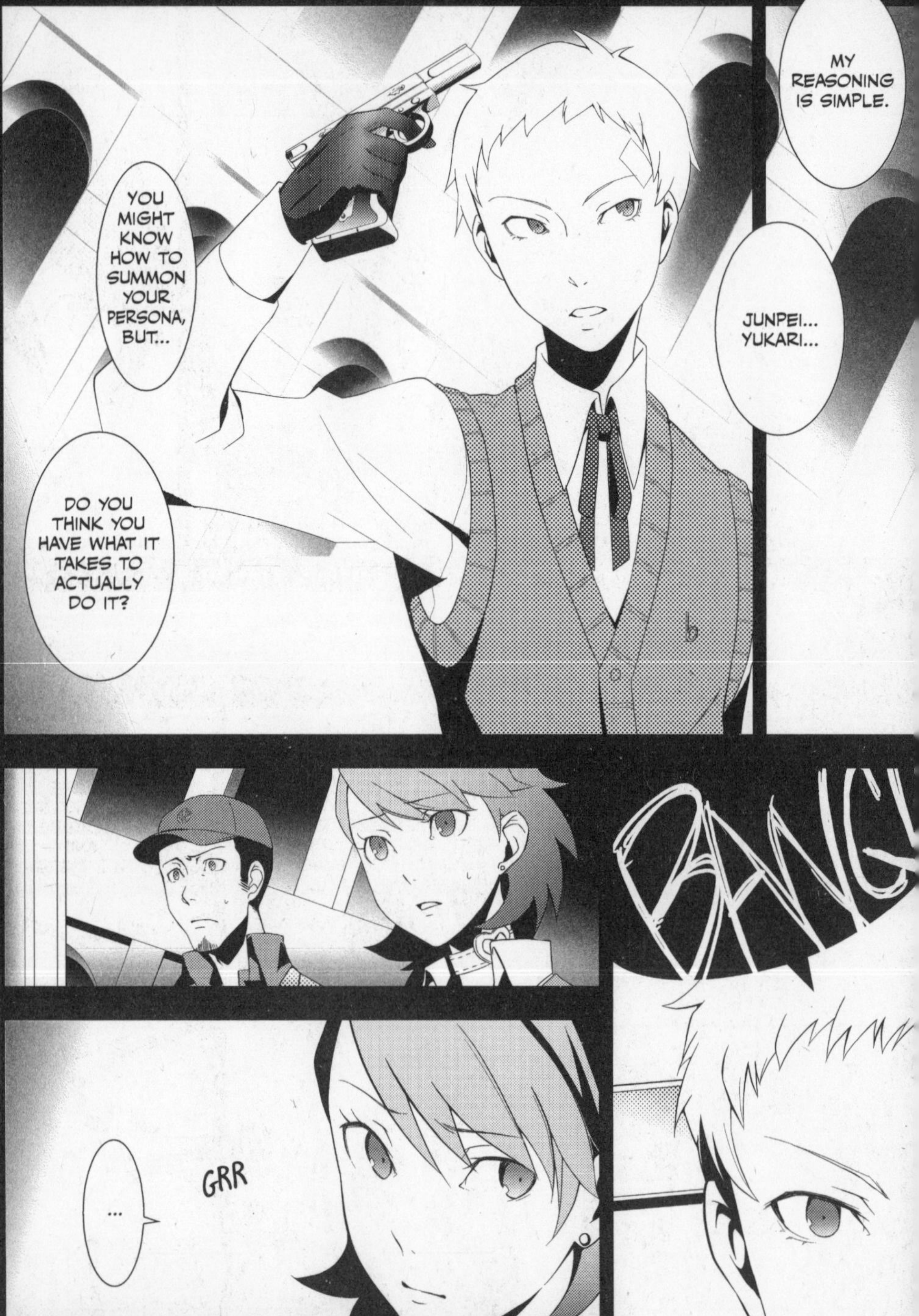
MY REASONING IS SIMPLE.
JUNPEI... YUKARI...
YOU MIGHT KNOW HOW TO SUMMON YOUR PERSONA, BUT...
DO YOU THINK YOU HAVE WHAT IT TAKES TO ACTUALLY DO IT?
BANG
...
GRR

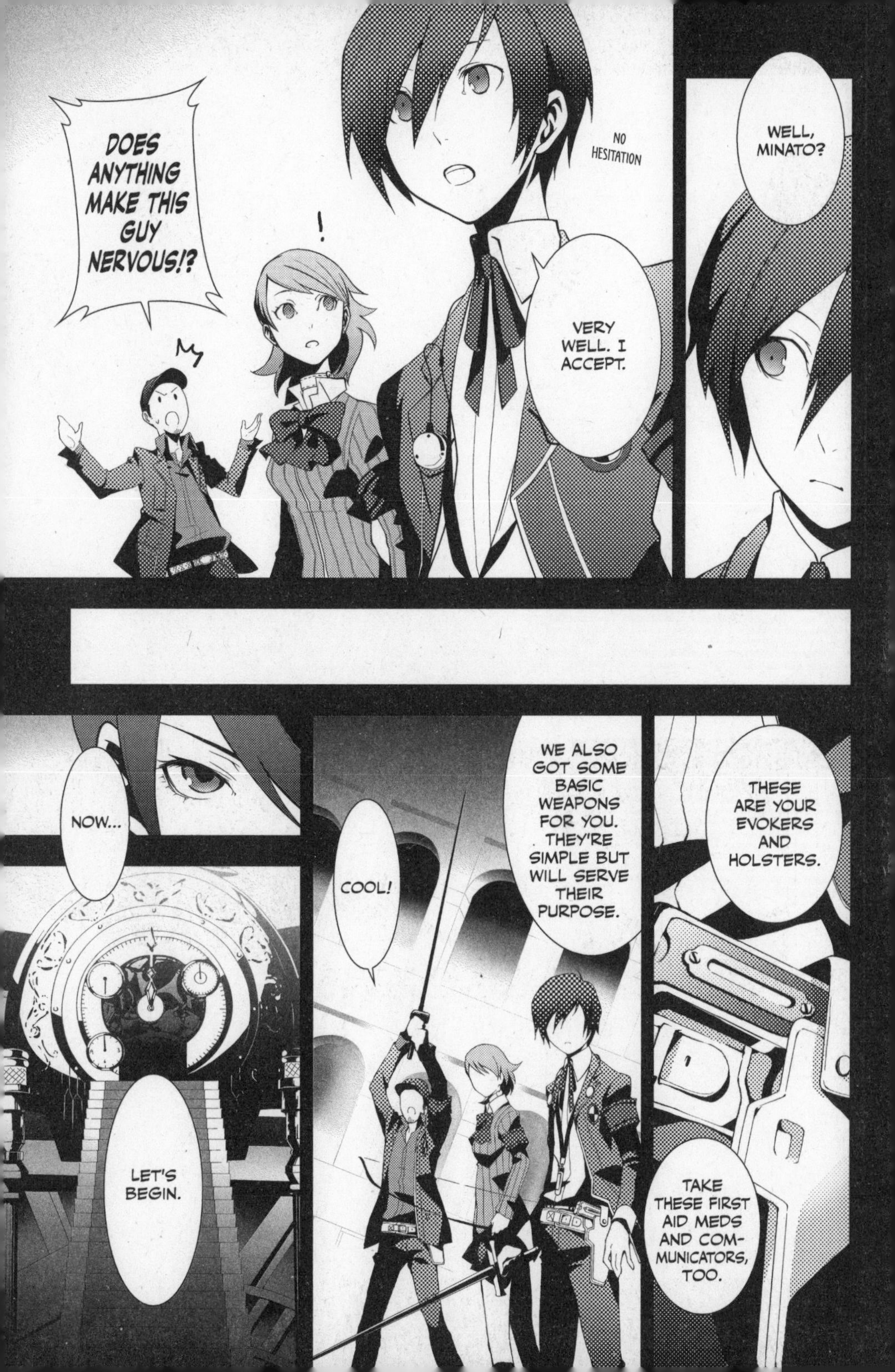
WELL, MINATO?
NO HESITATION
VERY WELL. I ACCEPT.
!
DOES ANYTHING MAKE THIS GUY NERVOUS!?
THESE ARE YOUR EVOKERS AND HOLSTERS.
TAKE THESE FIRST AID MEDS AND COM- MUNICATORS, TOO.
WE ALSO GOT SOME BASIC WEAPONS FOR YOU. THEY'RE SIMPLE BUT WILL SERVE THEIR PURPOSE.
COOL!
NOW...
LET'S BEGIN.

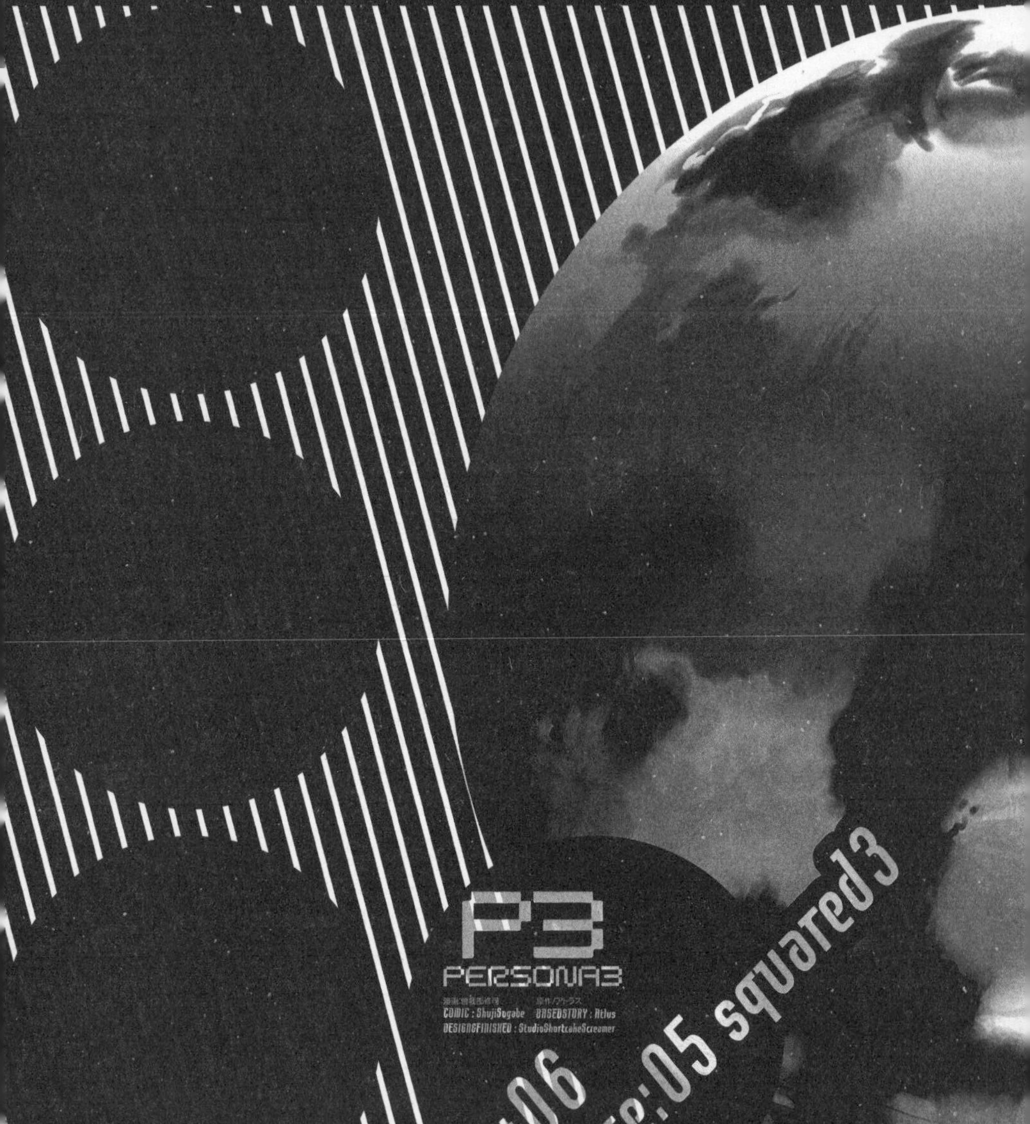
P3
PERSONA3
COMIC : ShujiSogabe
BASEDSTORY : Atlus
DESIGNGFINISHED : StudioShortcakeScreamer
#06
piece:05 squared3

P3
PERSONA3

漫画/曽我部修司　原作/アトラス
COMIC : Shuji Sogabe　BASED STORY : Atlus
DESIGN&FINISHED : Studio Shortcake Screamer

#06
piece:05 squared3

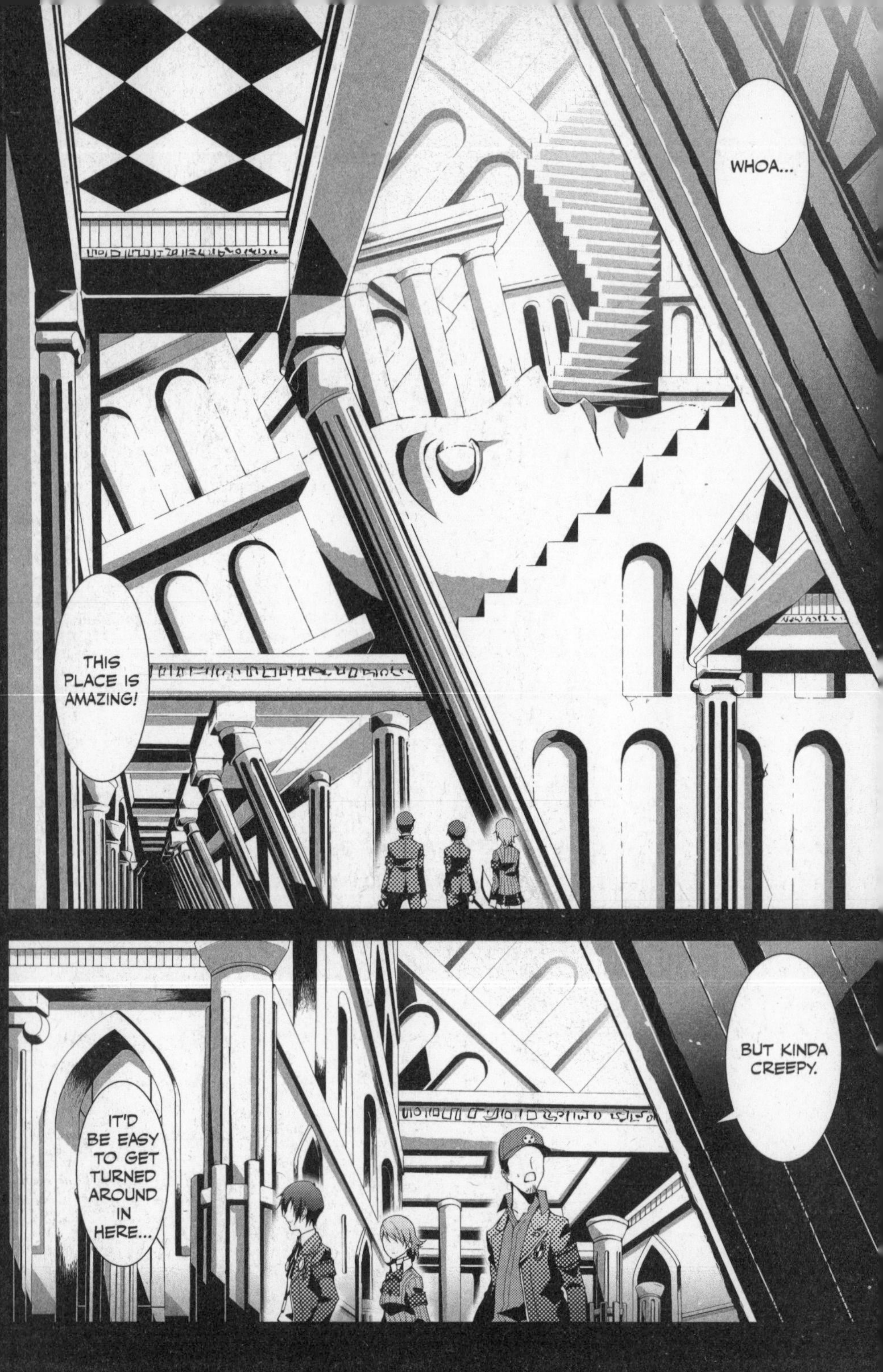
WHOA...
THIS PLACE IS AMAZING!
BUT KINDA CREEPY.
IT'D BE EASY TO GET TURNED AROUND IN HERE...

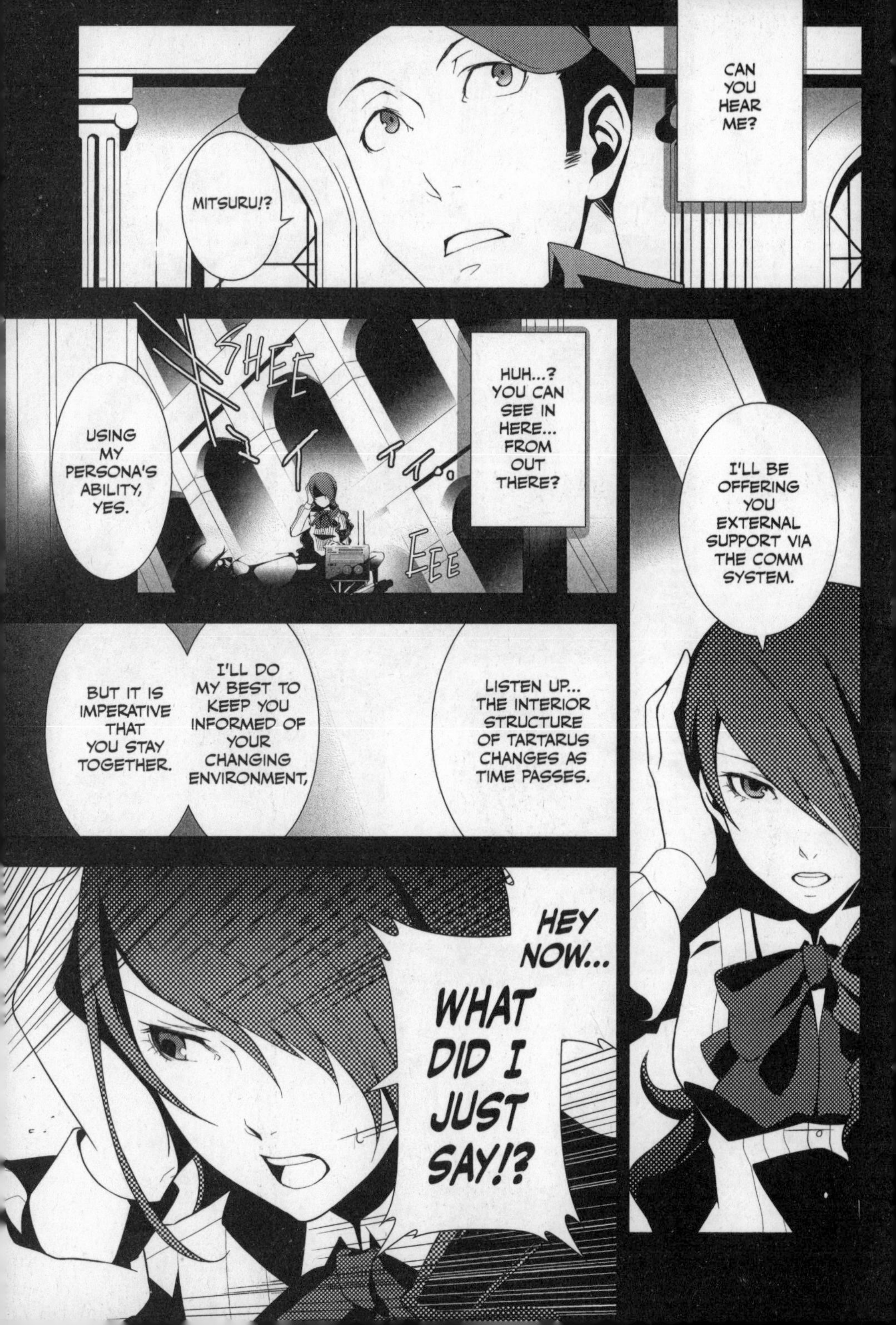
CAN YOU HEAR ME?
MITSURU!?
I'LL BE OFFERING YOU EXTERNAL SUPPORT VIA THE COMM SYSTEM.
HUH...? YOU CAN SEE IN HERE... FROM OUT THERE?
SHEE
EEE
USING MY PERSONA'S ABILITY, YES.
LISTEN UP... THE INTERIOR STRUCTURE OF TARTARUS CHANGES AS TIME PASSES.
I'LL DO MY BEST TO KEEP YOU INFORMED OF YOUR CHANGING ENVIRONMENT,
BUT IT IS IMPERATIVE THAT YOU STAY TOGETHER.
HEY NOW...
WHAT DID I JUST SAY!?

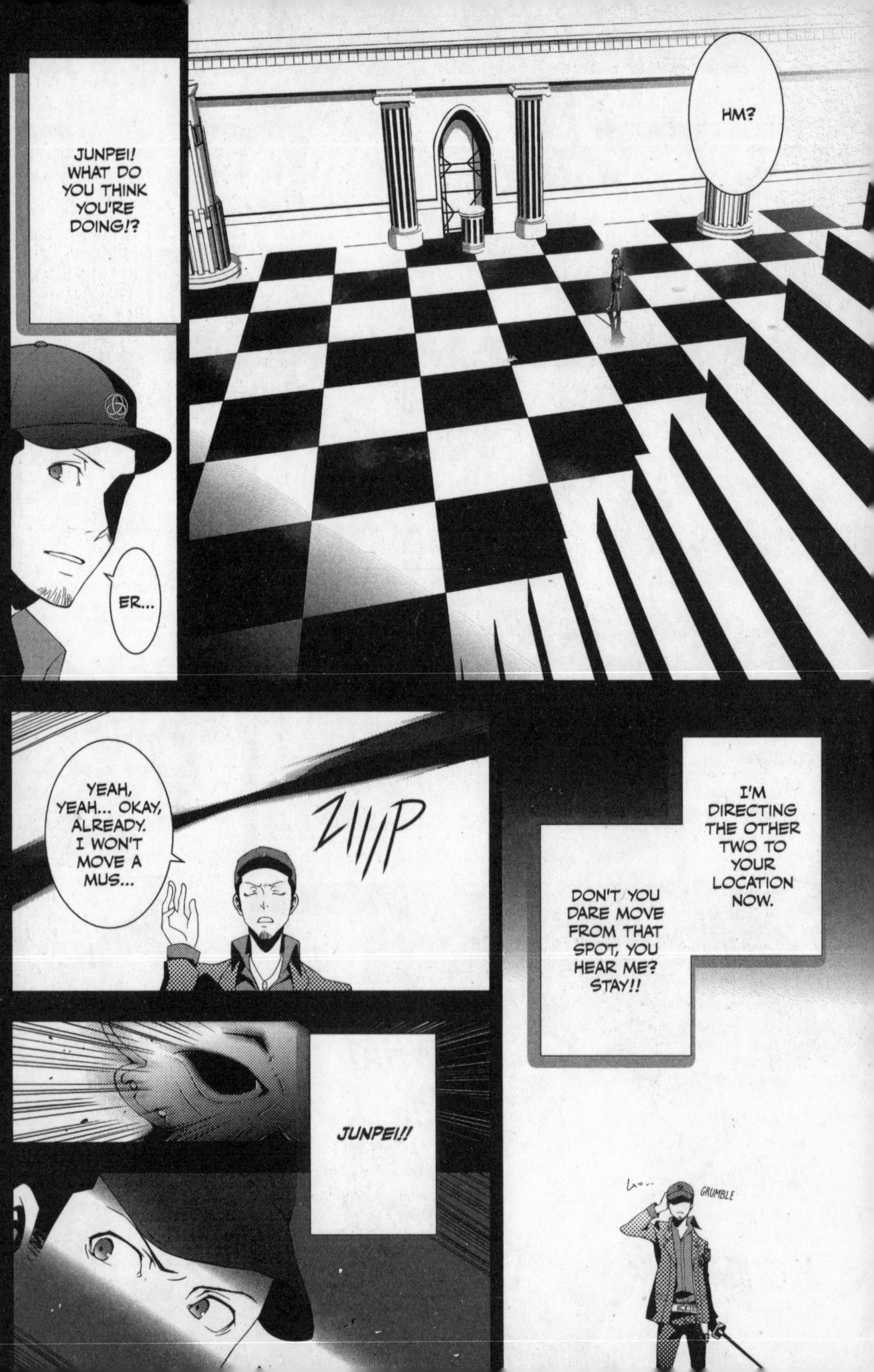
HM?
JUNPEI! WHAT DO YOU THINK YOU'RE DOING!?
ER...
I'M DIRECTING THE OTHER TWO TO YOUR LOCATION NOW.
DON'T YOU DARE MOVE FROM THAT SPOT, YOU HEAR ME? STAY!!
GRUMBLE
YEAH, YEAH... OKAY, ALREADY. I WON'T MOVE A MUS...
ZIIIP
JUNPEI!!

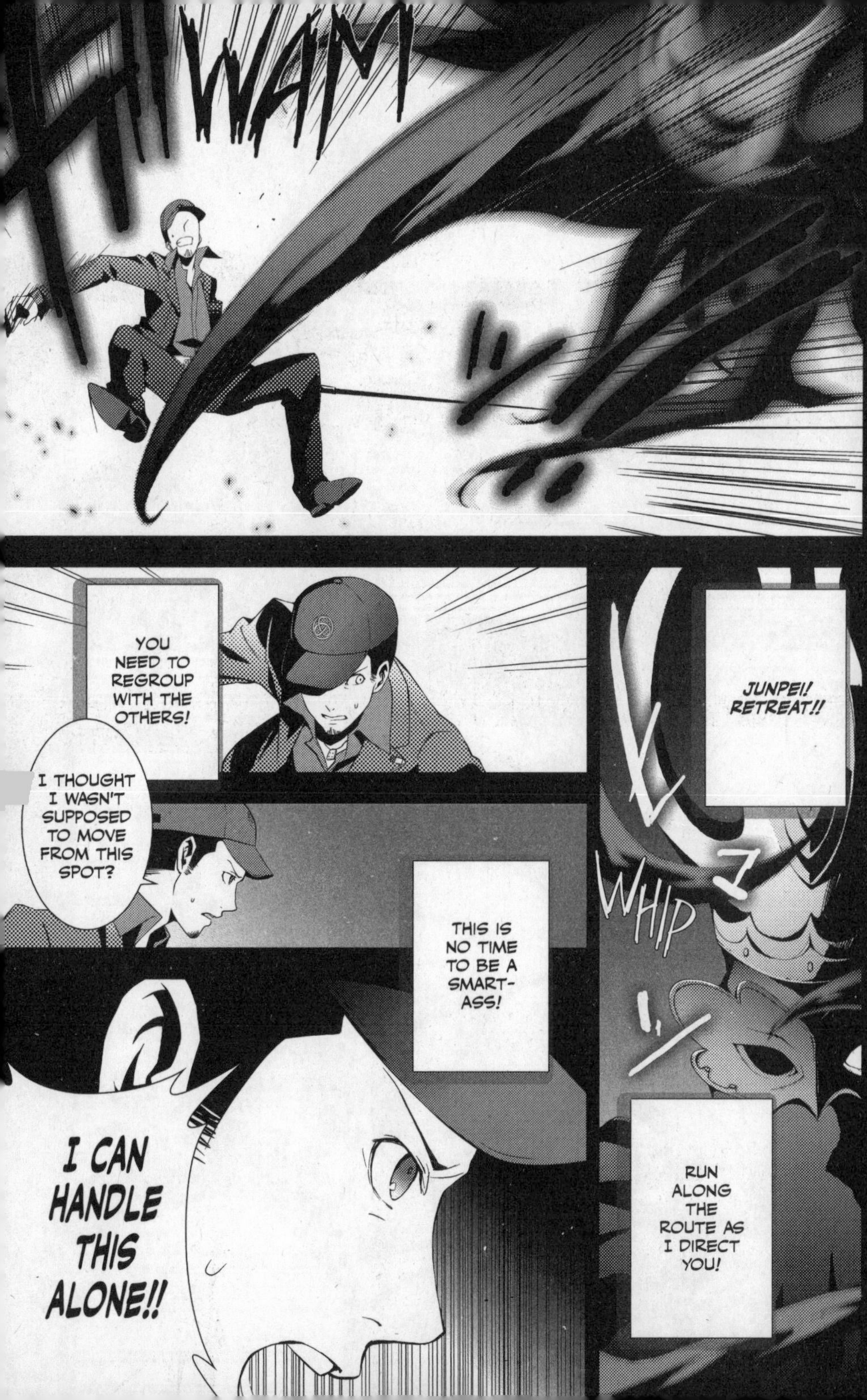
THWAM
JUNPEI! RETREAT!!
WHIP
RUN ALONG THE ROUTE AS I DIRECT YOU!
YOU NEED TO REGROUP WITH THE OTHERS!
I THOUGHT I WASN'T SUPPOSED TO MOVE FROM THIS SPOT?
THIS IS NO TIME TO BE A SMART-ASS!
I CAN HANDLE THIS ALONE!!

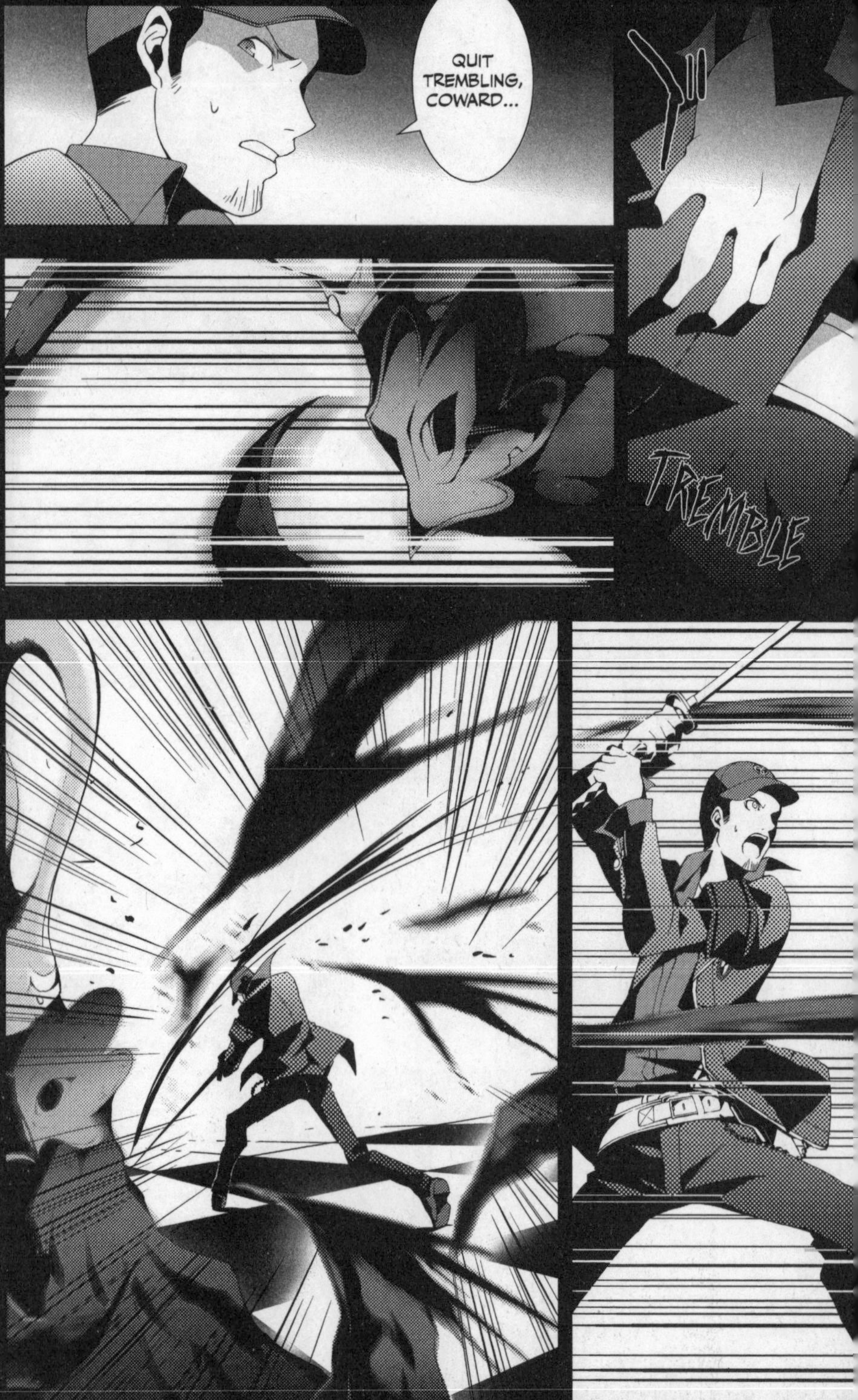
QUIT TREMBLING, COWARD...
TREMBLE

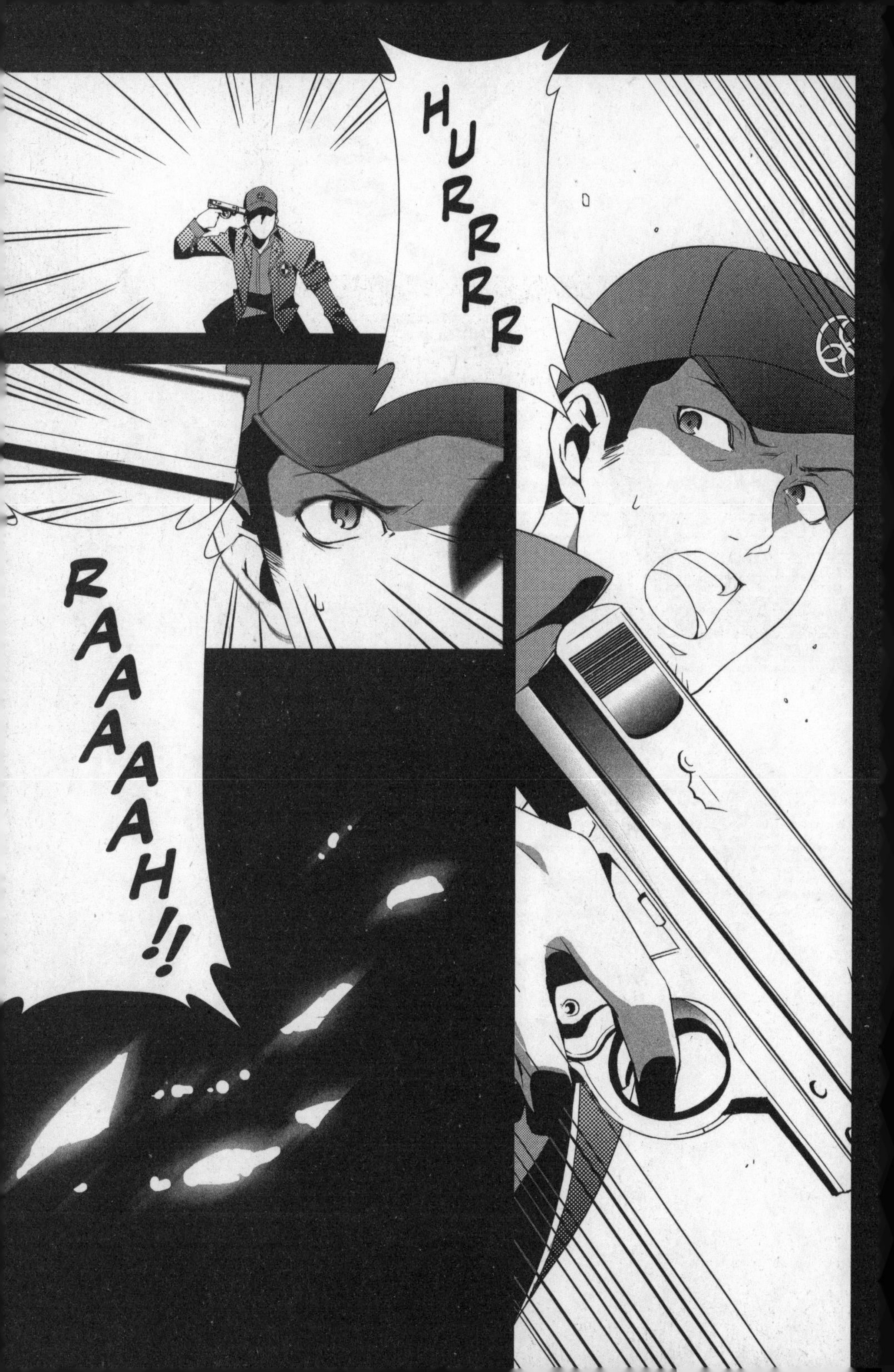
HURRRR
RAAAAAH!!

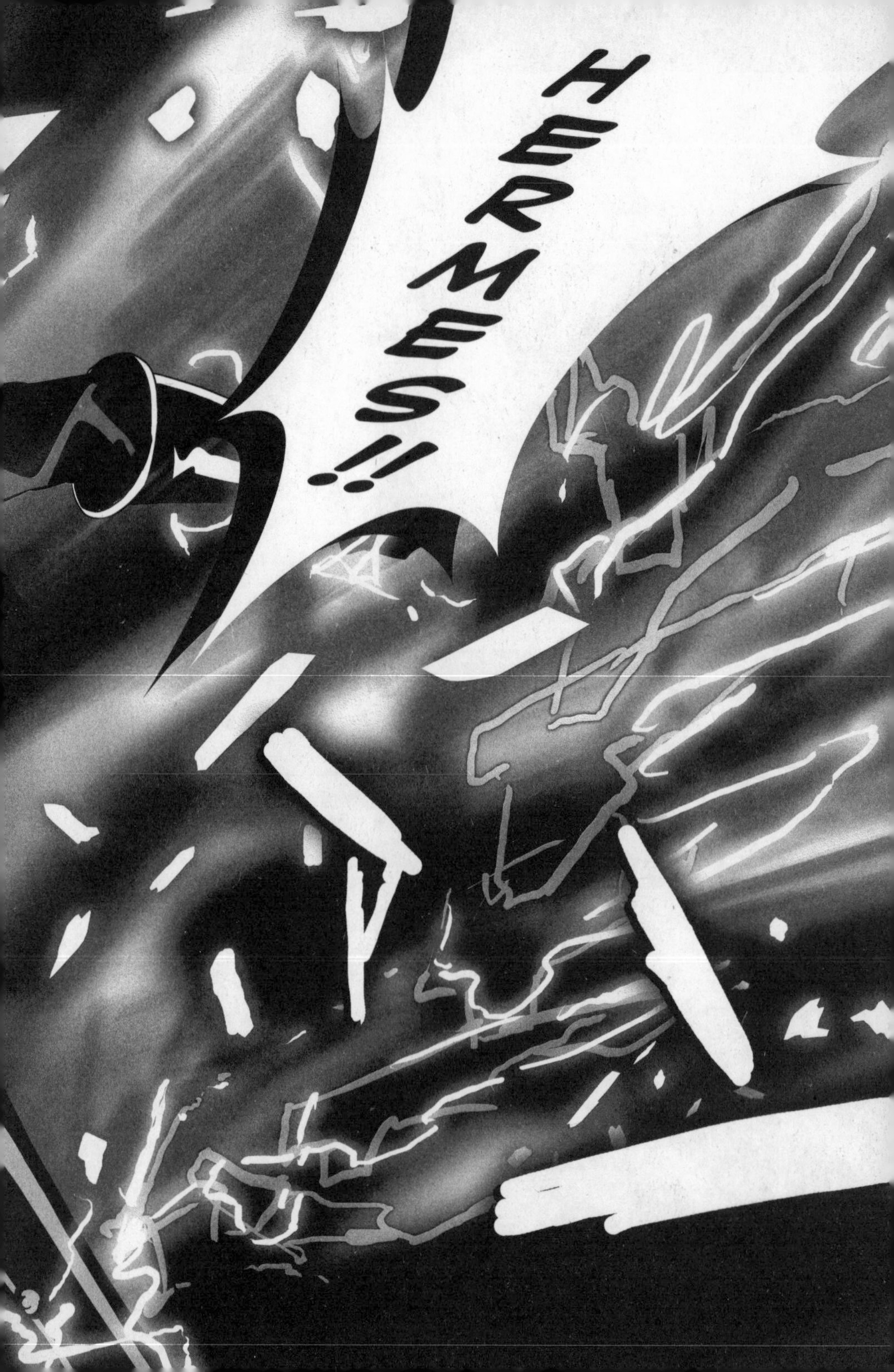
HERMES!!

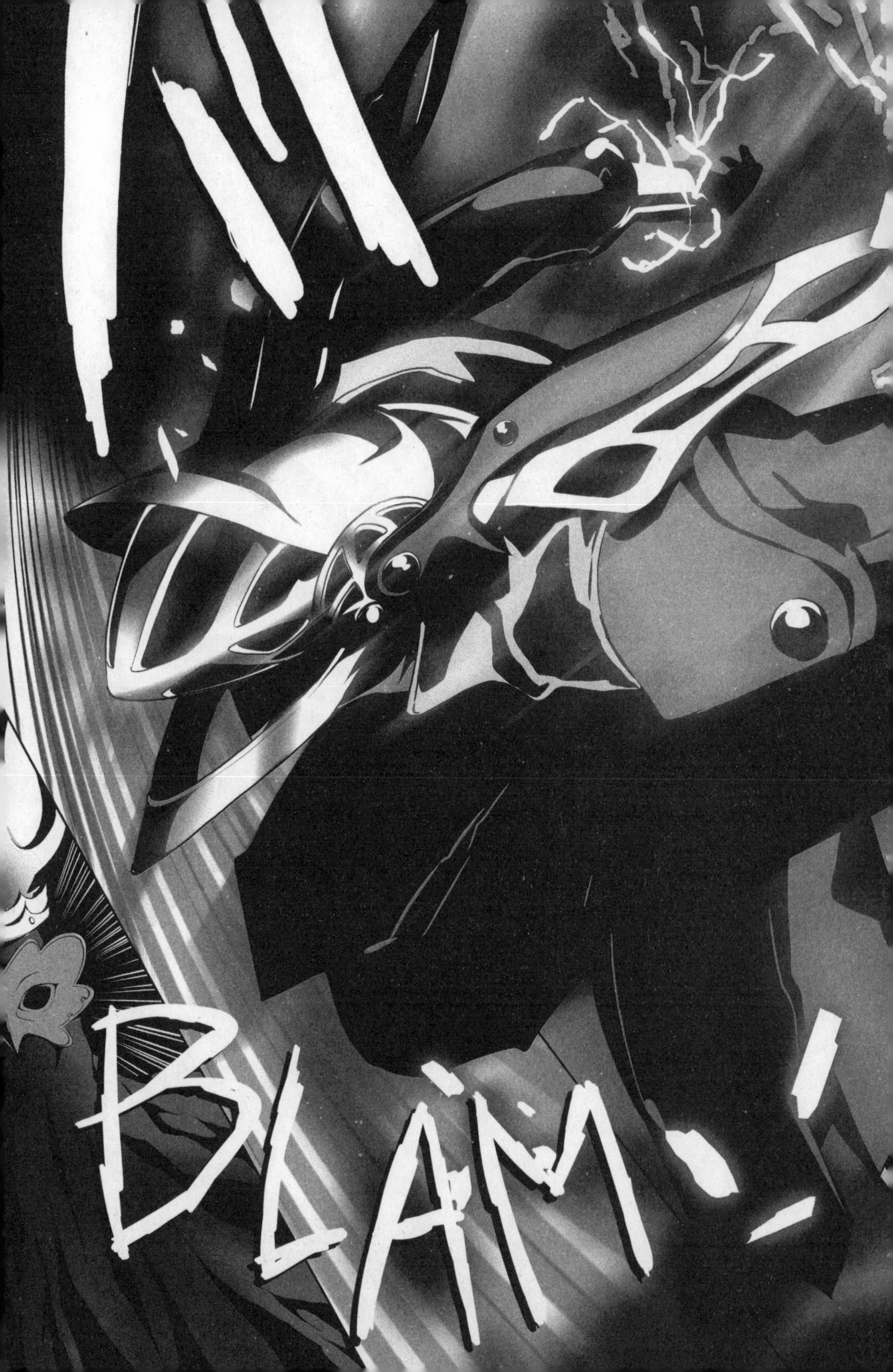
BLAM!

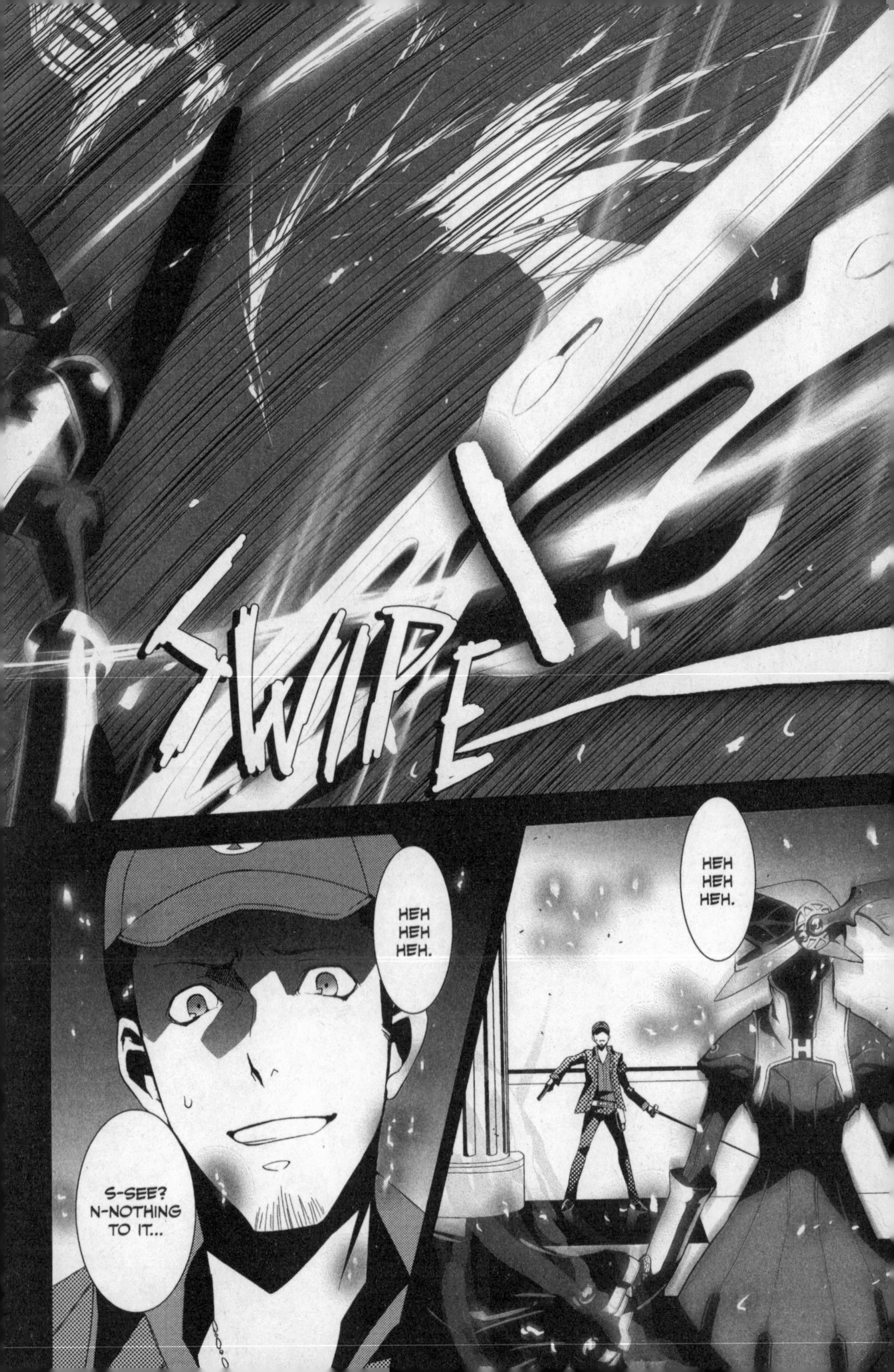
SWIPE
HEH HEH HEH.
HEH HEH HEH.
S-SEE? N-NOTHING TO IT...

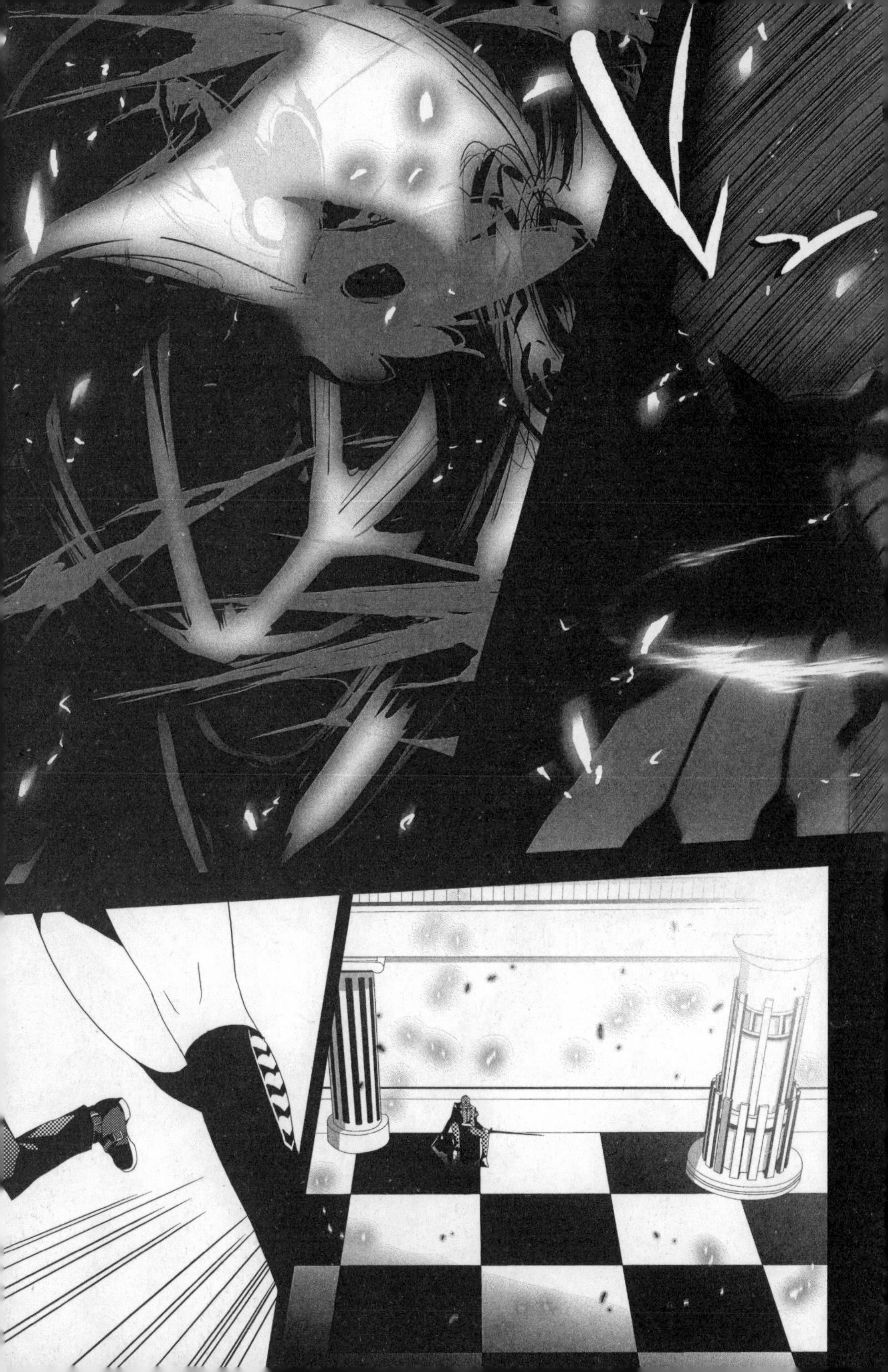

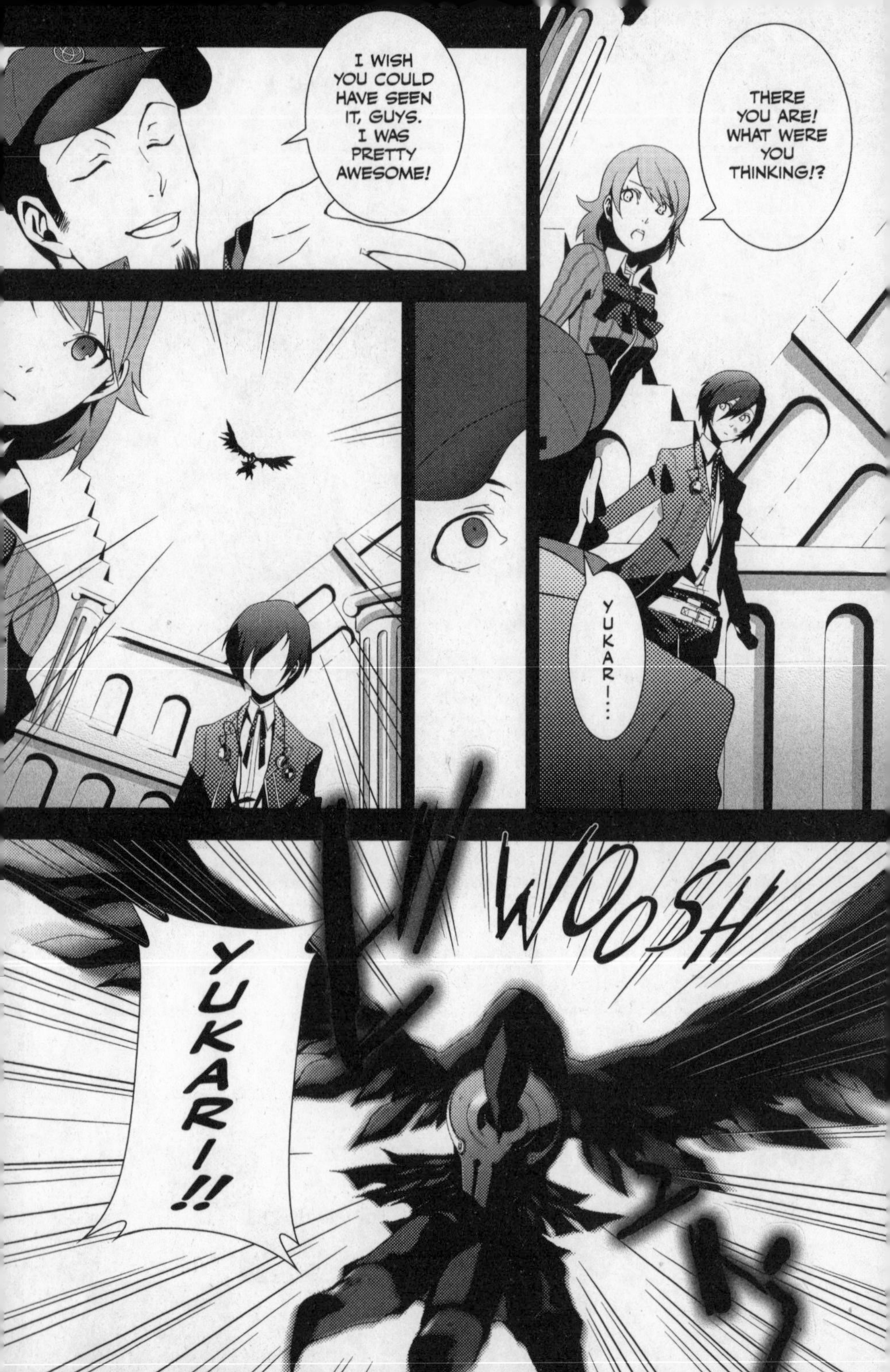
THERE YOU ARE! WHAT WERE YOU THINKING!?
YUKARI...!
I WISH YOU COULD HAVE SEEN IT, GUYS. I WAS PRETTY AWESOME!
WOOSH
YUKARI!!

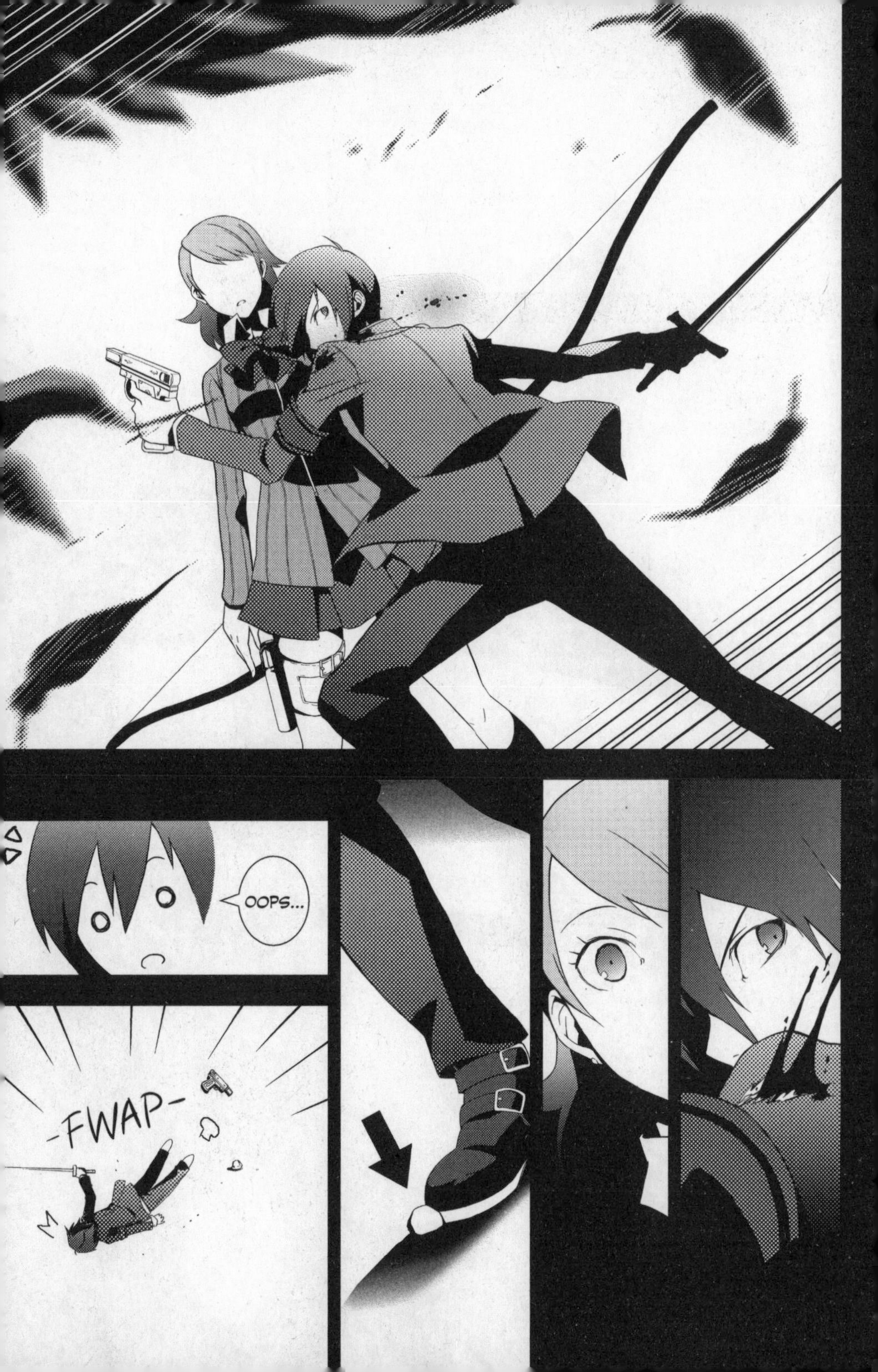
OOPS...
-FWAP-

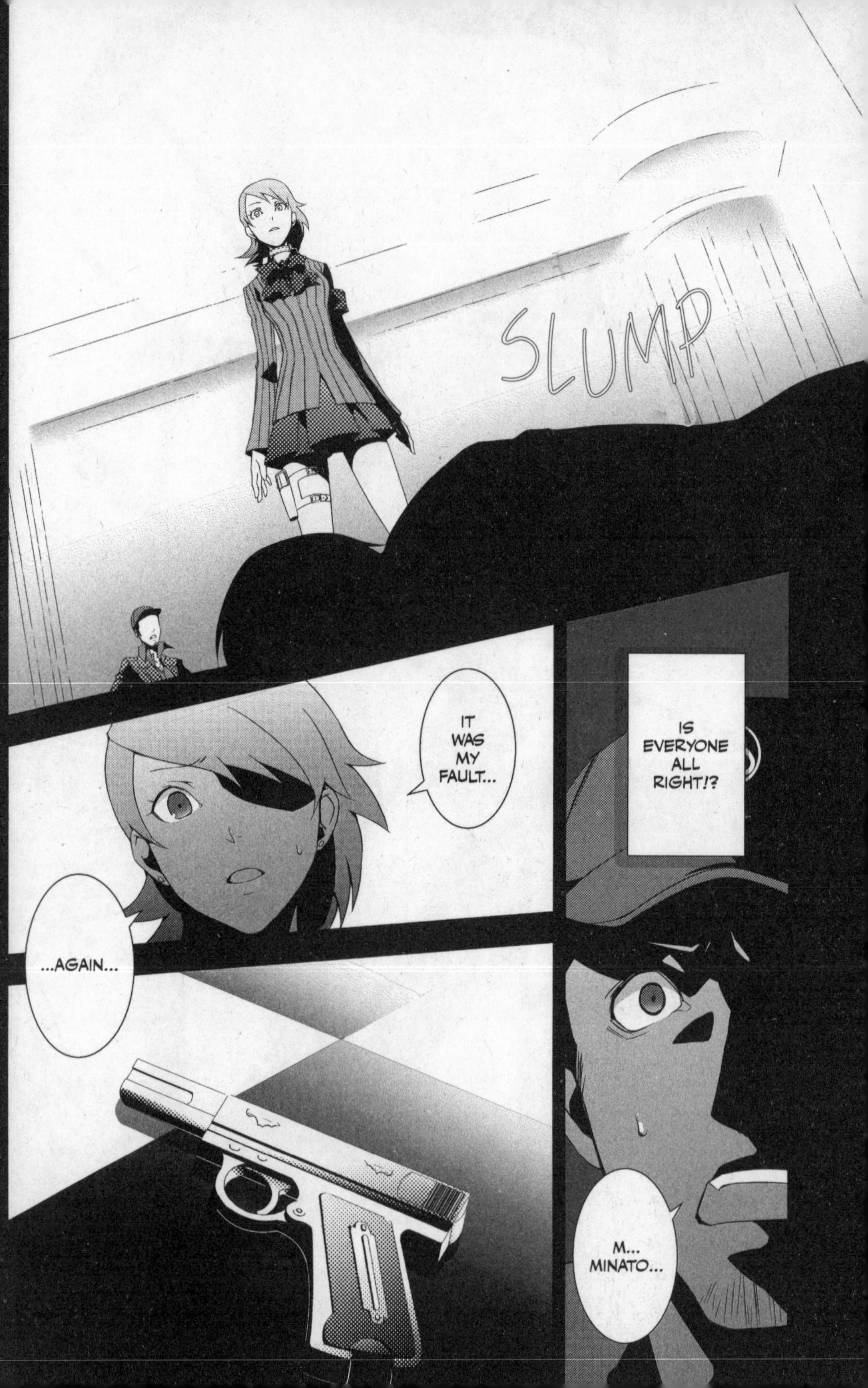
SLUMP
IS EVERYONE ALL RIGHT!?
IT WAS MY FAULT...
...AGAIN...
M... MINATO...

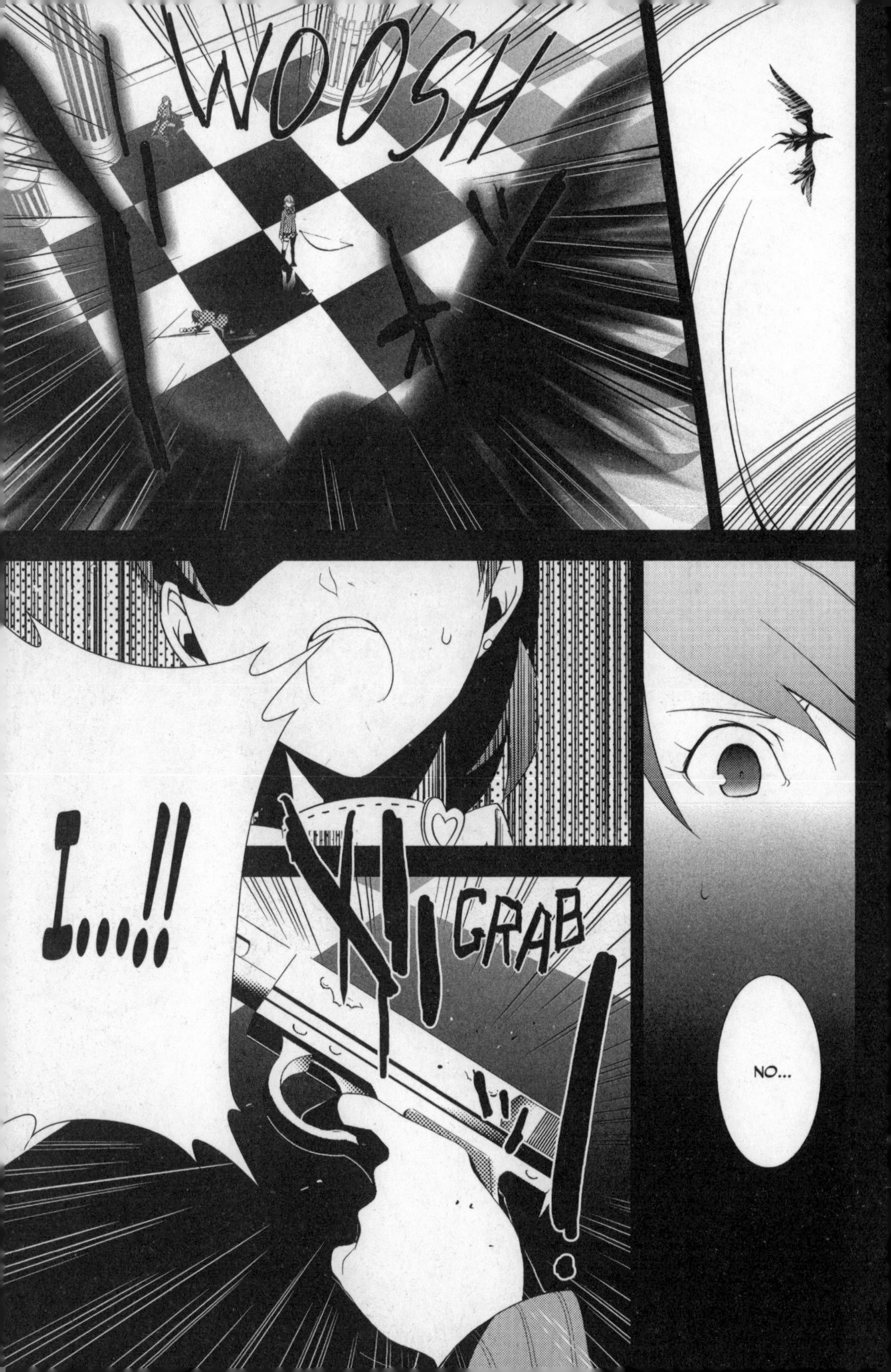
WOOSH
NO...
I....!!
GRAB

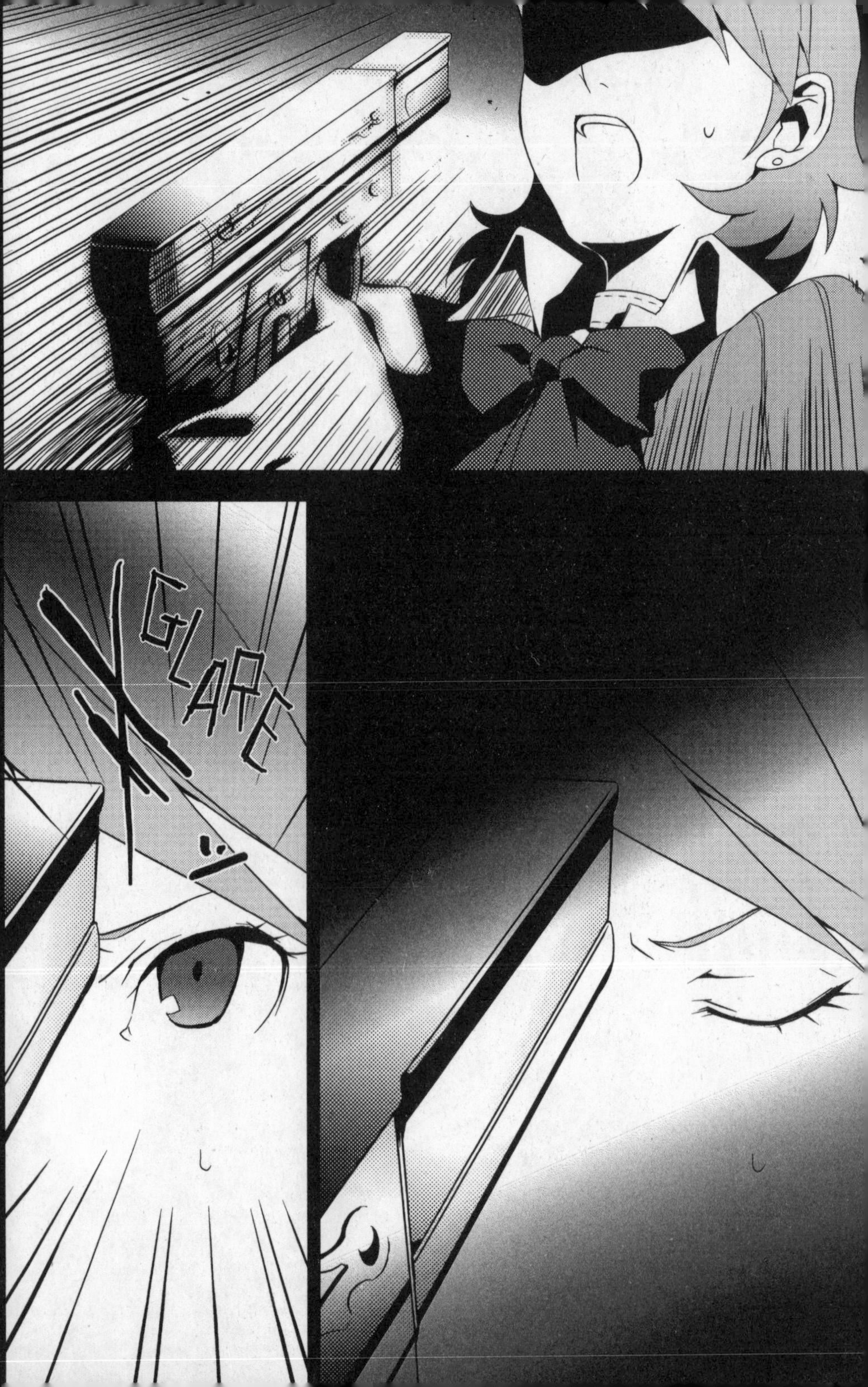
GLARE

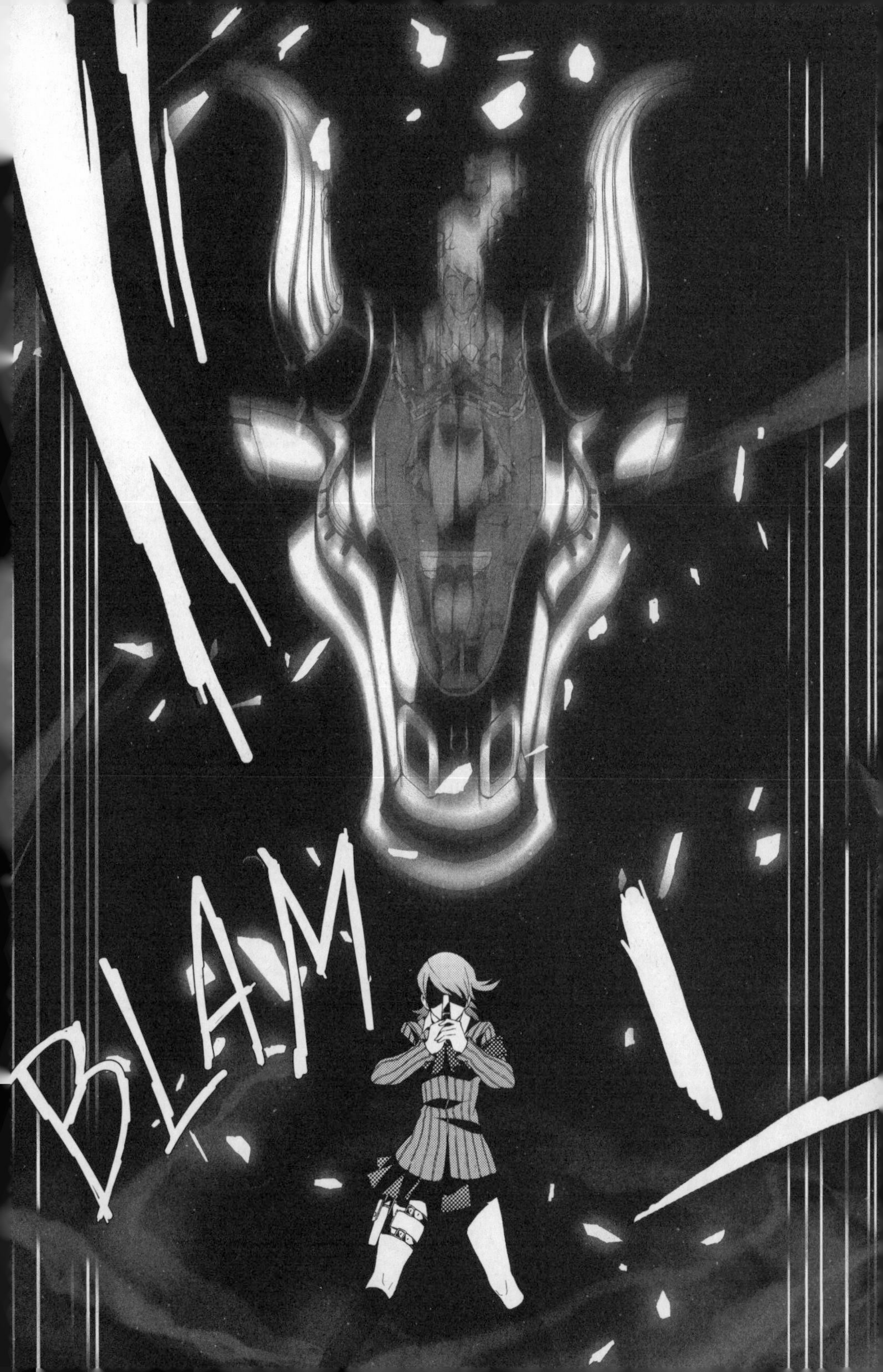
BLAM

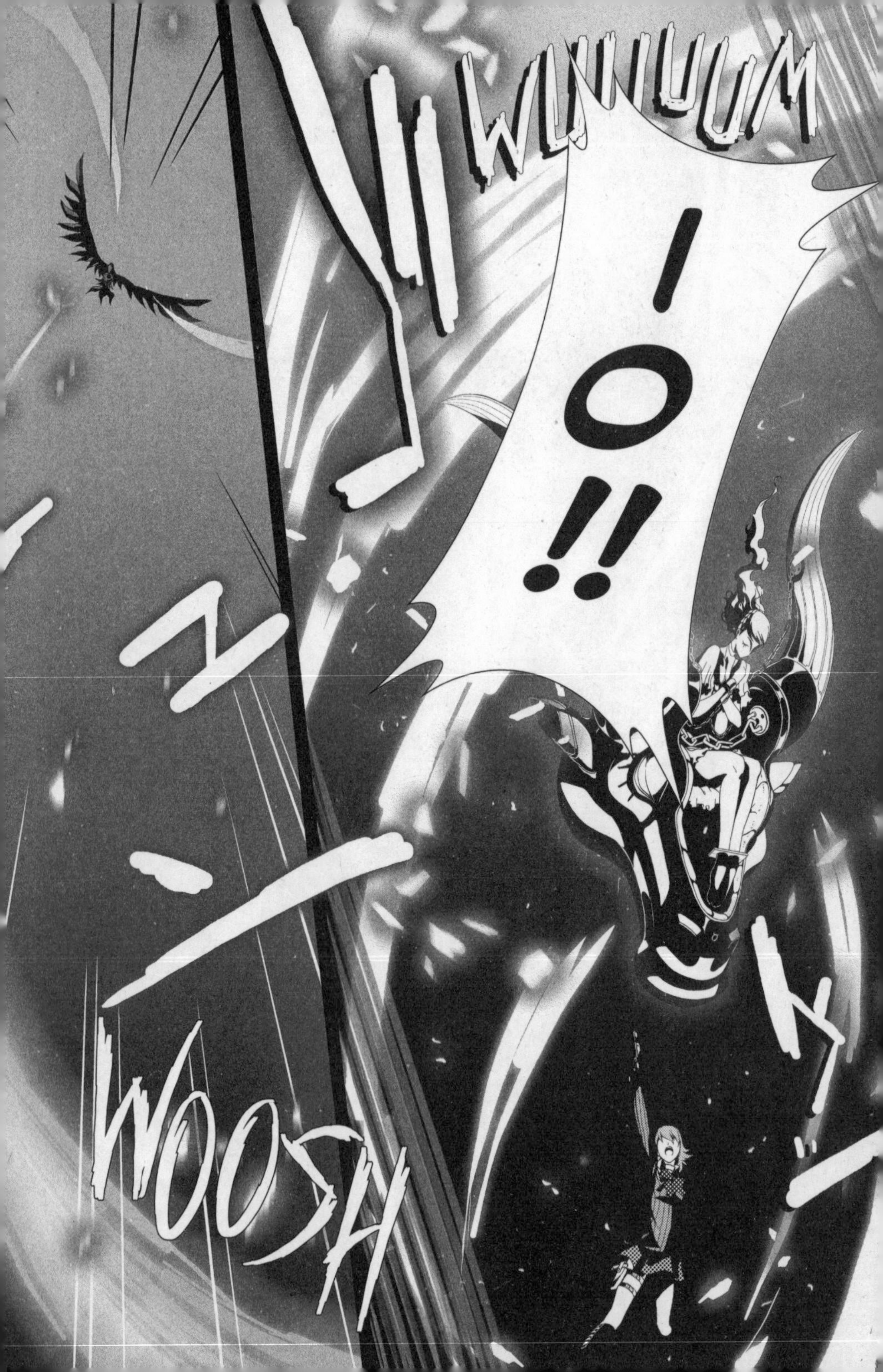
WUUUUM
!!
WOOSH

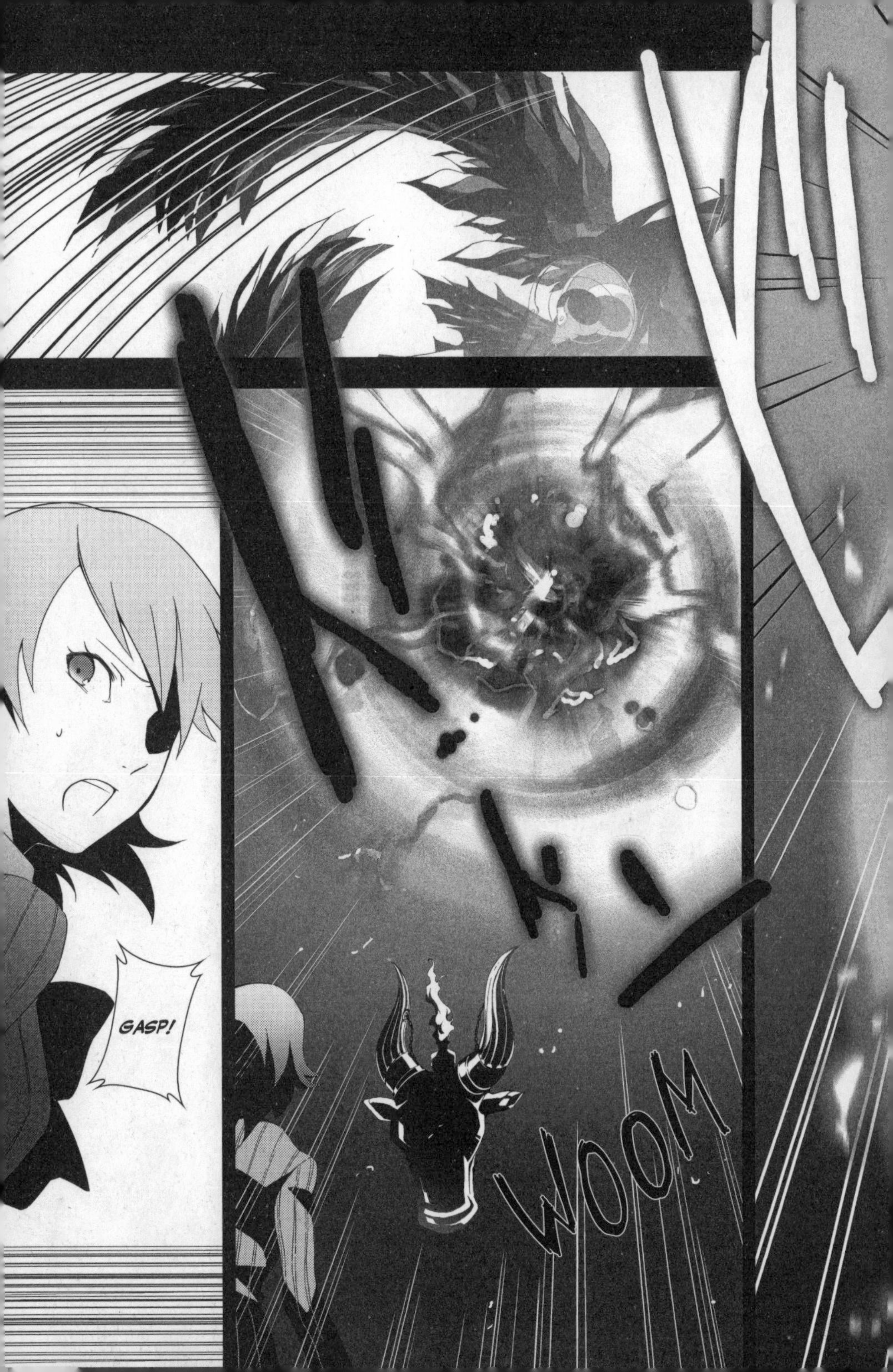
WOOM
GASP!

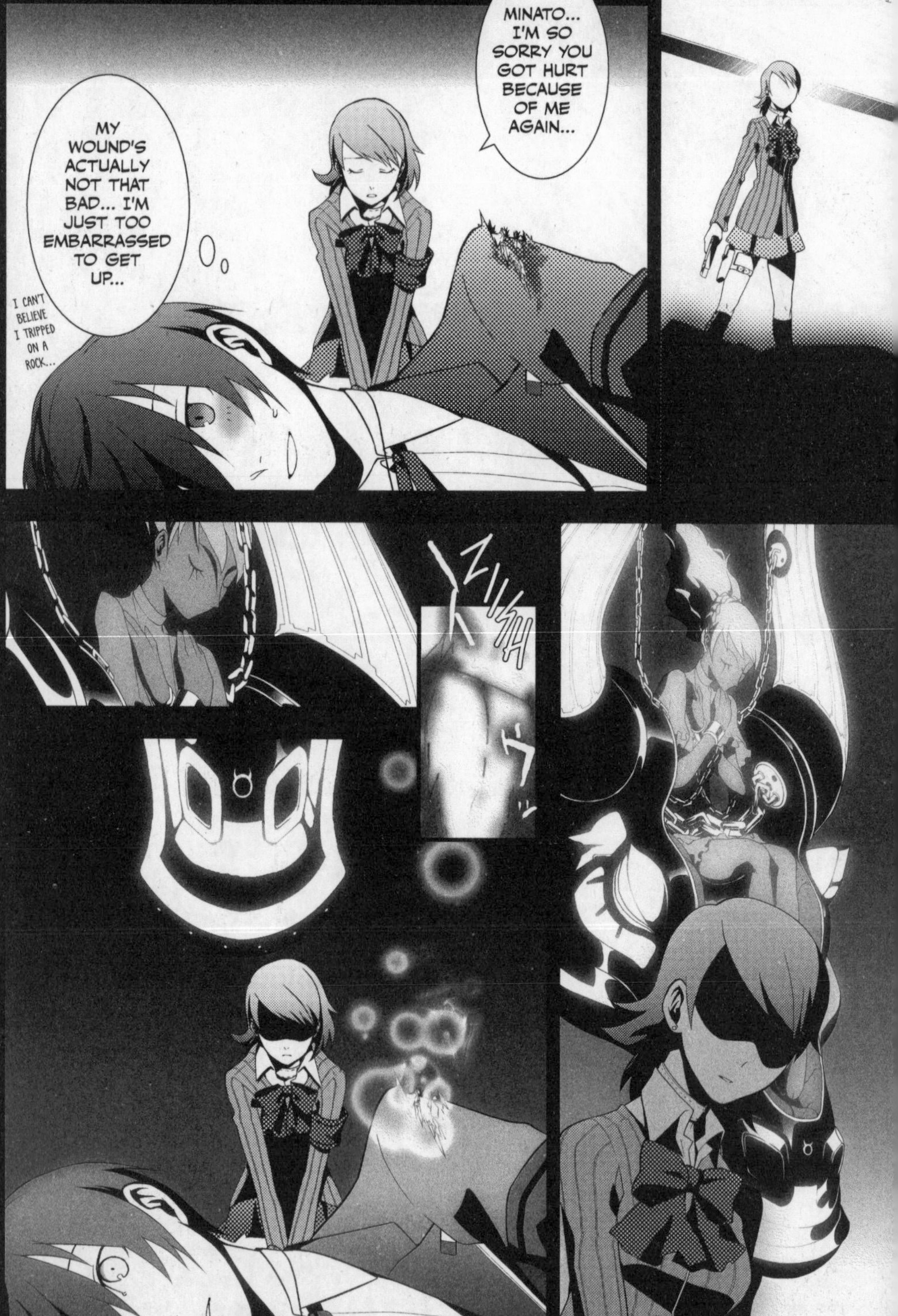
MINATO... I'M SO SORRY YOU GOT HURT BECAUSE OF ME AGAIN...
MY WOUND'S ACTUALLY NOT THAT BAD... I'M JUST TOO EMBARRASSED TO GET UP...
I CAN'T BELIEVE I TRIPPED ON A ROCK...

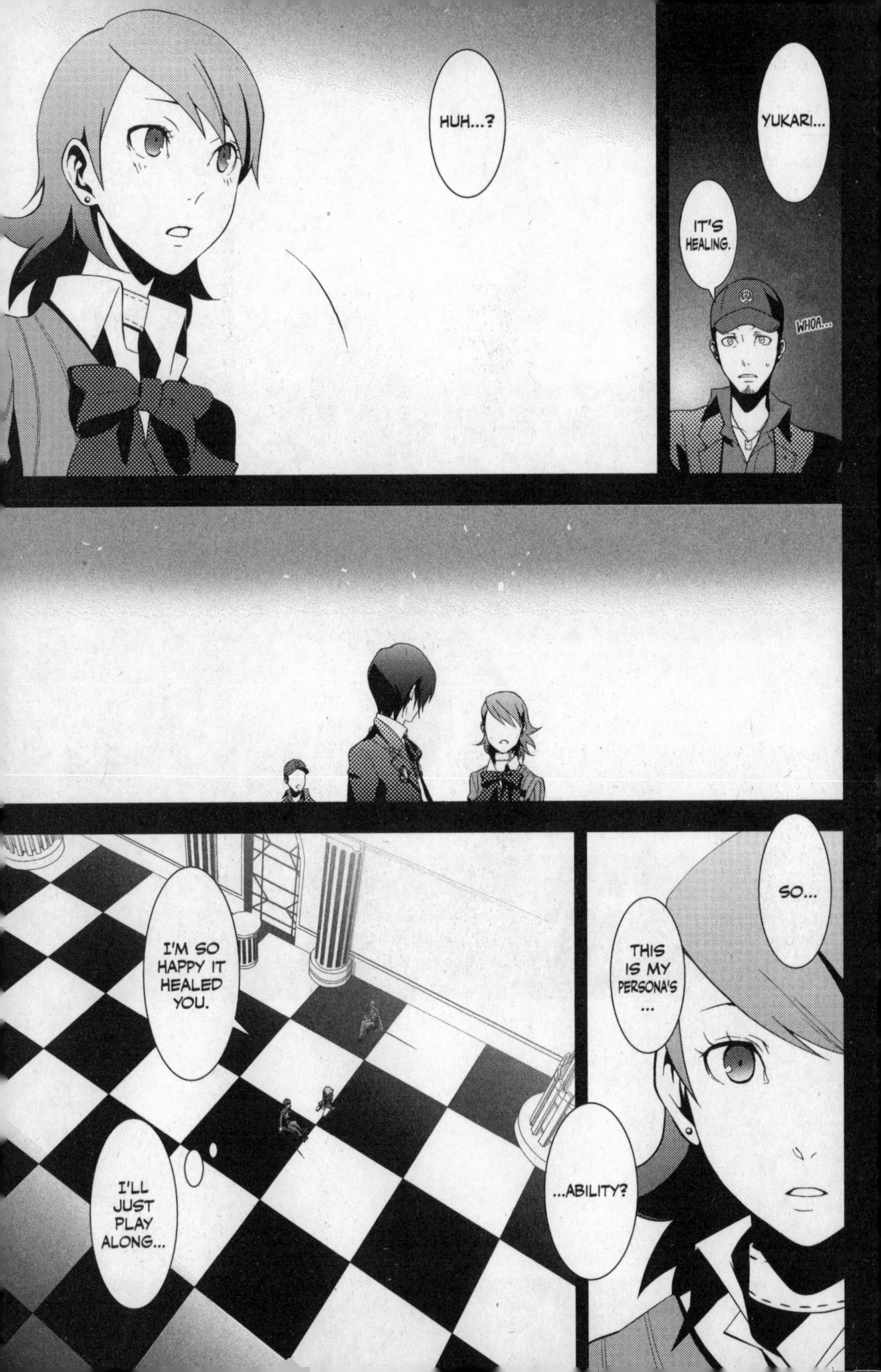
YUKARI...
IT'S HEALING.
WHOA...
HUH...?
SO...
THIS IS MY PERSONA'S ...
...ABILITY?
I'M SO HAPPY IT HEALED YOU.
I'LL JUST PLAY ALONG...

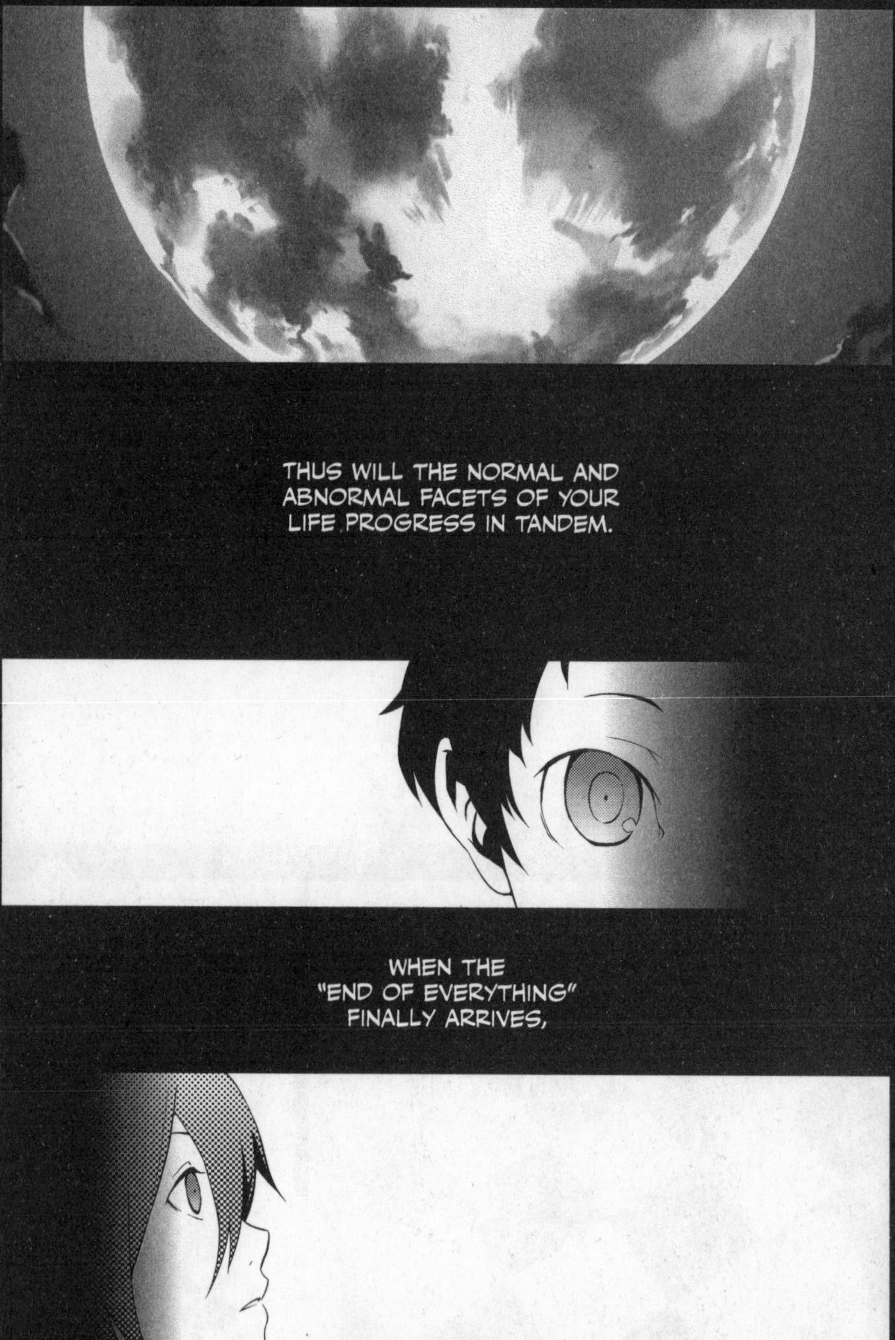
THUS WILL THE NORMAL AND ABNORMAL FACETS OF YOUR LIFE PROGRESS IN TANDEM.
WHEN THE "END OF EVERYTHING" FINALLY ARRIVES,

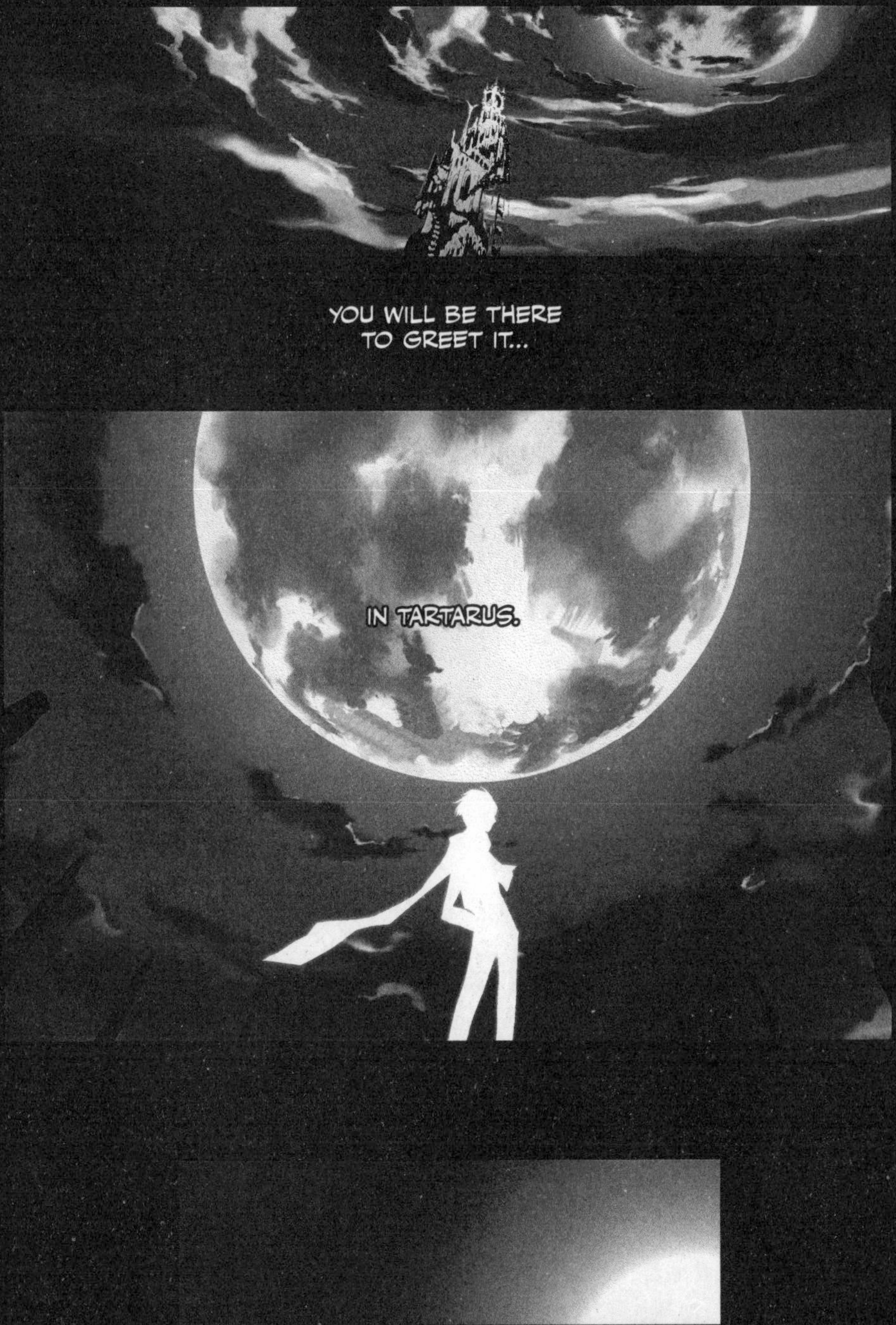
YOU WILL BE THERE TO GREET IT...
IN TARTARUS.

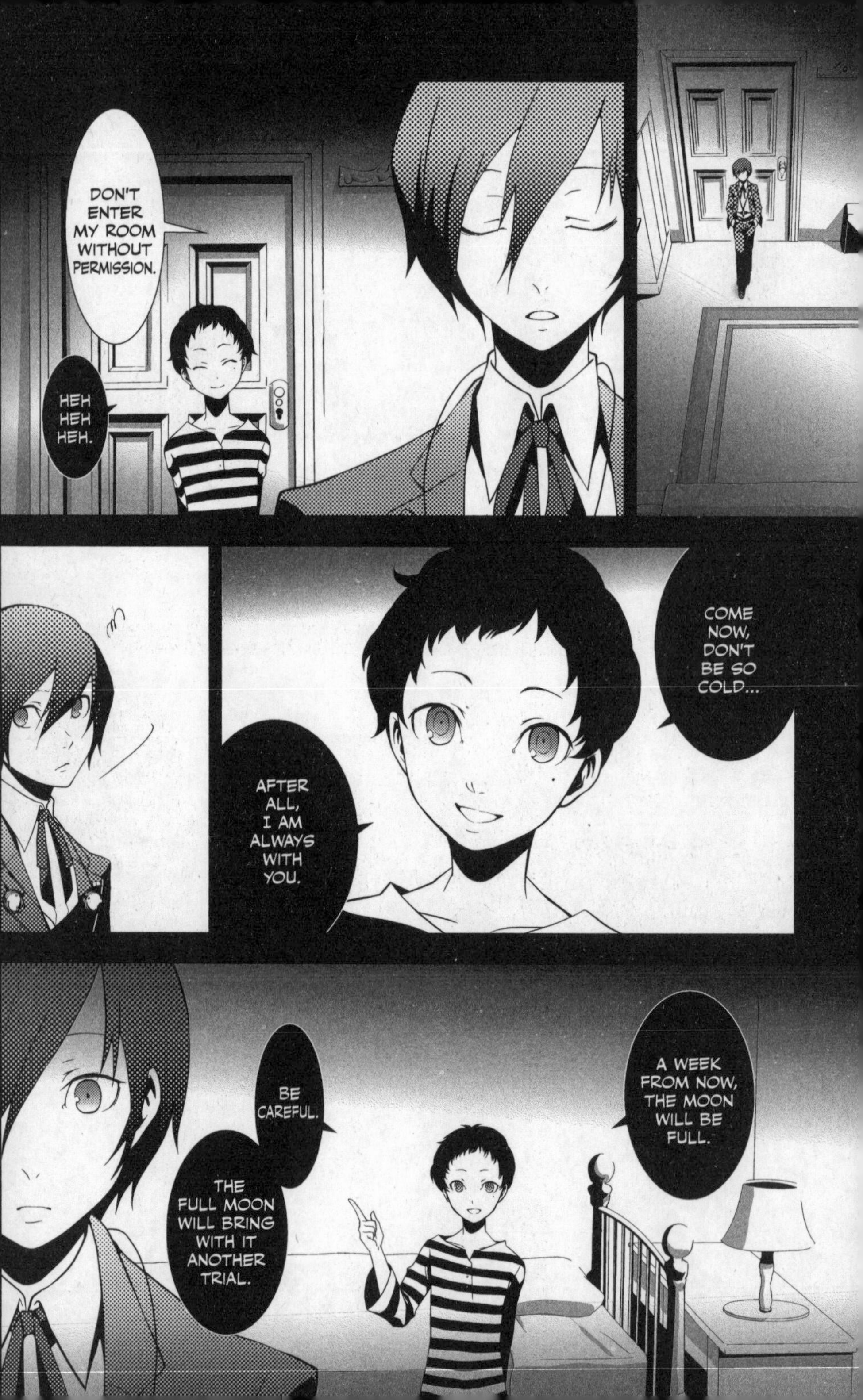
DON'T ENTER MY ROOM WITHOUT PERMISSION.
HEH HEH HEH.
COME NOW, DON'T BE SO COLD...
AFTER ALL, I AM ALWAYS WITH YOU.
A WEEK FROM NOW, THE MOON WILL BE FULL.
BE CAREFUL.
THE FULL MOON WILL BRING WITH IT ANOTHER TRIAL.

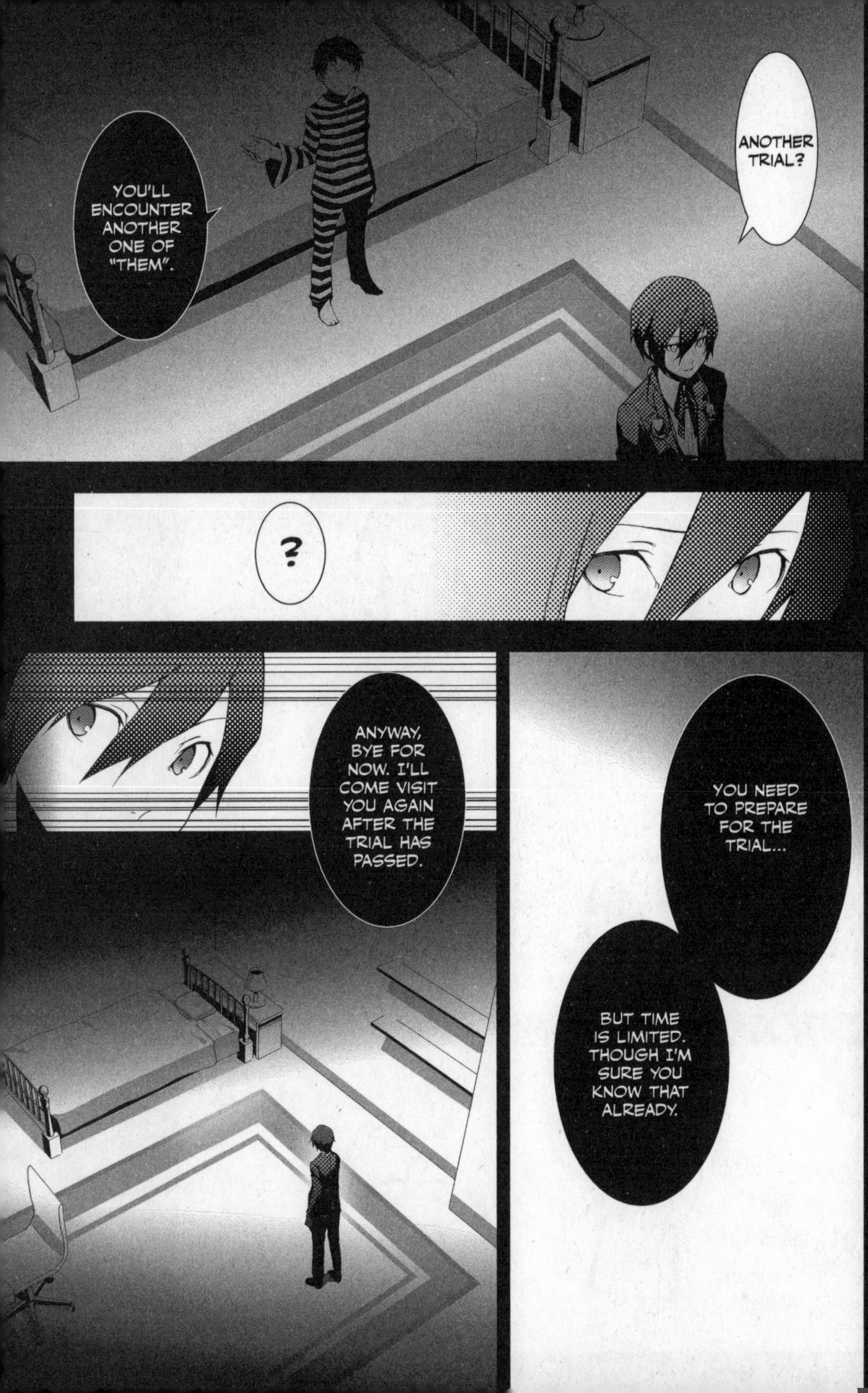
ANOTHER TRIAL?
YOU'LL ENCOUNTER ANOTHER ONE OF "THEM".
?
YOU NEED TO PREPARE FOR THE TRIAL...
BUT TIME IS LIMITED. THOUGH I'M SURE YOU KNOW THAT ALREADY.
ANYWAY, BYE FOR NOW. I'LL COME VISIT YOU AGAIN AFTER THE TRIAL HAS PASSED.

PSN 3

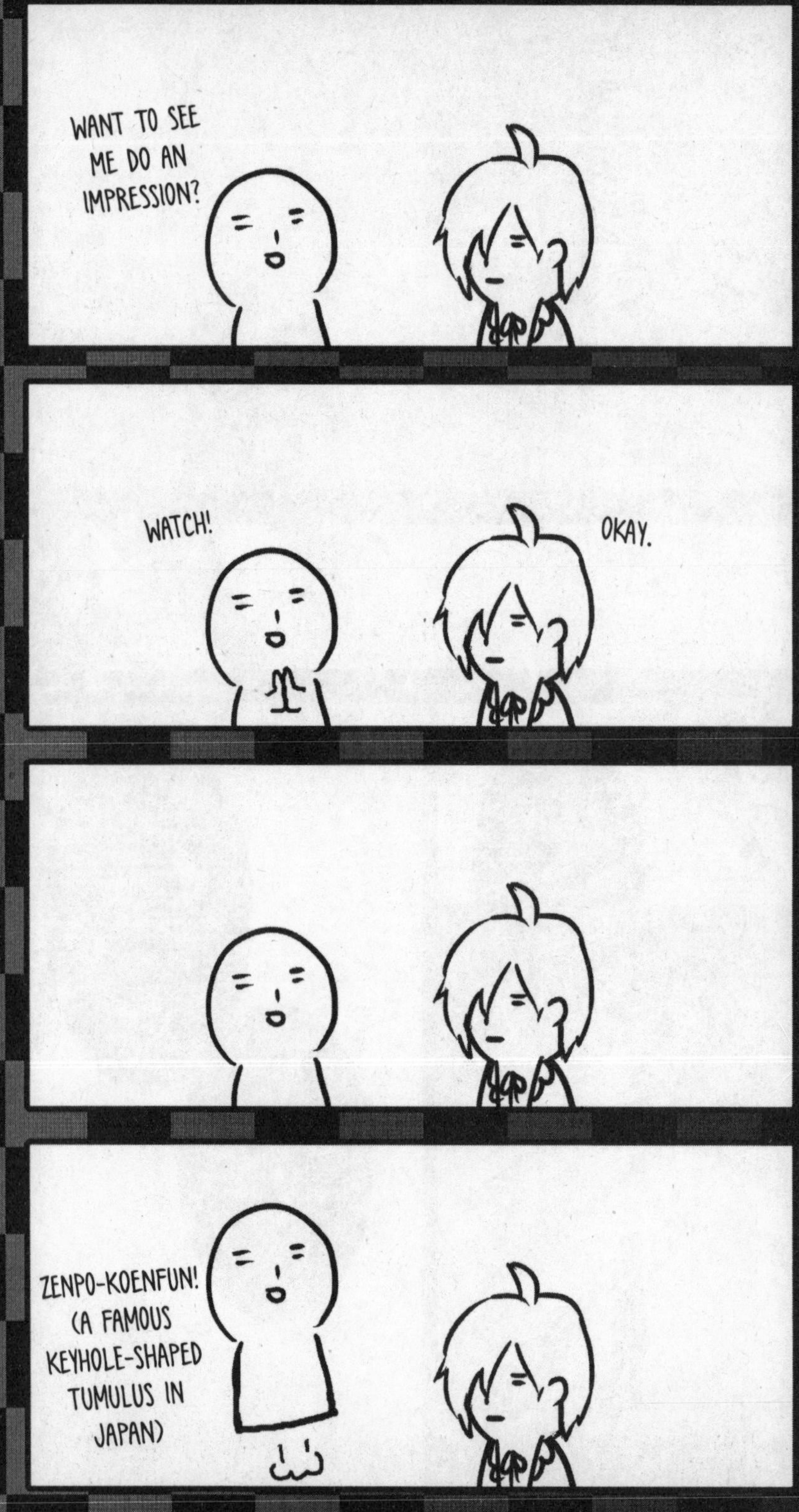
WANT TO SEE ME DO AN IMPRESSION?
OKAY.
WATCH!
ZENPO-KOENFUN! (A FAMOUS KEYHOLE-SHAPED TUMULUS IN JAPAN)

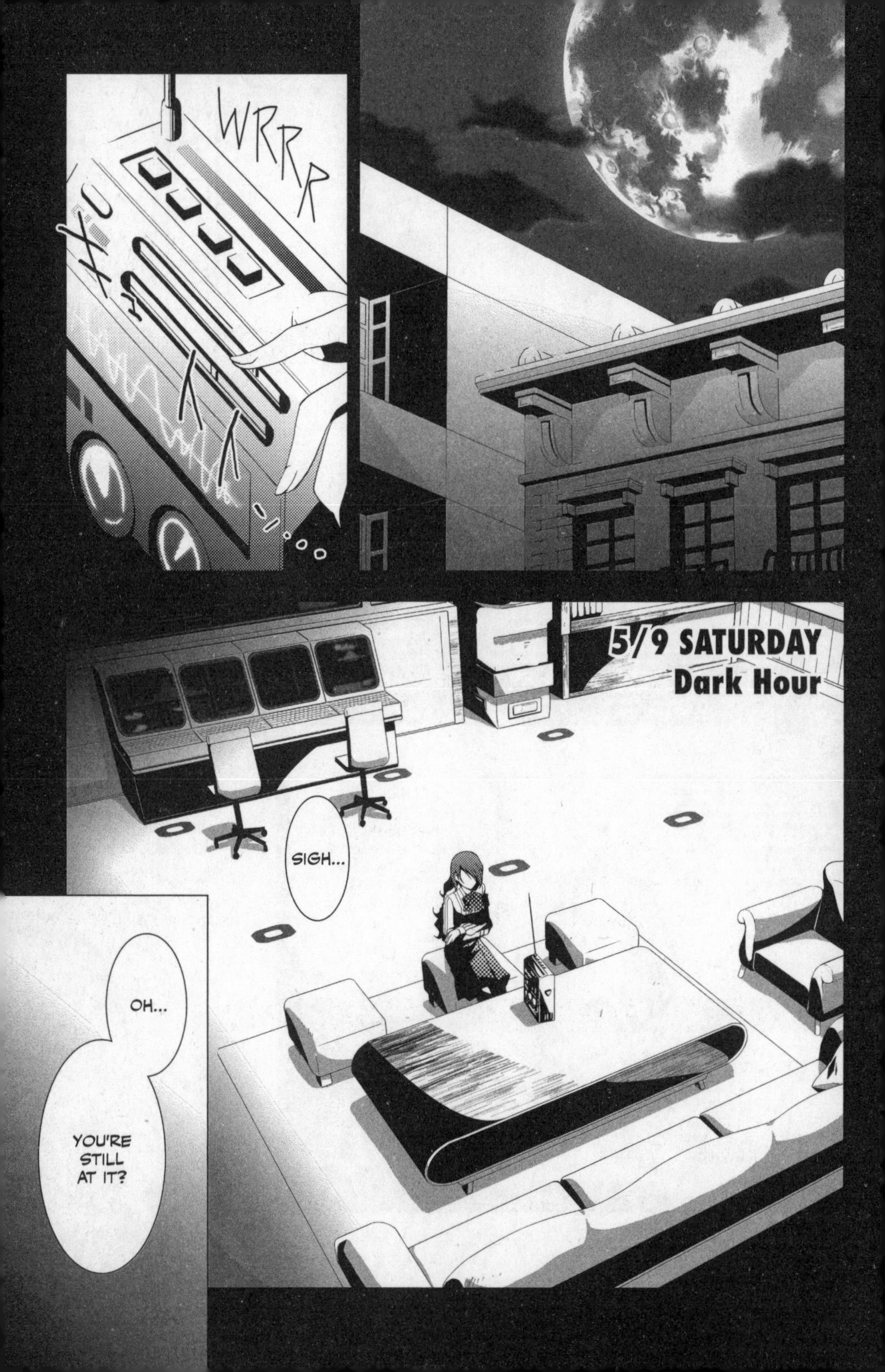
WRRR
5/9 SATURDAY
Dark Hour
SIGH...
OH...
YOU'RE STILL AT IT?

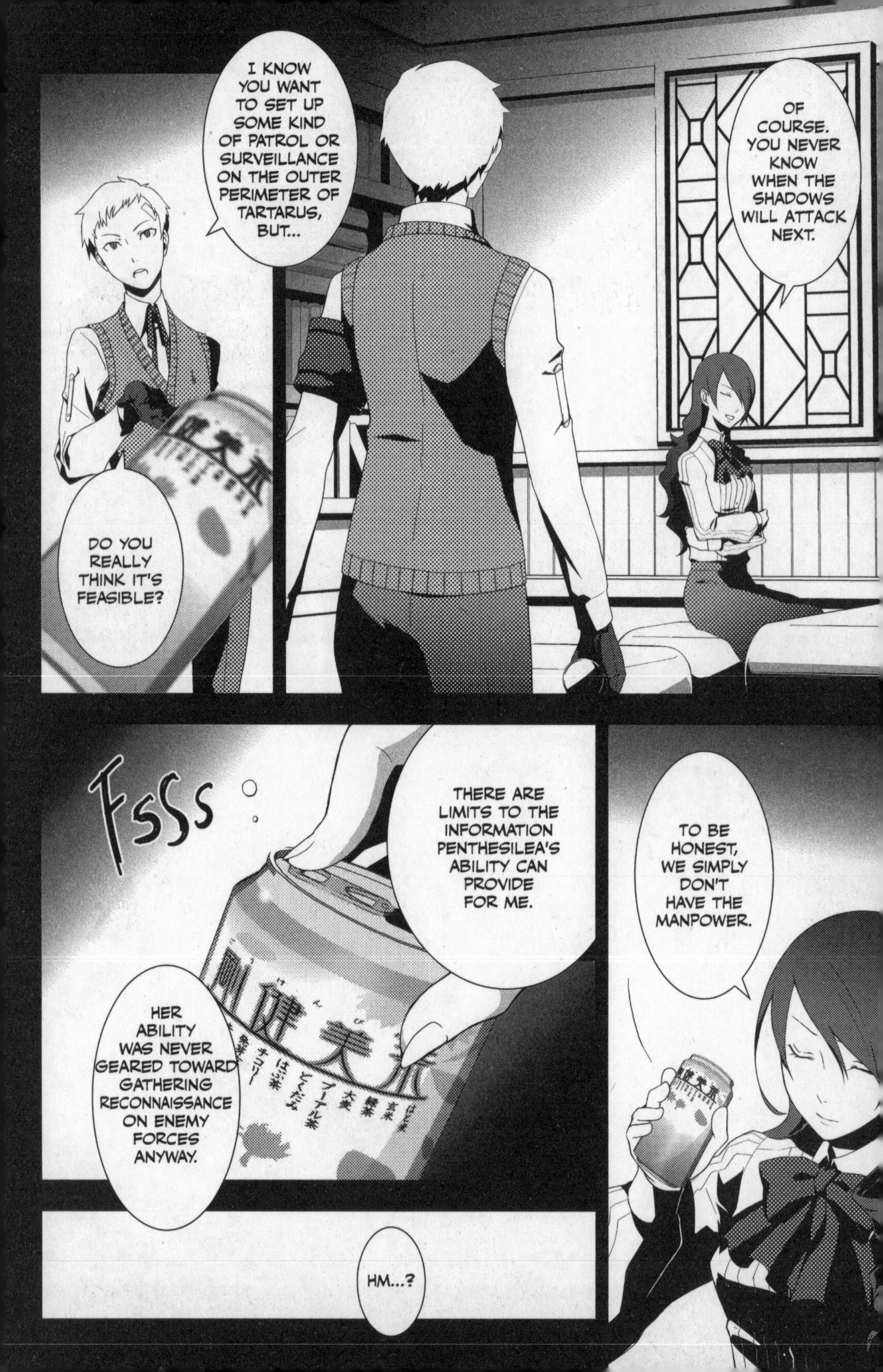
OF COURSE. YOU NEVER KNOW WHEN THE SHADOWS WILL ATTACK NEXT.
I KNOW YOU WANT TO SET UP SOME KIND OF PATROL OR SURVEILLANCE ON THE OUTER PERIMETER OF TARTARUS, BUT...
DO YOU REALLY THINK IT'S FEASIBLE?
TO BE HONEST, WE SIMPLY DON'T HAVE THE MANPOWER.
THERE ARE LIMITS TO THE INFORMATION PENTHESILEA'S ABILITY CAN PROVIDE FOR ME.
FSSS
HER ABILITY WAS NEVER GEARED TOWARD GATHERING RECONNAISSANCE ON ENEMY FORCES ANYWAY.
HM...?

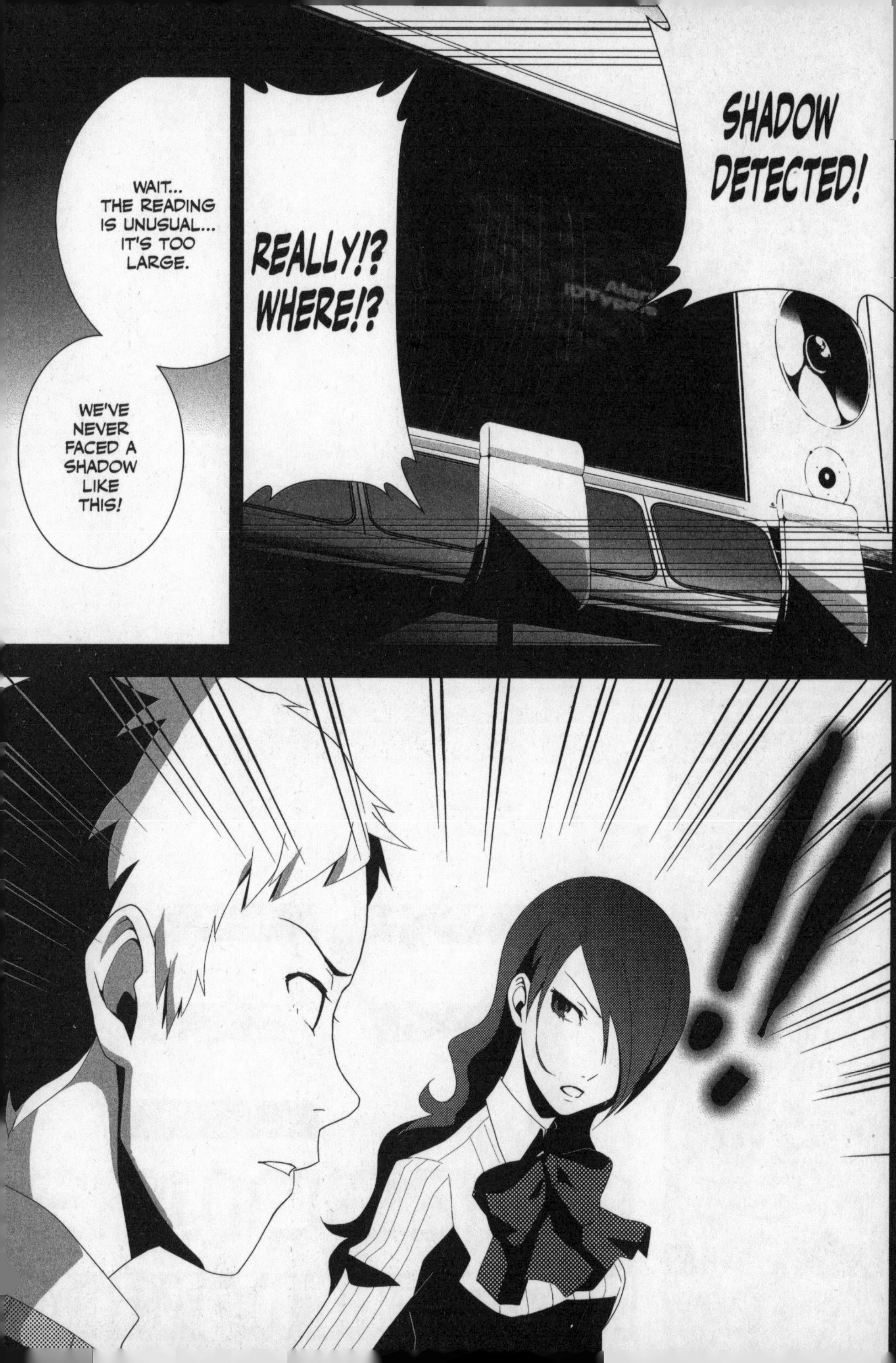
SHADOW DETECTED!
REALLY!? WHERE!?
WAIT... THE READING IS UNUSUAL... IT'S TOO LARGE.
WE'VE NEVER FACED A SHADOW LIKE THIS!
!!

P3

PERSONA3

piece:06
#07 Tight high tide

Design&Finished : StudioShortcakeScreamer

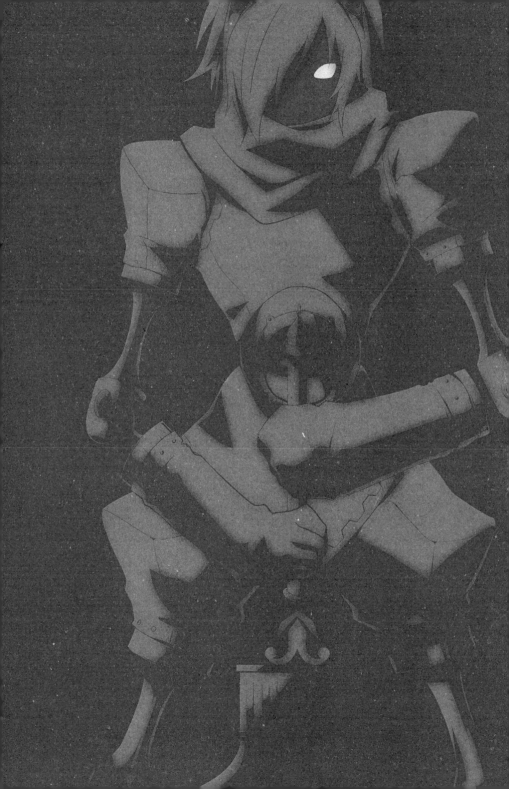

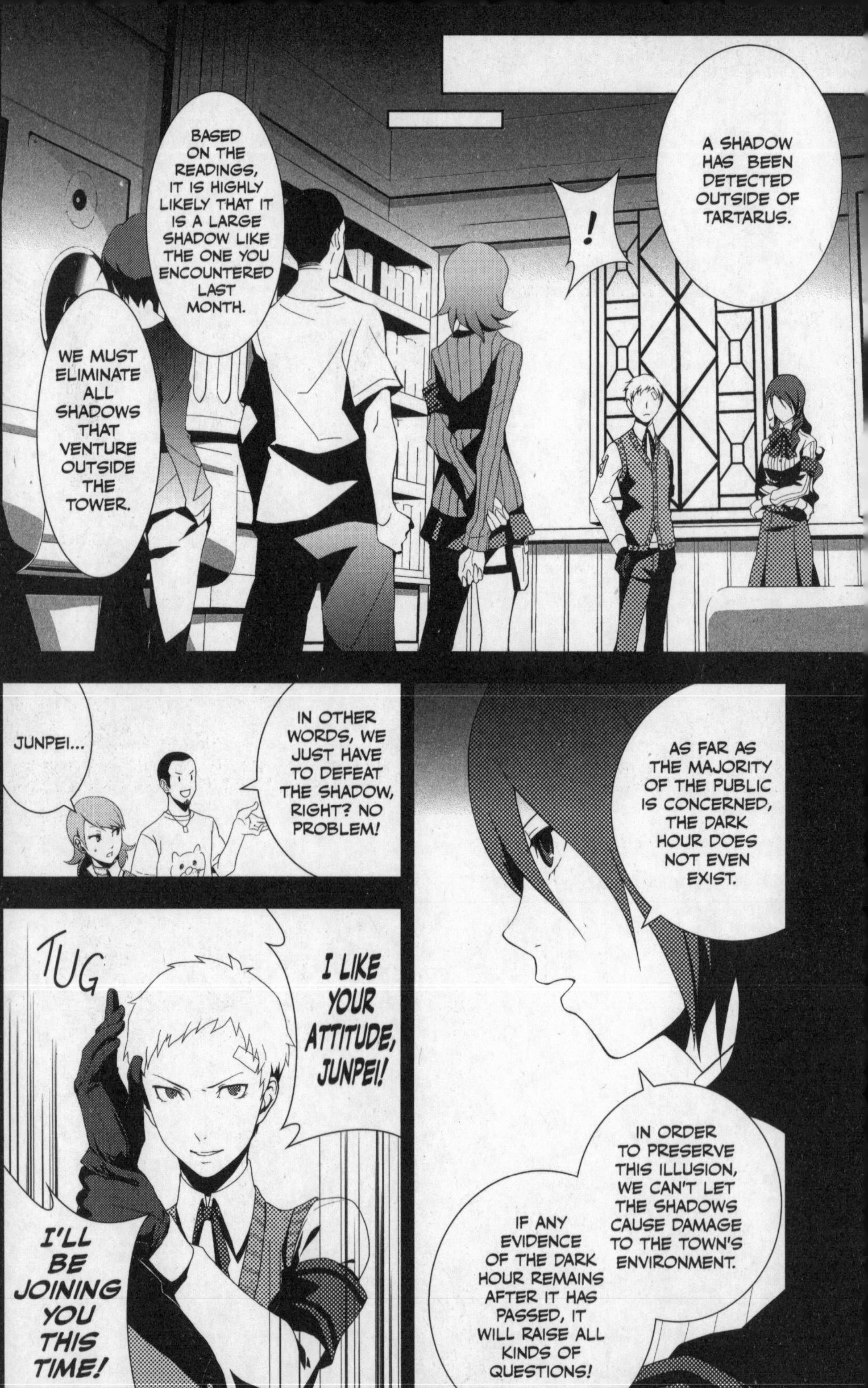
A SHADOW HAS BEEN DETECTED OUTSIDE OF TARTARUS.
!
BASED ON THE READINGS, IT IS HIGHLY LIKELY THAT IT IS A LARGE SHADOW LIKE THE ONE YOU ENCOUNTERED LAST MONTH.
WE MUST ELIMINATE ALL SHADOWS THAT VENTURE OUTSIDE THE TOWER.
AS FAR AS THE MAJORITY OF THE PUBLIC IS CONCERNED, THE DARK HOUR DOES NOT EVEN EXIST.
IN ORDER TO PRESERVE THIS ILLUSION, WE CAN'T LET THE SHADOWS CAUSE DAMAGE TO THE TOWN'S ENVIRONMENT.
IF ANY EVIDENCE OF THE DARK HOUR REMAINS AFTER IT HAS PASSED, IT WILL RAISE ALL KINDS OF QUESTIONS!
IN OTHER WORDS, WE JUST HAVE TO DEFEAT THE SHADOW, RIGHT? NO PROBLEM!
JUNPEI...
I LIKE YOUR ATTITUDE, JUNPEI!
TUG
I'LL BE JOINING YOU THIS TIME!

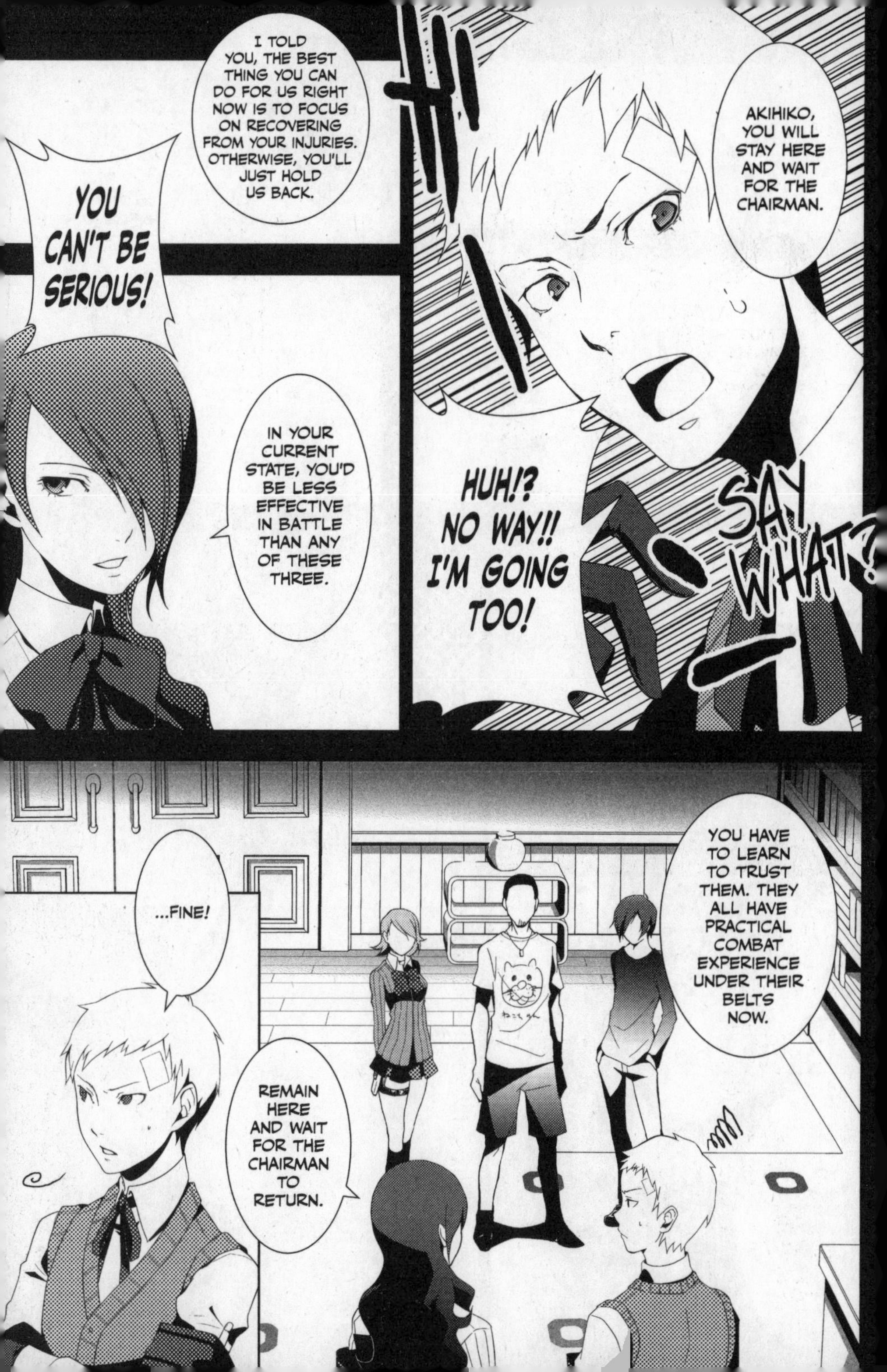
AKIHIKO, YOU WILL STAY HERE AND WAIT FOR THE CHAIRMAN.
SAY WHAT?
HUH!? NO WAY!! I'M GOING TOO!
I TOLD YOU, THE BEST THING YOU CAN DO FOR US RIGHT NOW IS TO FOCUS ON RECOVERING FROM YOUR INJURIES. OTHERWISE, YOU'LL JUST HOLD US BACK.
YOU CAN'T BE SERIOUS!
IN YOUR CURRENT STATE, YOU'D BE LESS EFFECTIVE IN BATTLE THAN ANY OF THESE THREE.
YOU HAVE TO LEARN TO TRUST THEM. THEY ALL HAVE PRACTICAL COMBAT EXPERIENCE UNDER THEIR BELTS NOW.
REMAIN HERE AND WAIT FOR THE CHAIRMAN TO RETURN.
...FINE!

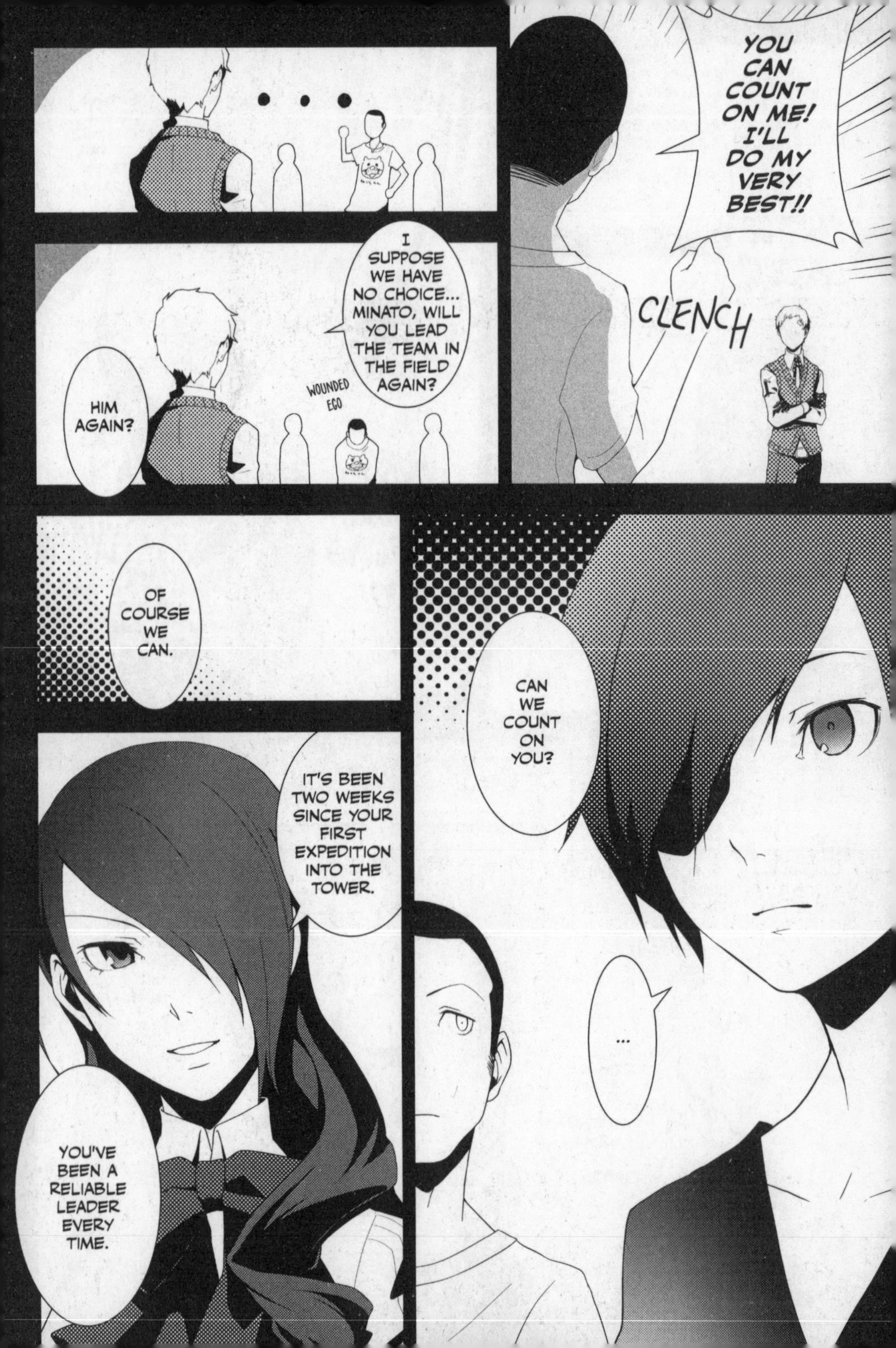
YOU CAN COUNT ON ME! I'LL DO MY VERY BEST!!
CLENCH
• • •
I SUPPOSE WE HAVE NO CHOICE... MINATO, WILL YOU LEAD THE TEAM IN THE FIELD AGAIN?
WOUNDED EGO
HIM AGAIN?
CAN WE COUNT ON YOU?
...
OF COURSE WE CAN.
IT'S BEEN TWO WEEKS SINCE YOUR FIRST EXPEDITION INTO THE TOWER.
YOU'VE BEEN A RELIABLE LEADER EVERY TIME.

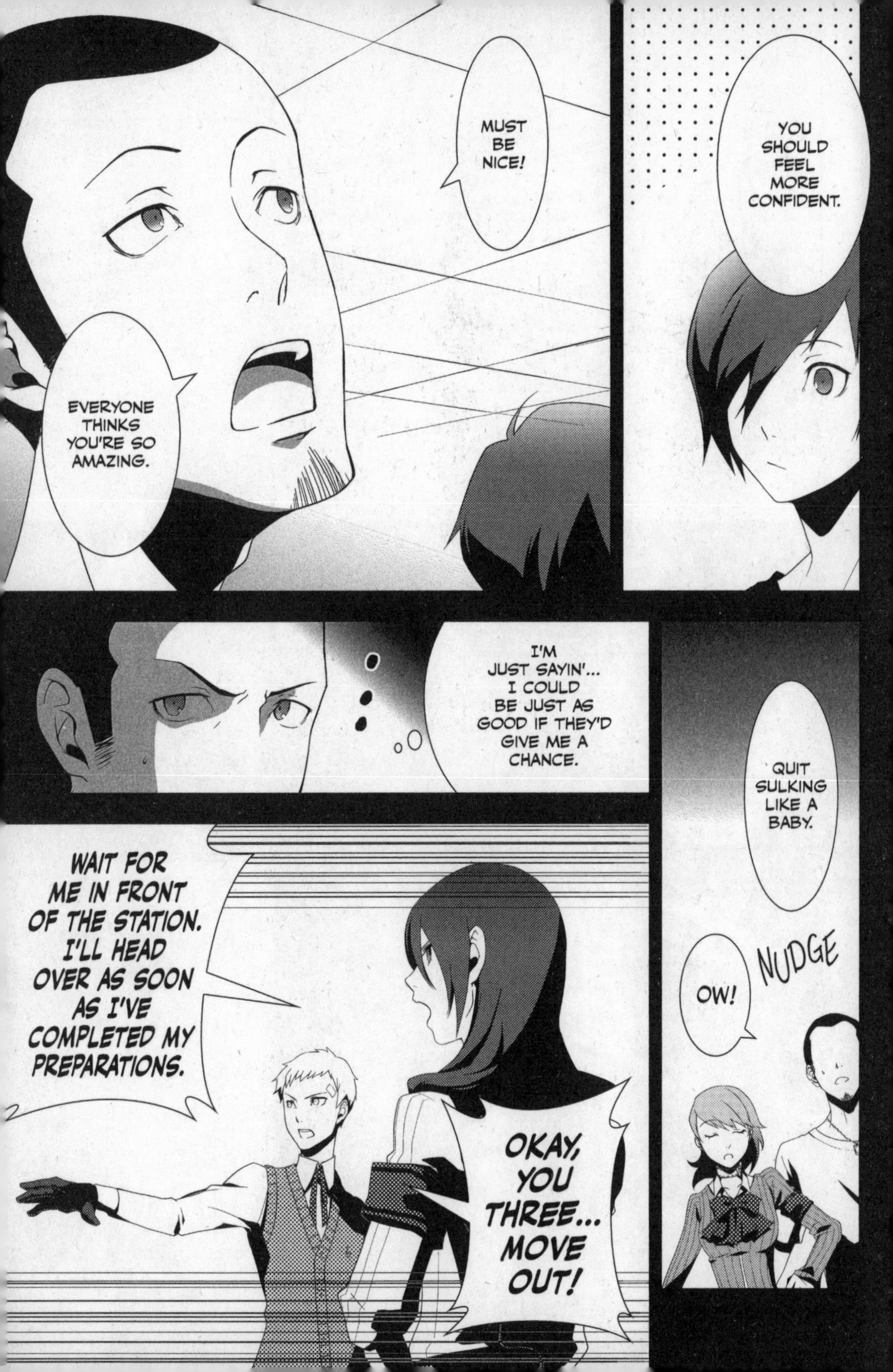
YOU SHOULD FEEL MORE CONFIDENT.
MUST BE NICE!
EVERYONE THINKS YOU'RE SO AMAZING.
QUIT SULKING LIKE A BABY.
NUDGE
OW!
I'M JUST SAYIN'... I COULD BE JUST AS GOOD IF THEY'D GIVE ME A CHANCE.
OKAY, YOU THREE... MOVE OUT!
WAIT FOR ME IN FRONT OF THE STATION. I'LL HEAD OVER AS SOON AS I'VE COMPLETED MY PREPARATIONS.

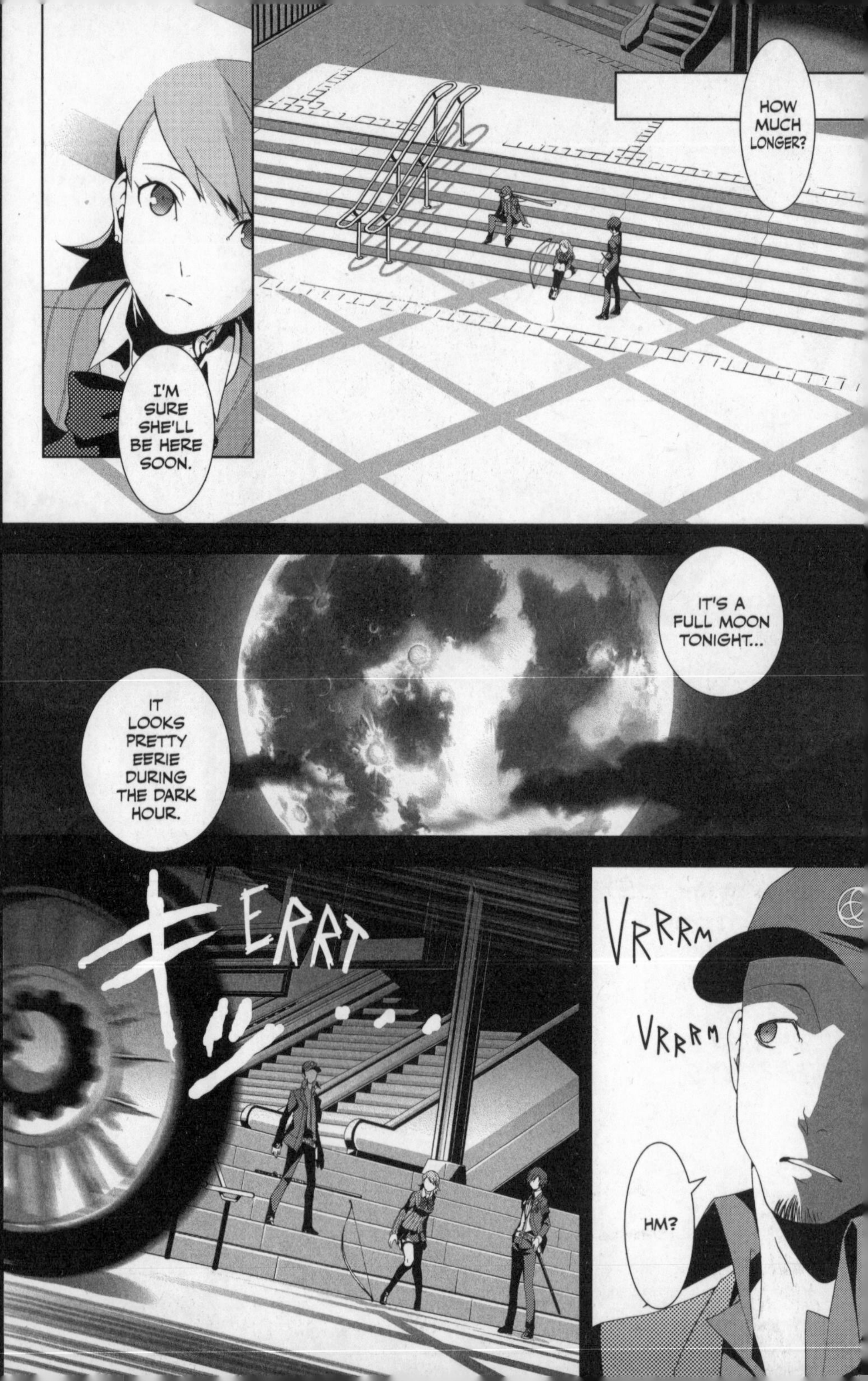
HOW MUCH LONGER?
I'M SURE SHE'LL BE HERE SOON.
IT'S A FULL MOON TONIGHT...
IT LOOKS PRETTY EERIE DURING THE DARK HOUR.
VRRRM
VRRRM
HM?
ERRT

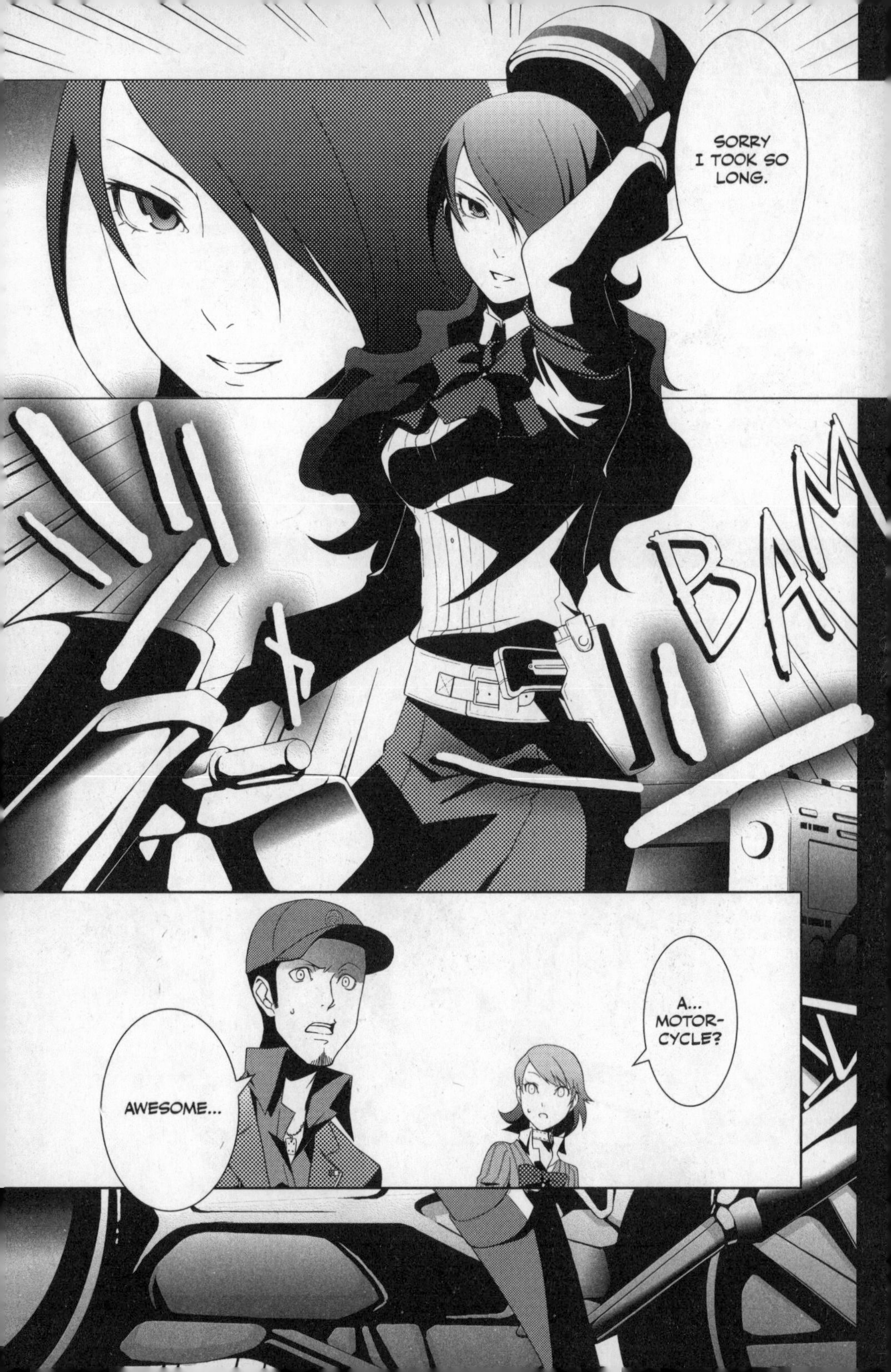
SORRY I TOOK SO LONG.
BAM
A... MOTOR-CYCLE?
AWESOME...

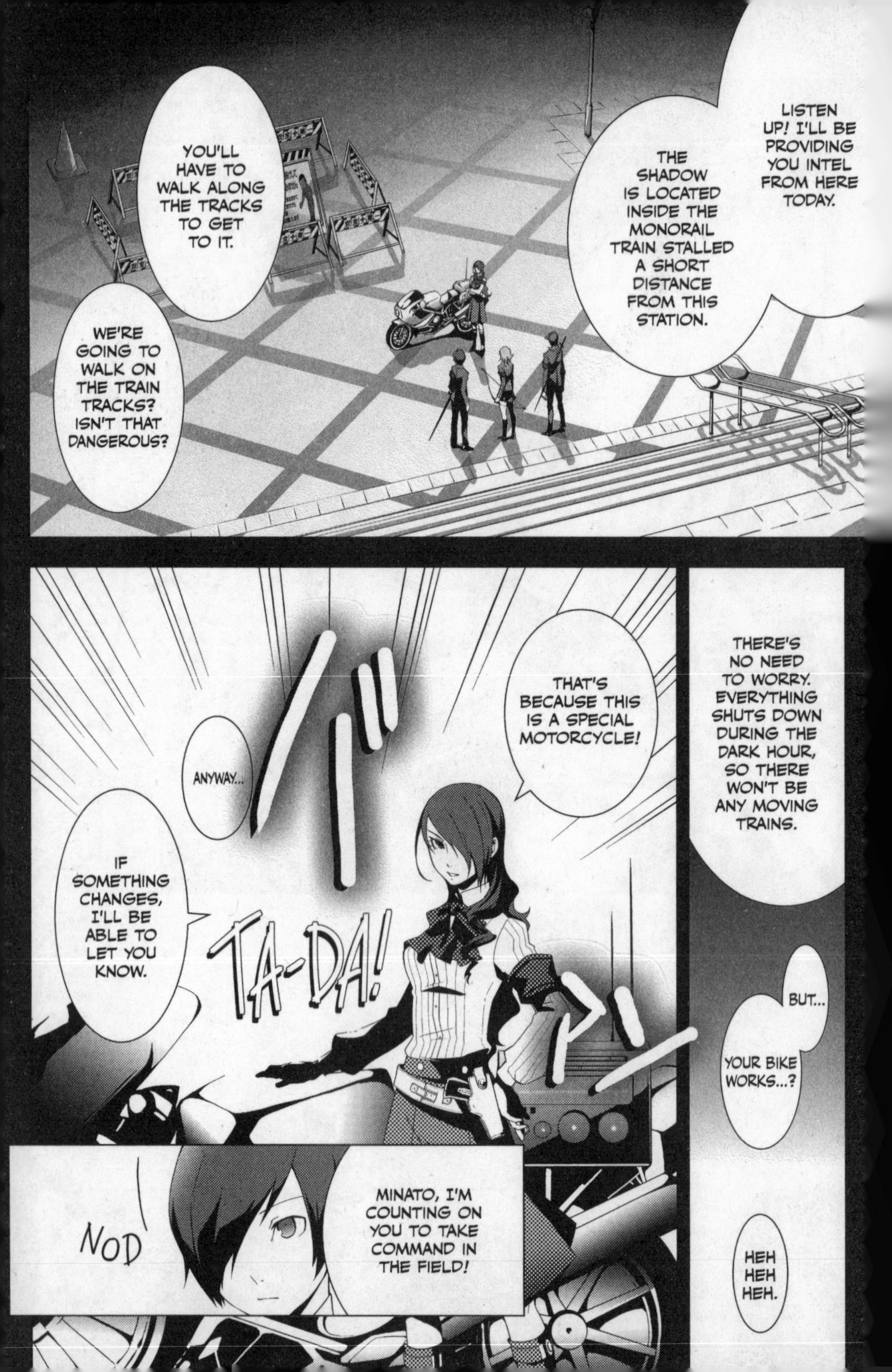

LISTEN UP! I'LL BE PROVIDING YOU INTEL FROM HERE TODAY.
THE SHADOW IS LOCATED INSIDE THE MONORAIL TRAIN STALLED A SHORT DISTANCE FROM THIS STATION.
YOU'LL HAVE TO WALK ALONG THE TRACKS TO GET TO IT.
WE'RE GOING TO WALK ON THE TRAIN TRACKS? ISN'T THAT DANGEROUS?
THERE'S NO NEED TO WORRY. EVERYTHING SHUTS DOWN DURING THE DARK HOUR, SO THERE WON'T BE ANY MOVING TRAINS.
BUT...
YOUR BIKE WORKS...?
HEH HEH HEH.
THAT'S BECAUSE THIS IS A SPECIAL MOTORCYCLE!
TA-DA!
ANYWAY...
IF SOMETHING CHANGES, I'LL BE ABLE TO LET YOU KNOW.
MINATO, I'M COUNTING ON YOU TO TAKE COMMAND IN THE FIELD!
NOD

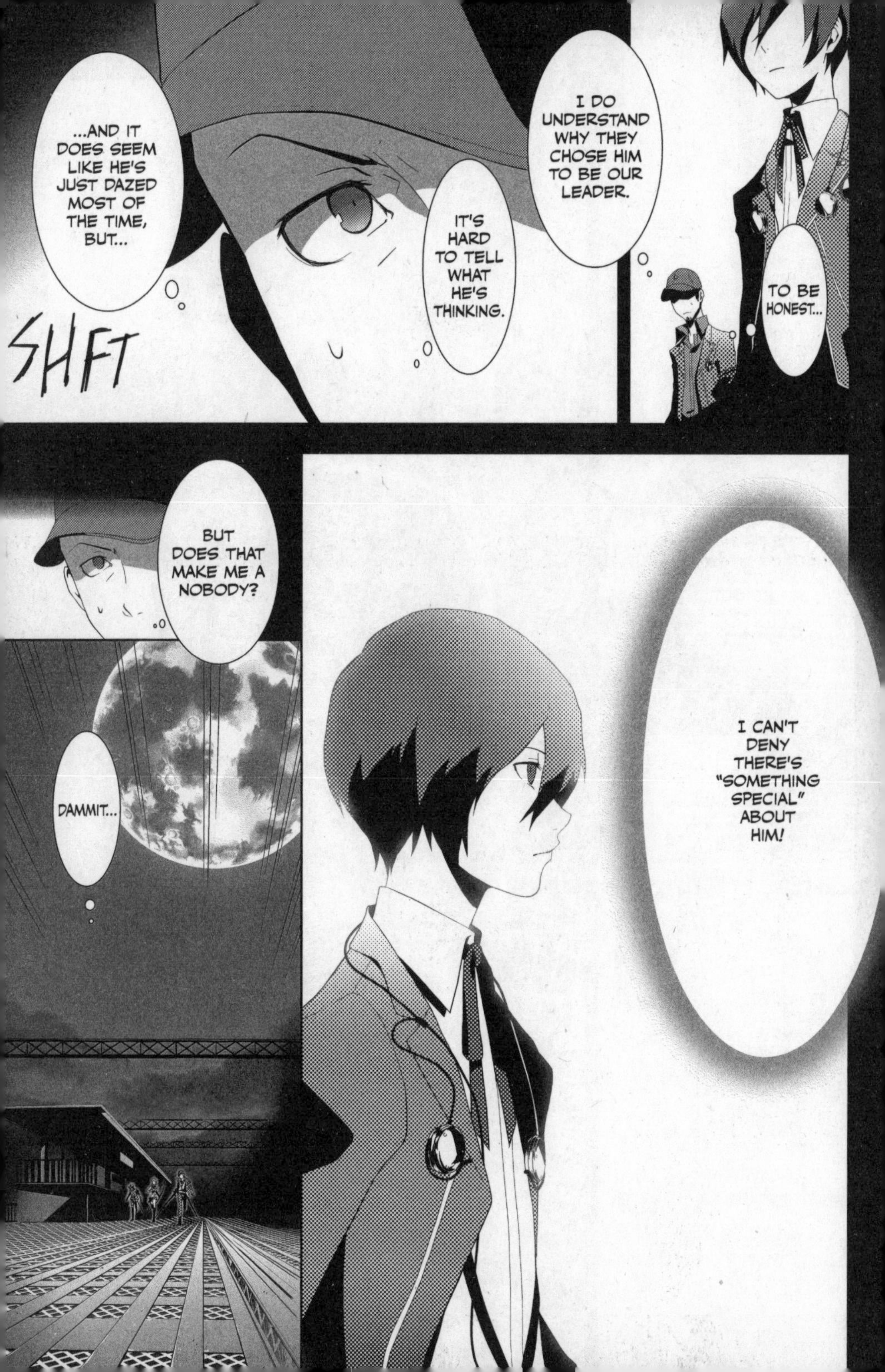
TO BE HONEST...
I DO UNDERSTAND WHY THEY CHOSE HIM TO BE OUR LEADER.
IT'S HARD TO TELL WHAT HE'S THINKING.
...AND IT DOES SEEM LIKE HE'S JUST DAZED MOST OF THE TIME, BUT...
SHFT
I CAN'T DENY THERE'S "SOMETHING SPECIAL" ABOUT HIM!
BUT DOES THAT MAKE ME A NOBODY?
DAMMIT...

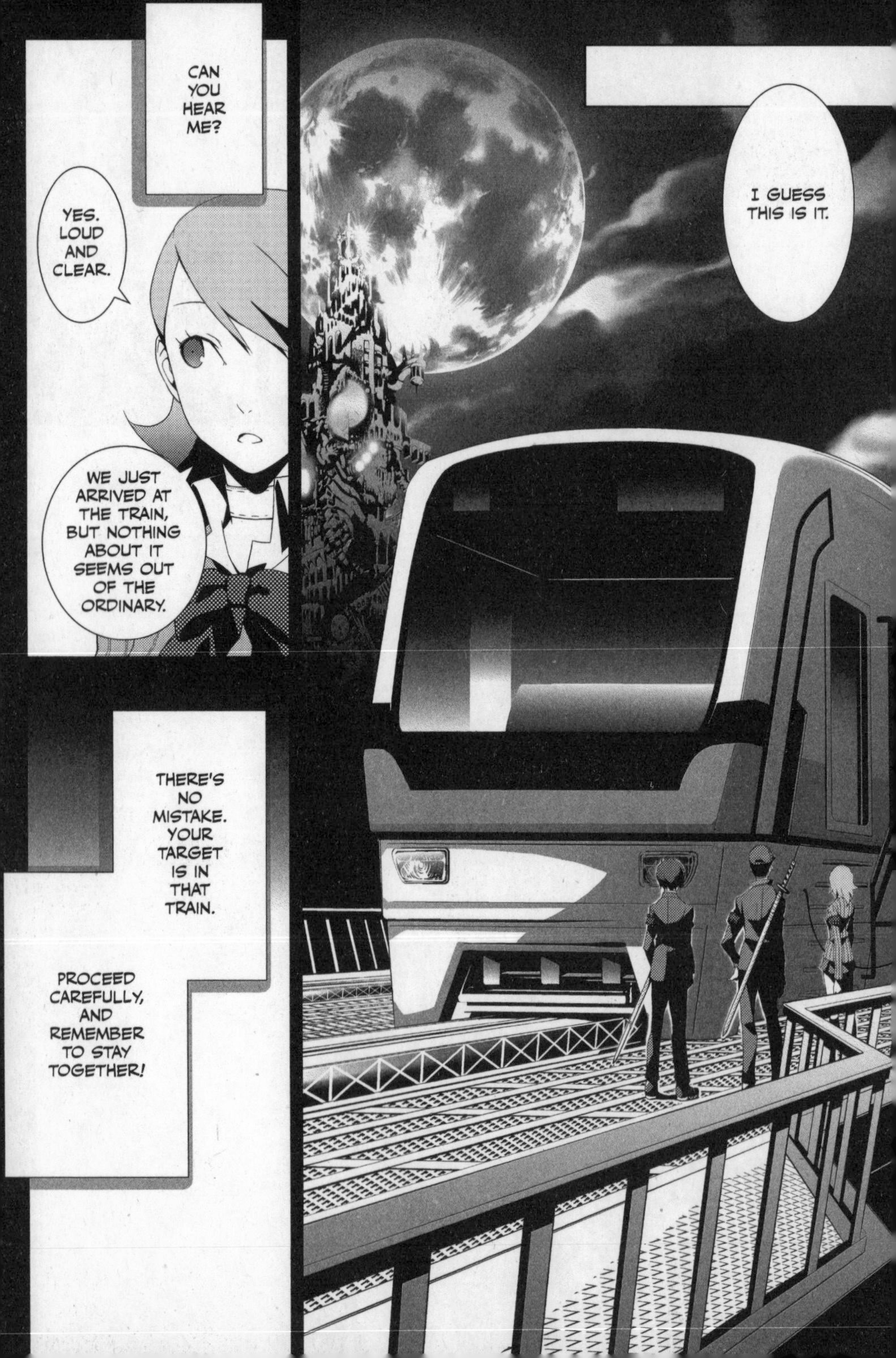
I GUESS THIS IS IT.
CAN YOU HEAR ME?
YES. LOUD AND CLEAR.
WE JUST ARRIVED AT THE TRAIN, BUT NOTHING ABOUT IT SEEMS OUT OF THE ORDINARY.
THERE'S NO MISTAKE. YOUR TARGET IS IN THAT TRAIN.
PROCEED CAREFULLY, AND REMEMBER TO STAY TOGETHER!

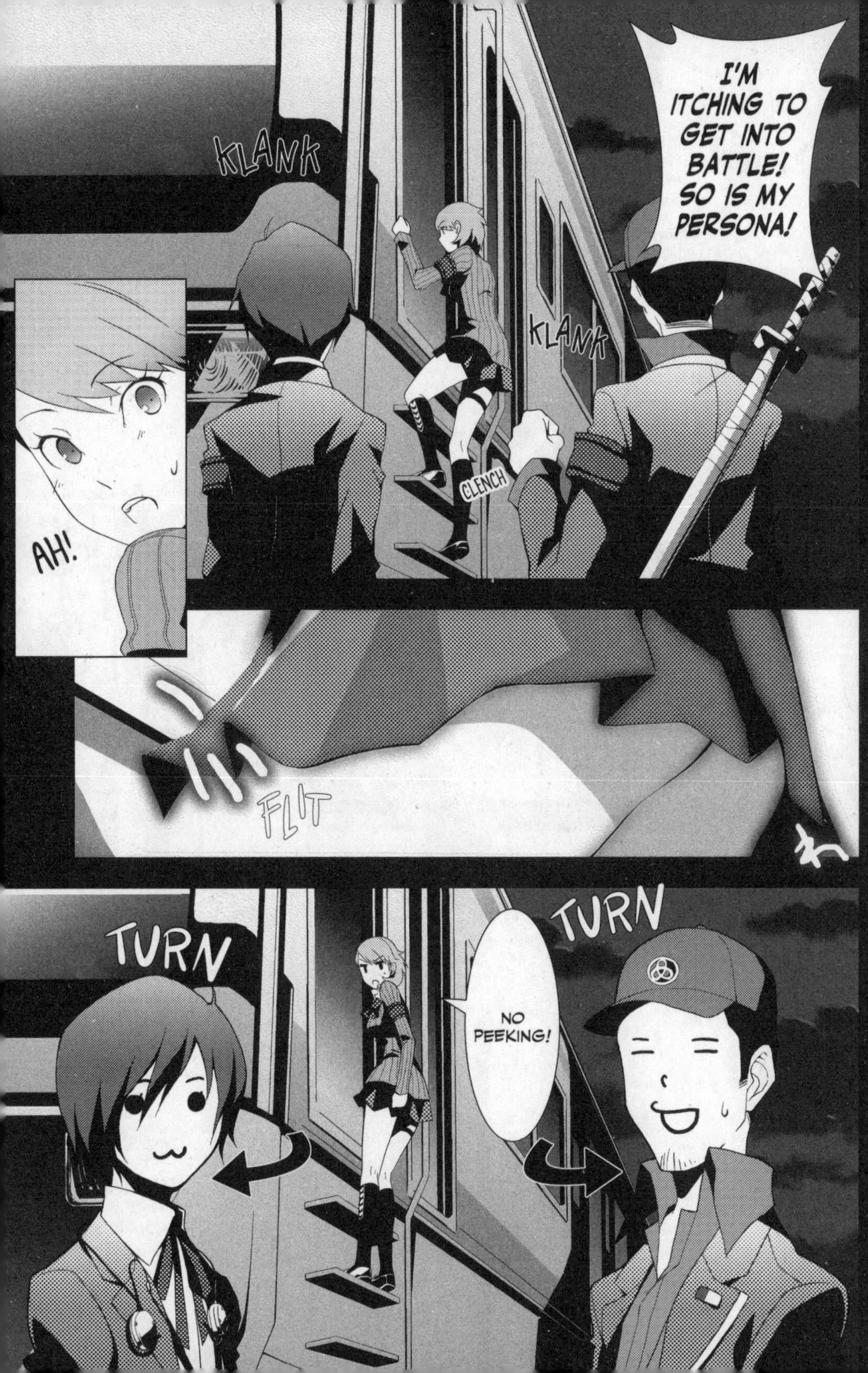
I'M ITCHING TO GET INTO BATTLE! SO IS MY PERSONA!
KLANK
KLANK
CLENCH
AH!
FLIT
TURN
NO PEEKING!
TURN

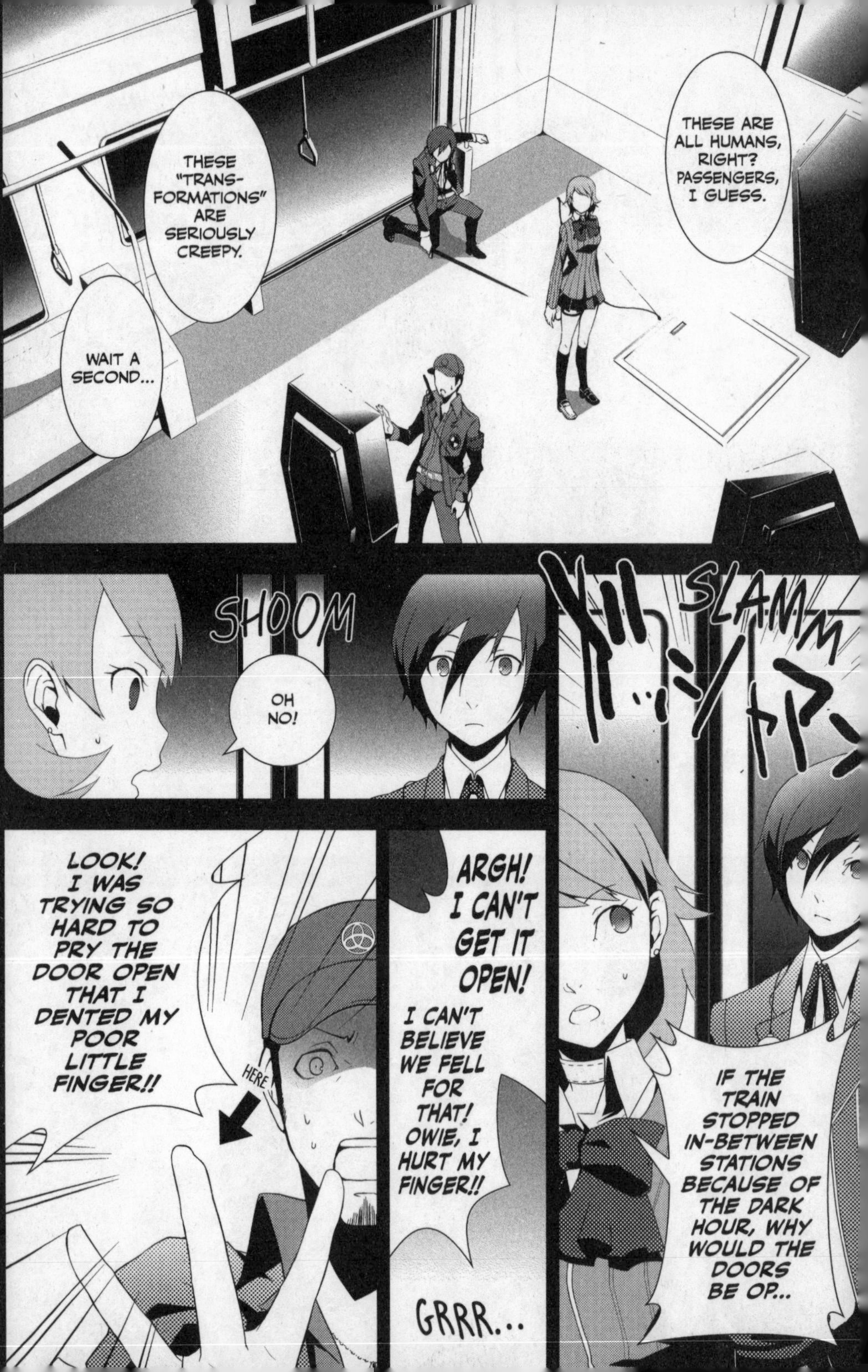
THESE ARE ALL HUMANS, RIGHT? PASSENGERS, I GUESS.
THESE "TRANS-FORMATIONS" ARE SERIOUSLY CREEPY.
WAIT A SECOND...
SLAMM
IF THE TRAIN STOPPED IN-BETWEEN STATIONS BECAUSE OF THE DARK HOUR, WHY WOULD THE DOORS BE OP...
SHOOM
OH NO!
ARGH! I CAN'T GET IT OPEN!
I CAN'T BELIEVE WE FELL FOR THAT! OWIE, I HURT MY FINGER!!
GRRR...
LOOK! I WAS TRYING SO HARD TO PRY THE DOOR OPEN THAT I DENTED MY POOR LITTLE FINGER!!
HERE

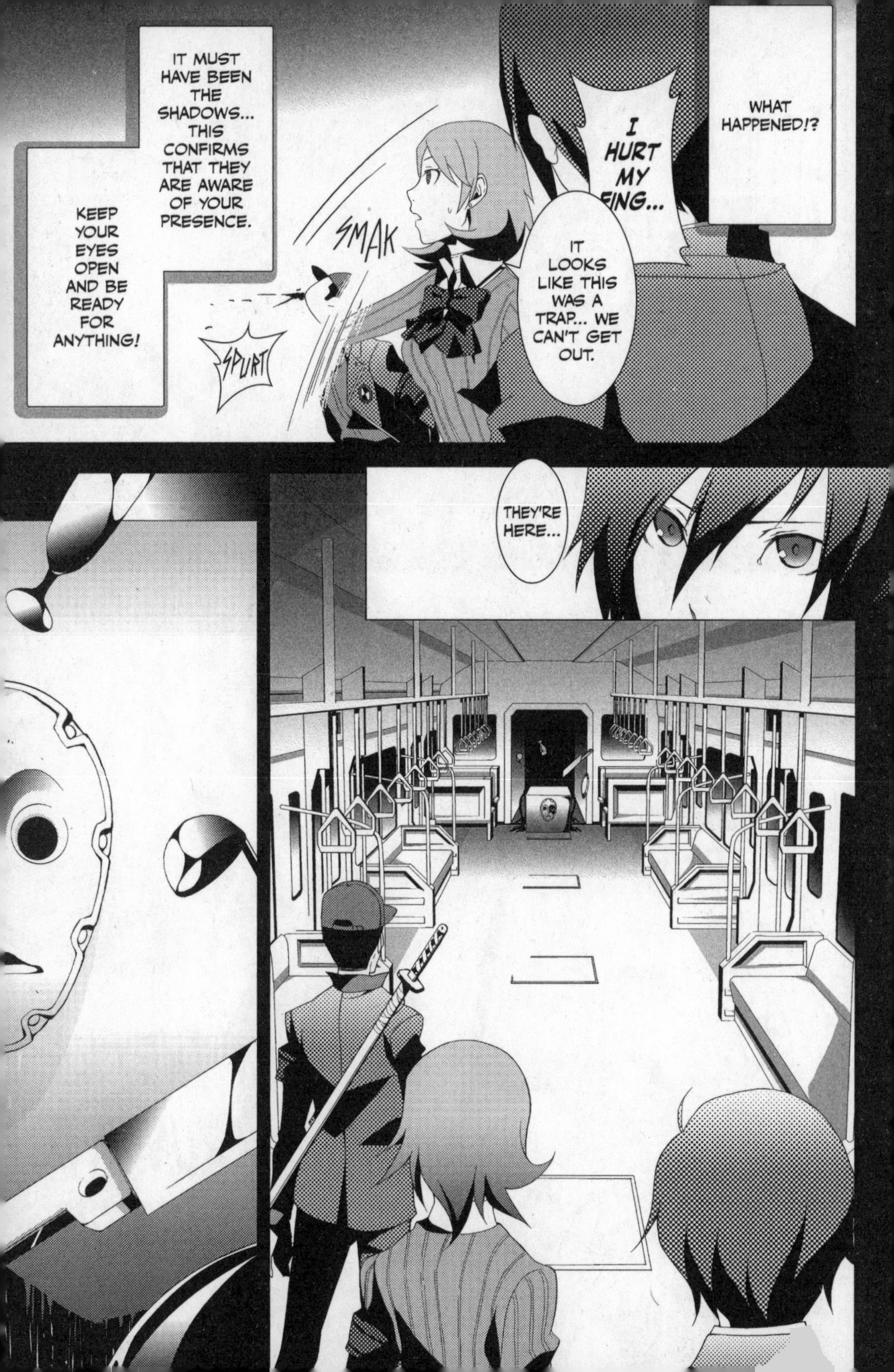
WHAT HAPPENED!?
I HURT MY FING...
IT LOOKS LIKE THIS WAS A TRAP... WE CAN'T GET OUT.
SMAK
SPURT
IT MUST HAVE BEEN THE SHADOWS... THIS CONFIRMS THAT THEY ARE AWARE OF YOUR PRESENCE.
KEEP YOUR EYES OPEN AND BE READY FOR ANYTHING!
THEY'RE HERE...

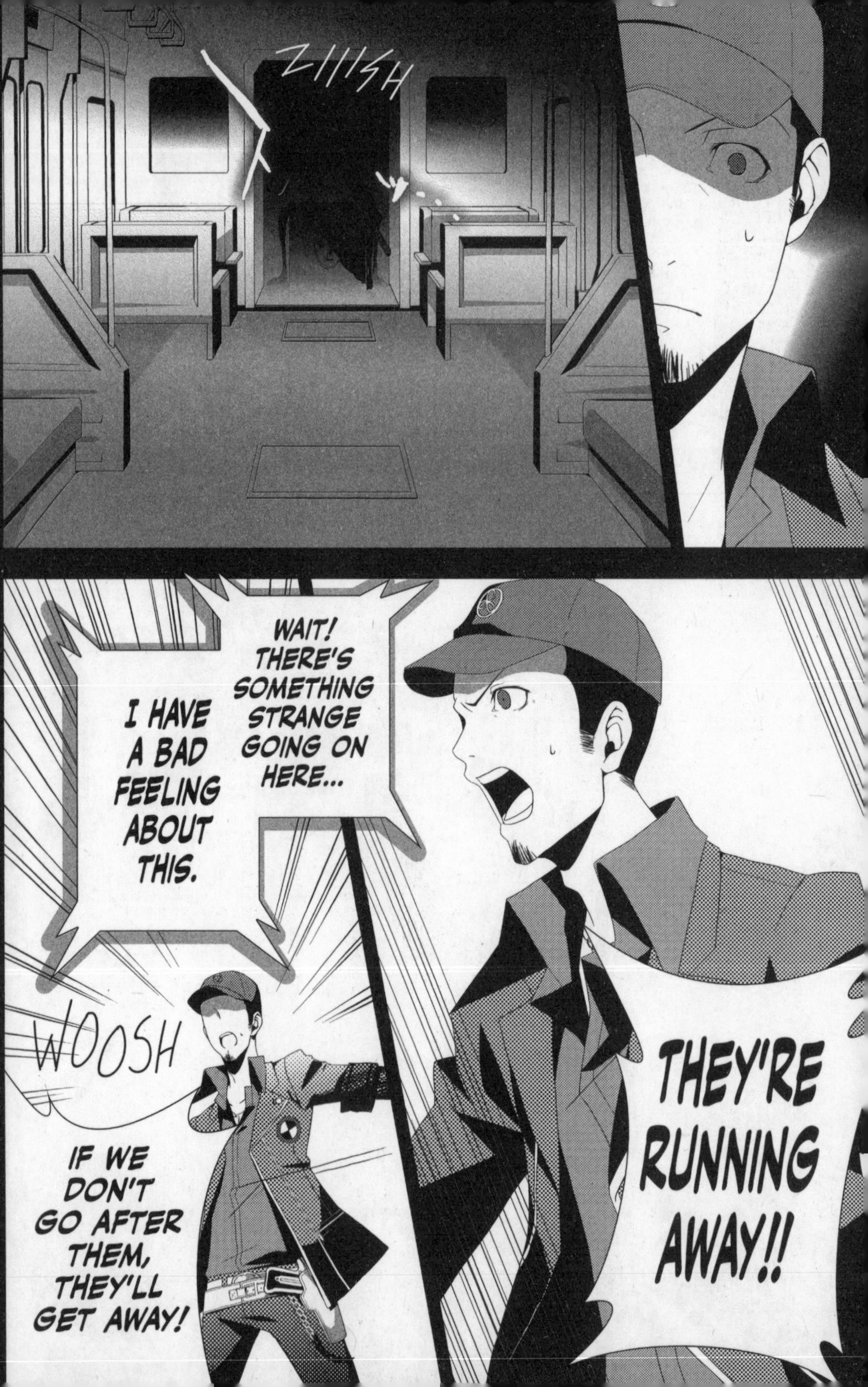
ZIIISH
WAIT! THERE'S SOMETHING STRANGE GOING ON HERE...
I HAVE A BAD FEELING ABOUT THIS.
THEY'RE RUNNING AWAY!!
WOOSH
IF WE DON'T GO AFTER THEM, THEY'LL GET AWAY!

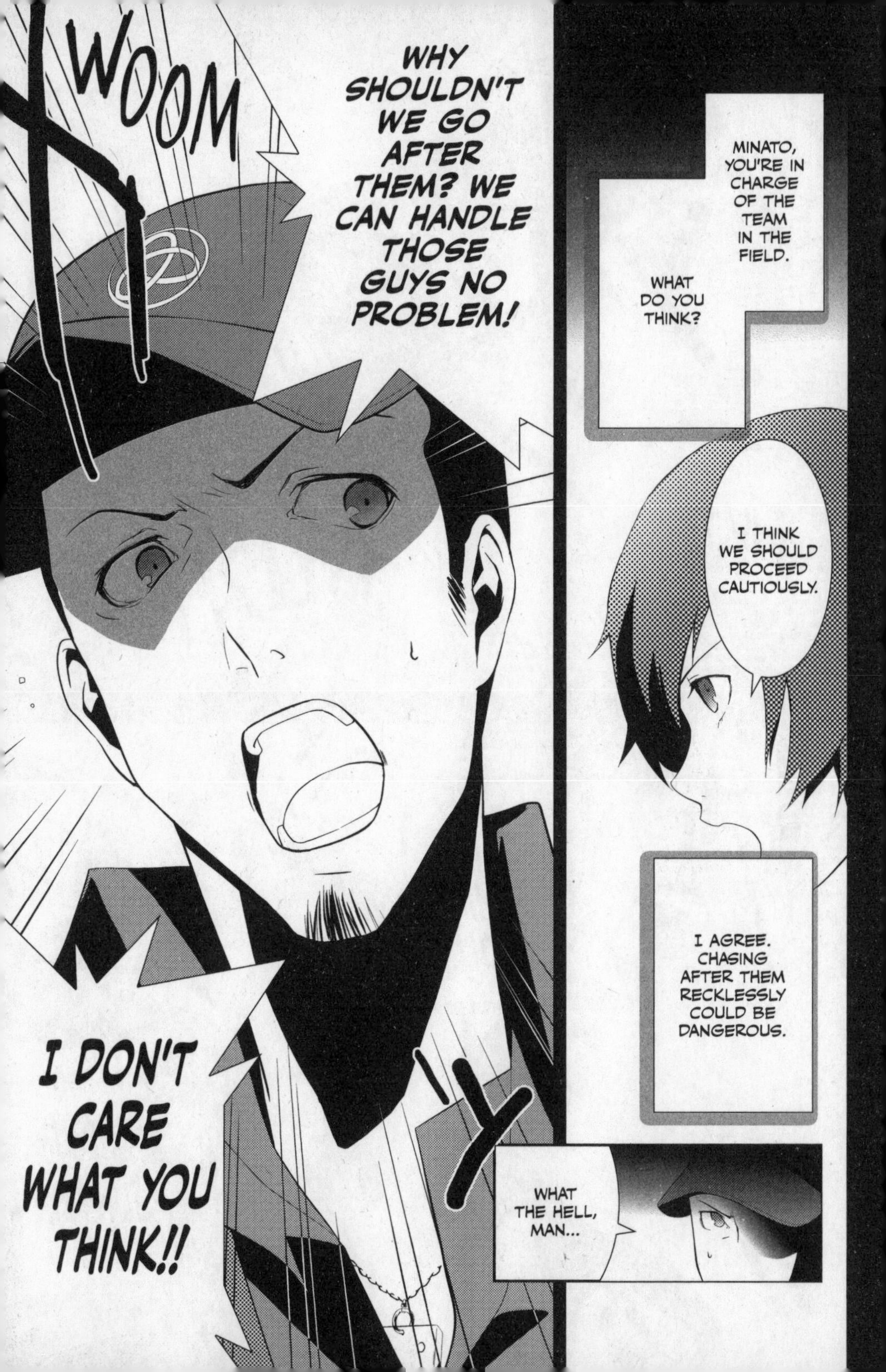
MINATO, YOU'RE IN CHARGE OF THE TEAM IN THE FIELD.
WHAT DO YOU THINK?
I THINK WE SHOULD PROCEED CAUTIOUSLY.
I AGREE. CHASING AFTER THEM RECKLESSLY COULD BE DANGEROUS.
WHAT THE HELL, MAN...
WOOM
WHY SHOULDN'T WE GO AFTER THEM? WE CAN HANDLE THOSE GUYS NO PROBLEM!
I DON'T CARE WHAT YOU THINK!!

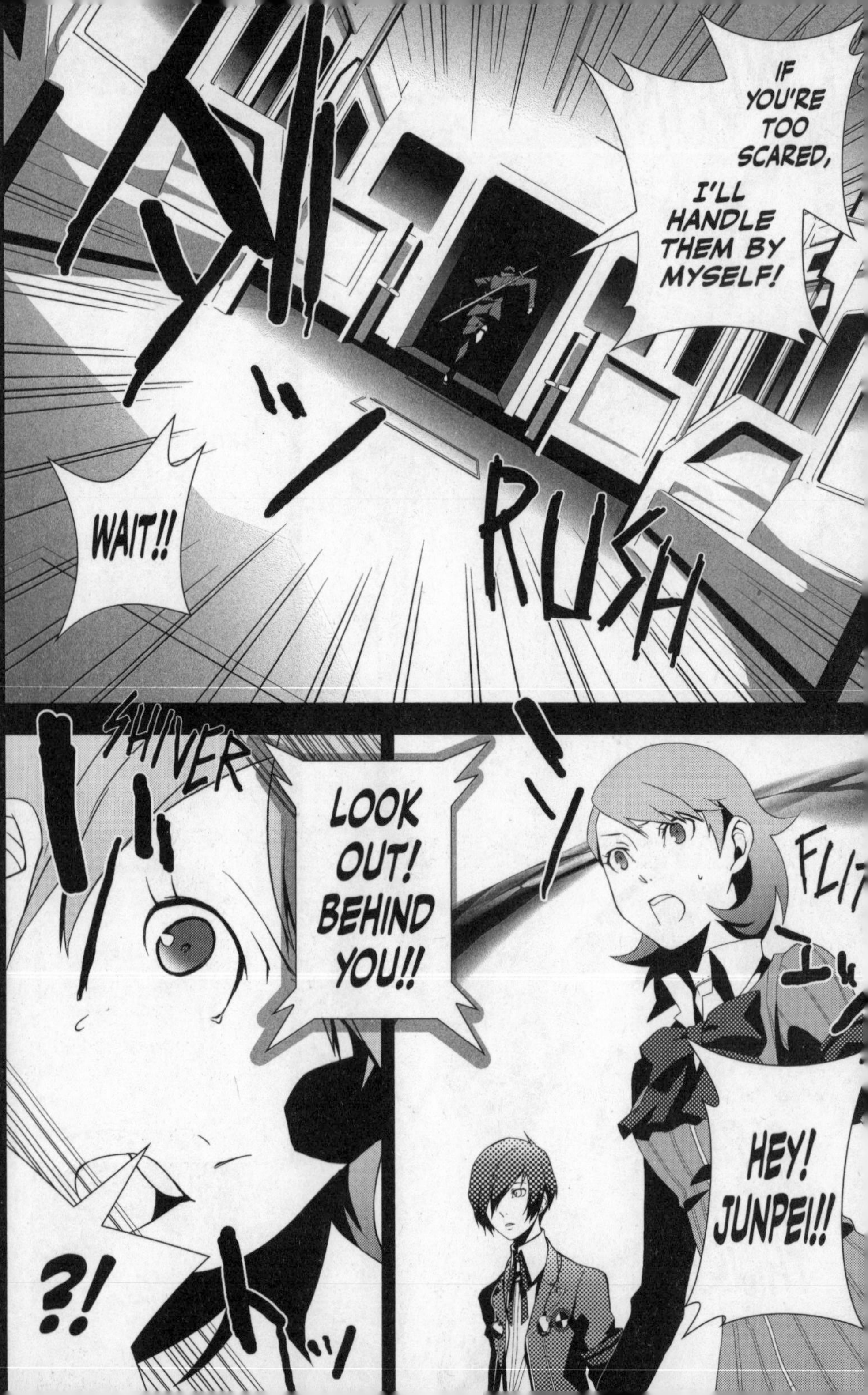
IF YOU'RE TOO SCARED, I'LL HANDLE THEM BY MYSELF!
RUSH
WAIT!!
FLIT
HEY! JUNPEI!!
SHIVER
LOOK OUT! BEHIND YOU!!
?!

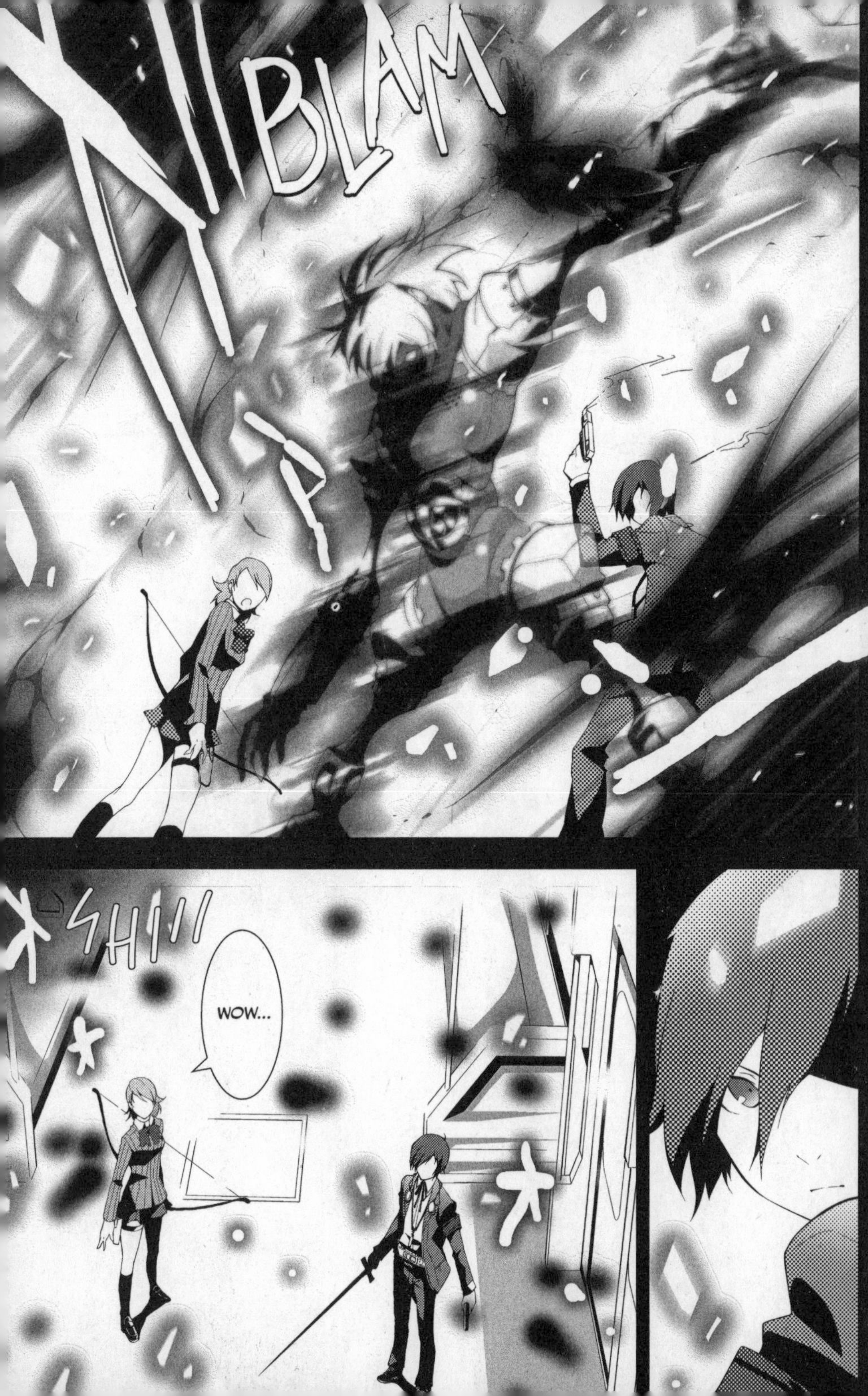
BLAM
SHI
WOW...

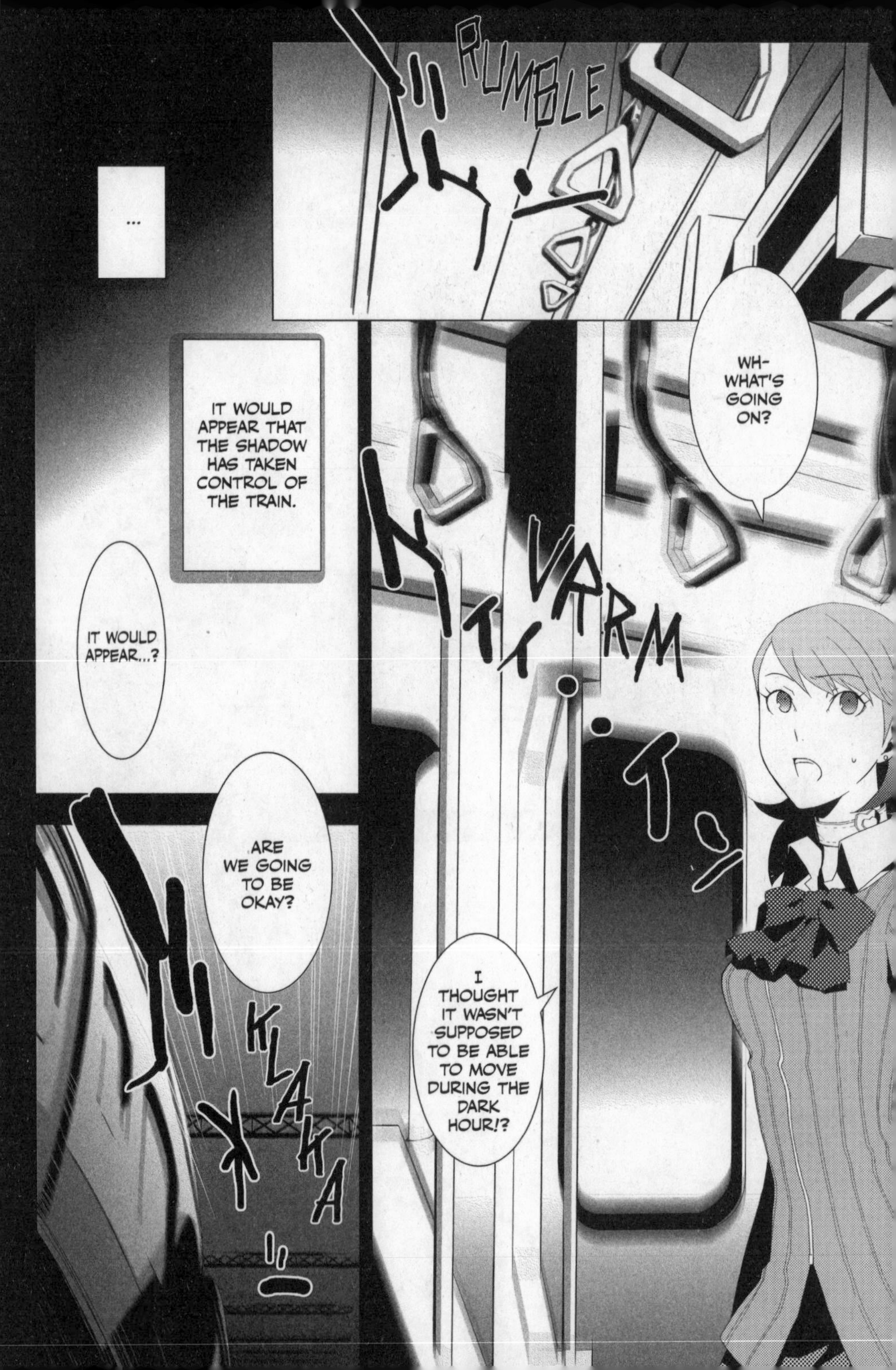
RUMBLE
WH- WHAT'S GOING ON?
VRRM
I THOUGHT IT WASN'T SUPPOSED TO BE ABLE TO MOVE DURING THE DARK HOUR!?
...
IT WOULD APPEAR THAT THE SHADOW HAS TAKEN CONTROL OF THE TRAIN.
IT WOULD APPEAR...?
ARE WE GOING TO BE OKAY?
KLAKA
K

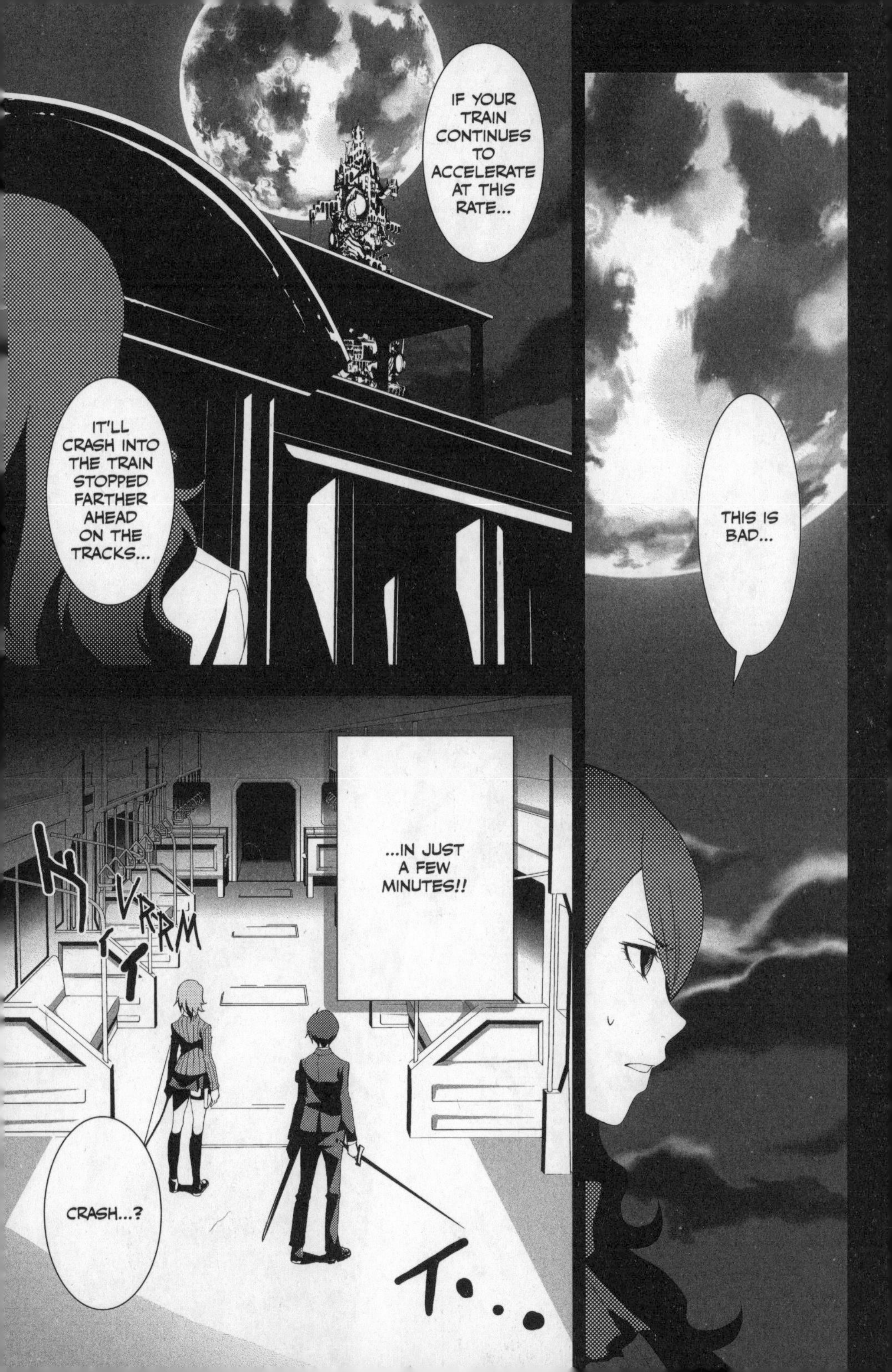
THIS IS BAD...
IF YOUR TRAIN CONTINUES TO ACCELERATE AT THIS RATE...
IT'LL CRASH INTO THE TRAIN STOPPED FARTHER AHEAD ON THE TRACKS...
...IN JUST A FEW MINUTES!!
VRRM
CRASH...?
T...

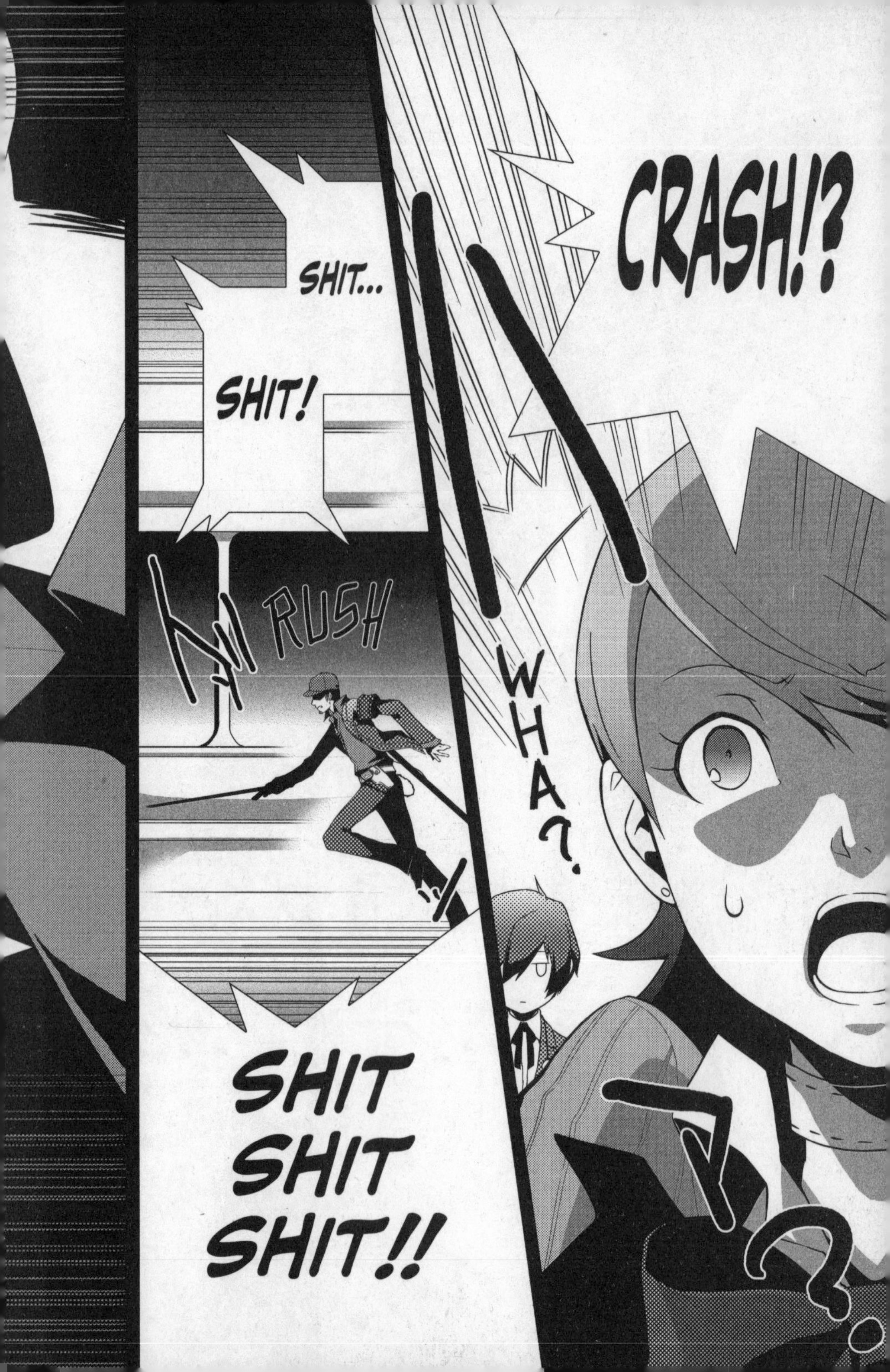
CRASH!?
WHA?
SHIT...
SHIT!
RUSH
SHIT SHIT SHIT!!
?

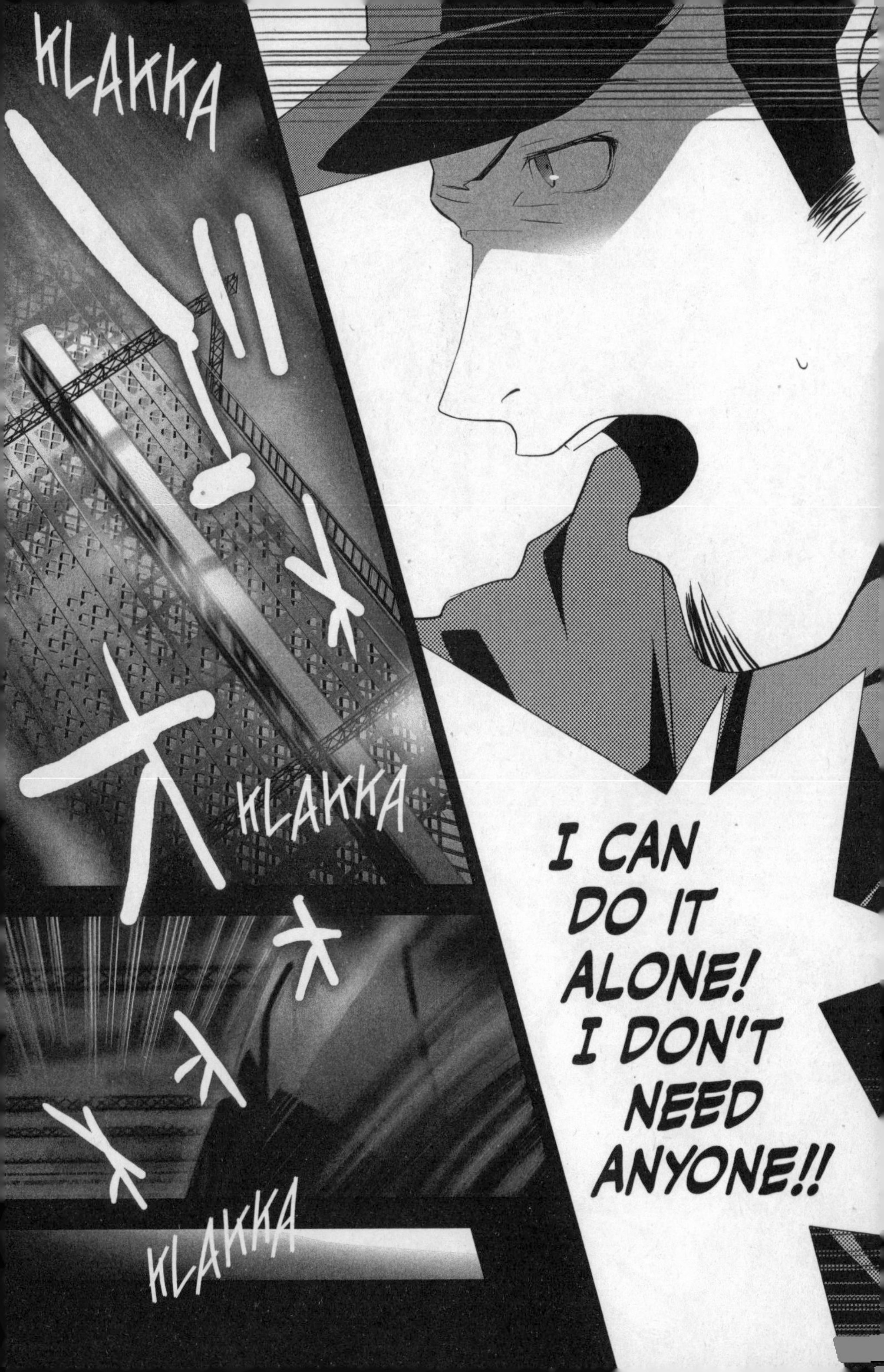
KLAKKA
I CAN DO IT ALONE! I DON'T NEED ANYONE!!
KLAKKA
KLAKKA

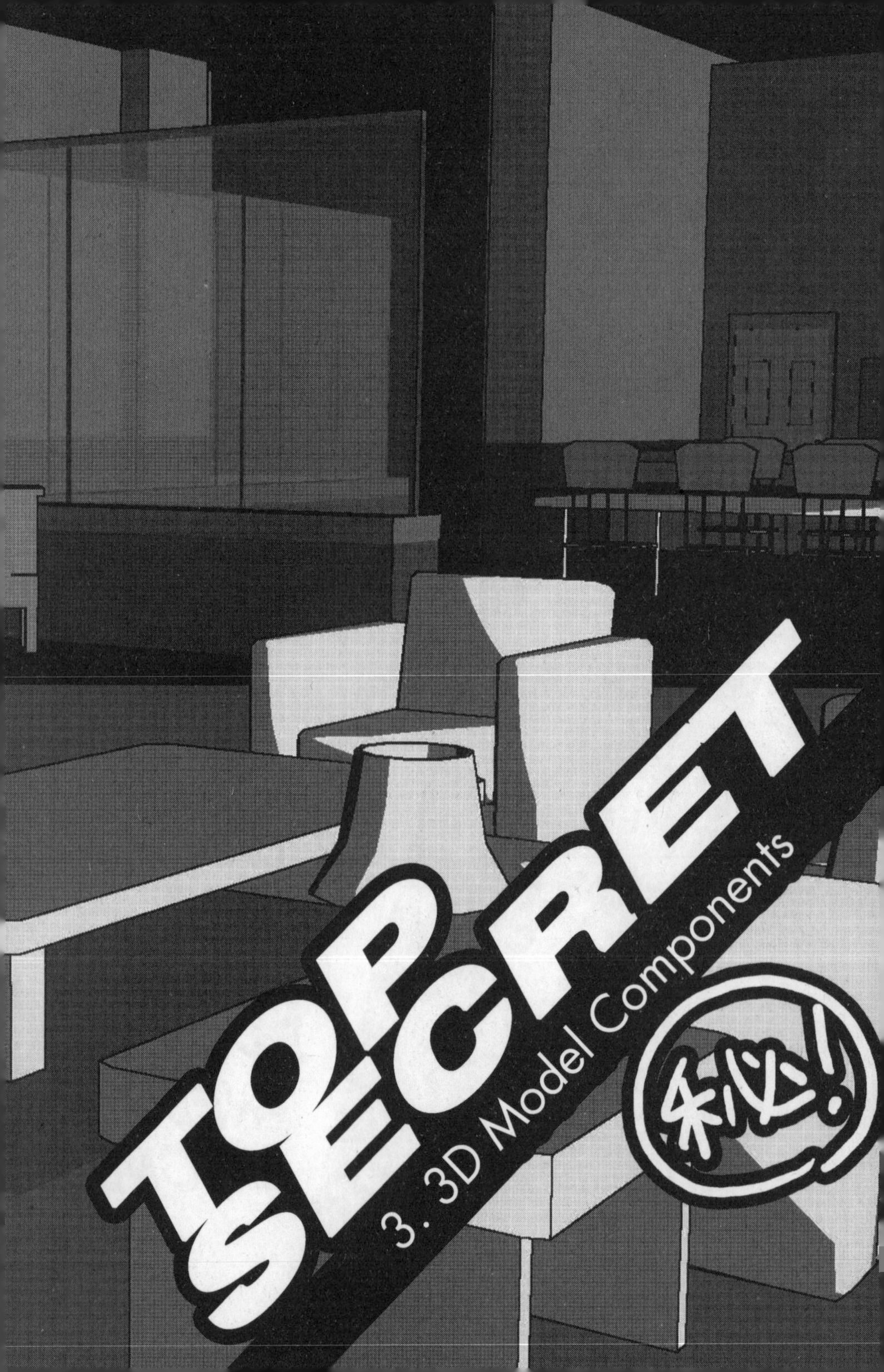
TOP SECRET
3. 3D Model Components
秘!

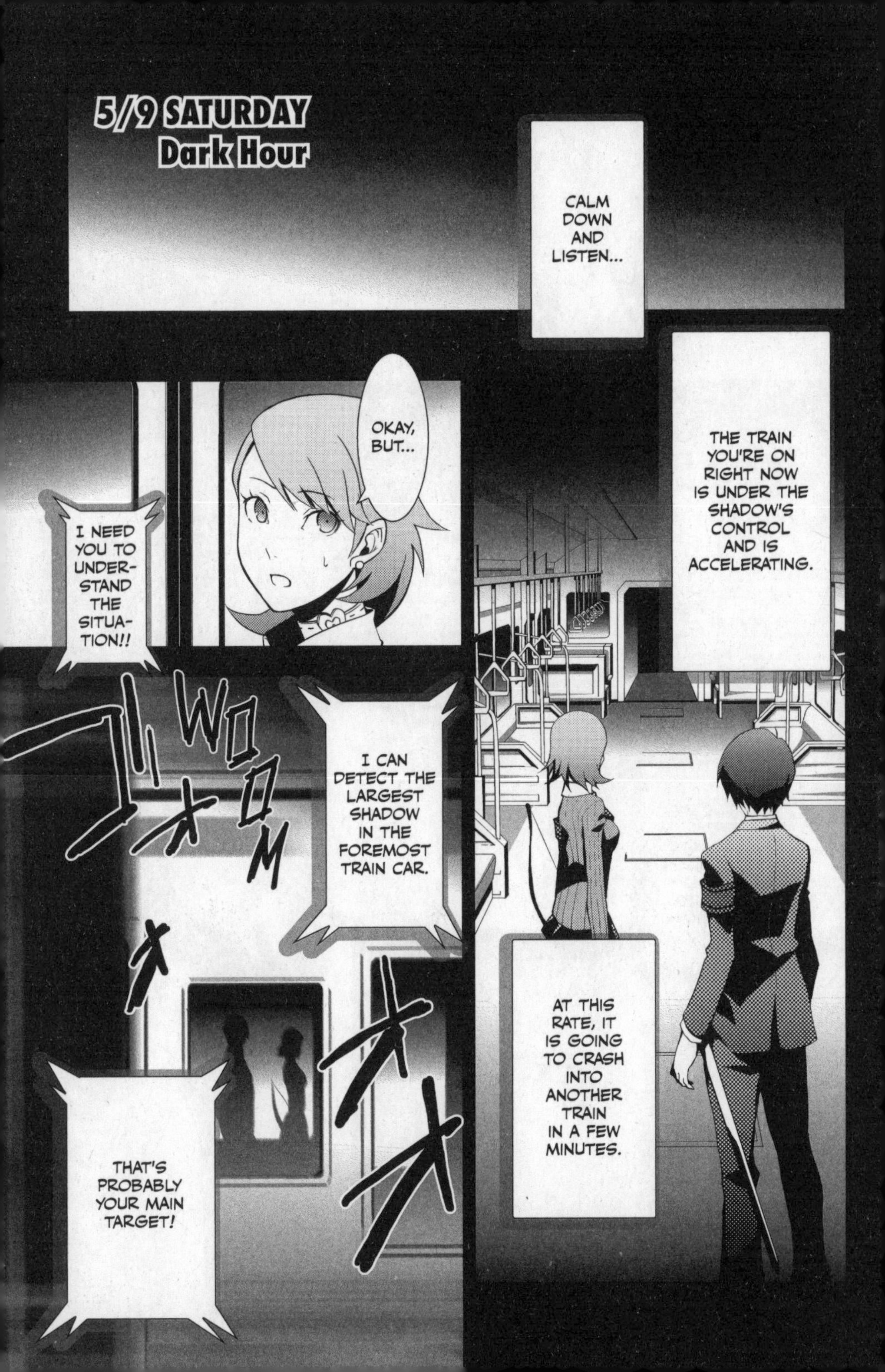
5/9 SATURDAY
Dark Hour
CALM DOWN AND LISTEN...
THE TRAIN YOU'RE ON RIGHT NOW IS UNDER THE SHADOW'S CONTROL AND IS ACCELERATING.
AT THIS RATE, IT IS GOING TO CRASH INTO ANOTHER TRAIN IN A FEW MINUTES.
OKAY, BUT...
I NEED YOU TO UNDER-STAND THE SITUA-TION!!
I CAN DETECT THE LARGEST SHADOW IN THE FOREMOST TRAIN CAR.
WOOOM
THAT'S PROBABLY YOUR MAIN TARGET!

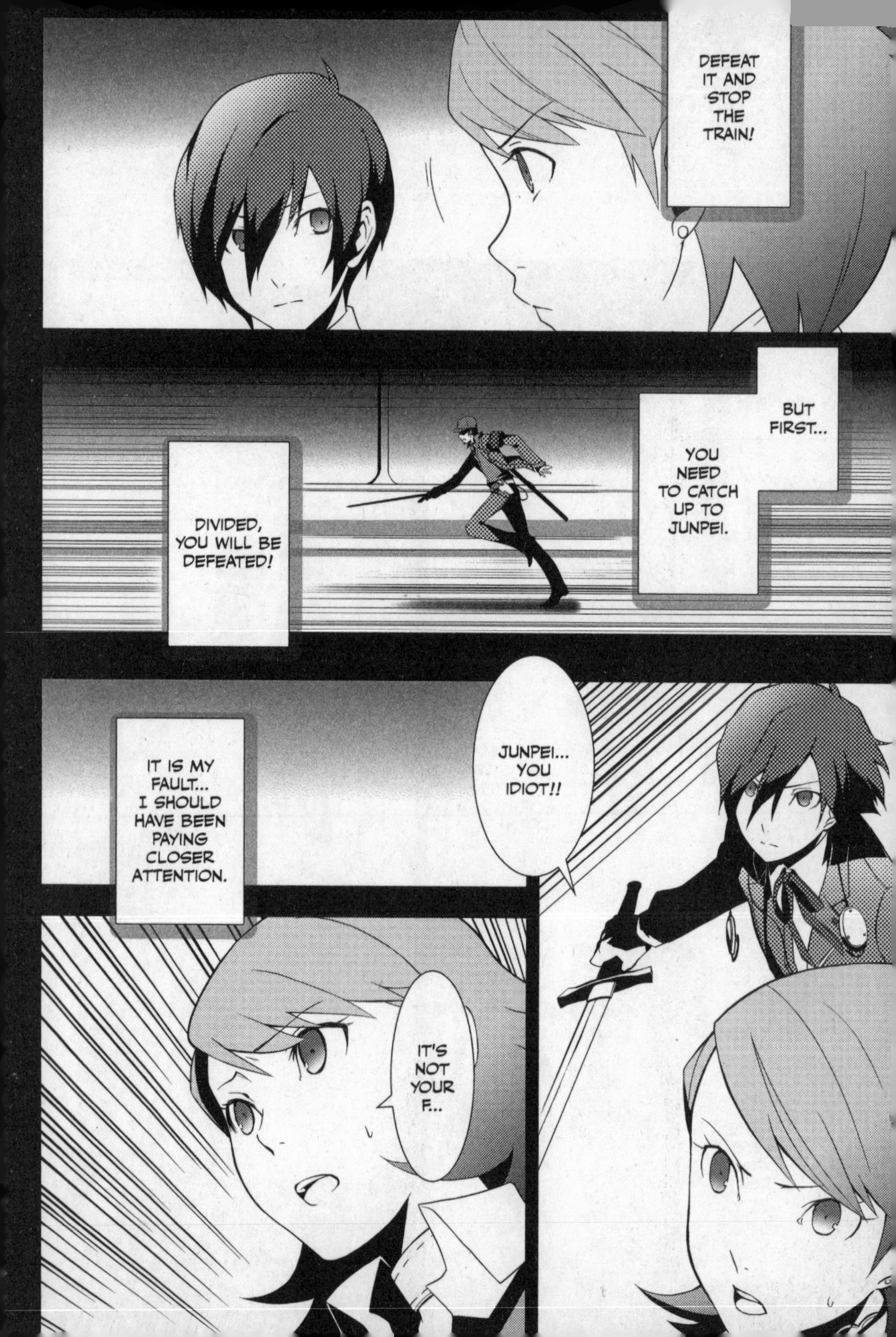
DEFEAT IT AND STOP THE TRAIN!
BUT FIRST...
YOU NEED TO CATCH UP TO JUNPEI.
DIVIDED, YOU WILL BE DEFEATED!
JUNPEI... YOU IDIOT!!
IT IS MY FAULT... I SHOULD HAVE BEEN PAYING CLOSER ATTENTION.
IT'S NOT YOUR F...

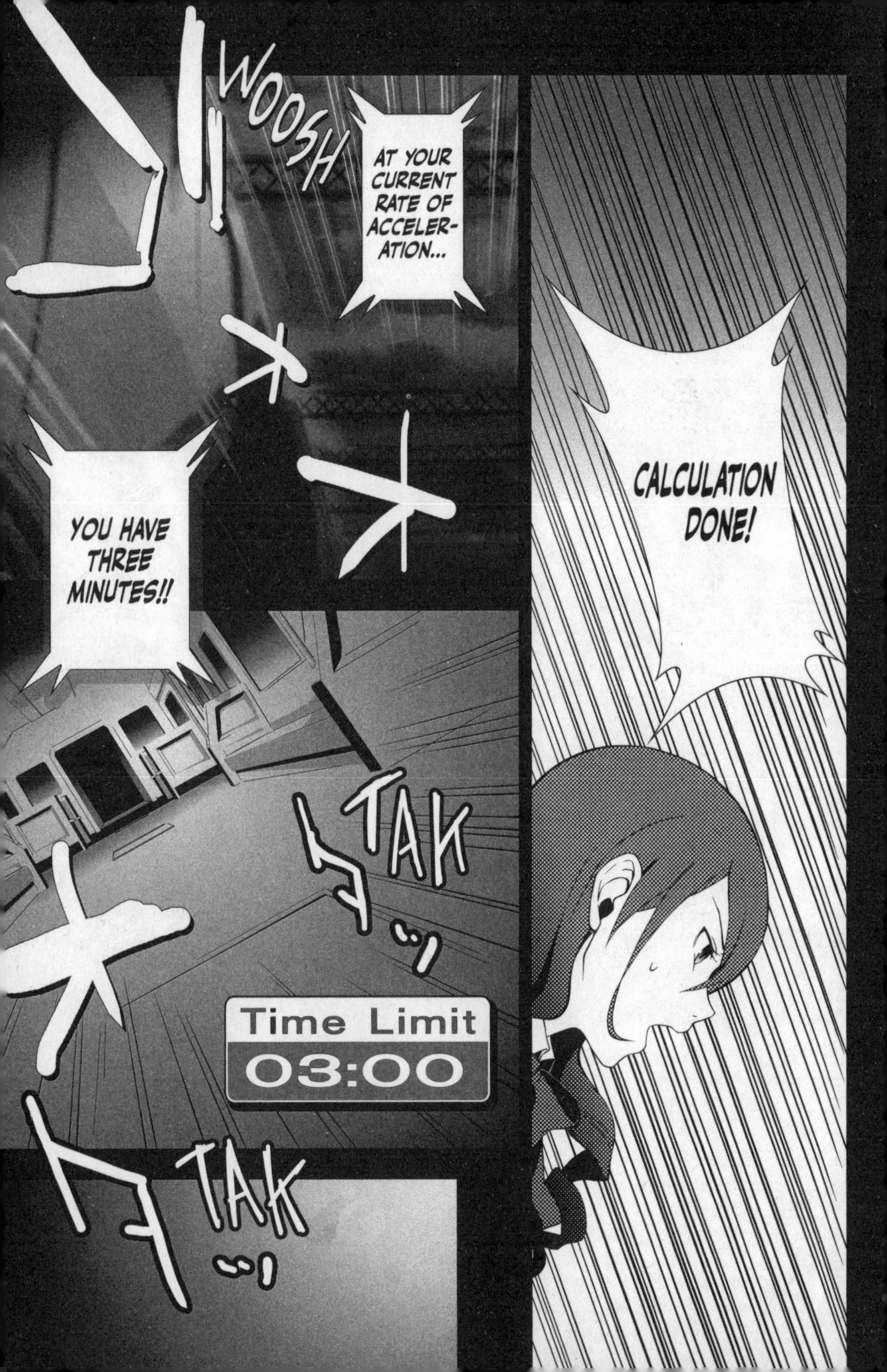
CALCULATION DONE!
WOOSH
AT YOUR CURRENT RATE OF ACCELER-ATION...
YOU HAVE THREE MINUTES!!
TAK
Time Limit
03:00
TAK

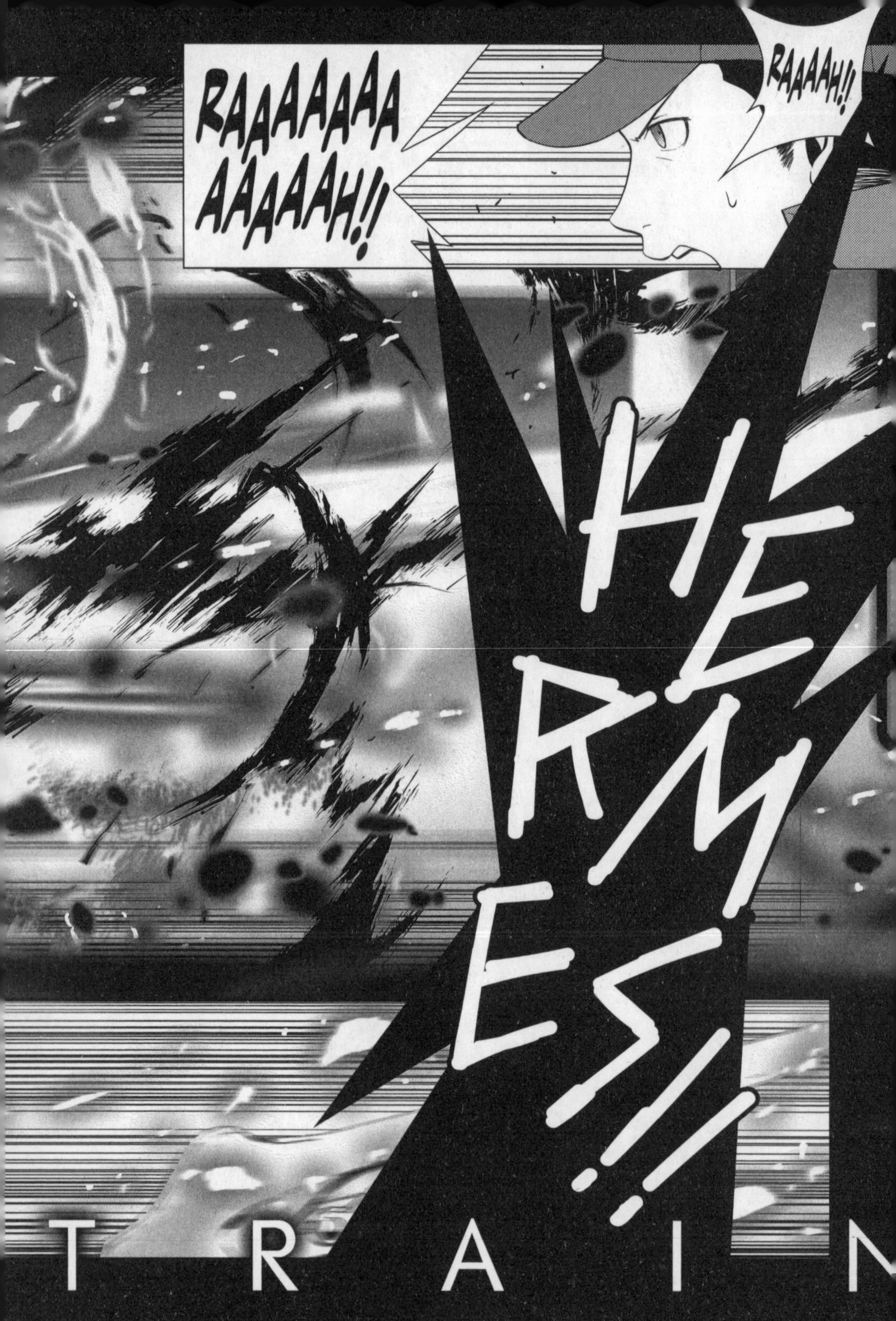

RAAAAH!!
RAAAAAAA AAAAAH!!
HERMES!!!
TRAIN

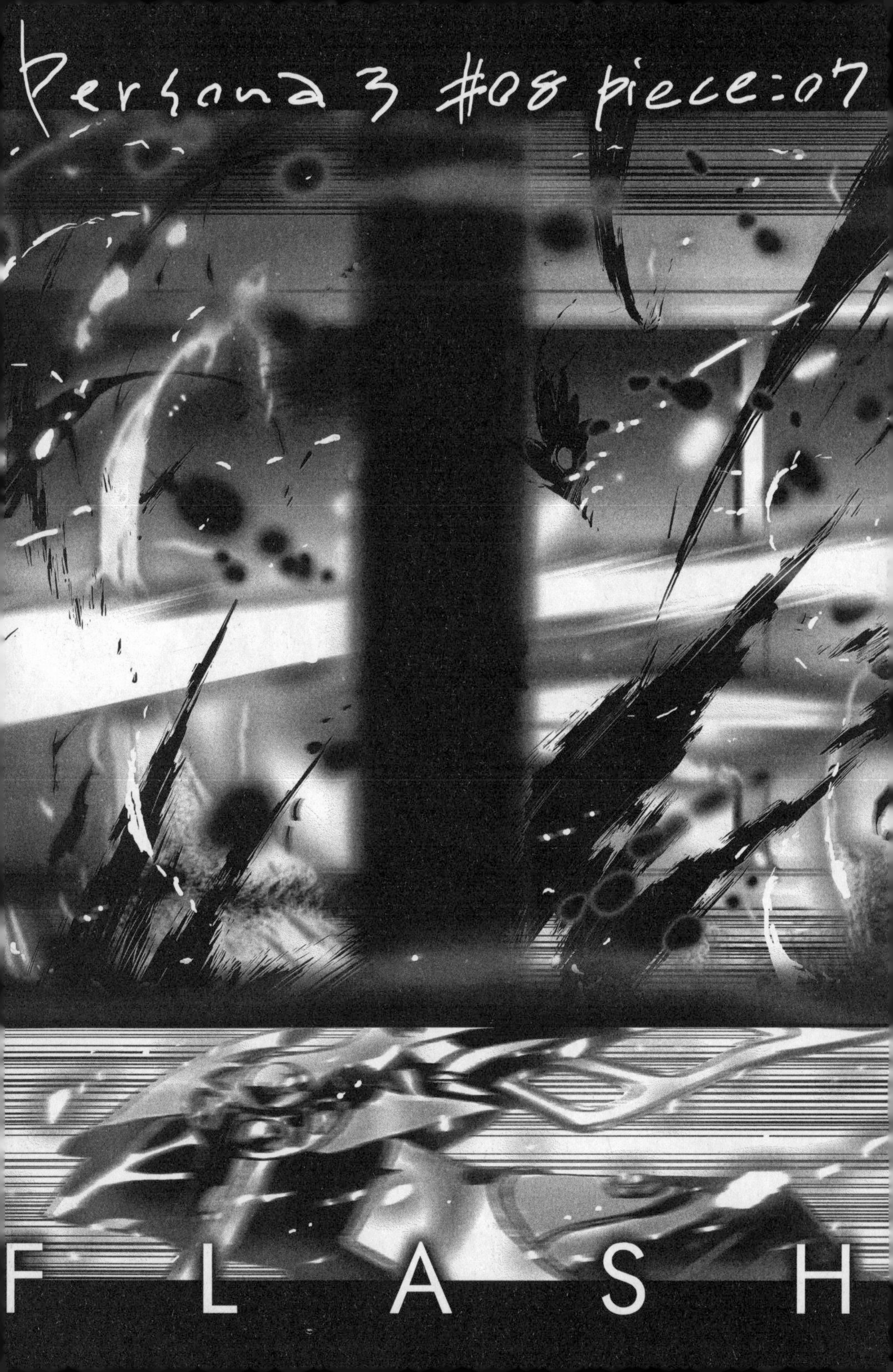
persona 3 #08 piece:07
FLASH

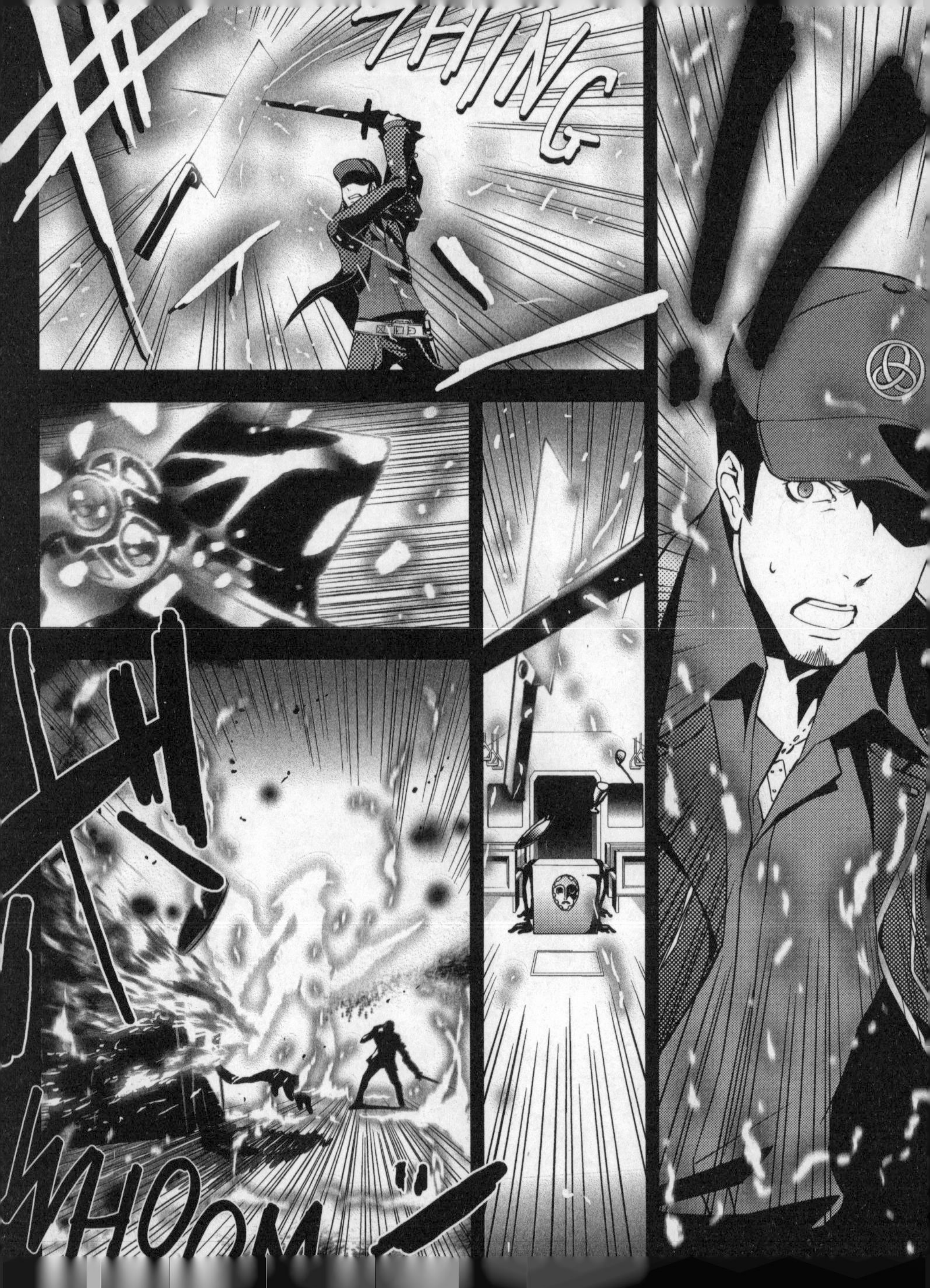
THING
WHOOM

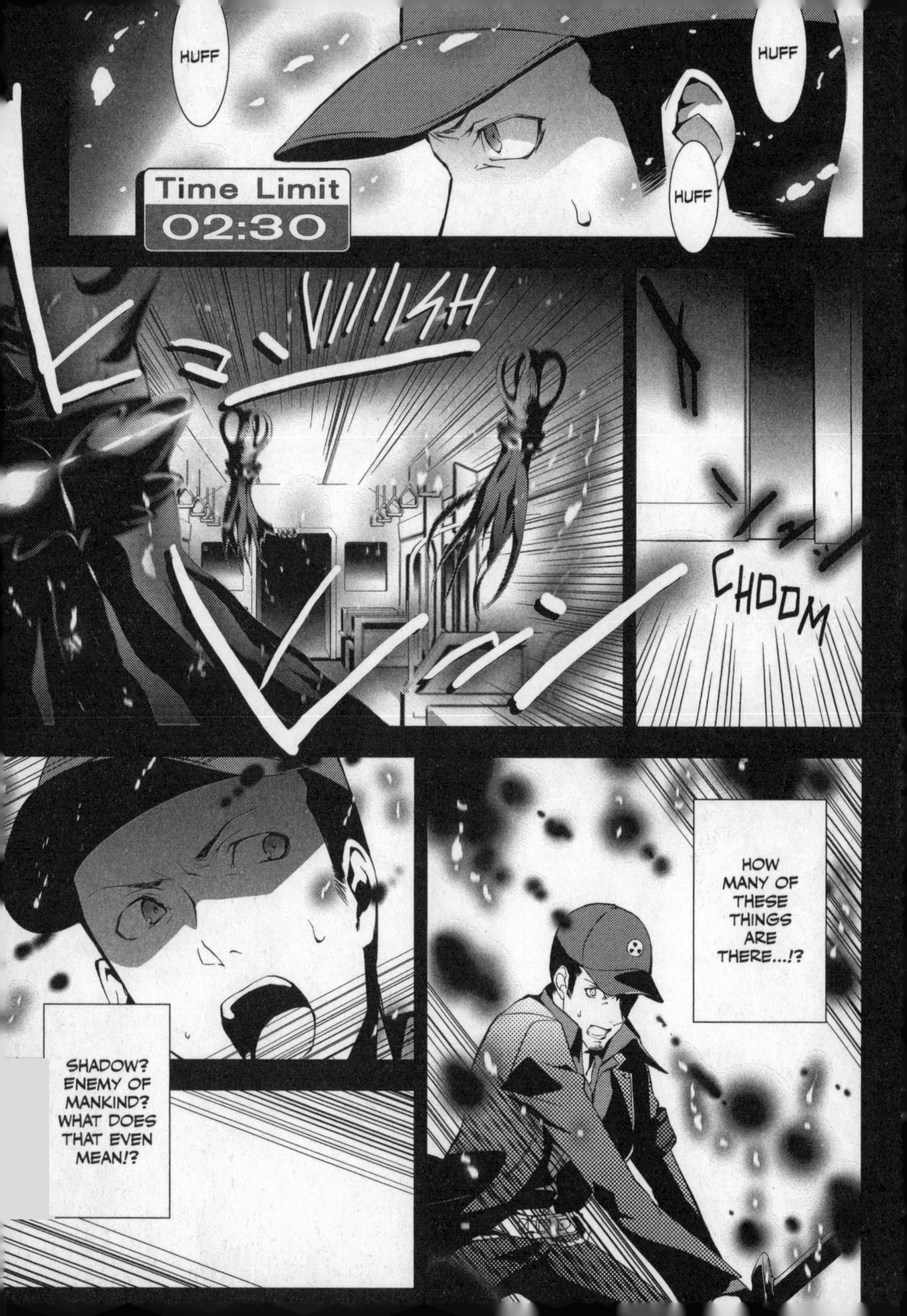
HUFF
HUFF
HUFF
Time Limit
02:30
CHOOM
VIIISH
HOW MANY OF THESE THINGS ARE THERE...!?
SHADOW? ENEMY OF MANKIND? WHAT DOES THAT EVEN MEAN!?

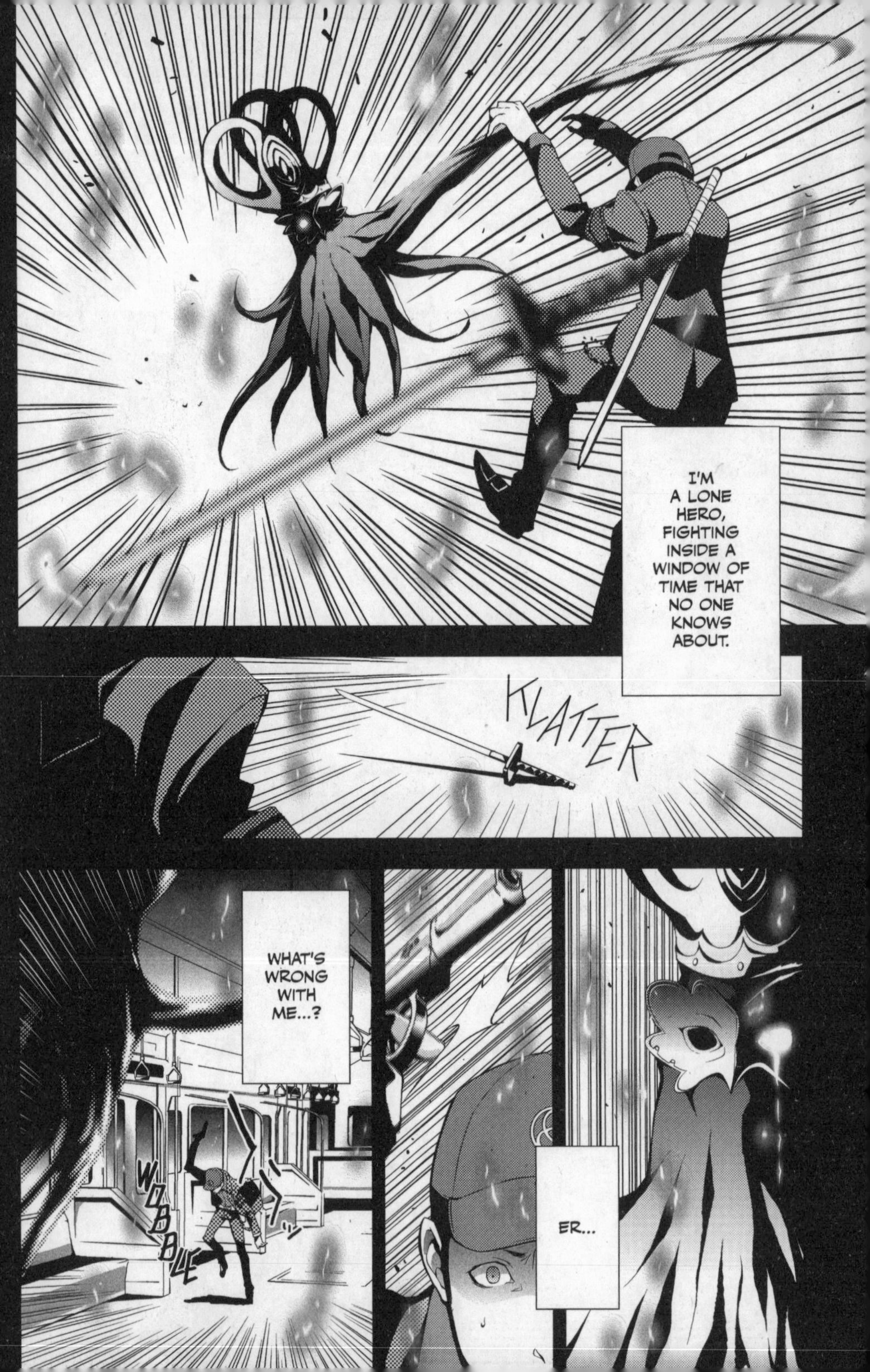
I'M A LONE HERO, FIGHTING INSIDE A WINDOW OF TIME THAT NO ONE KNOWS ABOUT.
KLATTER
ER...
WHAT'S WRONG WITH ME...?
WOBBLE

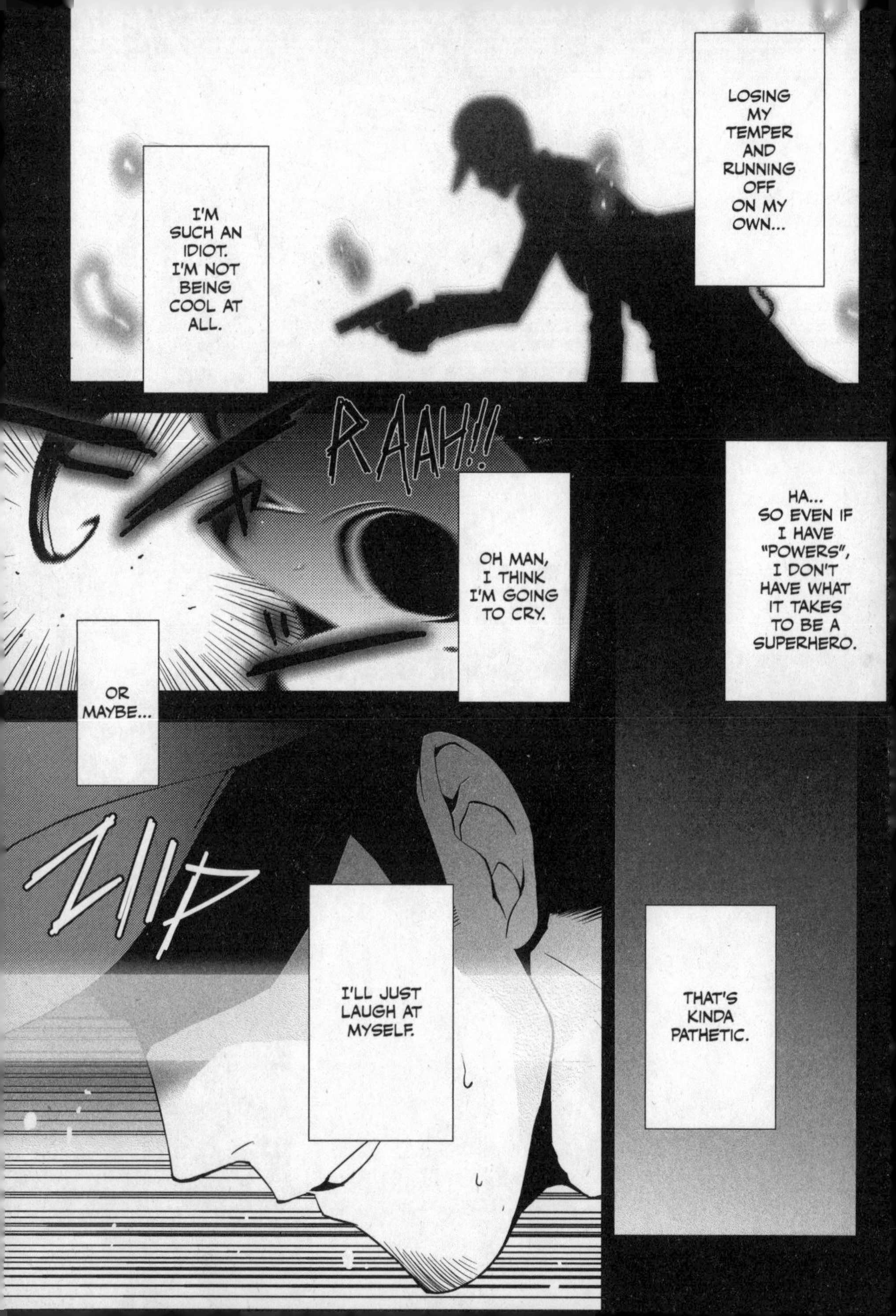

LOSING MY TEMPER AND RUNNING OFF ON MY OWN...
I'M SUCH AN IDIOT. I'M NOT BEING COOL AT ALL.
HA... SO EVEN IF I HAVE "POWERS", I DON'T HAVE WHAT IT TAKES TO BE A SUPERHERO.
THAT'S KINDA PATHETIC.
RAAH!!
OH MAN, I THINK I'M GOING TO CRY.
OR MAYBE...
ZIP
I'LL JUST LAUGH AT MYSELF.

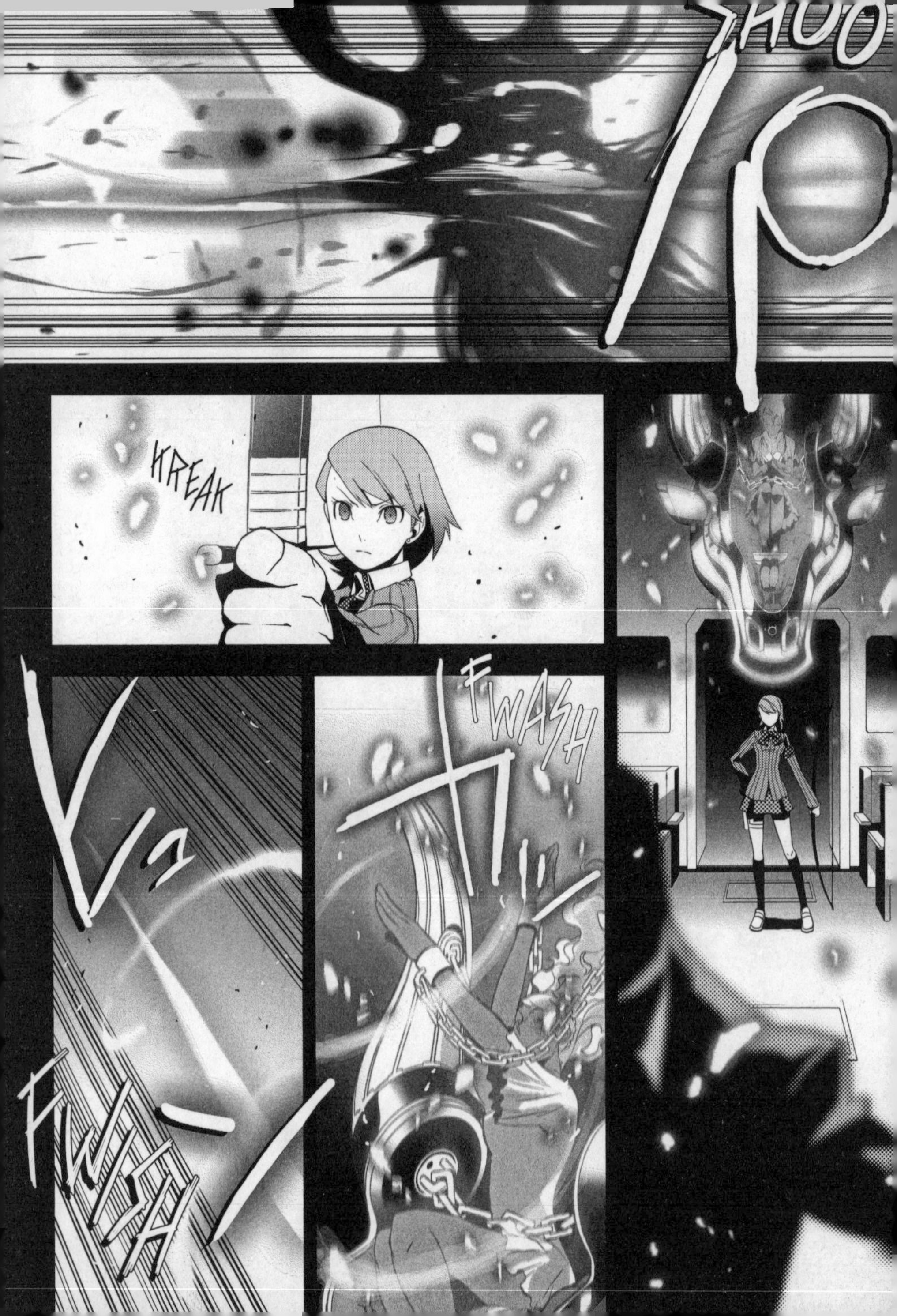
SHOOP
KREAK
FWASH
FWISH

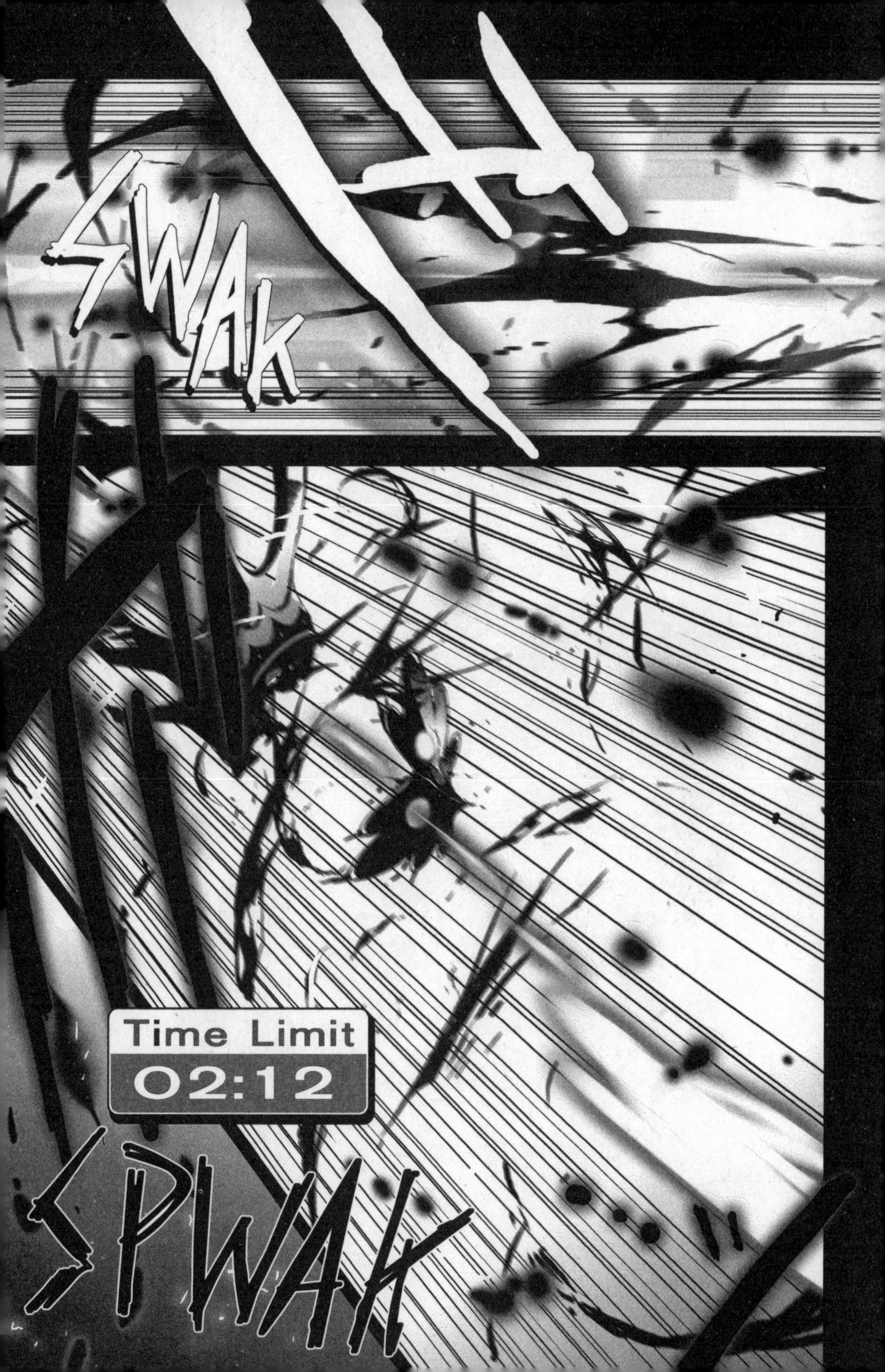
SWAK
Time Limit
02:12
SPWAK

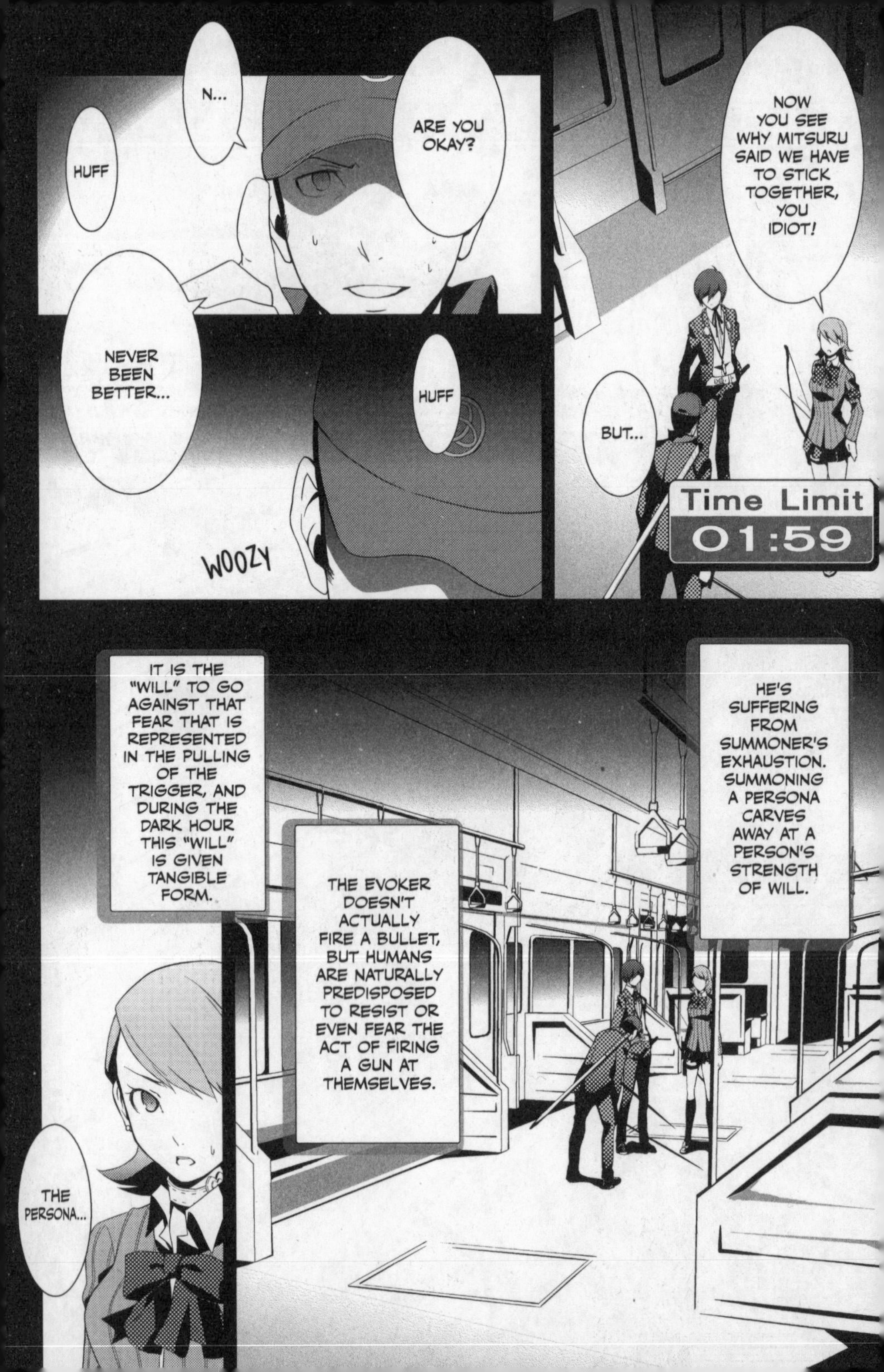
NOW YOU SEE WHY MITSURU SAID WE HAVE TO STICK TOGETHER, YOU IDIOT!
BUT...
Time Limit
01:59
ARE YOU OKAY?
N...
HUFF
NEVER BEEN BETTER...
HUFF
WOOZY
HE'S SUFFERING FROM SUMMONER'S EXHAUSTION. SUMMONING A PERSONA CARVES AWAY AT A PERSON'S STRENGTH OF WILL.
THE EVOKER DOESN'T ACTUALLY FIRE A BULLET, BUT HUMANS ARE NATURALLY PREDISPOSED TO RESIST OR EVEN FEAR THE ACT OF FIRING A GUN AT THEMSELVES.
IT IS THE "WILL" TO GO AGAINST THAT FEAR THAT IS REPRESENTED IN THE PULLING OF THE TRIGGER, AND DURING THE DARK HOUR THIS "WILL" IS GIVEN TANGIBLE FORM.
THE PERSONA...

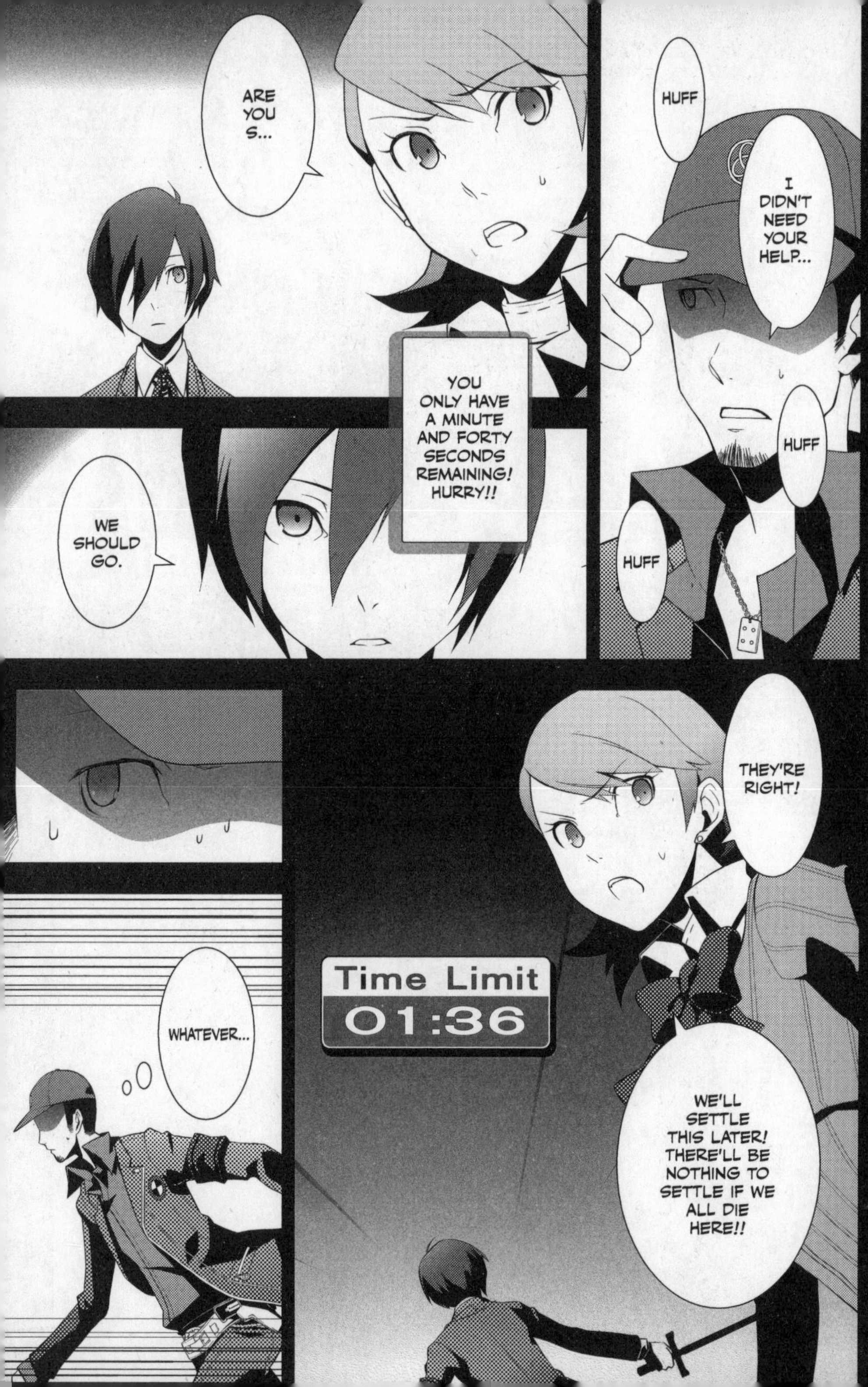
HUFF
I DIDN'T NEED YOUR HELP...
HUFF
HUFF
ARE YOU S...
YOU ONLY HAVE A MINUTE AND FORTY SECONDS REMAINING! HURRY!!
WE SHOULD GO.
THEY'RE RIGHT!
Time Limit
01:36
WE'LL SETTLE THIS LATER! THERE'LL BE NOTHING TO SETTLE IF WE ALL DIE HERE!!
WHATEVER...

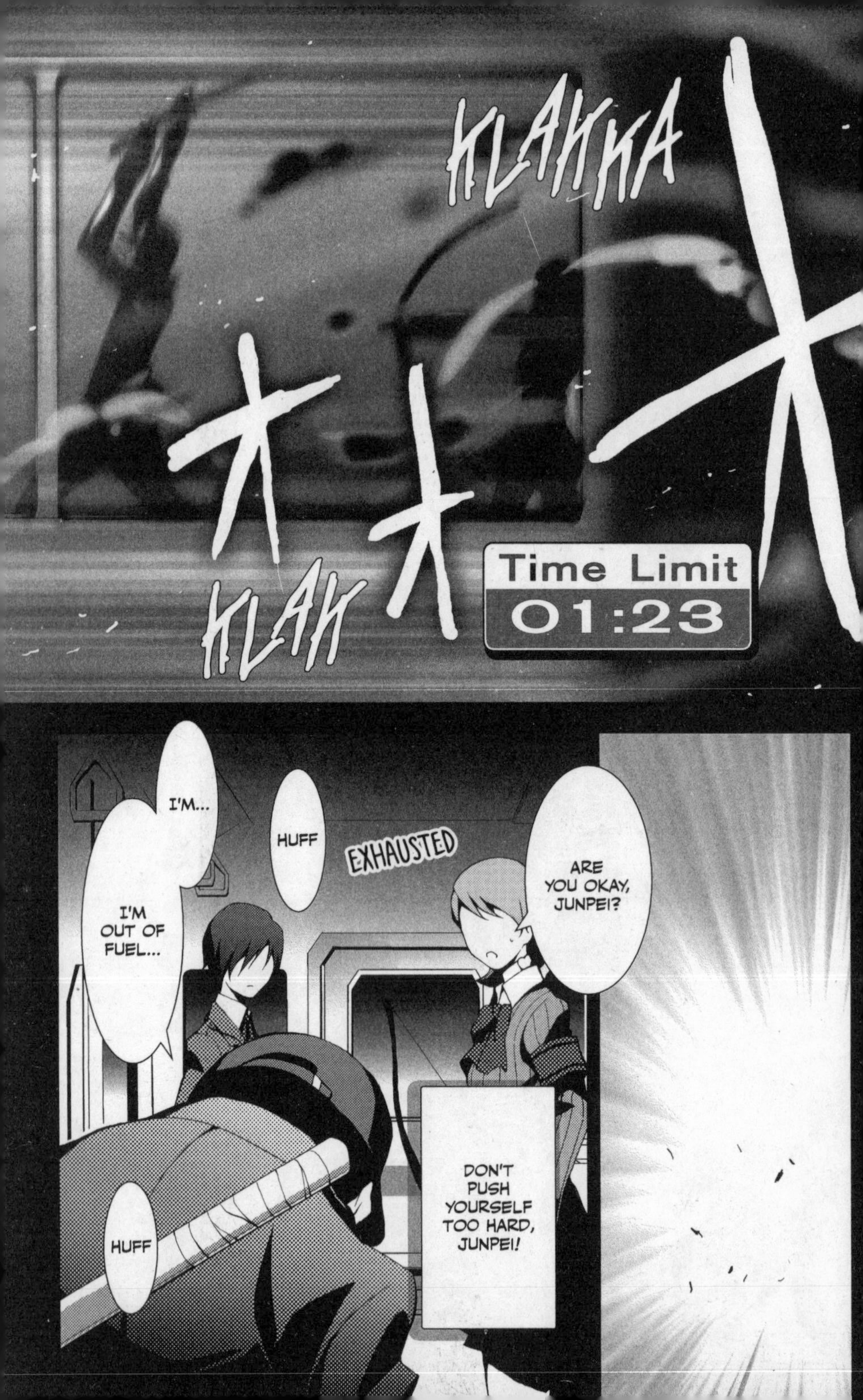
KLAKKA
KLAK
Time Limit
01:23
ARE YOU OKAY, JUNPEI?
DON'T PUSH YOURSELF TOO HARD, JUNPEI!
EXHAUSTED
HUFF
I'M...
I'M OUT OF FUEL...
HUFF

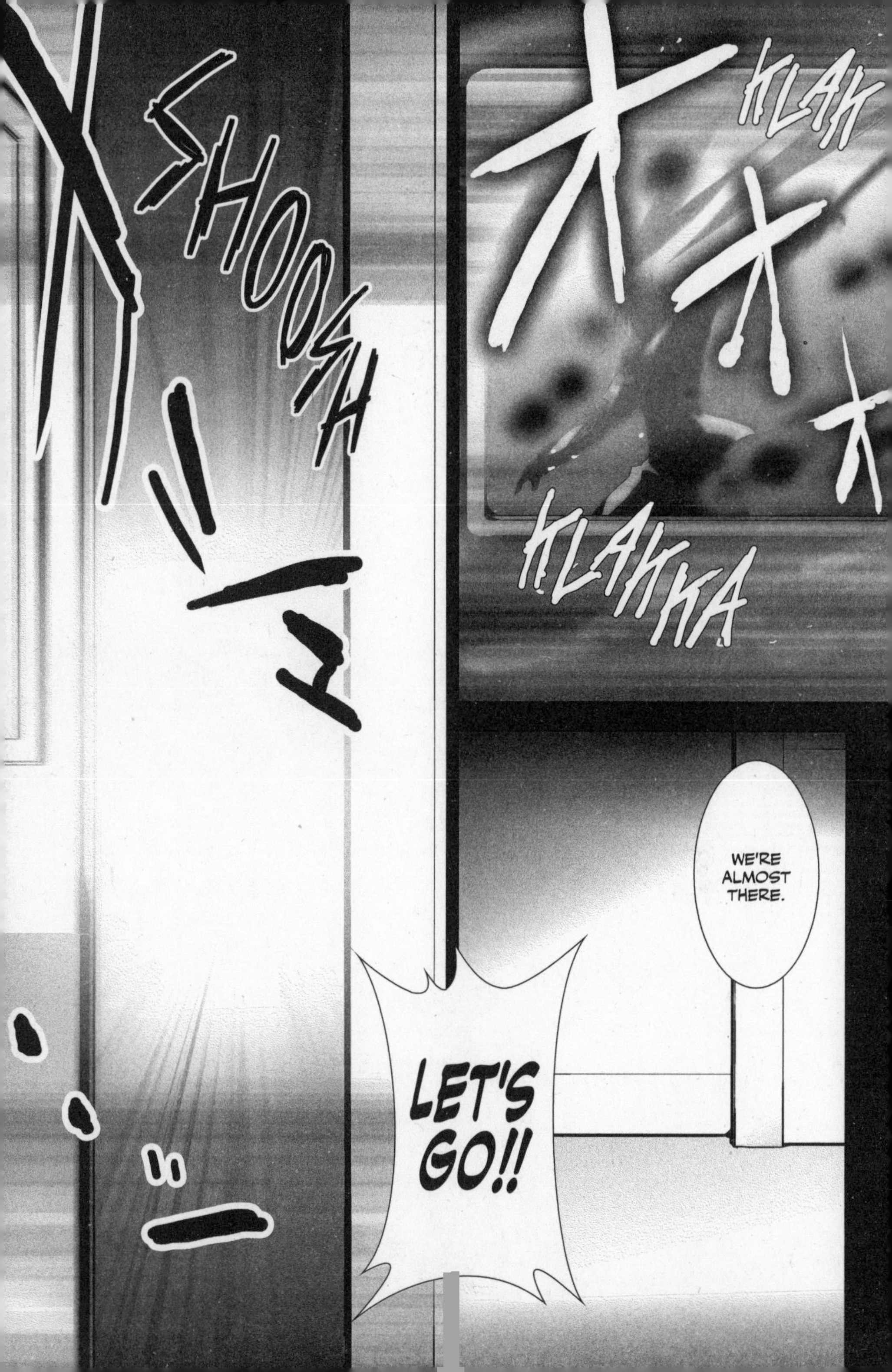
KLAK
KLAKKA
WE'RE ALMOST THERE.
LET'S GO!!
SHOOSH

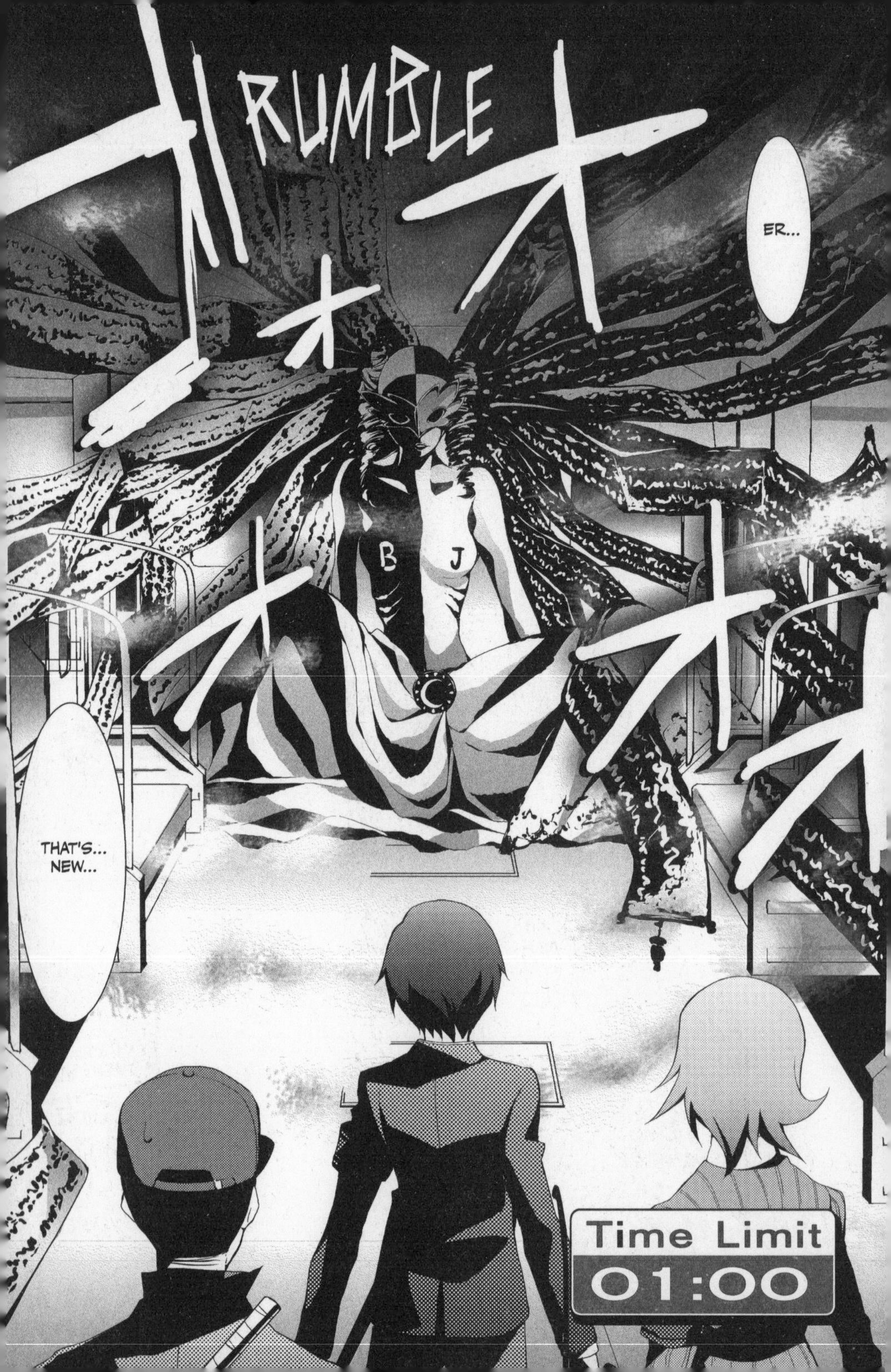
RUMBLE
ER...
THAT'S... NEW...
Time Limit
01:00

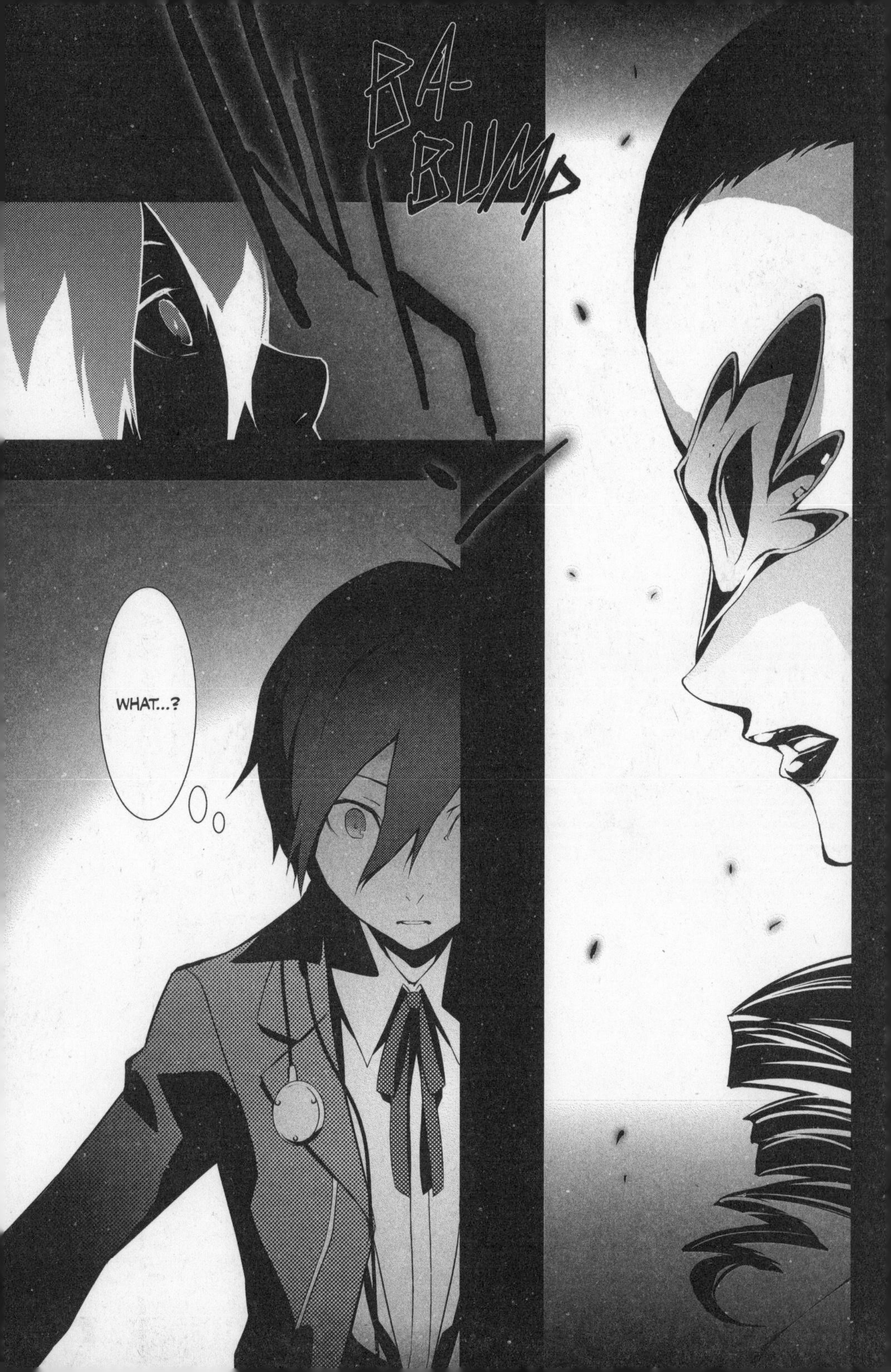
BA-BUMP
WHAT...?

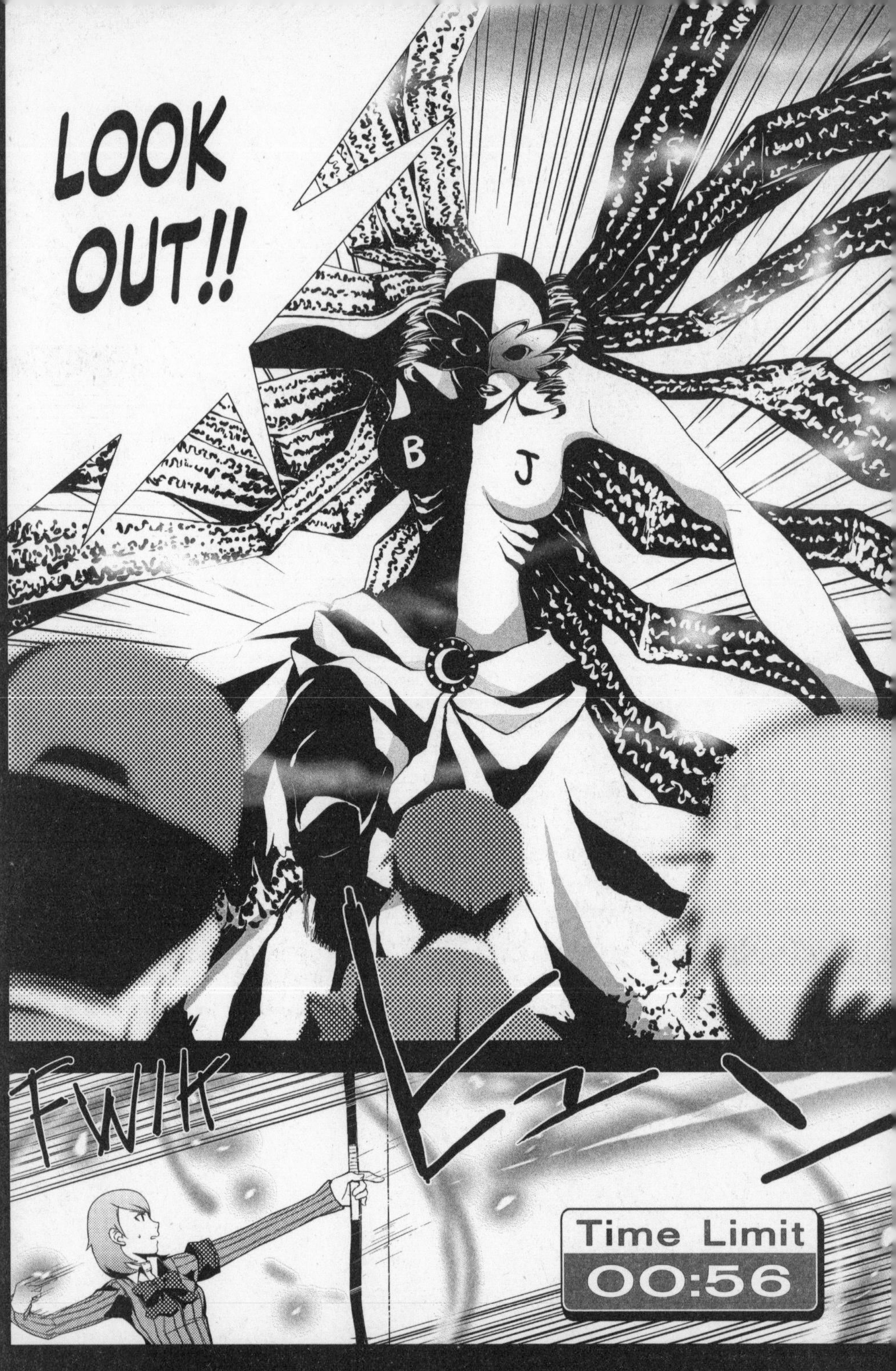
LOOK OUT!!
B
J
FWIK
Time Limit
00:56

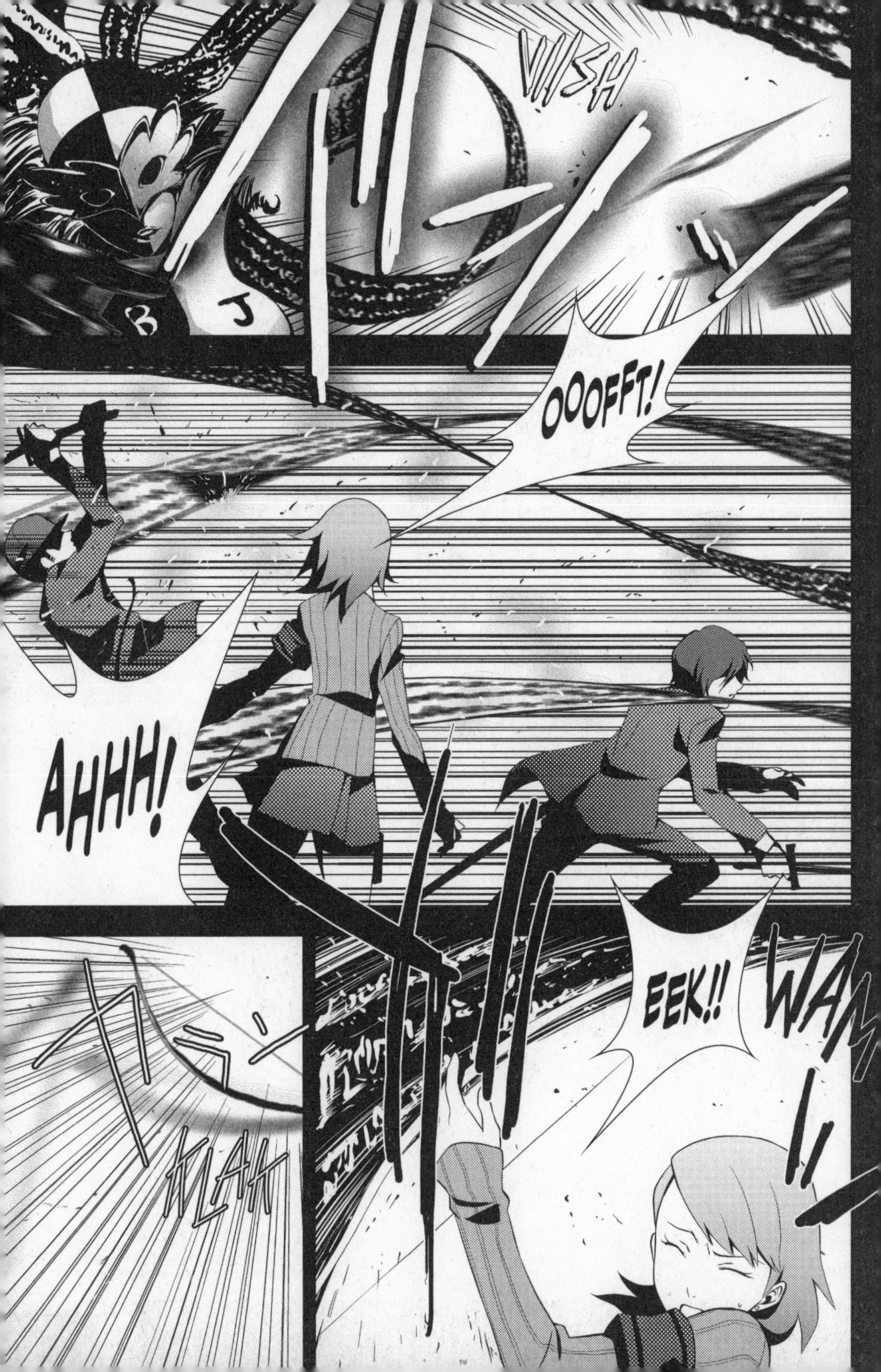
VIISH
B J
OOOFFT!
AHHH!
WAM
EEK!!
KLAK

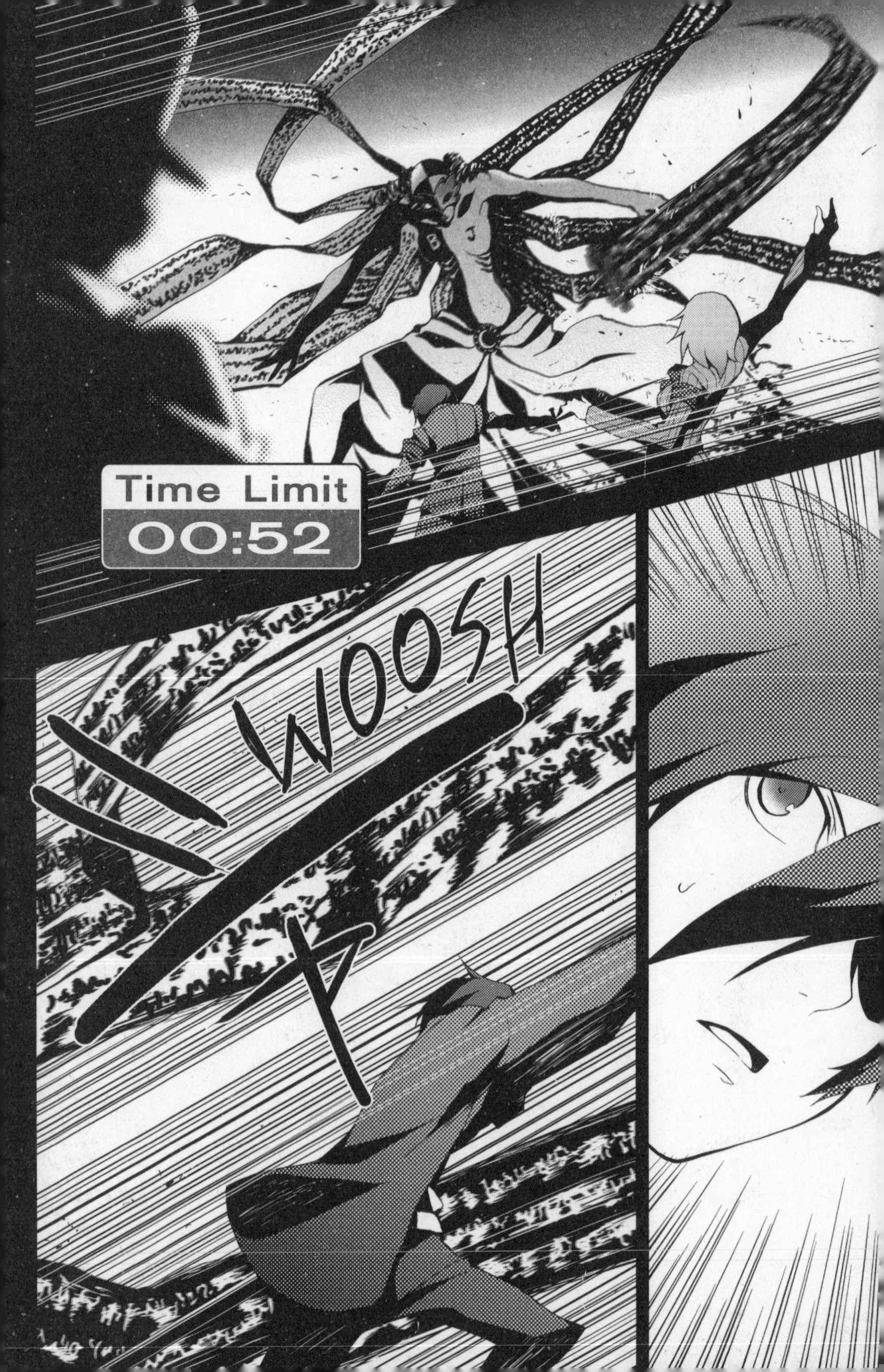
Time Limit
00:52
WOOSH

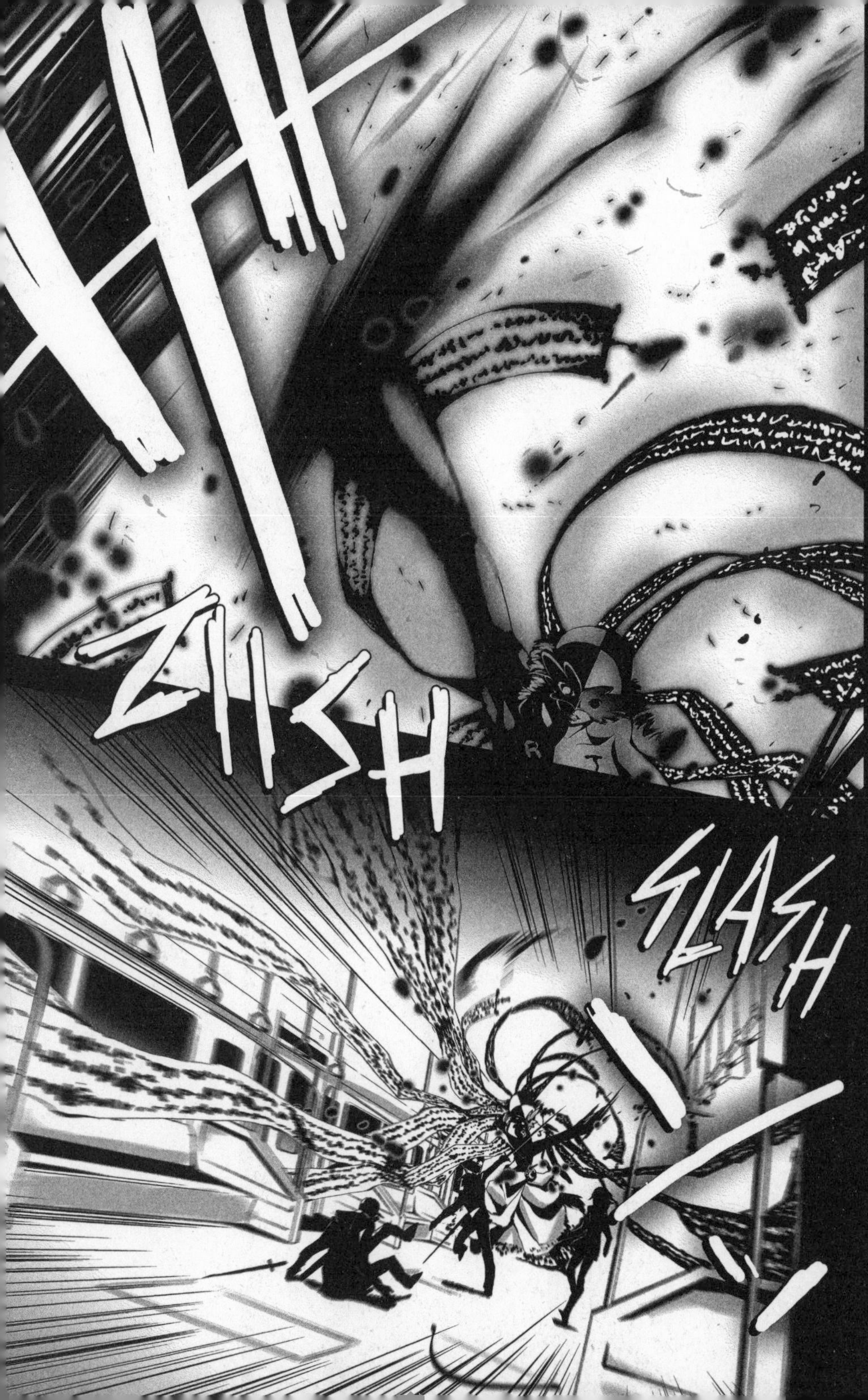
ZIISH
SLASH

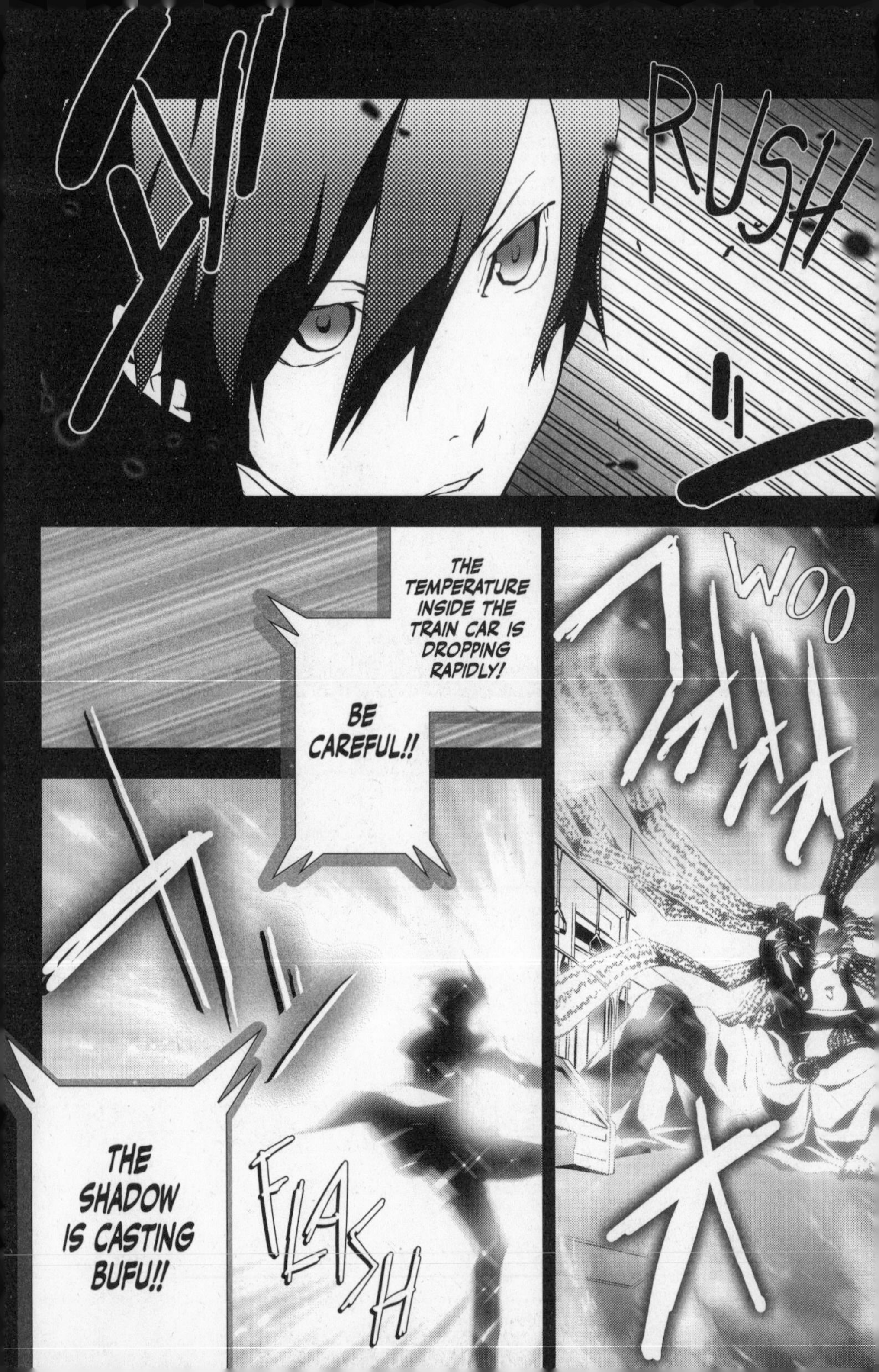
RUSH
WOO
THE TEMPERATURE INSIDE THE TRAIN CAR IS DROPPING RAPIDLY!
BE CAREFUL!!
THE SHADOW IS CASTING BUFU!!
FLASH

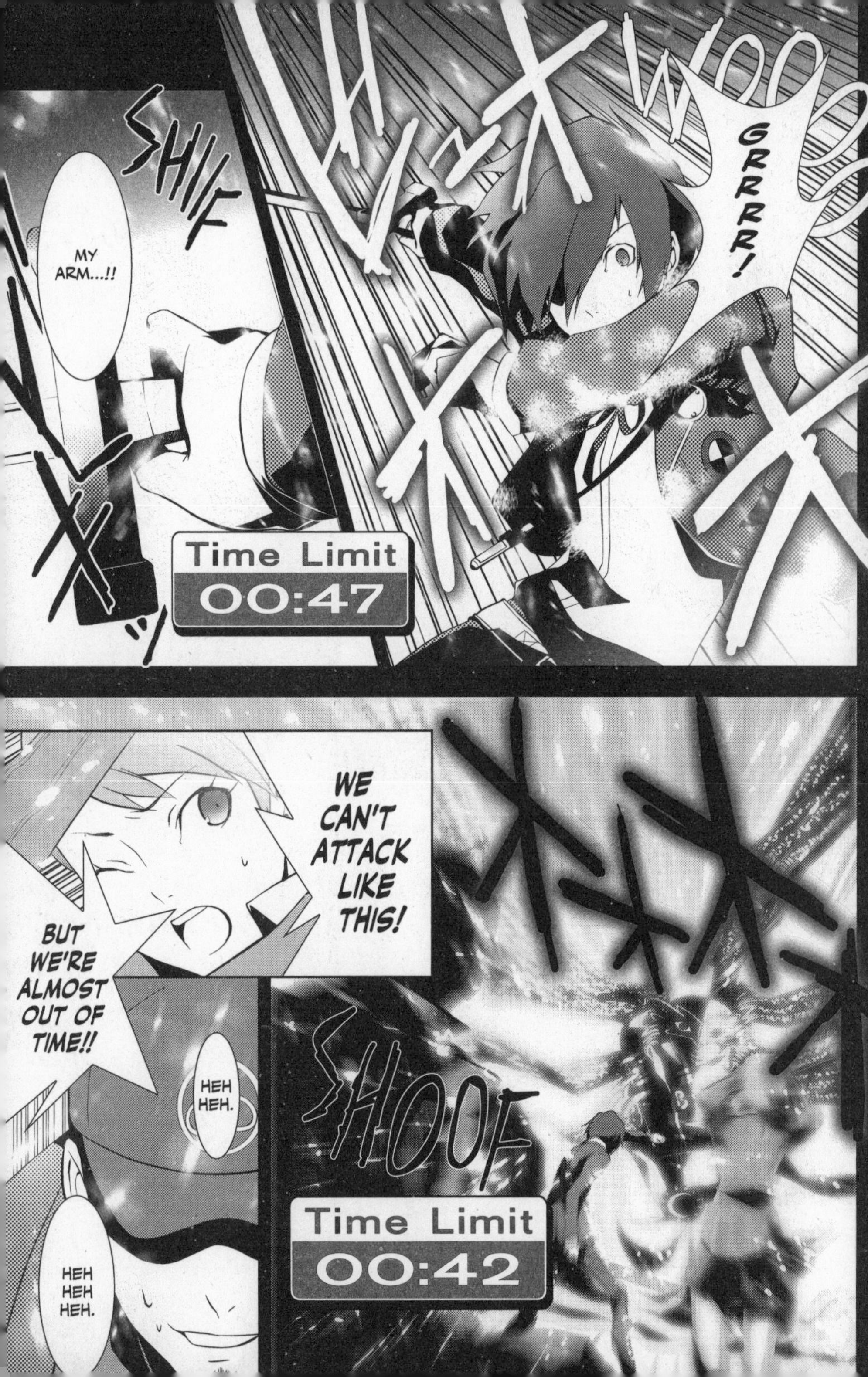
GRRRR!
SHIF
MY ARM...!!
Time Limit
00:47
SHOOF
Time Limit
00:42
WE CAN'T ATTACK LIKE THIS!
BUT WE'RE ALMOST OUT OF TIME!!
HEH HEH.
HEH HEH HEH.

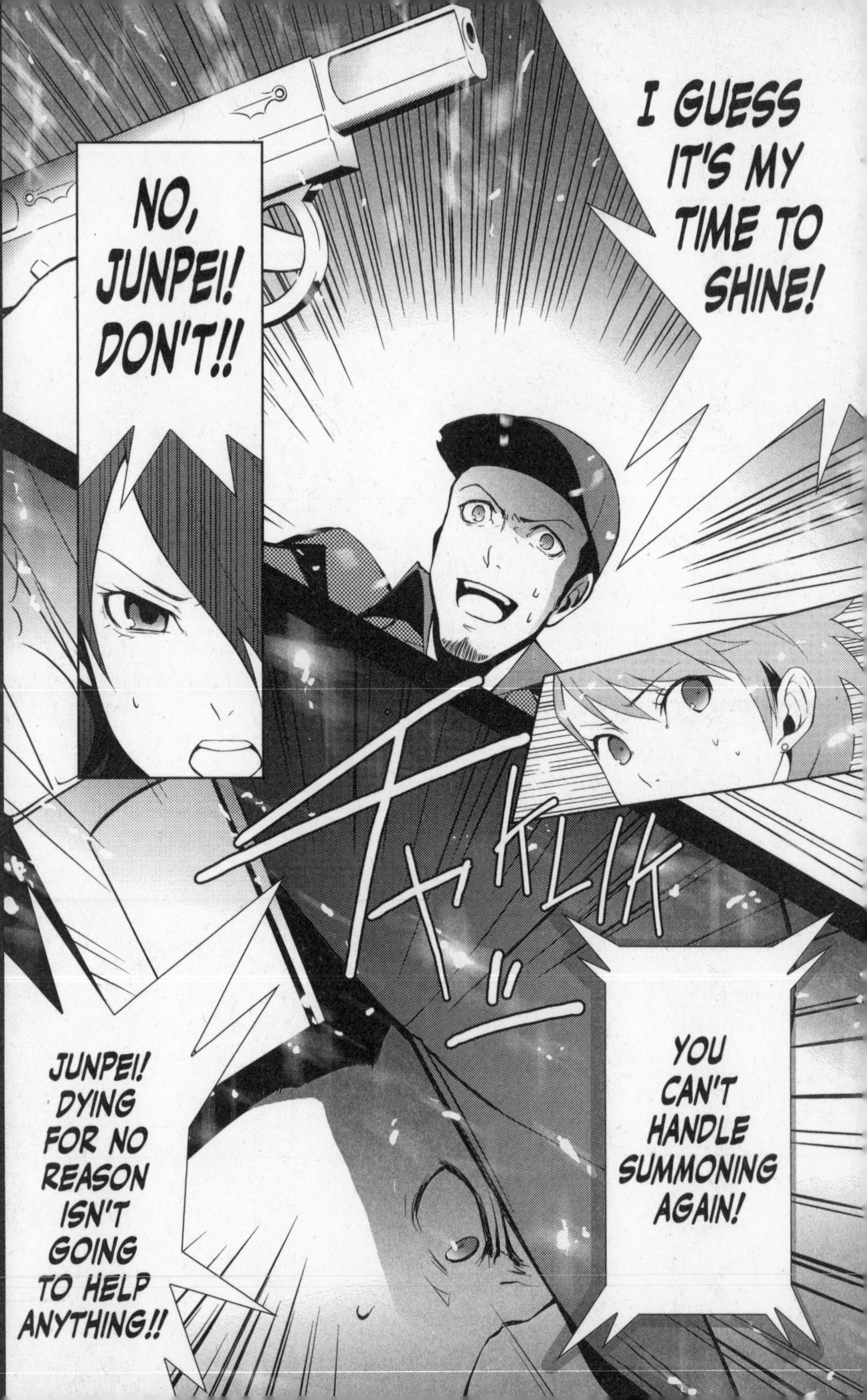
I GUESS IT'S MY TIME TO SHINE!
NO, JUNPEI! DON'T!!
KLIK
YOU CAN'T HANDLE SUMMONING AGAIN!
JUNPEI! DYING FOR NO REASON ISN'T GOING TO HELP ANYTHING!!

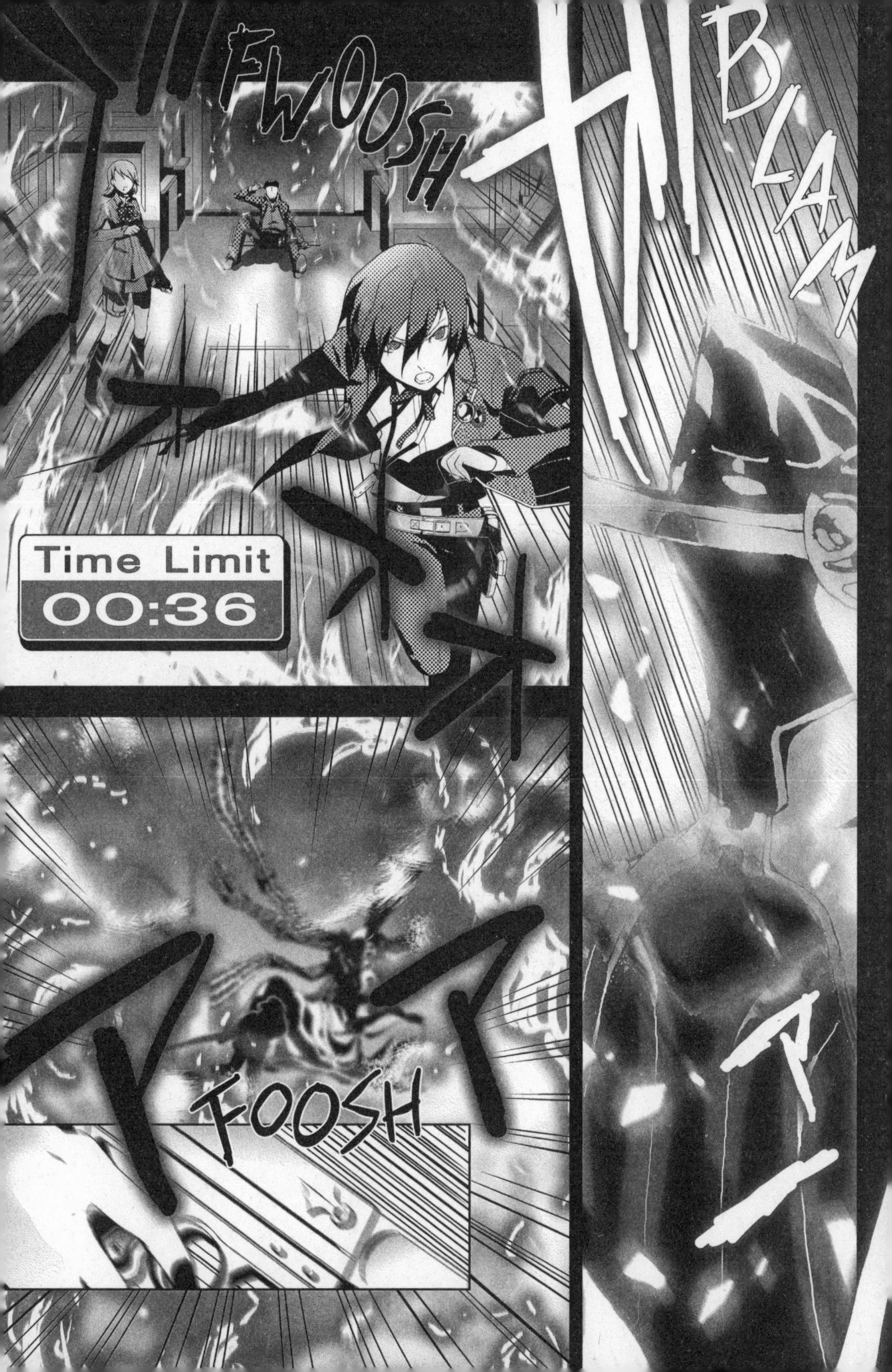
BLAM
FWOOSH
Time Limit
00:36
FOOSH

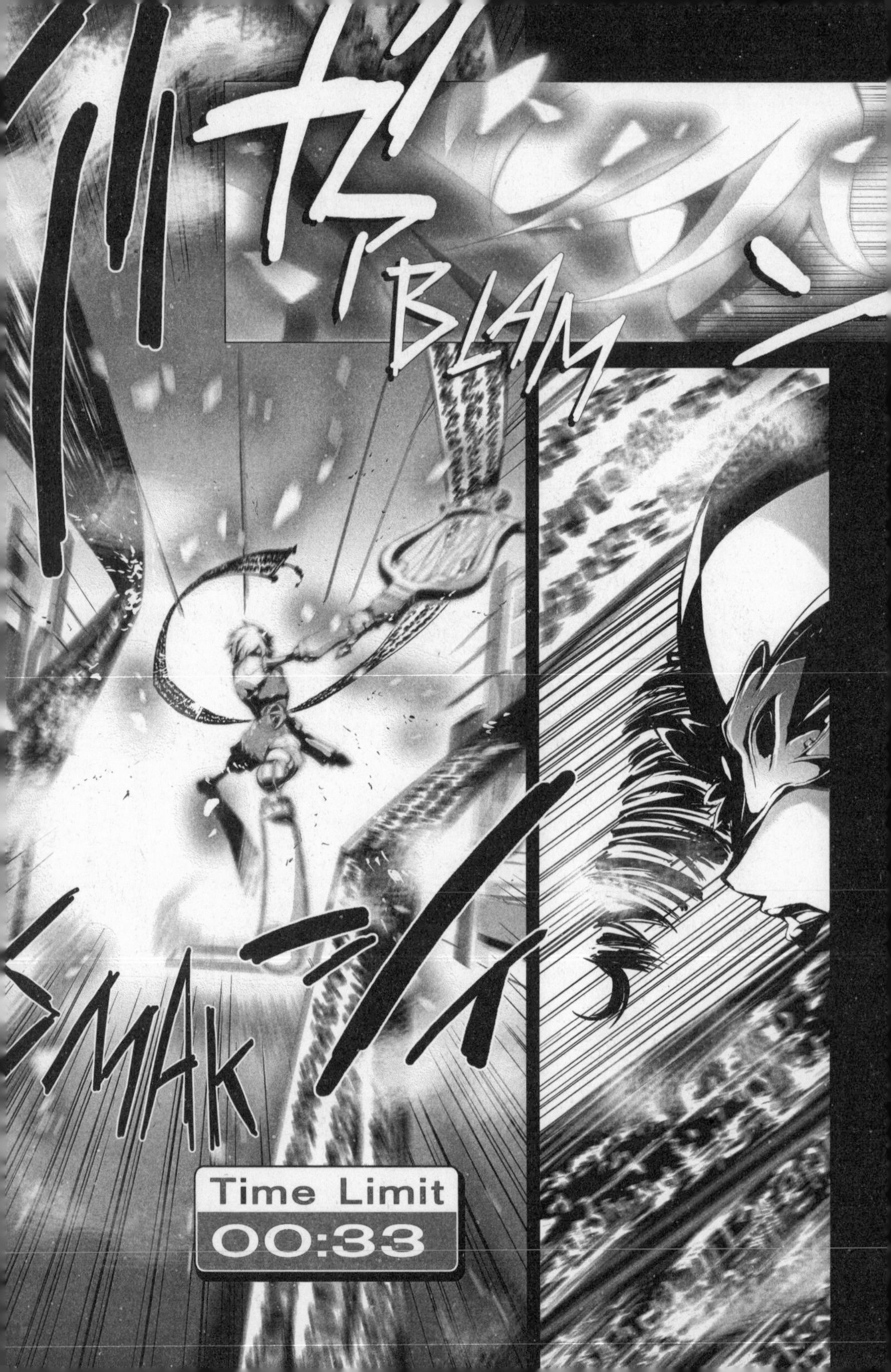
BLAM
SMAK
Time Limit
00:33

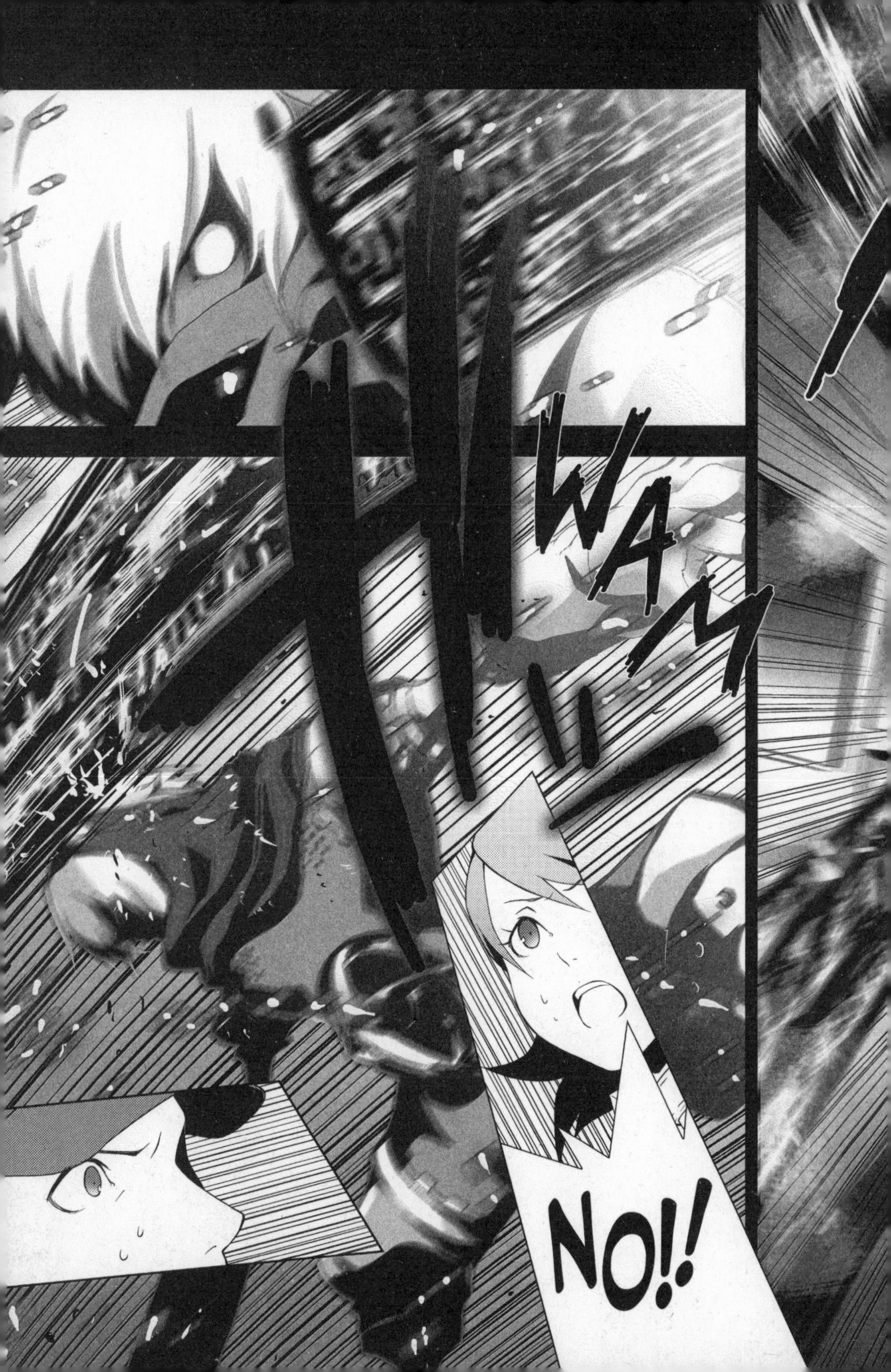
WAM
NO!!

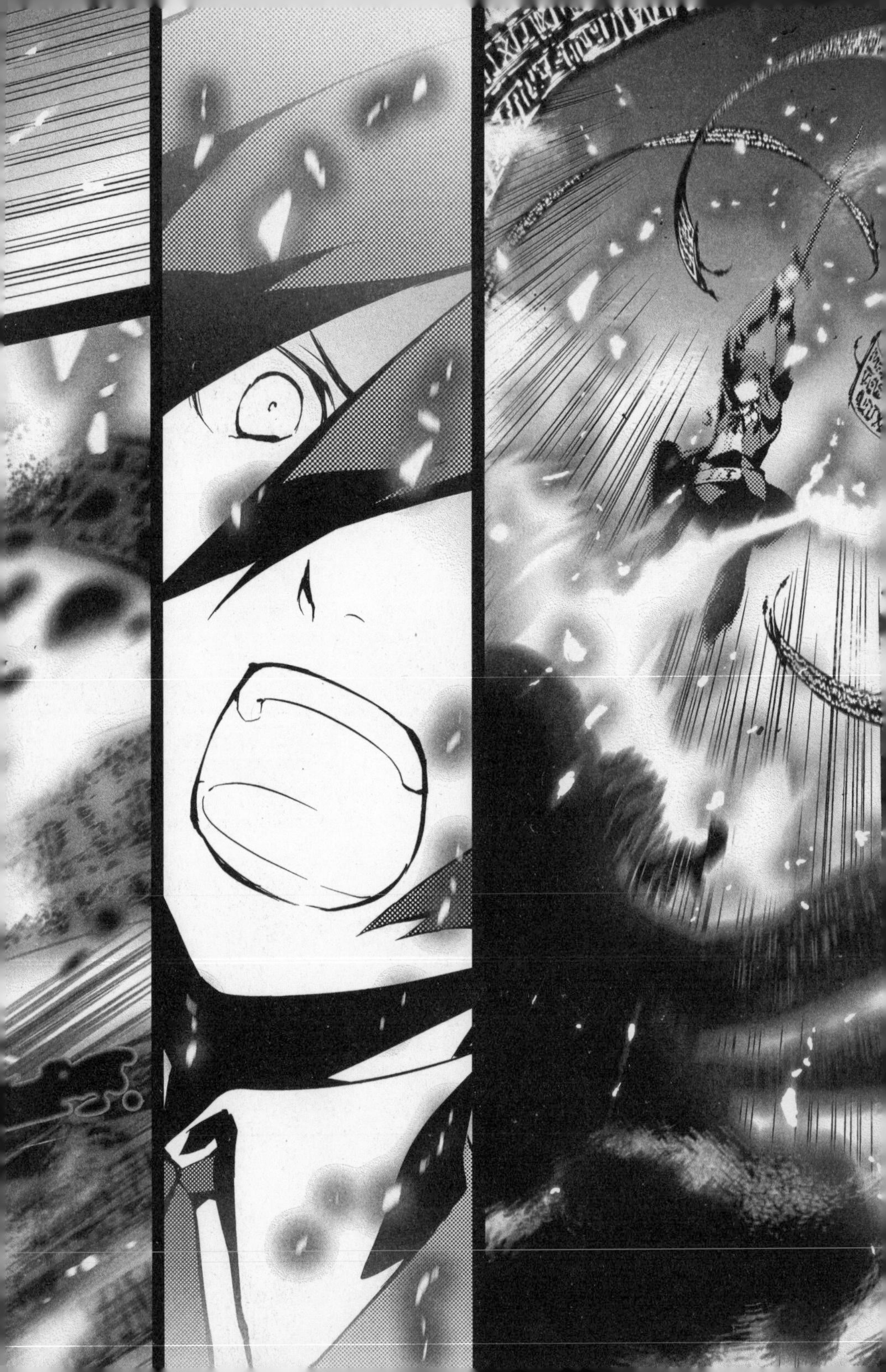

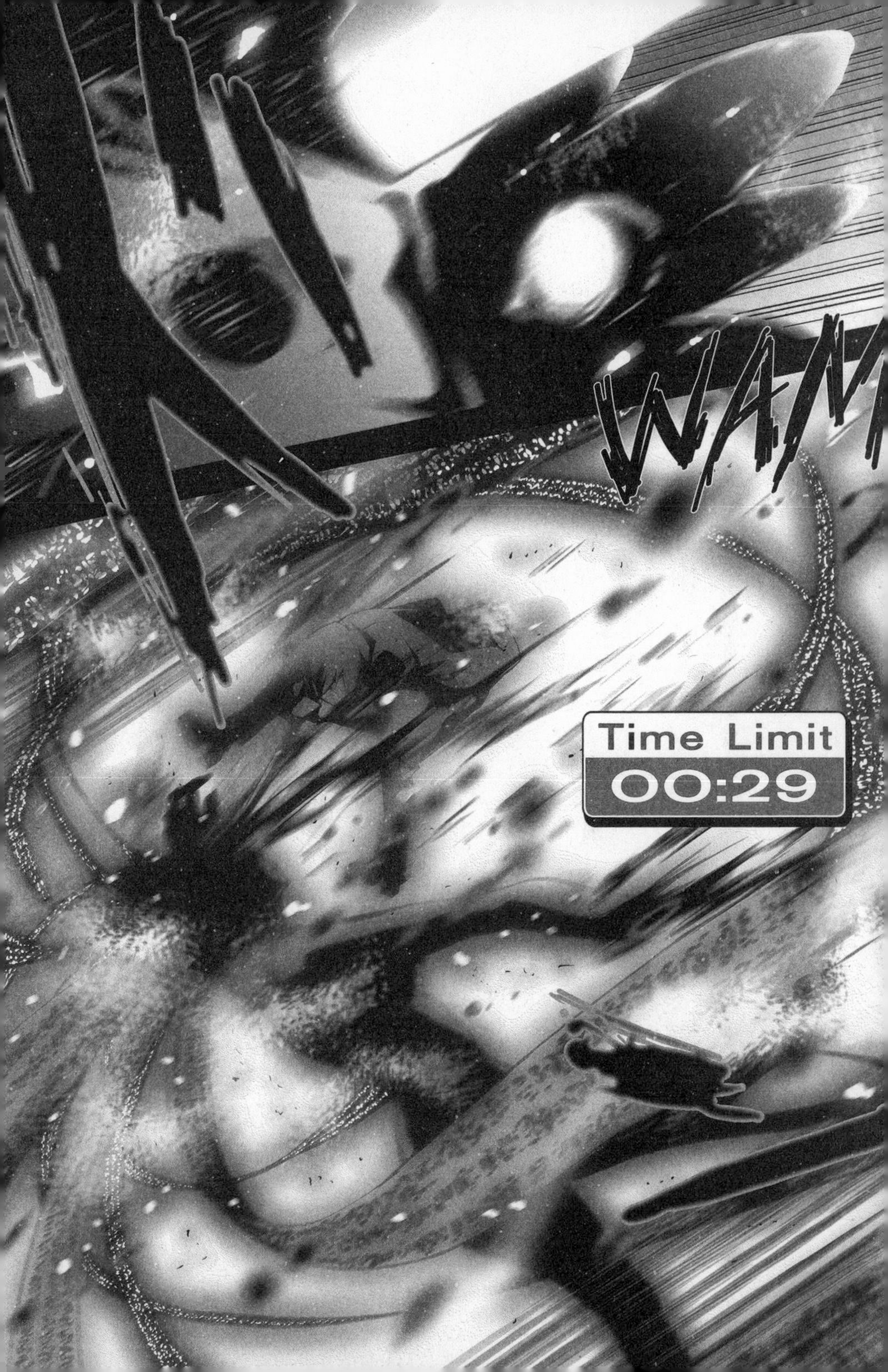
WAM
Time Limit
00:29

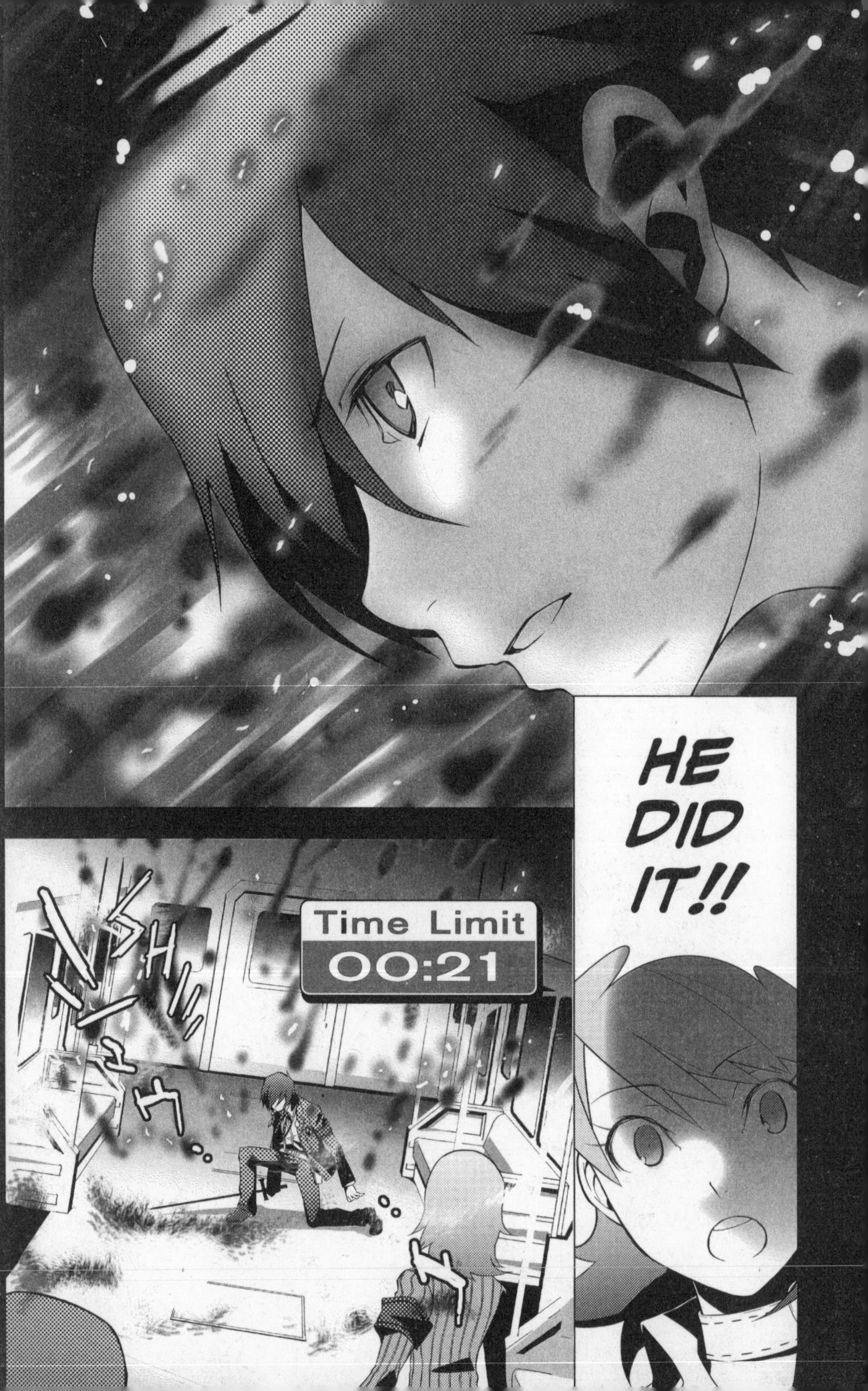
HE DID IT!!
Time Limit
00:21

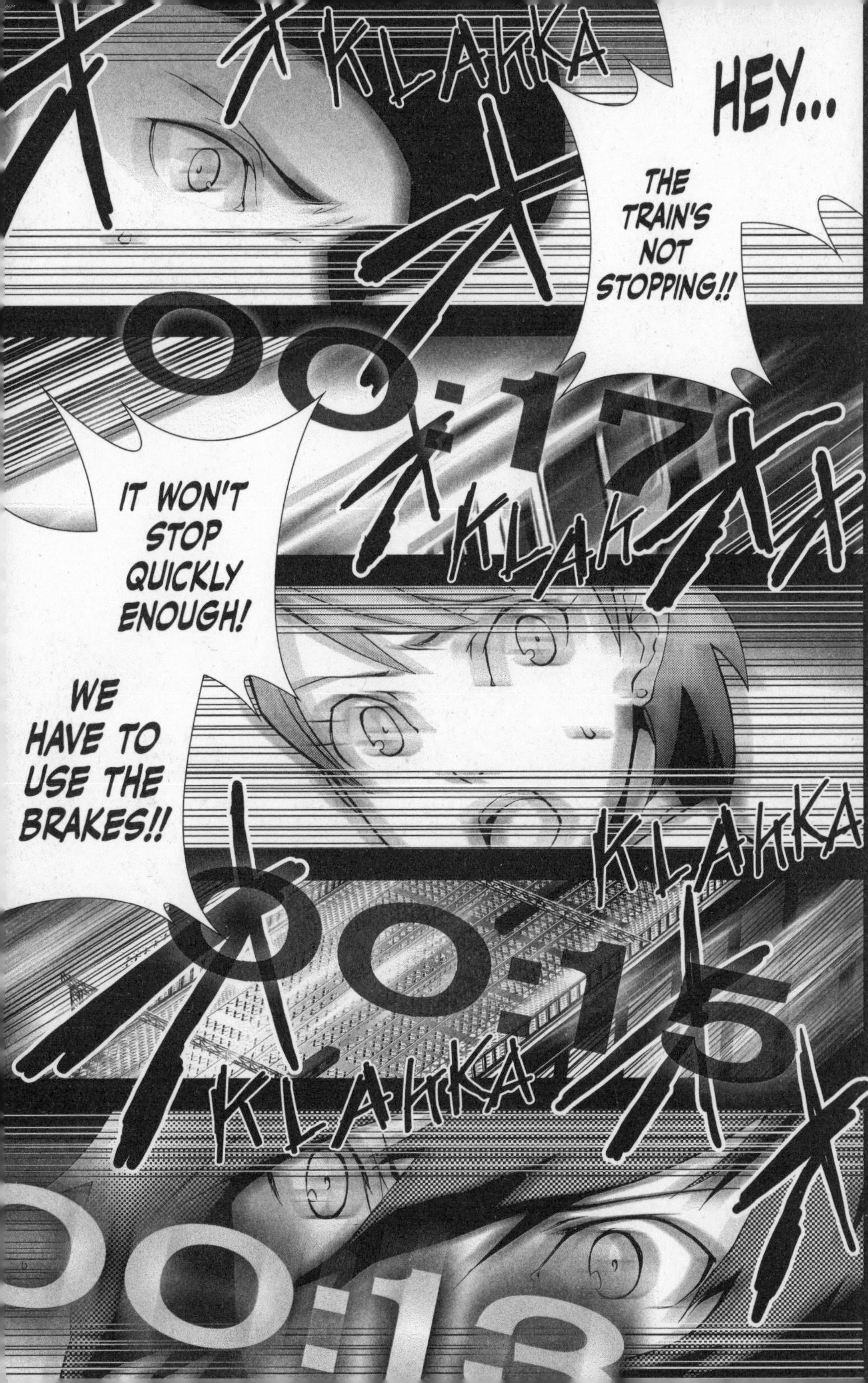
KLAKKA
HEY...
THE TRAIN'S NOT STOPPING!!
00:17
KLAKKA
IT WON'T STOP QUICKLY ENOUGH!
WE HAVE TO USE THE BRAKES!!
KLAKKA
00:15
KLAKKA
00:13

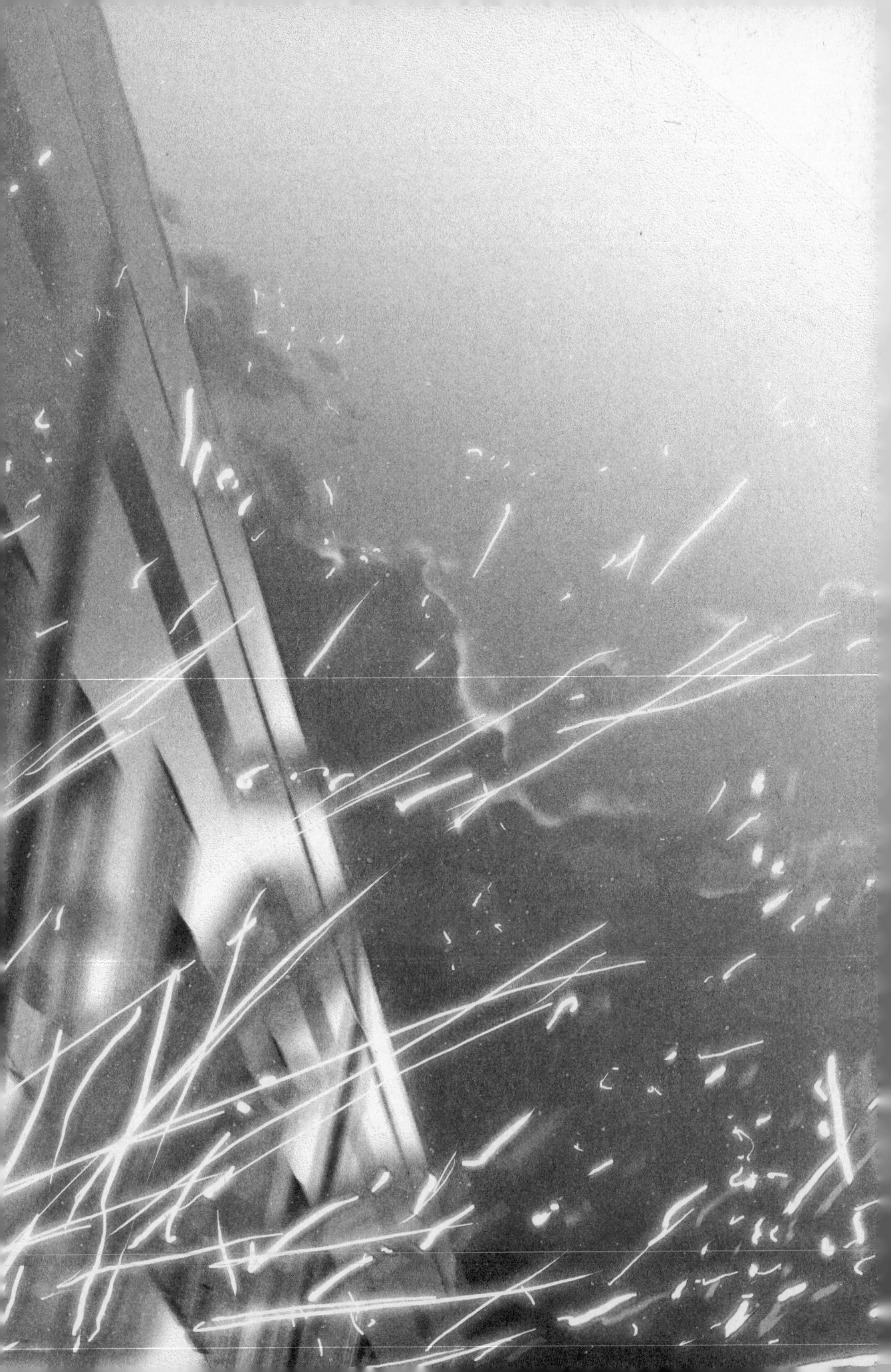

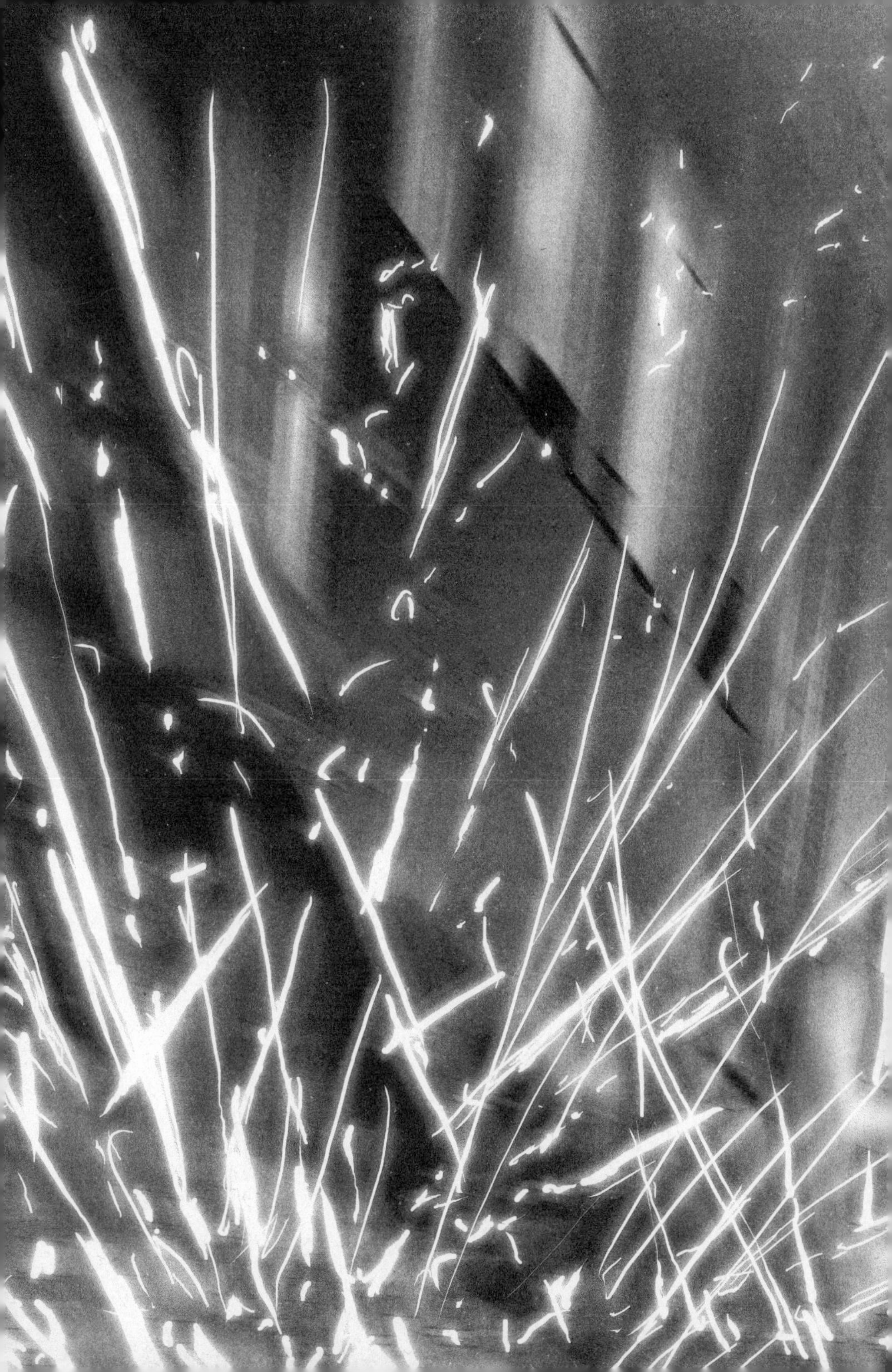

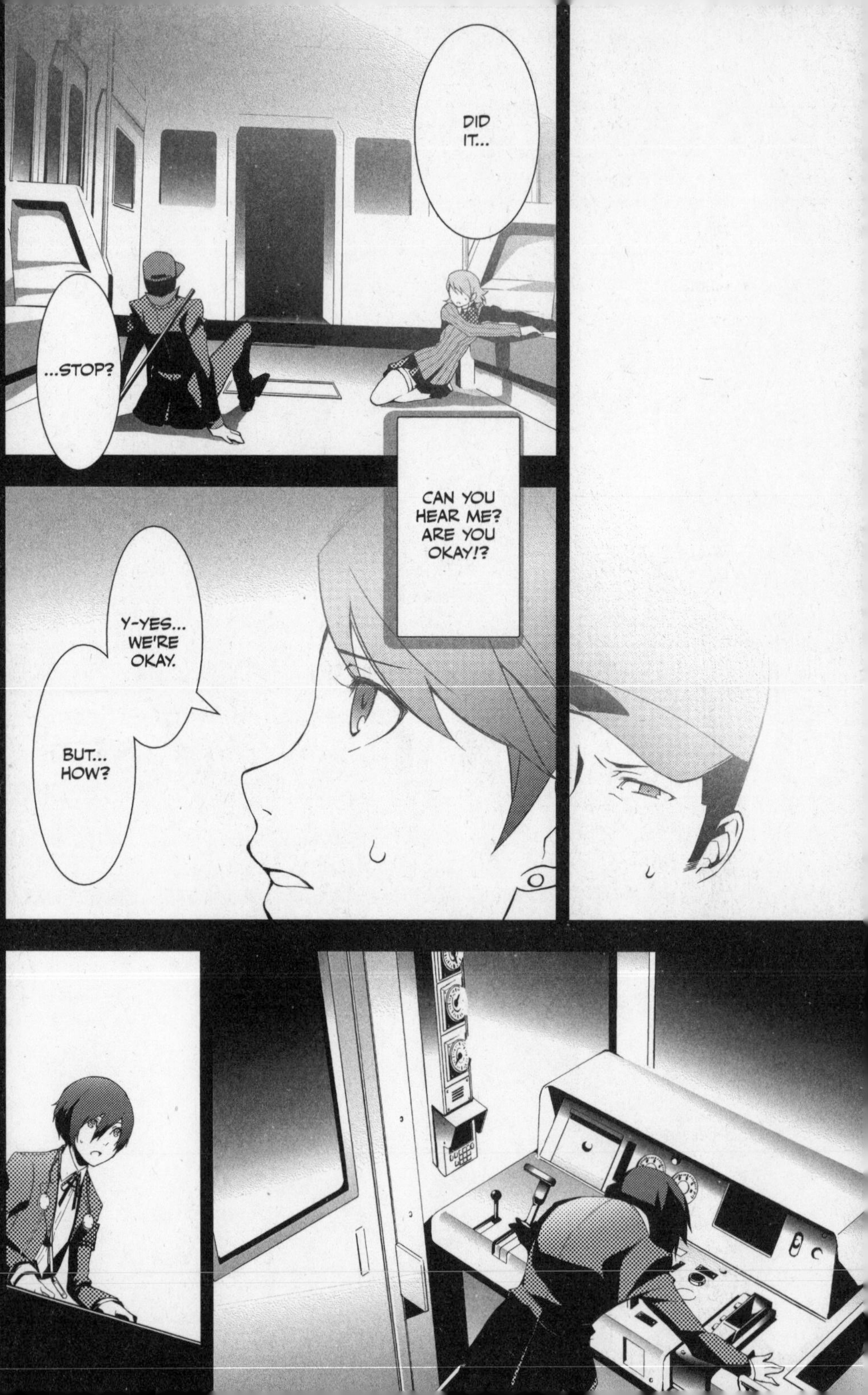
DID IT...
...STOP?
CAN YOU HEAR ME? ARE YOU OKAY!?
Y-YES... WE'RE OKAY.
BUT... HOW?

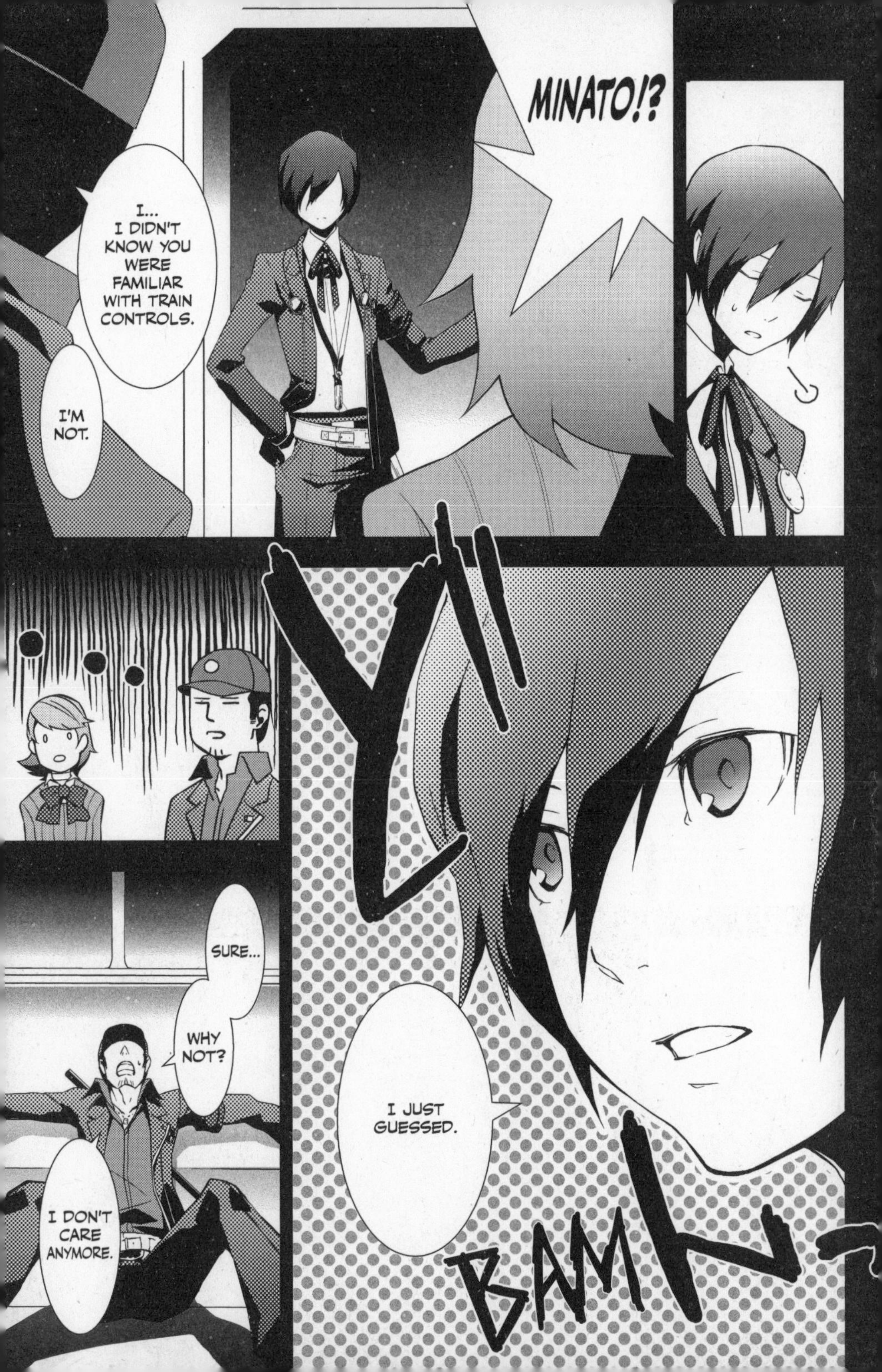
MINATO!?
I... I DIDN'T KNOW YOU WERE FAMILIAR WITH TRAIN CONTROLS.
I'M NOT.
I JUST GUESSED.
BAM
SURE...
WHY NOT?
I DON'T CARE ANYMORE.

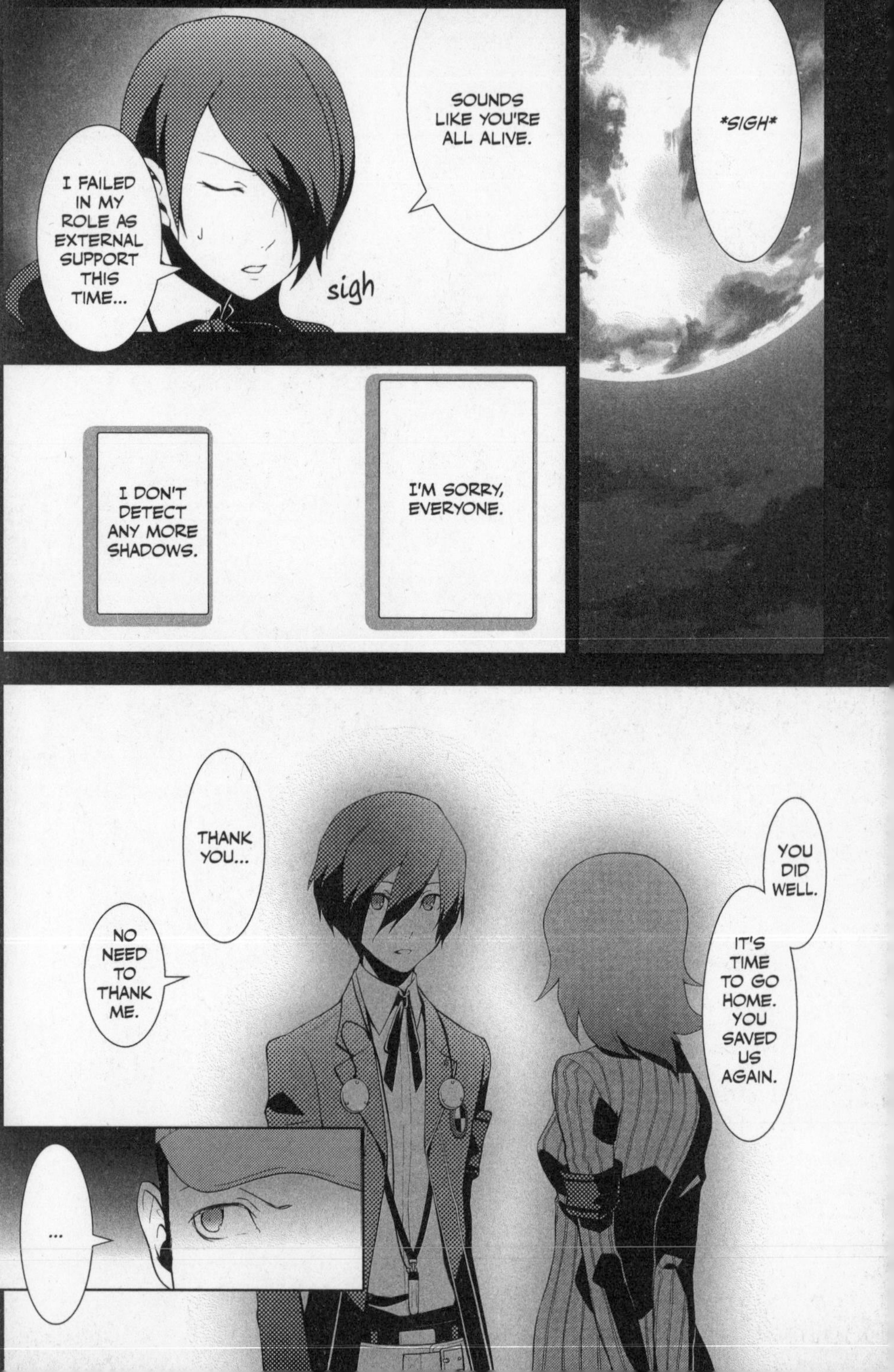
SIGH
SOUNDS LIKE YOU'RE ALL ALIVE.
sigh
I FAILED IN MY ROLE AS EXTERNAL SUPPORT THIS TIME...
I'M SORRY, EVERYONE.
I DON'T DETECT ANY MORE SHADOWS.
YOU DID WELL.
IT'S TIME TO GO HOME. YOU SAVED US AGAIN.
THANK YOU...
NO NEED TO THANK ME.
...

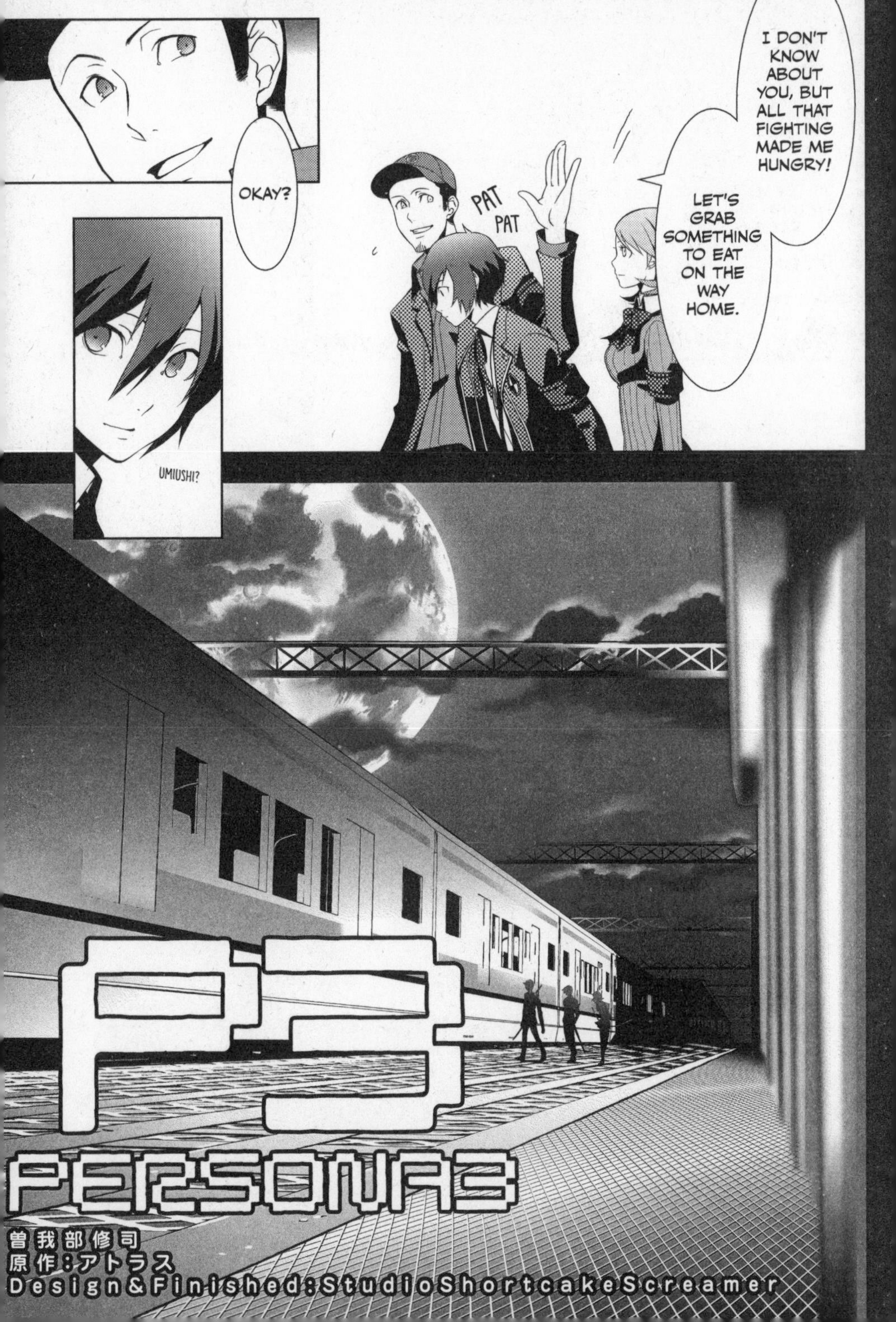
I DON'T KNOW ABOUT YOU, BUT ALL THAT FIGHTING MADE ME HUNGRY!
LET'S GRAB SOMETHING TO EAT ON THE WAY HOME.
PAT PAT
OKAY?
UMIUSHI?
P3
PERSONA3
曽我部修司
原作:アトラス
Design&Finished:StudioShortcakeScreamer

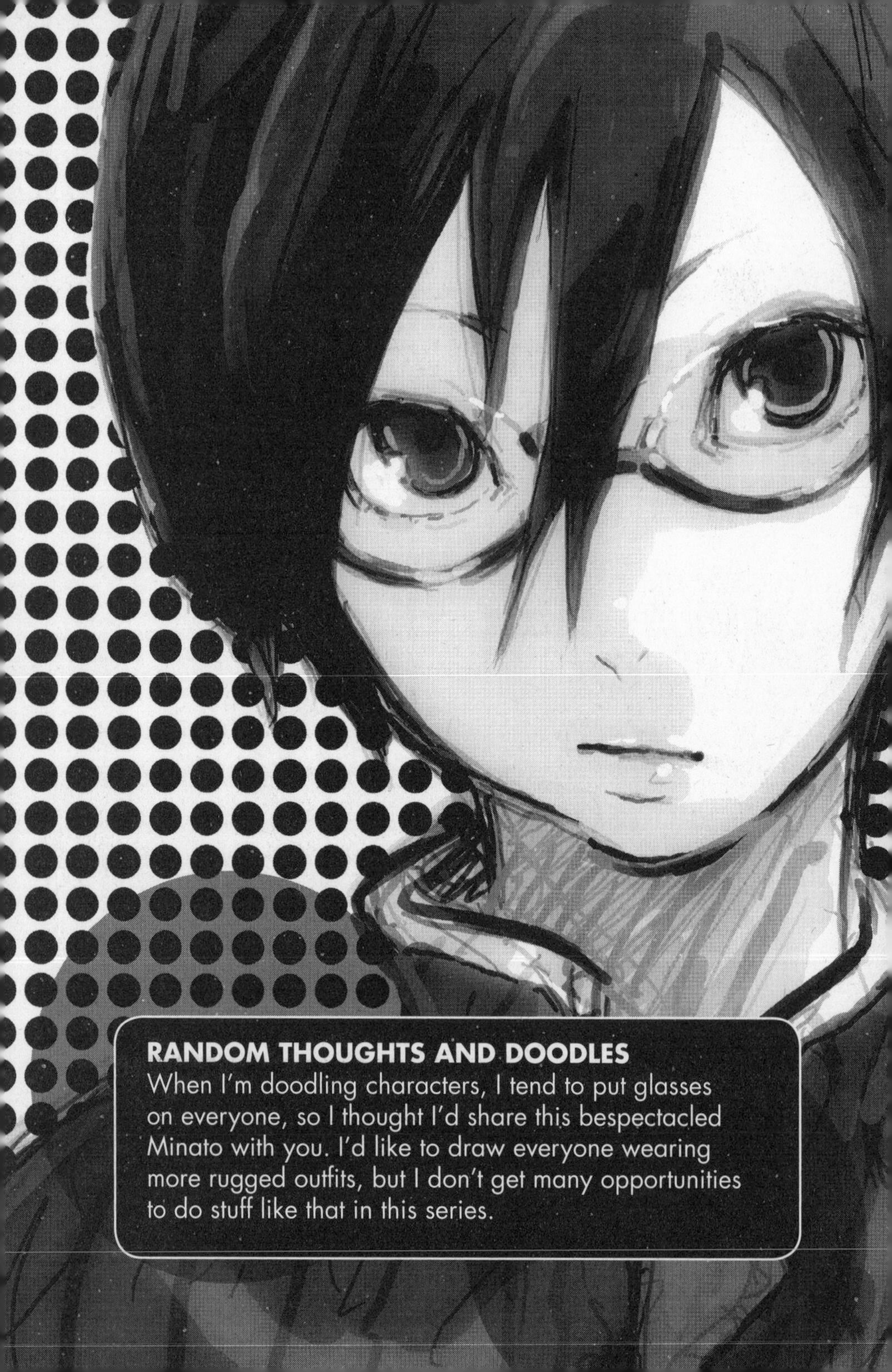

RANDOM THOUGHTS AND DOODLES

When I'm doodling characters, I tend to put glasses on everyone, so I thought I'd share this bespectacled Minato with you. I'd like to draw everyone wearing more rugged outfits, but I don't get many opportunities to do stuff like that in this series.

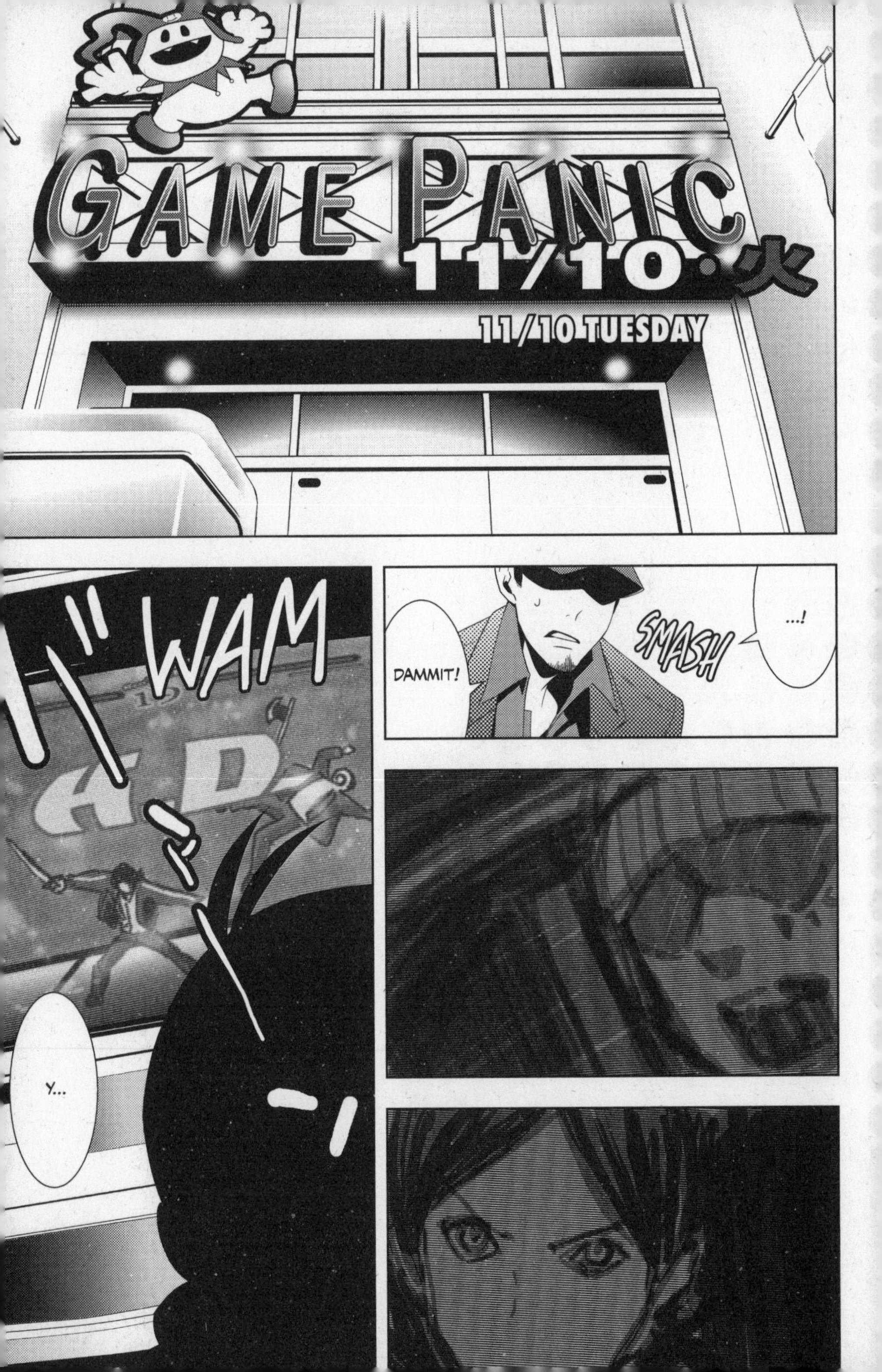
GAME PANIC
11/10·火
11/10 TUESDAY
...!
SMASH
DAMMIT!
WAM
Y...

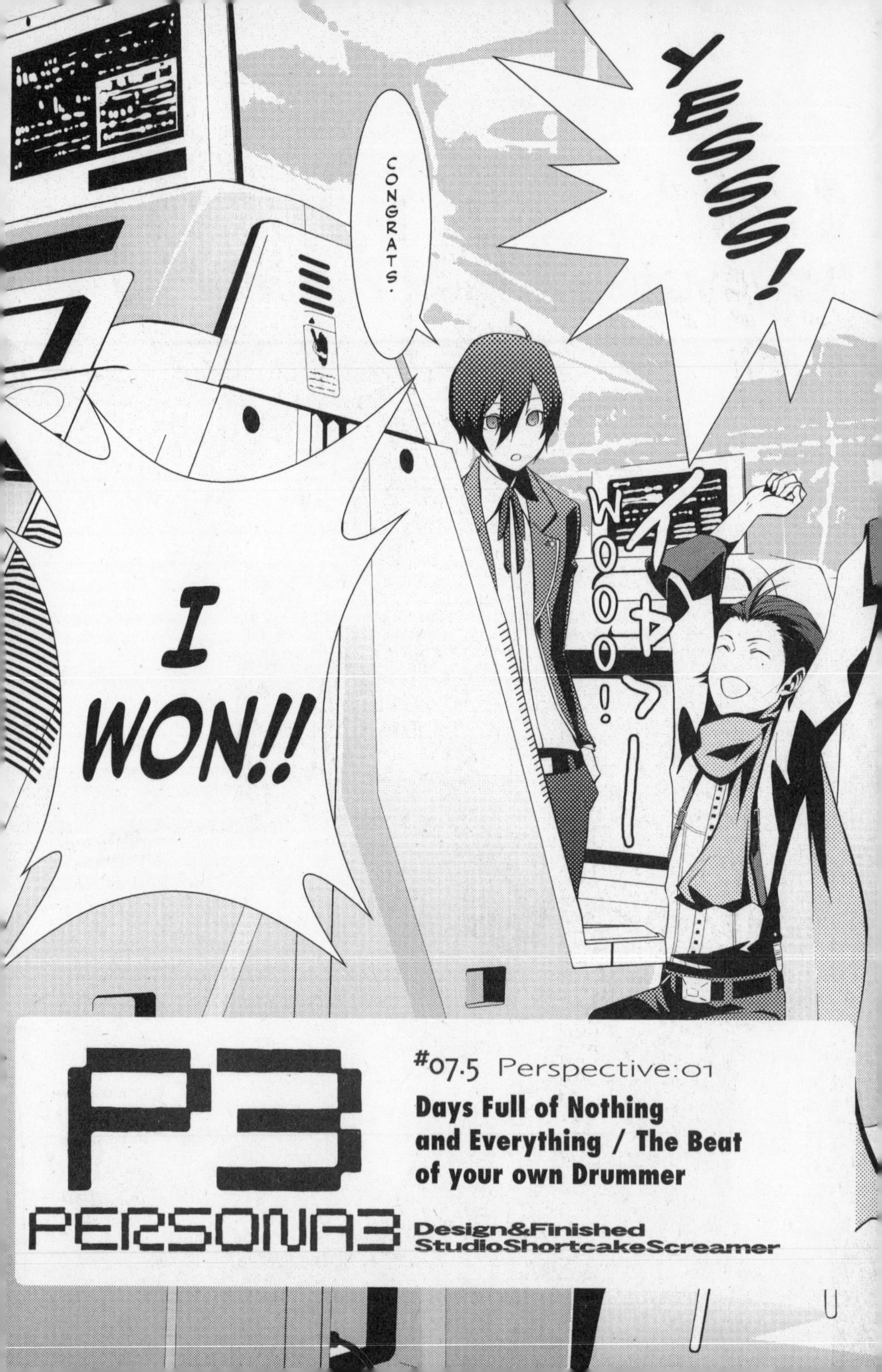
YESSS!
WOOOO!
CONGRATS.
I WON!!

P3
PERSONA3

#07.5 Perspective:01

Days Full of Nothing and Everything / The Beat of your own Drummer

Design&Finished
StudioShortcakeScreamer

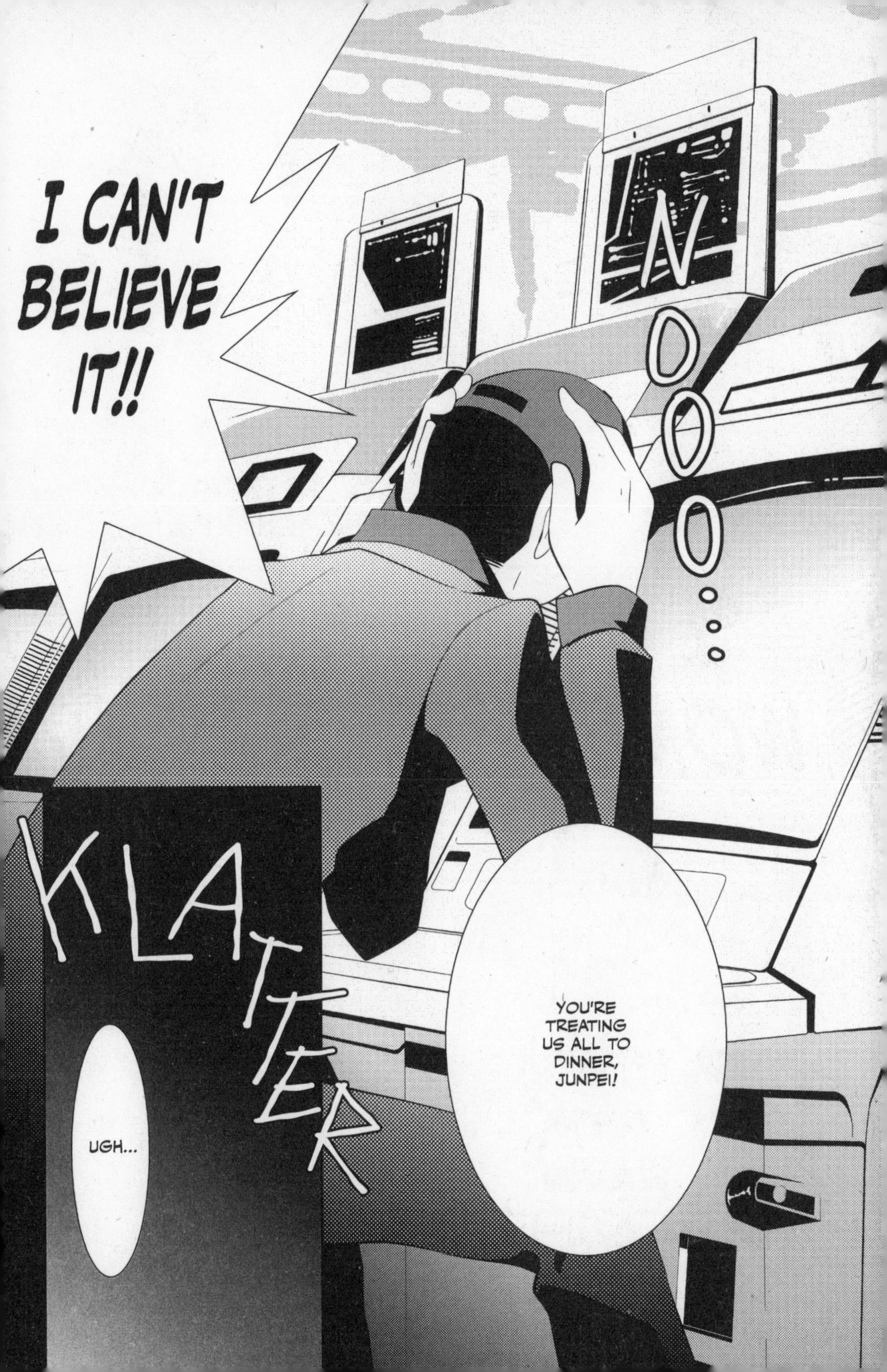
NOOOooo
I CAN'T BELIEVE IT!!
YOU'RE TREATING US ALL TO DINNER, JUNPEI!
KLATTER
UGH...

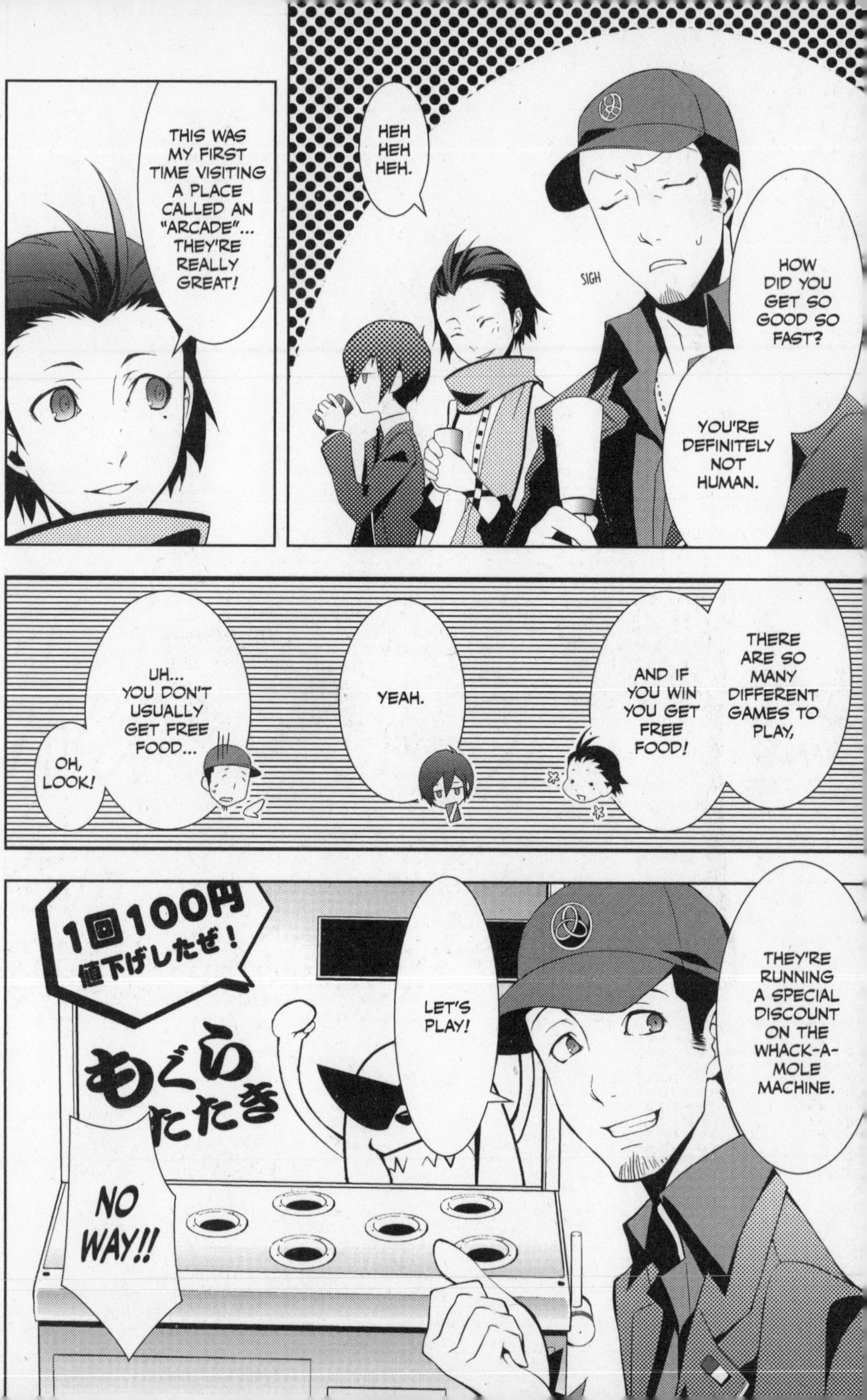
HOW DID YOU GET SO GOOD SO FAST?
SIGH
YOU'RE DEFINITELY NOT HUMAN.
HEH HEH HEH.
THIS WAS MY FIRST TIME VISITING A PLACE CALLED AN "ARCADE"... THEY'RE REALLY GREAT!
THERE ARE SO MANY DIFFERENT GAMES TO PLAY,
AND IF YOU WIN YOU GET FREE FOOD!
YEAH.
UH... YOU DON'T USUALLY GET FREE FOOD...
OH, LOOK!
THEY'RE RUNNING A SPECIAL DISCOUNT ON THE WHACK-A-MOLE MACHINE.
LET'S PLAY!
1回100円 値下げしたぜ！
もぐらたたき
NO WAY!!

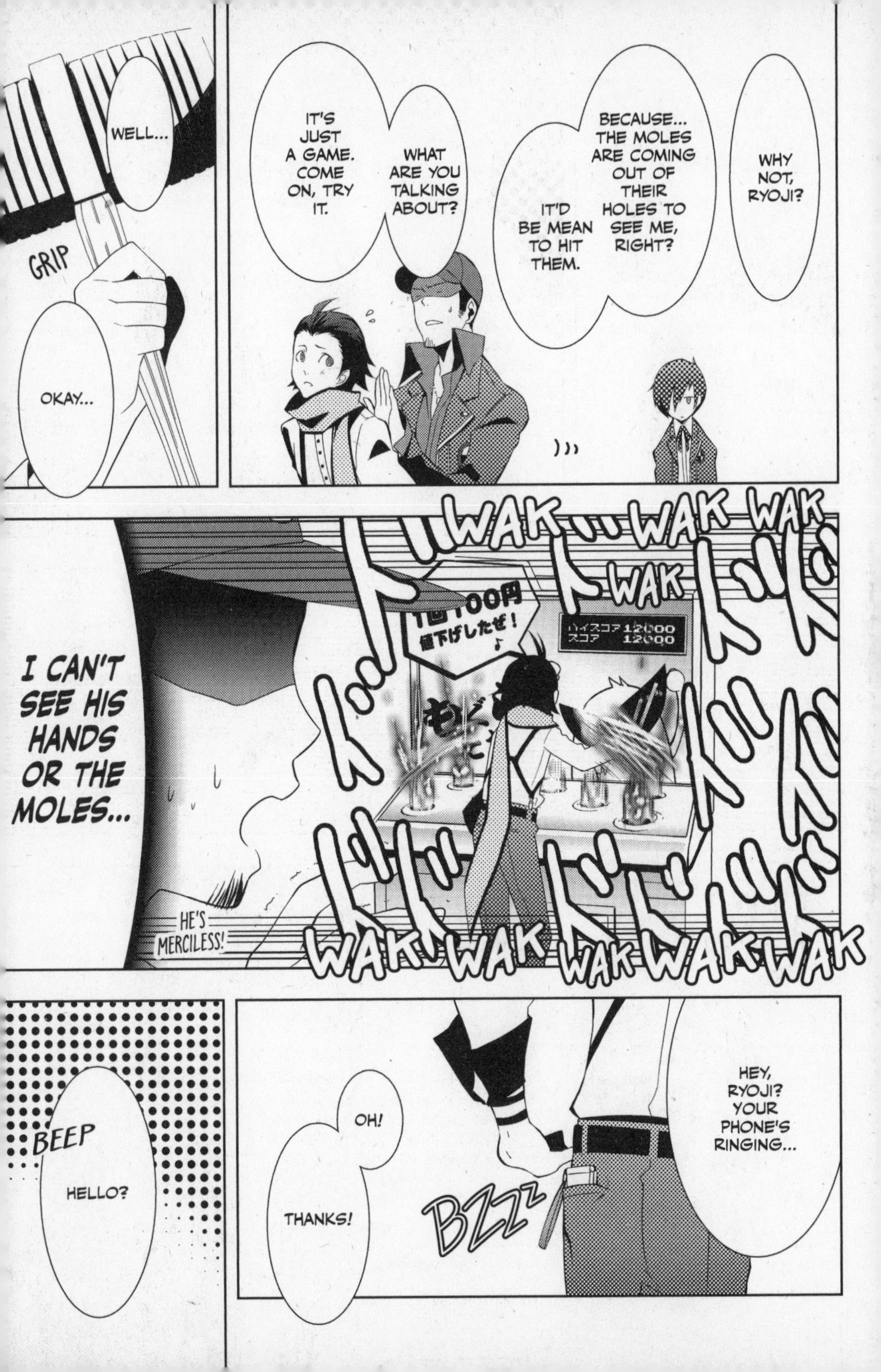
WHY NOT, RYOJI?
BECAUSE... THE MOLES ARE COMING OUT OF THEIR HOLES TO SEE ME, RIGHT?
IT'D BE MEAN TO HIT THEM.
WHAT ARE YOU TALKING ABOUT?
IT'S JUST A GAME. COME ON, TRY IT.
WELL...
GRIP
OKAY...
WAK WAK WAK
WAK
1回100円 値下げしたぜ！♪
ハイスコア 12000
スコア 12000
I CAN'T SEE HIS HANDS OR THE MOLES...
HE'S MERCILESS!
WAK WAK WAK WAK WAK
HEY, RYOJI? YOUR PHONE'S RINGING...
BZZZ
OH!
THANKS!
BEEP
HELLO?

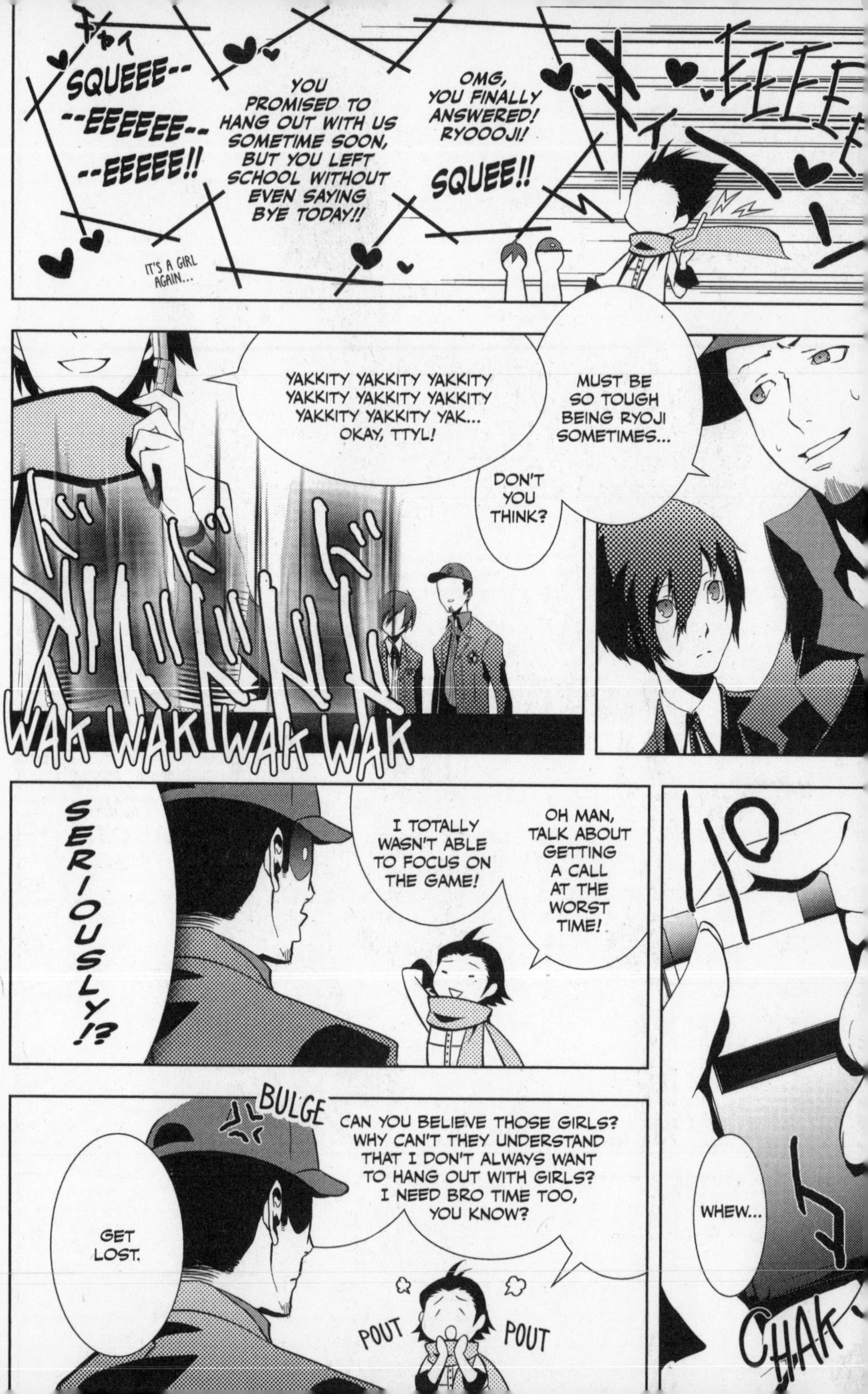
EEEEE
OMG, YOU FINALLY ANSWERED! RYOOOJI!
SQUEE!!
YOU PROMISED TO HANG OUT WITH US SOMETIME SOON, BUT YOU LEFT SCHOOL WITHOUT EVEN SAYING BYE TODAY!!
SQUEEE----EEEEEE----EEEEE!!
IT'S A GIRL AGAIN...
MUST BE SO TOUGH BEING RYOJI SOMETIMES...
DON'T YOU THINK?
YAKKITY YAKKITY YAKKITY YAKKITY YAKKITY YAKKITY YAKKITY YAKKITY YAK... OKAY, TTYL!
WAK WAK WAK WAK
WHEW...
CHAK
OH MAN, TALK ABOUT GETTING A CALL AT THE WORST TIME!
I TOTALLY WASN'T ABLE TO FOCUS ON THE GAME!
SERIOUSLY!?
BULGE
CAN YOU BELIEVE THOSE GIRLS? WHY CAN'T THEY UNDERSTAND THAT I DON'T ALWAYS WANT TO HANG OUT WITH GIRLS? I NEED BRO TIME TOO, YOU KNOW?
POUT POUT
GET LOST.

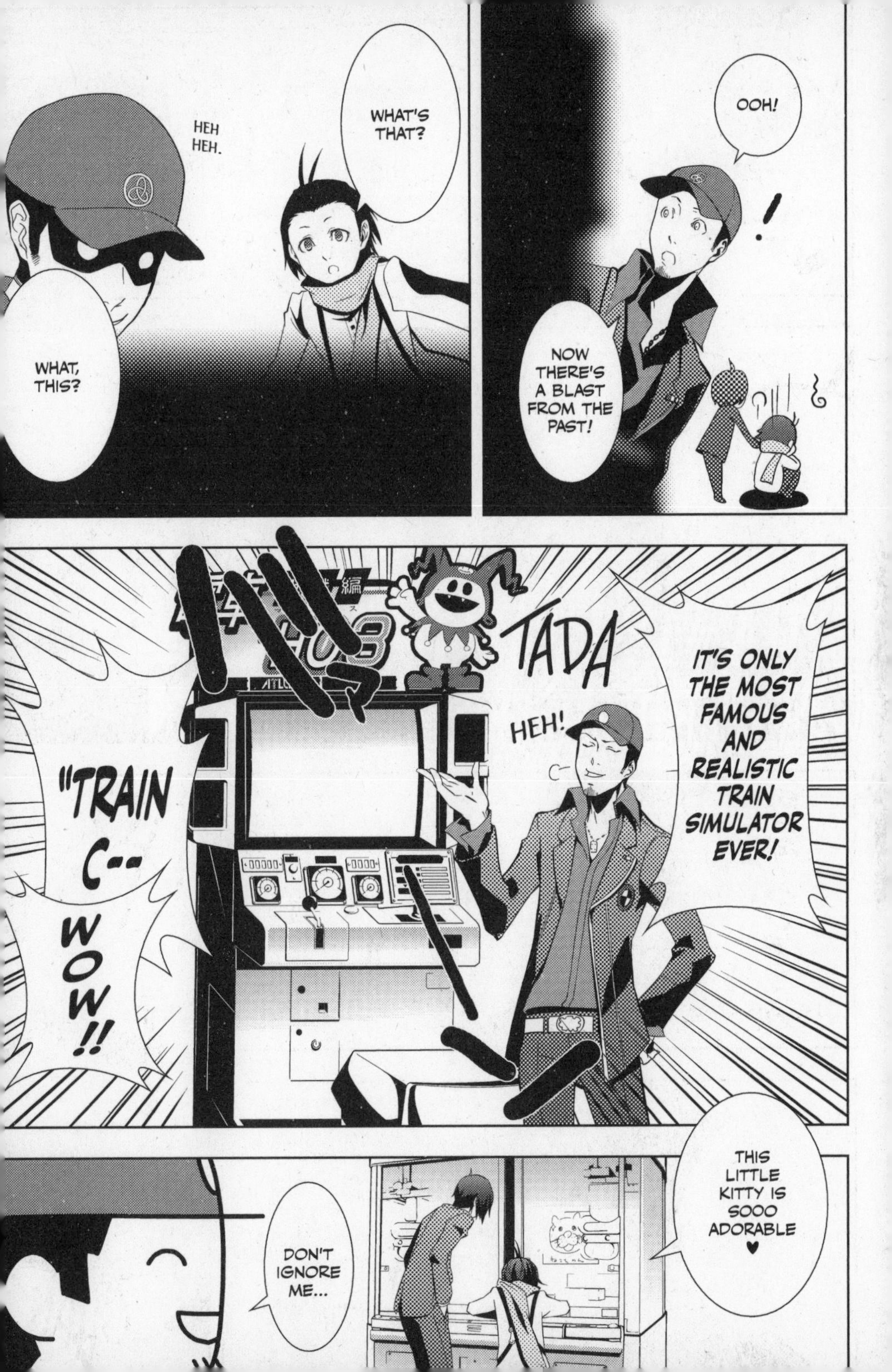
OOH!
!
NOW THERE'S A BLAST FROM THE PAST!
WHAT'S THAT?
HEH HEH.
WHAT, THIS?
TADA
IT'S ONLY THE MOST FAMOUS AND REALISTIC TRAIN SIMULATOR EVER!
HEH!
"TRAIN C--
WOW!!
THIS LITTLE KITTY IS SOOO ADORABLE ♥
DON'T IGNORE ME...

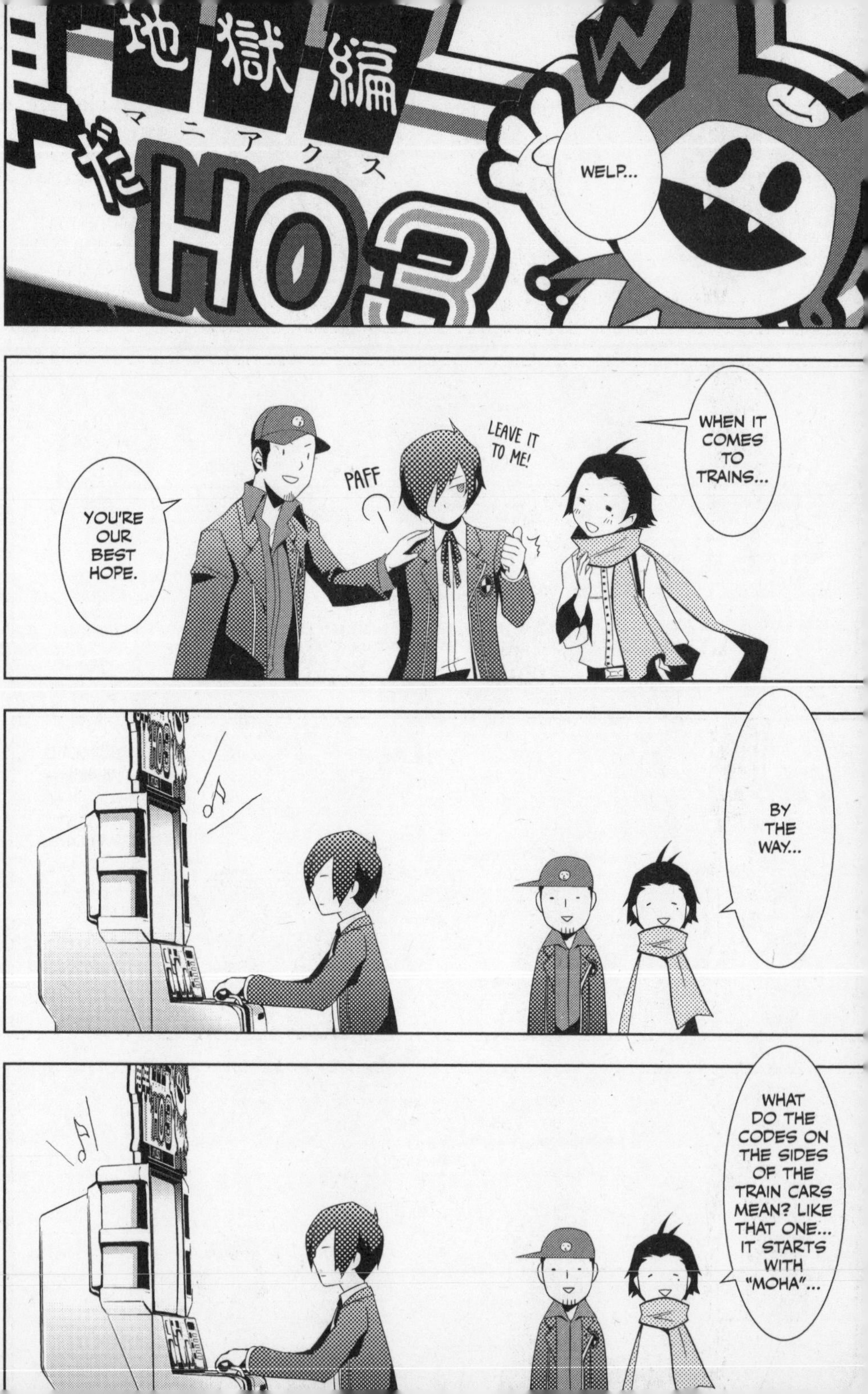
地獄編
マニアクス
WELP...
WHEN IT COMES TO TRAINS...
LEAVE IT TO ME!
PAFF
YOU'RE OUR BEST HOPE.
BY THE WAY...
WHAT DO THE CODES ON THE SIDES OF THE TRAIN CARS MEAN? LIKE THAT ONE... IT STARTS WITH "MOHA"...

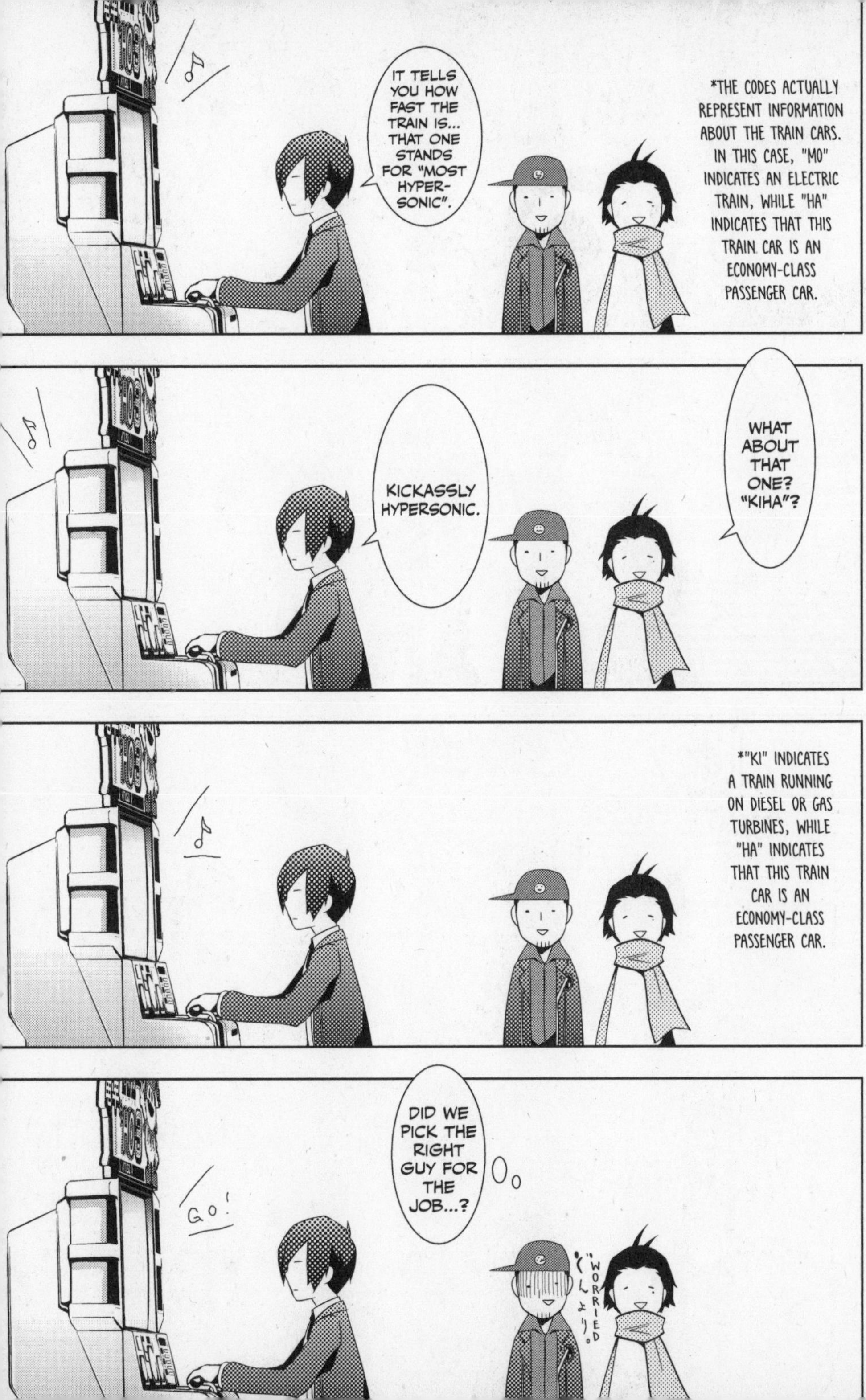
*THE CODES ACTUALLY REPRESENT INFORMATION ABOUT THE TRAIN CARS. IN THIS CASE, "MO" INDICATES AN ELECTRIC TRAIN, WHILE "HA" INDICATES THAT THIS TRAIN CAR IS AN ECONOMY-CLASS PASSENGER CAR.
IT TELLS YOU HOW FAST THE TRAIN IS... THAT ONE STANDS FOR "MOST HYPER-SONIC".
WHAT ABOUT THAT ONE? "KIHA"?
KICKASSLY HYPERSONIC.
*"KI" INDICATES A TRAIN RUNNING ON DIESEL OR GAS TURBINES, WHILE "HA" INDICATES THAT THIS TRAIN CAR IS AN ECONOMY-CLASS PASSENGER CAR.
DID WE PICK THE RIGHT GUY FOR THE JOB...?
WORRIED
GO!

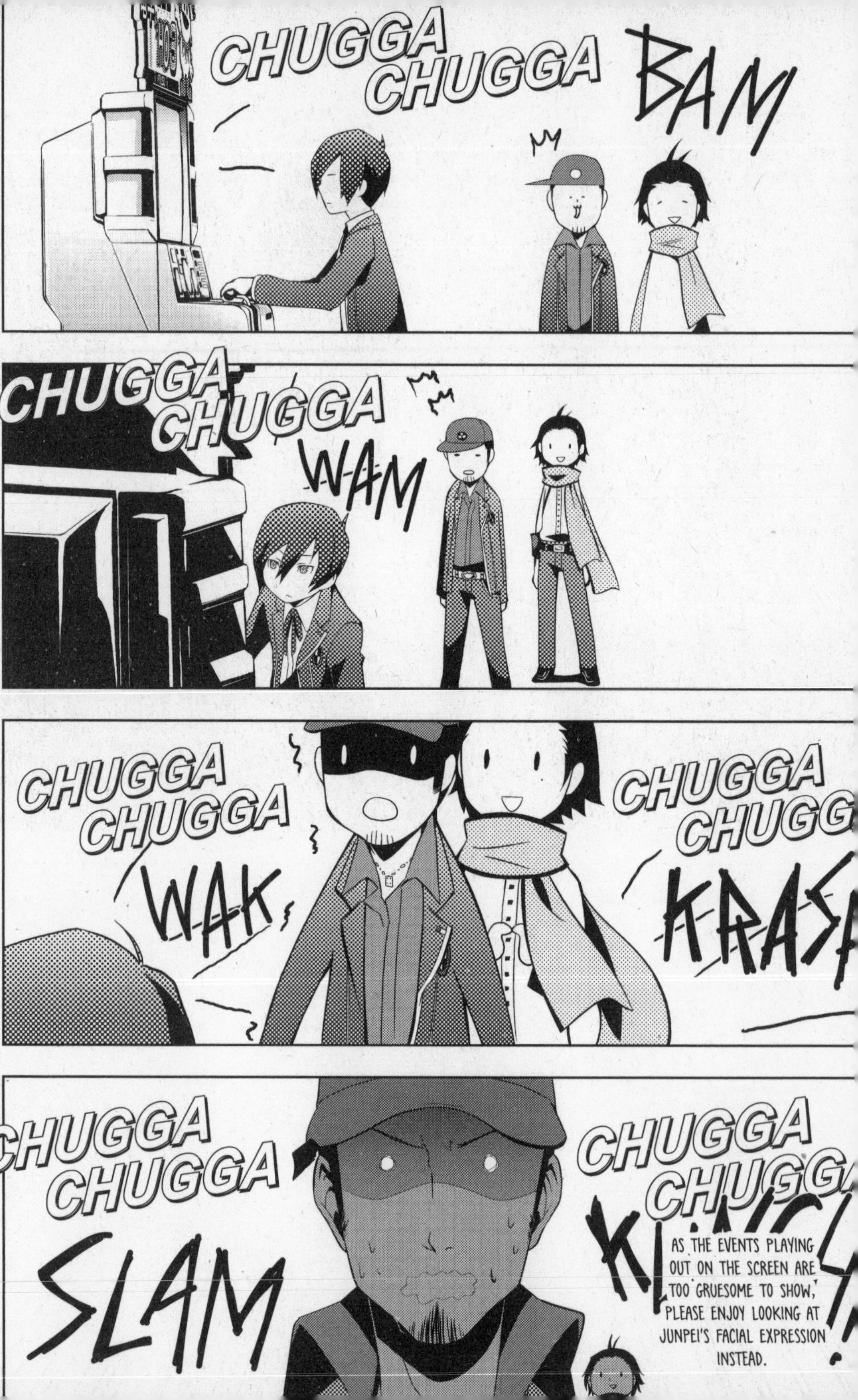

CHUGGA
CHUGGA
BAM
CHUGGA
CHUGGA
WAM
CHUGGA
CHUGG
CHUGGA
CHUGGA
WAK
CHUGGA
CHUGG
AS THE EVENTS PLAYING OUT ON THE SCREEN ARE TOO GRUESOME TO SHOW, PLEASE ENJOY LOOKING AT JUNPEI'S FACIAL EXPRESSION INSTEAD.
CHUGGA
CHUGGA
SLAM

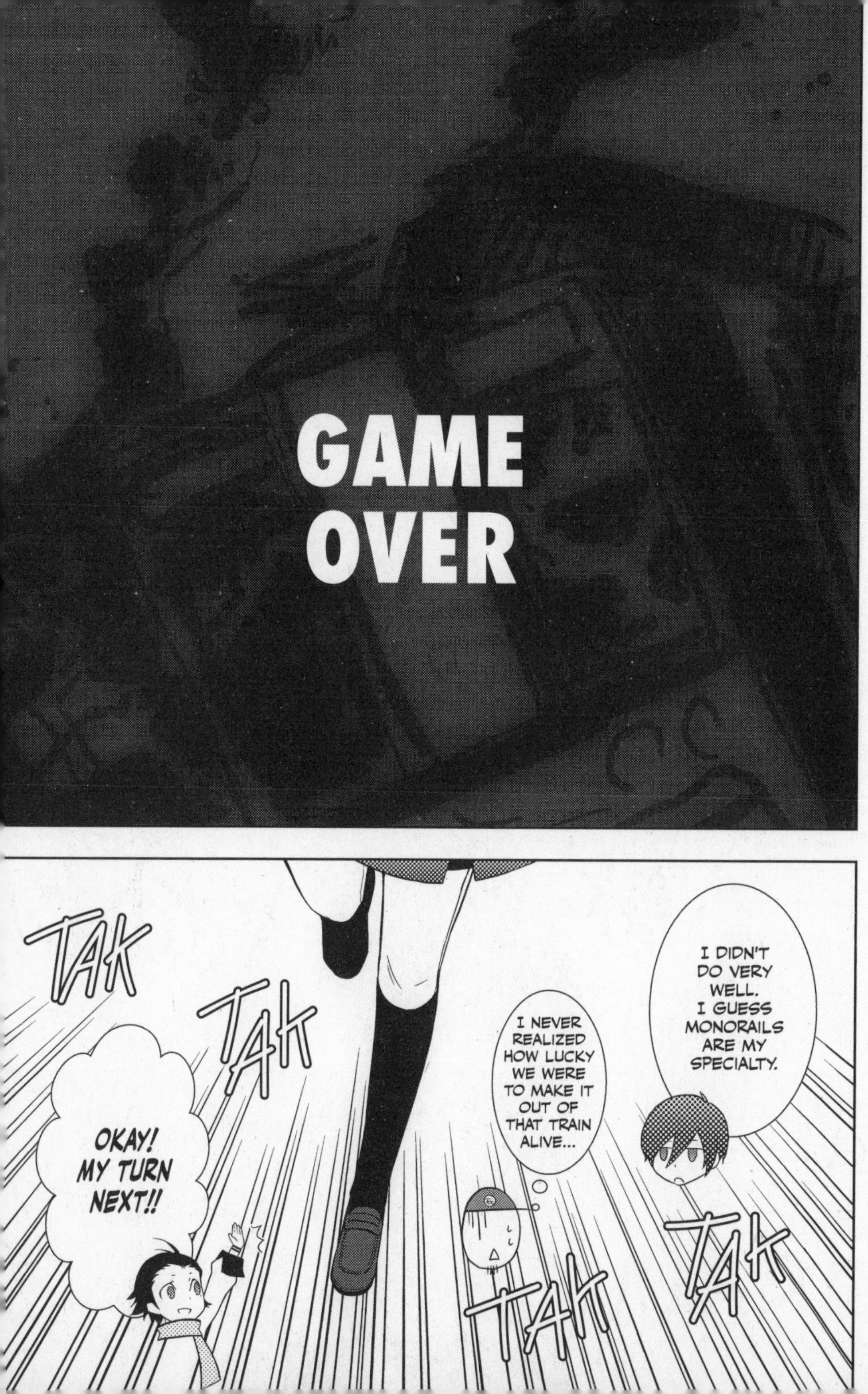
GAME OVER
I DIDN'T DO VERY WELL. I GUESS MONORAILS ARE MY SPECIALTY.
I NEVER REALIZED HOW LUCKY WE WERE TO MAKE IT OUT OF THAT TRAIN ALIVE...
TAK
TAK
OKAY! MY TURN NEXT!!
TAK
TAK

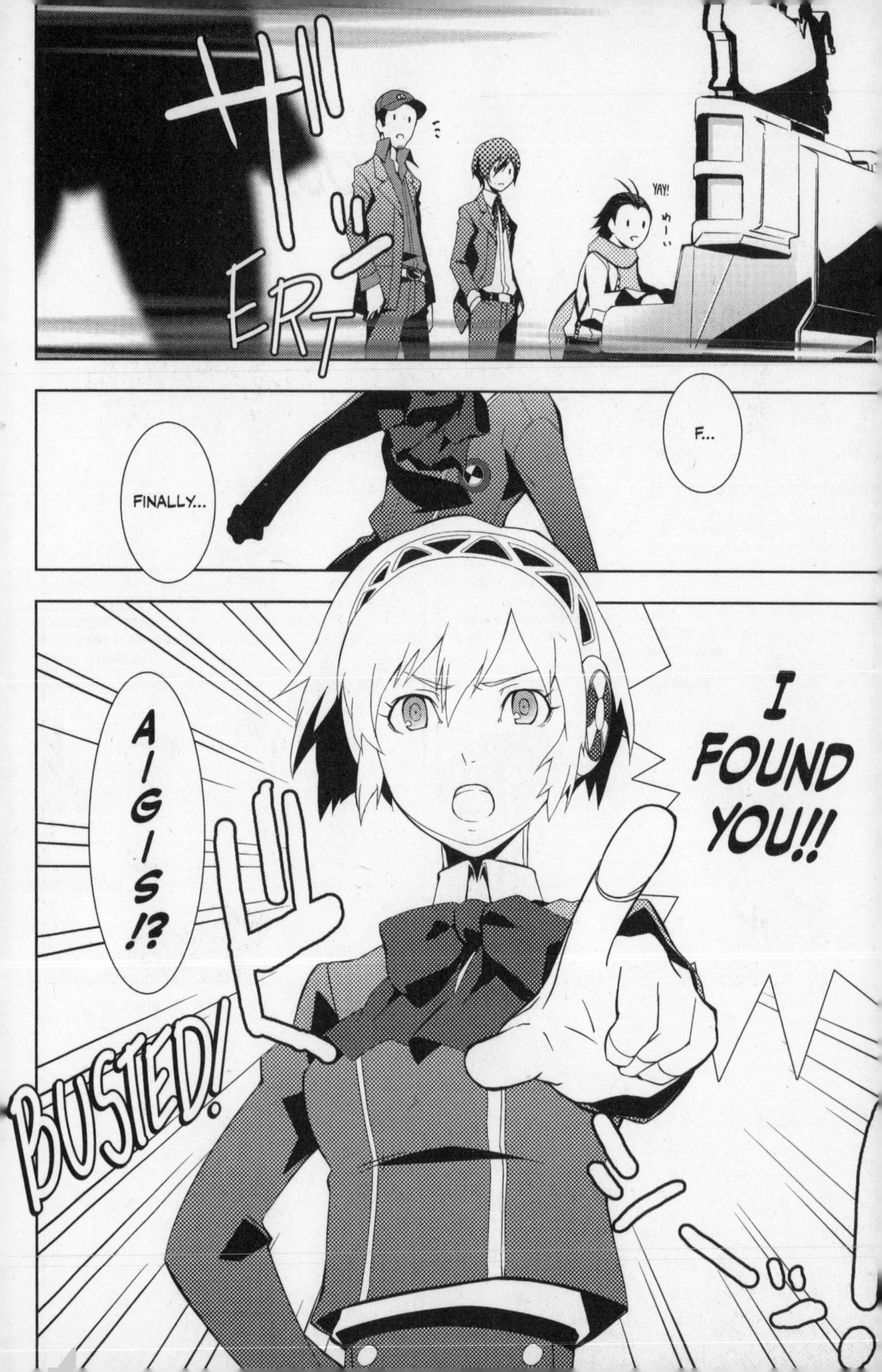
YAY!
ERT
F...
FINALLY...
I FOUND YOU!!
AIGIS!?
BUSTED!

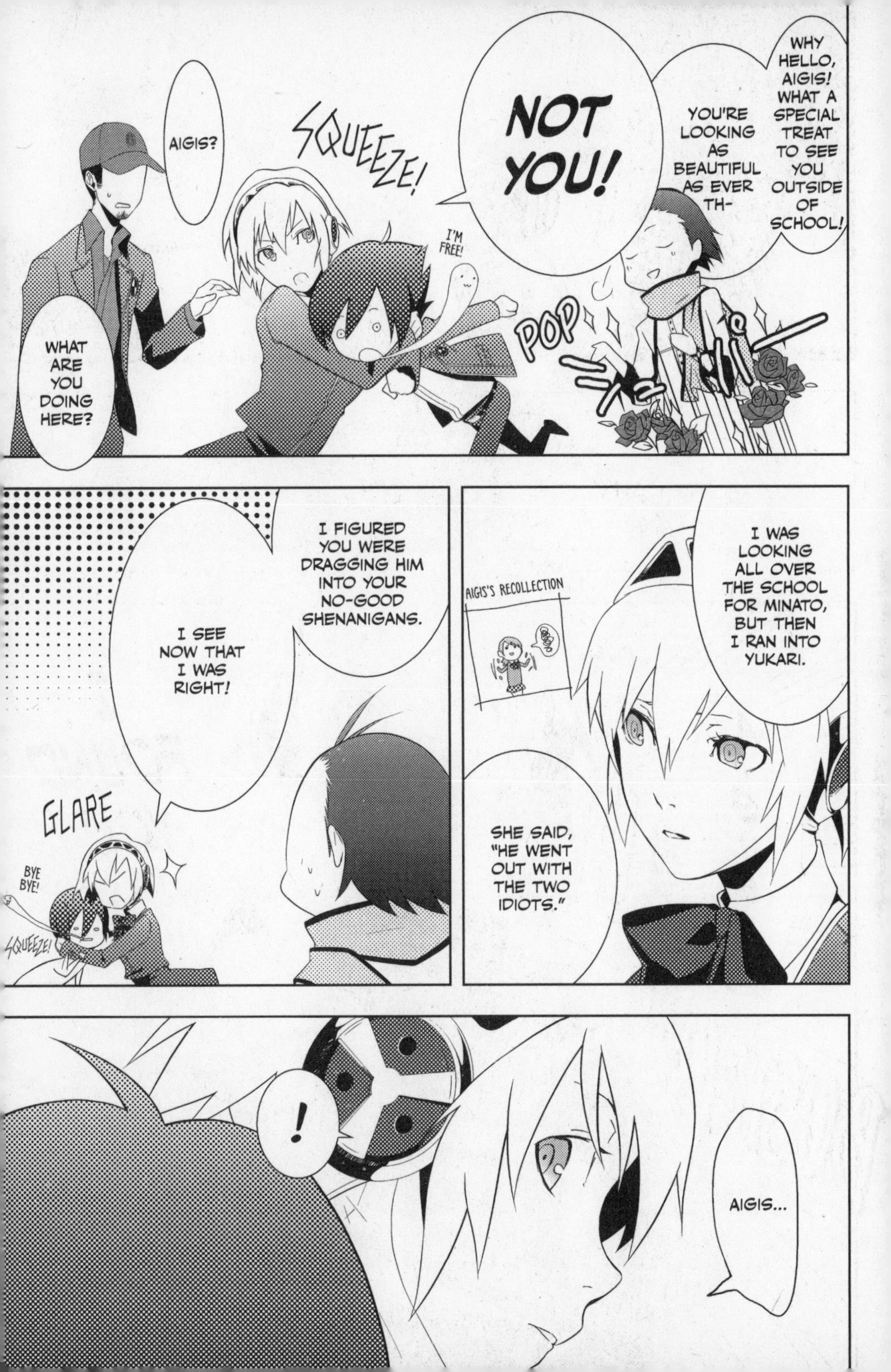
WHY HELLO, AIGIS! WHAT A SPECIAL TREAT TO SEE YOU OUTSIDE OF SCHOOL!
YOU'RE LOOKING AS BEAUTIFUL AS EVER TH-
NOT YOU!
POP
SQUEEZE!
I'M FREE!
AIGIS?
WHAT ARE YOU DOING HERE?
I WAS LOOKING ALL OVER THE SCHOOL FOR MINATO, BUT THEN I RAN INTO YUKARI.
AIGIS'S RECOLLECTION
SHE SAID, "HE WENT OUT WITH THE TWO IDIOTS."
I FIGURED YOU WERE DRAGGING HIM INTO YOUR NO-GOOD SHENANIGANS.
I SEE NOW THAT I WAS RIGHT!
GLARE
BYE BYE!
SQUEEZE!
AIGIS...
!

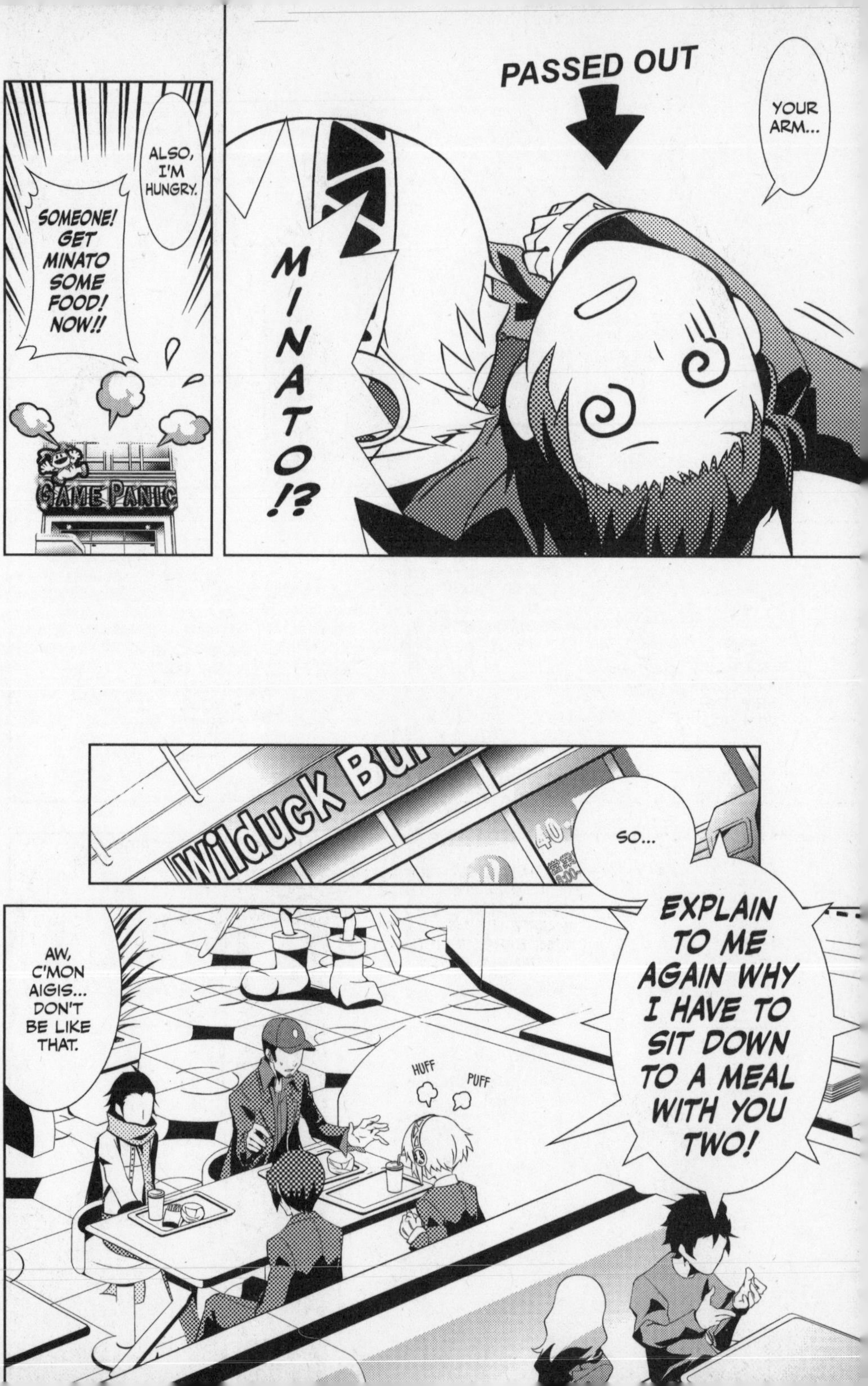
YOUR ARM...
PASSED OUT
MINATO!?
ALSO, I'M HUNGRY.
SOMEONE! GET MINATO SOME FOOD! NOW!!
GAME PANIC
SO...
EXPLAIN TO ME AGAIN WHY I HAVE TO SIT DOWN TO A MEAL WITH YOU TWO!
HUFF
PUFF
AW, C'MON AIGIS... DON'T BE LIKE THAT.

I KNOW THAT I AM BEING RUDE AND EVEN HARSH TO YOU...

BUT I CAN'T CHANGE HOW I FEEL.

I...

HMM... I DON'T UNDERSTAND WHY SHE'S REJECTING ME SO HARD WHEN WE'VE ONLY JUST MET.

DEJECTED.

BUT YOU KNOW, I'M GLAD THAT WE MET.

I'D REALLY LIKE TO BECOME FRIENDS WITH YOU.

I CAN UNDERSTAND THAT... I GUESS ALL I CAN DO IS WORK HARD TO CHANGE YOUR MIND.

HE'S RIGHT!

LET'S EAT!!

Y-YOU'D BETTER EAT UP BEFORE IT GETS ALL SOGGY IN THE WRAPPER! I MEAN, IT'S PROBABLY A LITTLE DAMP ALREADY, BUT...

YAY!

ER...

THAT'S WHAT I WANT, ANYWAY.

...

HM?

MIND YOUR OWN BUSINESS!

AREN'T YOU GOING TO EAT, AIGIS?

NOM NOM

ARE YOU HOLDING BACK OUT OF CONSIDERATION FOR ME BECAUSE I'M PAYING FOR EVERYONE?

THAT'S REALLY NICE OF YOU, BUT YOU REALLY DON'T HAVE TO WORRY! ORDER WHATEVER YOU WANT!

MINATO...

YOU ONLY ORDERED A DRINK?

THUD

I APOLOGIZE FOR THE WAIT.

I...

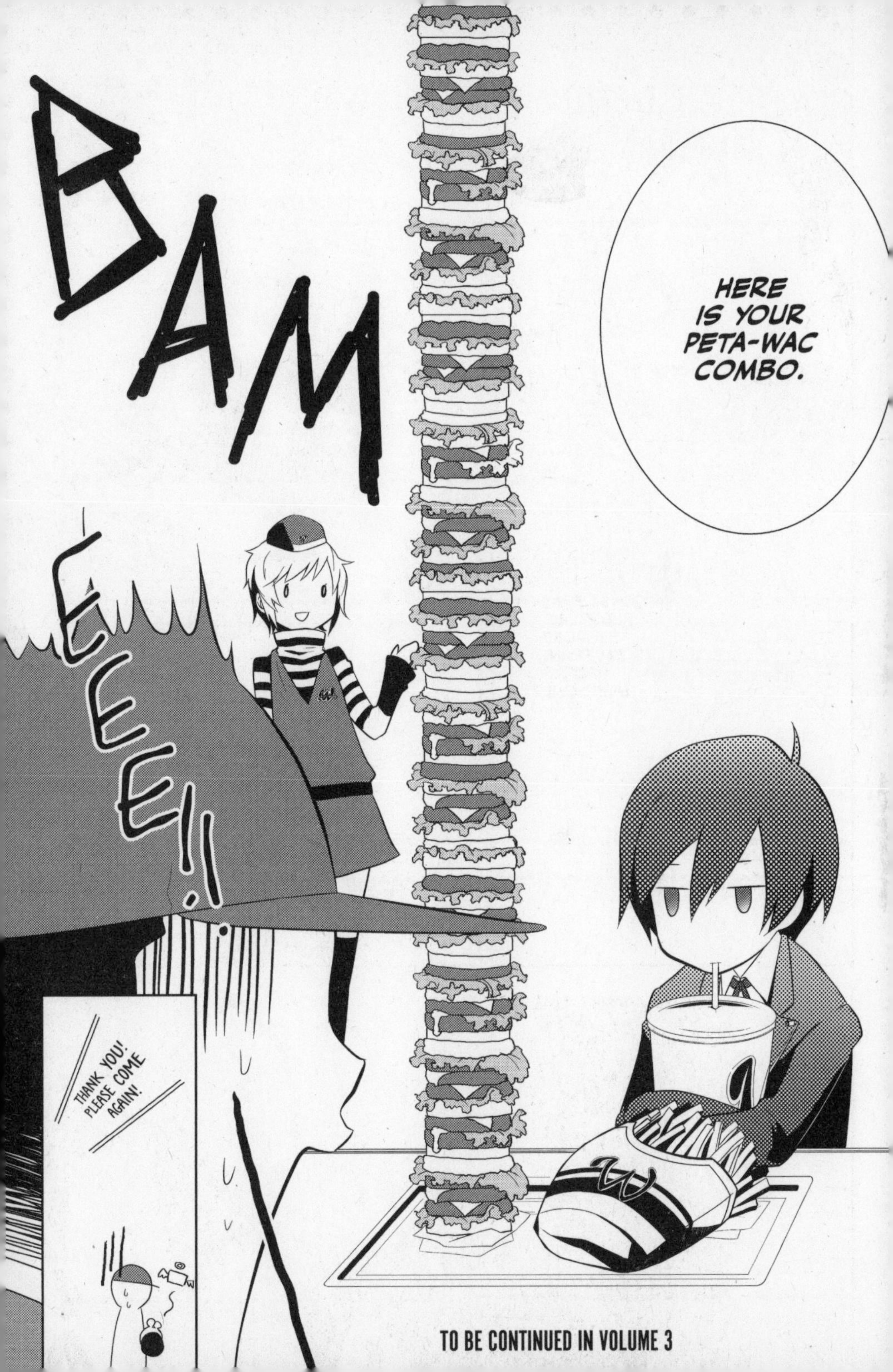
HERE IS YOUR PETA-WAC COMBO.
BAM
EEEEE!!
THANK YOU! PLEASE COME AGAIN!
TO BE CONTINUED IN VOLUME 3

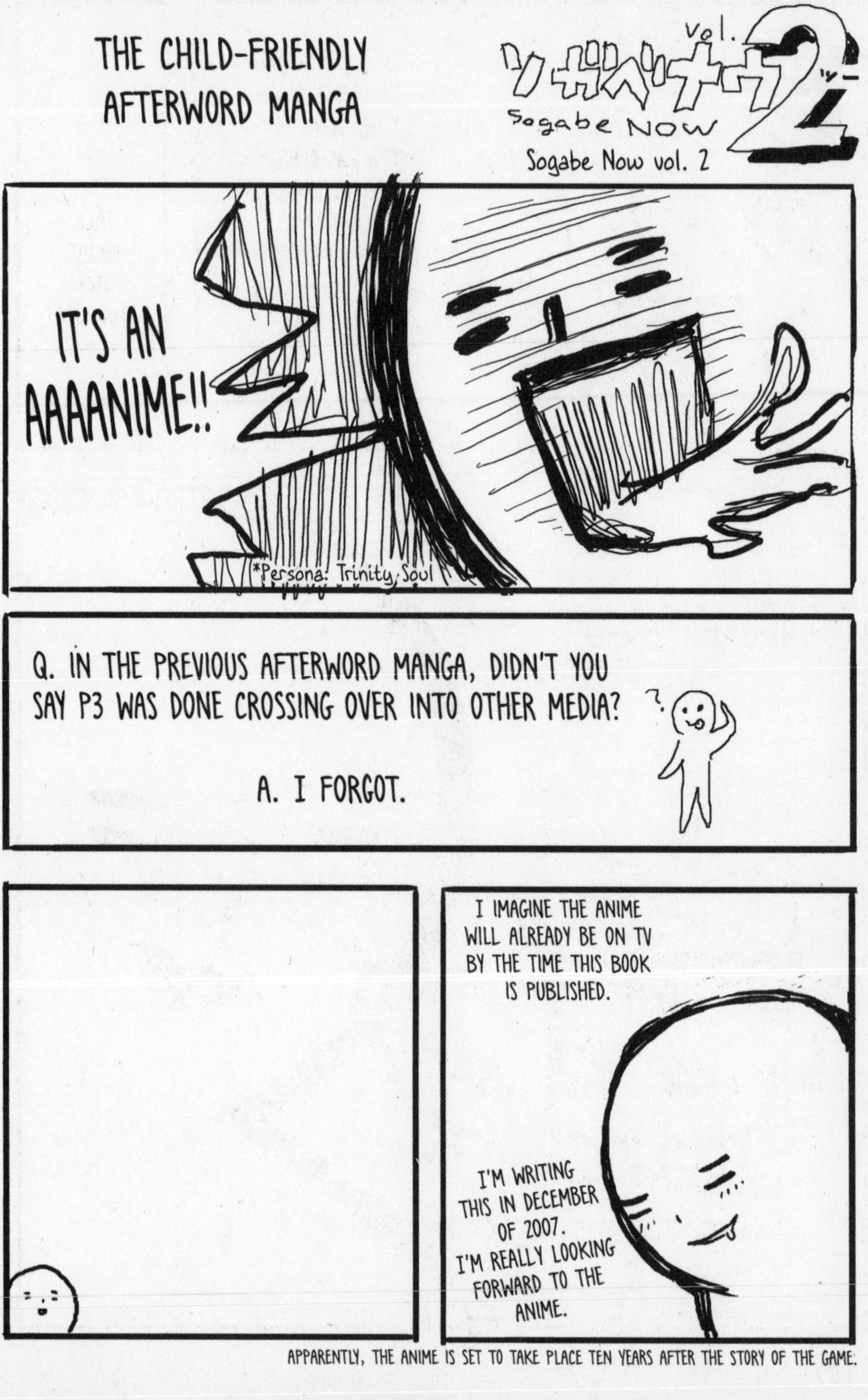

Sogabe NOW
Sogabe Now vol. 2
THE CHILD-FRIENDLY AFTERWORD MANGA
IT'S AN AAAANIME!!
*Persona: Trinity Soul
Q. IN THE PREVIOUS AFTERWORD MANGA, DIDN'T YOU SAY P3 WAS DONE CROSSING OVER INTO OTHER MEDIA?
A. I FORGOT.
I IMAGINE THE ANIME WILL ALREADY BE ON TV BY THE TIME THIS BOOK IS PUBLISHED.
I'M WRITING THIS IN DECEMBER OF 2007. I'M REALLY LOOKING FORWARD TO THE ANIME.
APPARENTLY, THE ANIME IS SET TO TAKE PLACE TEN YEARS AFTER THE STORY OF THE GAME.

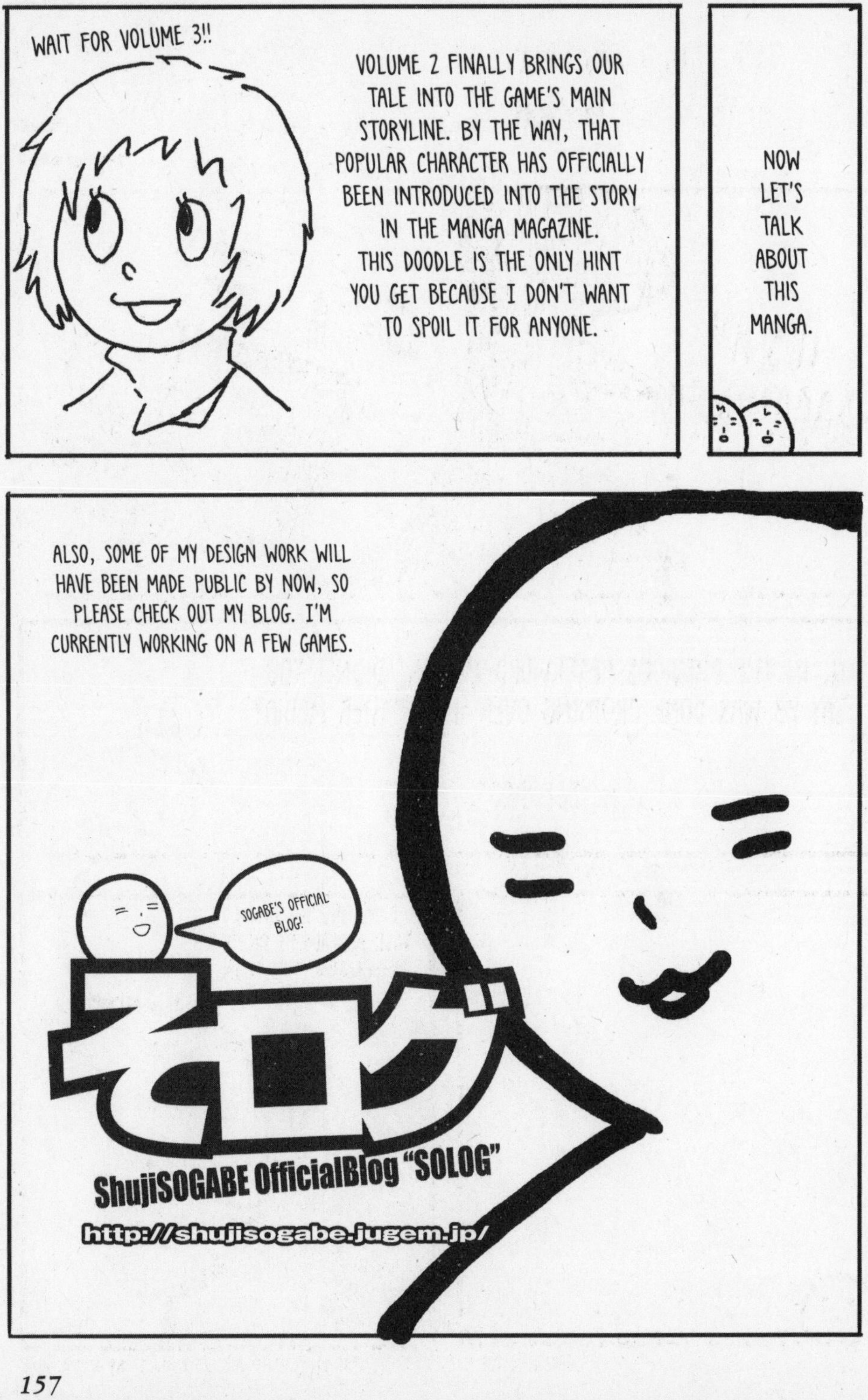
NOW LET'S TALK ABOUT THIS MANGA.
VOLUME 2 FINALLY BRINGS OUR TALE INTO THE GAME'S MAIN STORYLINE. BY THE WAY, THAT POPULAR CHARACTER HAS OFFICIALLY BEEN INTRODUCED INTO THE STORY IN THE MANGA MAGAZINE. THIS DOODLE IS THE ONLY HINT YOU GET BECAUSE I DON'T WANT TO SPOIL IT FOR ANYONE.
WAIT FOR VOLUME 3!!
ALSO, SOME OF MY DESIGN WORK WILL HAVE BEEN MADE PUBLIC BY NOW, SO PLEASE CHECK OUT MY BLOG. I'M CURRENTLY WORKING ON A FEW GAMES.
SOGABE'S OFFICIAL BLOG!
ShujiSOGABE OfficialBlog "SOLOG"
http://shujisogabe.jugem.jp/

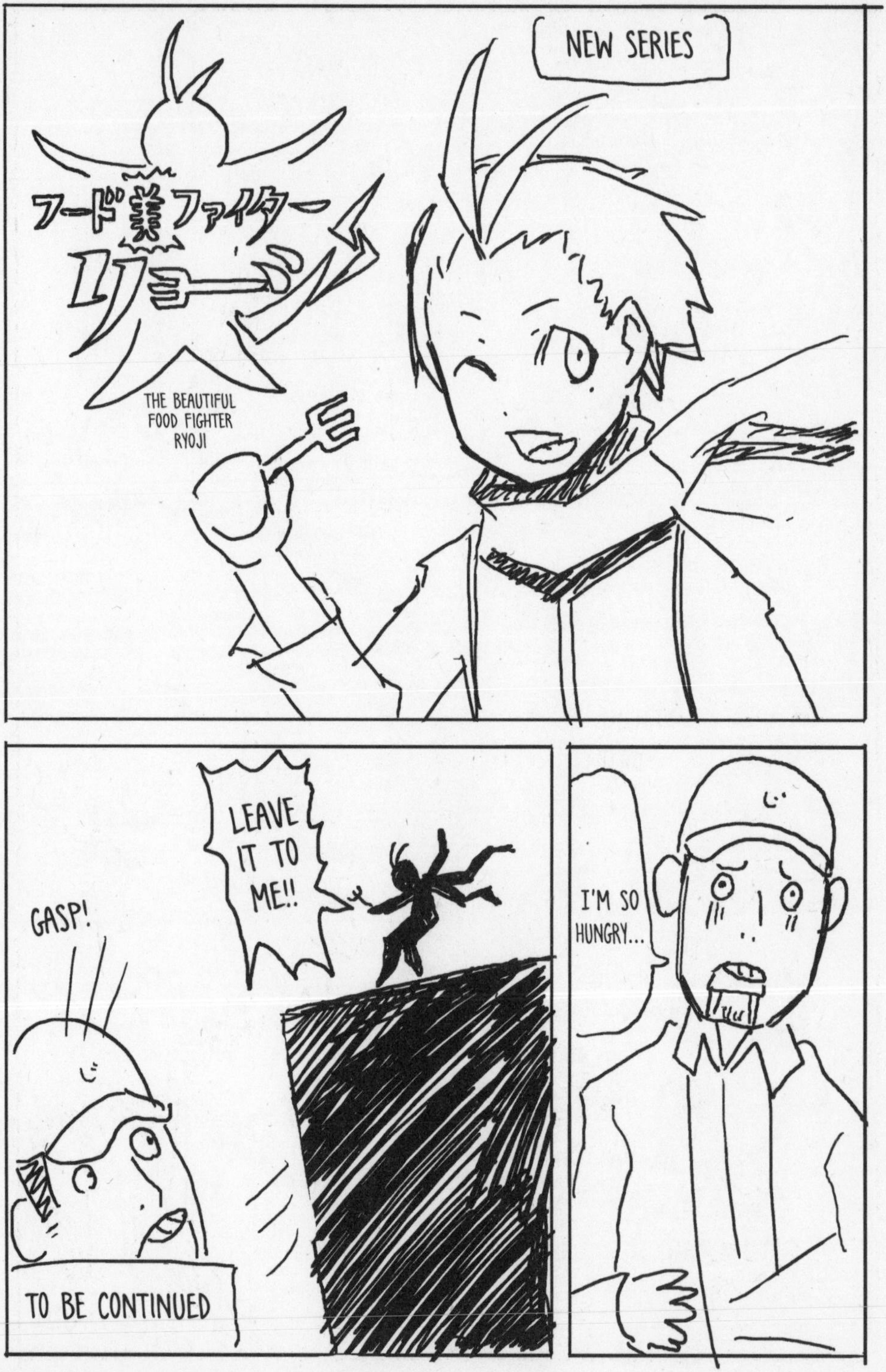
NEW SERIES
フード美ファイターリョージ
THE BEAUTIFUL FOOD FIGHTER RYOJI
I'M SO HUNGRY...
LEAVE IT TO ME!!
GASP!
TO BE CONTINUED

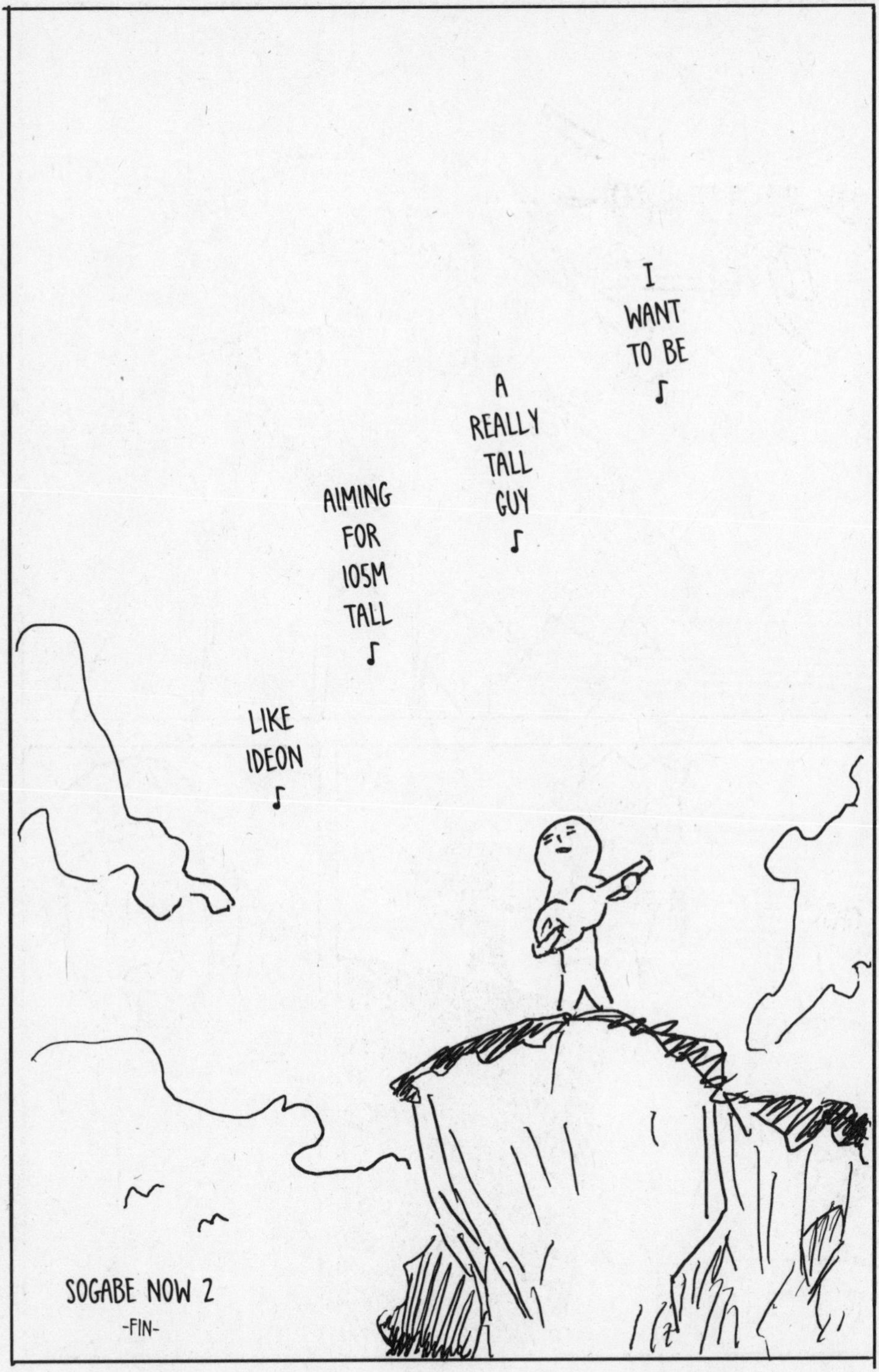
I WANT TO BE ♪
A REALLY TALL GUY ♪
AIMING FOR 105M TALL ♪
LIKE IDEON ♪
SOGABE NOW 2
-FIN-

HIGH SCHOOL

Original Work by:
アトラス
ATLUS

Original Art Director:
副島成記（ATLUS）
Shigenori SOEJIMA

Original Scenario Writer:
田中裕一郎（ATLUS）
Yuichiro TANAKA

Manga/Story Composition:
曽我部修司
Shuji SOGABE

Production (Supervisor)/Layout/Advisor:
Studio Shortcake Screamer
青木春菜 (#07.5)
Haruna AOKI

本間良太 (#05~'08)
Ryota HONMA

Special Thanks
ゲームファクトリーマグマ川越店
GAME FACTORY MAGMA

森純一（ATLUS）
Junichi MORI

ペルソナ3 オリジナルスタッフ
PERSONA3 ORIGINAL STAFF

Design
スタジオショートケーキスクリーマー
Studio Shortcake Screamer

Translation
タノヴァン・フィリップ
TANOVAN Phillippe

フィードバック
Feedback

Backgrounds/Coloring:
Studio Shortcake Screamer
菅野友美
Tomomi KANNO

野本李紗
Risa NOMOTO

堀晴子
Haruko HORI

Grayscale Painting:
Studio Shortcake Screamer
佐久間あさみ
Asami SAKUMA

3D Modeling and Layout:
Studio Shortcake Screamer
夏目彰浩
Akihiro NATSUME

Editing
飯島直樹
Naoki IIJIMA

今井洸一
Kouichi IMAI

照沼美和
Miwa TERUNUMA

Since 1982

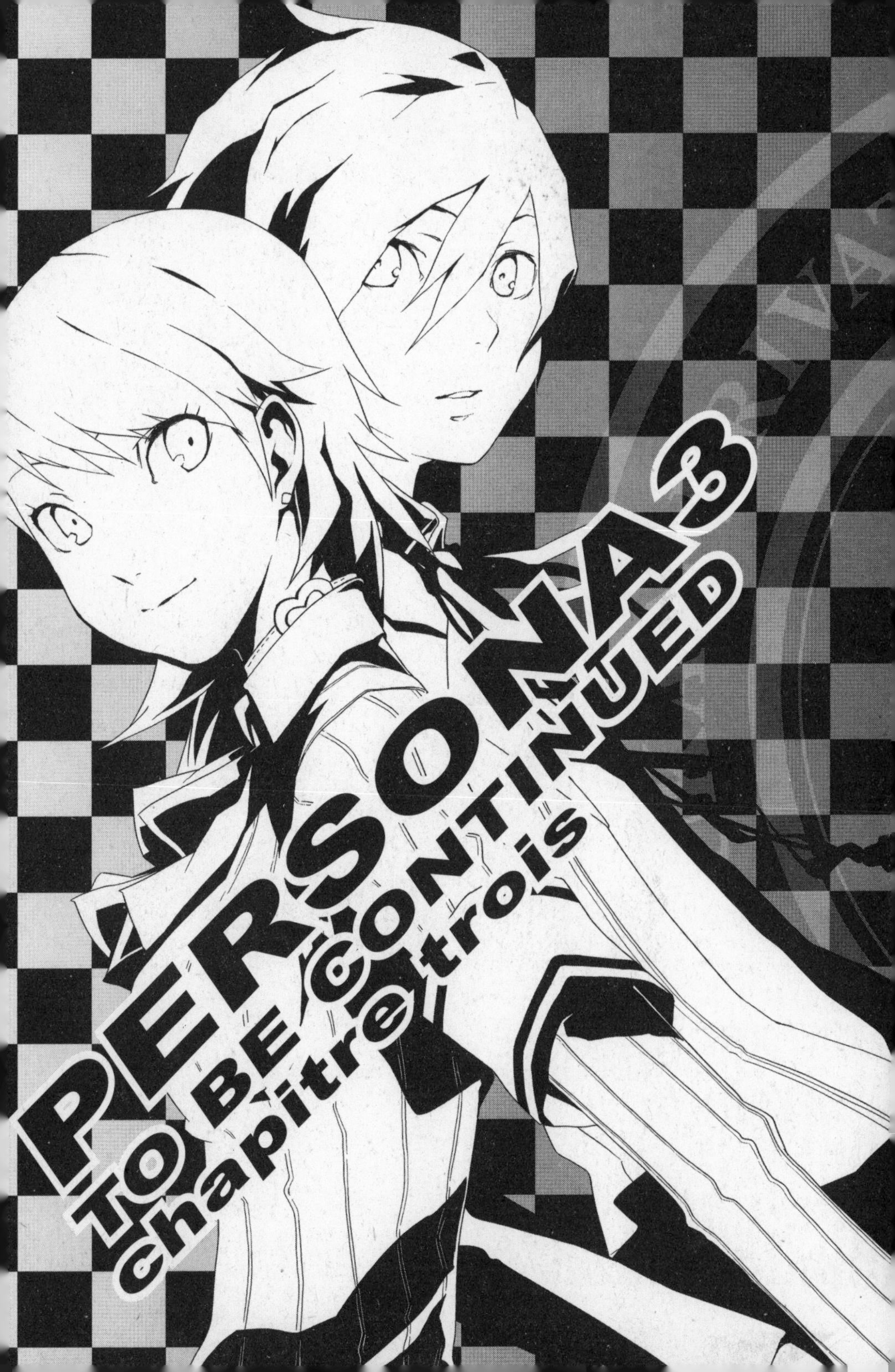
PERSONA 3
TO BE CONTINUED
chapitre trois

Persona3

Vol.2: Shuji SOGABE / ATLUS

ENGLISH EDITION
Translation: M. KIRIE HAYASHI
Lettering: MARSHALL DILLON
Copy Editor: ASH PAULSEN

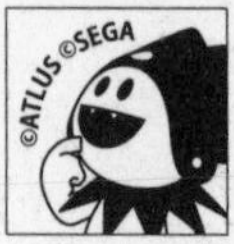
©ATLUS ©SEGA

UDON STAFF
Chief of Operations: ERIK KO
Director of Publishing: MATT MOYLAN
VP of Business Development: CORY CASONI
Director of Marketing: MEGAN MAIDEN
Japanese Liaisons: STEVEN CUMMINGS
ANNA KAWASHIMA

ペルソナ３２
PERSONA 3 Volume 2

First published in 2008 by KADOKAWA CORPORATION, Tokyo.
English translation rights arranged with KADOKAWA CORPORATION, Tokyo

English language version published by UDON Entertainment Inc.
118 Tower Hill Road, C1, PO Box 20008
Richmond Hill, Ontario, L4K 0K0 CANADA

www.UDONentertainment.com

Second Printing: April 2020
ISBN-13: 978-1-927925-86-7
ISBN-10: 1-927925-86-X

Printed in Canada